SPACED OUT

How the NBA's Three-Point Revolution
Changed Everything You Thought
You Knew About Basketball

Mike Prada

TRIUMPH
B O O K S

No part of this publication may be reproduced, stored in a retrieval system, or transmitted in any form by any means, electronic, mechanical, photocopying, or otherwise, without the prior written permission of the publisher, Triumph Books LLC, 814 North Franklin Street, Chicago, Illinois 60610.

Library of Congress Cataloging-in-Publication Data available upon request.

This book is available in quantity at special discounts for your group or organization. For further information, contact:

Triumph Books LLC
814 North Franklin Street
Chicago, Illinois 60610
(312) 337-0747
www.triumphbooks.com

Printed in U.S.A.
ISBN: 978-1-62937-886-2
Design by Patricia Frey

For Vincent Prada, who introduced me
to this amazing sport, among many other things.
I miss you every day. RIP

Contents

Introduction
The Game Done Changed

What happens when the same sport is suddenly played on twice
as large a playing surface with the same number of players?

An NBA regulation court measures 94 feet long, 50 feet wide, and 10 feet high, plus a few feet to account for aerial acrobatics. That multiplies to a surface area of nearly 13,000 square feet—12,280 if you only count up to the 10-foot rim, up to 13,144 if you include the three extra feet to the top of the backboard. Those have been basketball's official spatial dimensions for a century, back in the days of "cage leagues" and annual *Spalding's Official Basketball Guides.*

For most of that time, the sport's *practical* playing surface was nowhere near that lofty figure. From the first days of the 10-second[1] and backcourt violations in 1932, through the widening of the lane from six to 16 feet, beyond 1955's invention of the 24-second shot clock, a typical basketball sequence smushed the sport's 10 combatants into a geometric shape that was a fraction of its maximum size.

Those rules and cultural changes each made a significant long-term impact, of course. Widening the lane to 16 feet created perimeter play. The 24-second shot clock popularized the fast break, a de facto speedway for

---

1. Limited to eight seconds in 2001.

players to zip through the middle two quadrants of the floor into the smaller scoring zone. The three-point line, first introduced in 1979, demarcated remote suburbs that a growing, but limited subset of ambitious players began to colonize.

But those nudges, until as recently as a decade ago, had only extended the practical geometric shape of the sport to a quarter of its 13,000–square-foot surface. Basketball was evolving as most sports do: meaningfully, but gradually. It took eight decades for the 10 players to extend the danger zone's borders beyond the edge of the lane to the three-point arc. Even the widest broadcast camera angles stopped just beyond that point, knowing the 10 players on the floor would fit snugly into that space.

And then, everything changed.

At some point in the mid-2010s, the NBA rapidly went from living with the three-point shot to loving it. Teams hunted long balls, then longer balls, then even longer balls. They positioned players to help generate those long shots, placing them well beyond the outer borders of the previously understood confines. Twenty-five feet became 30, then 35, then 40, and now encroaches into the backcourt. Broadcast camera angles had to zoom out to half court to have a chance at capturing all 10 players in one frame.

You know this time period as the "three-point revolution," or some form of the term. All you have to do is scan a shot chart, peek at a box score, or watch a two-minute highlight clip to know that this is not the NBA you once knew. With the possible exception of the years following the implementation of the 24-second shot clock in 1954, the NBA has never faced as much upheaval as it has over the last decade, or even half decade.

The object of this book is to challenge that premise. Not because the sport isn't, in fact, transforming. Quite the opposite. Somehow, for all the justified attention the three-point revolution of the 2010s has received, its impact on every fabric of the sport itself has been *underplayed*.

The sport as once we knew it simply does not exist anymore. We—from players to coaches to analysts to fans—can no longer assume that *any* fundamental strategic, tactical, or individual skill tenant that we once held to be self-evident still applies. We—the *royal we*—must re-examine everything we thought we knew about the sport we hold so dear.

This book is an attempt to do just that. It is, first and foremost, a story of how and why the league's relationship with the long ball transformed from a prolonged 35-year courtship into the steamy love affair of the last half-decade. It will heavily feature three crucial rule alterations in a 25-year-span, the innovative figures that first capitalized on their chain reaction in the ensuing years, and the people still thrusting the game further forward.

But that is just the tip of the iceberg. In truth, this book is about all the *downstream effects* of this revolutionary moment in NBA history. It will illustrate all the ways a sport that still features five players a side, 48 minutes per game, and is decided by numbers on a scoreboard has become something far different, now that its players are occupying so much more of those 12,280 square feet on each sequence.

The new NBA is often described as a triumph of "pace and space," which is a useful shorthand as long as you understand that the league keeps raising the upper limit on both halves of that phrase. In the span of a few years, long-range shooting went from being a luxury of champions to a necessity for competitiveness, and then to the foundation of every single team in the sport. Size went from being an asset to a detriment and then back to being an asset, as long as it included a mastery of the smaller man's skill set. Good offense, once powered by inside play, rapidly changed focus to bomb away from the perimeter, and then just as quickly leveraged the threat of the latter to create easier pathways for the former. Effective defenses once prioritized brute physicality, then shifted into limiting a team's three-point attempts, and are now increasingly willing to live with certain types of threes as a means of deterring drives to the basket.

It's tempting to say that old, in some form, can again become new in the NBA. History tends to rhyme, if not repeat itself outright. The innovators that pushed and are still pushing the sport forward have built on the foundation of others.

But they've done so by recycling and reimagining the right elements of the sport's history. Some are timeless. Some are more important than before. Some are less important. Others are of similar import, but in different constructions. And some are brand new concepts that have surged from fringe to mainstream so quickly that they've become second nature to even the most inquisitive fans, hoopers, coaches, and analysts.

The sum of that work and the widening of the practical playing surface has blended the old and new together to create strategies, philosophies, tactics, schemes, skill sets, movement patterns, and measures of basketball intelligence that didn't exist in the past. It has become a completely different experience to play the game and an ever-complex one to strategize up close or analyze from afar. It has paradoxically become much easier for fans to consume while also being much harder to understand.

The goal of this book is to bridge that disconnect once and for all. It is for casuals and diehards, practitioners and consumers, pro and amateur analysts, Xs and Os aficionados and sneakerheads. It will feature on-court diagrams. It will occasionally veer into dense and overly technical language. But it's not intended only for League Pass junkies, nor is it tailored entirely to casual fans or folks who stopped watching years ago. Instead, it yearns to give a layperson a taste of the sport's granularity *and* help experts gain a new appreciation for how fundamentally it's changed in less than a decade.

Are you ready to fall back in love with the Spaced Out version of NBA basketball? Let's begin at the scene of its first domino.

Chapter 1
Carnival Basketball

The NBA's decades-long journey to accept the long ball,
and the team that finally saw its full potential.

The object of basketball is to score more points in a set amount of time than your opponent. That means a shot worth three points is more valuable than many shots worth two points. If you're good at making three-pointers, the defense must stretch out to honor that threat, which allows your team to get much easier two-point shots.

I've just described the basic theory of the modern NBA.

That's it?

Three … is greater than two? It's harder for five people to cover more space than … less space? That should've been easy to figure out.

But if the power of the three-point line was so evident, it sure took a while for the game's players and coaches to realize it. Specifically: half a decade to use it even sparingly, 20 more years to accept it, another decade to embrace it, and only *then* did they begin to maximize its full potential. A slow-but-steady rise in three-point attempts for 35 years suddenly transformed into explosive growth until present day. In 2012–13, the league averaged 20 three-point attempts per game for the first time ever. That number jumped to 24.1 per game in 2015–16. Six years later, the NBA exceeded *35 three-point attempts per contest.*

The people within the NBA's orbit decades ago weren't stupid. They knew three was worth more than two, and they intellectually understood that the three-point line could open up the rest of the floor. Yet it *still* took many of those same people and their descendants 35 years to dig the long ball in practice. That seems hard to believe in hindsight. But it happened.

From another lens, though, the widespread resistance to the power of the three-point line mirrors those of other new technologies in different fields. Change often seems to happen quickly, but that only appears true retrospectively. Truthfully, 35 years is fast compared to many of history's most important innovations.

Calestous Juma, an influential Harvard professor who authored a 2016 book titled *Innovation and Its Enemies,* identified three "sociopsychological factors" that slow the widespread adoption of innovations.

- A reluctance to break out of existing habits or routines.
- Perceived downstream risks associated with innovation.
- Public attitudes toward the technology in question at the time.

All three feature heavily in the story of the NBA's long resistance to the three-point shot. The first step to understand why today's NBA looks so different from prior eras is to understand how that resistance began.

THE YEAR WAS 1979. Magic Johnson and Larry Bird were about to begin their illustrious NBA careers after dazzling audiences in the spring's NCAA Tournament. The Seattle SuperSonics were the defending champions after defeating the aging Washington Bullets in a Finals rematch that generated little enthusiasm outside of the country's two Washingtons.

Yet neither topic dominated the lead-up to the upcoming 1979–80 NBA season. Everything took a backseat to the three-point line, which was finally coming to the NBA for good after years of intrigue, flirtation, and fiery debate.

After sampling the arc during the 1978 preseason, the league's coaches, general managers, and owners authorized it for all games on a one-year trial basis. The vote was far from unanimous. Many of the league's luminaries opposed it and were not shy about saying so. But now they had little choice but to grin, bear, and adjust.

The questions on everyone's mind were wide-ranging. What would this brand-new element do to the sport? Would the game ever be the same? How would coaches and players properly incorporate this new wrinkle into their strategies? Would the product become unrecognizable to longtime fans?

Those questions, the contentious debate of previous years, and everyone's natural fear of change put the rule's proponents and designers in an odd position. Their work over the previous years had (barely) convinced enough league power players to accept the three-point line as their best hope to fix the sport's lagging popularity. Now, these same people were forced to allay the skeptics' fear of chaos. That meant downplaying the impact of the very thing they had sold as essential to the game's growth.

"I'm convinced of one thing—it will not change the game," Jerry Colangelo, then the Phoenix Suns general manager and only at the start of a decades-long career in the sport, told the Associated Press in October 1979. "As a purist, I want to see the game left alone. But under the circumstances, we need to take a look at this for one year. But the basic structure of the game will not change at all, and that's the important thing."

One year turned into two, then three, and is now at 43 and counting. For much of that time, Colangelo was right. The basic structure of the game didn't change as significantly as its detractors feared. Not in 1979, 1989, 1999, or 2009. Heck, Colangelo at least had a kernel of a point in the spring of 2014.

Not so in 2022. From 2014 on, Colangelo's statement became exponentially more absurd with each calendar year, to the point where you wonder how it was ever right at any point. In the span of less than a decade, the three-point line *did* completely change the basic structure of the game in ways the 1979 version of Colangelo could never have anticipated. It's tempting to wonder why the NBA game transformed so quickly. The better question is why it took so long to transform at all.

For all the concern that the modern NBA is too soft or geared too much to the offense, it is closer to the platonic stylistic ideal the league's founders have long sought. Basketball was never meant to be a rough imitation of the king of the hill game you played as a kid. From the days of George Mikan in the 1950s through the dominance of Shaquille O'Neal at the turn of the century and beyond, league stakeholders have taken proactive measures to limit the overpowering influence its largest players have on the game.

In the early days of the NBA, the paint was just six feet wide. We call it "the key" because it originally looked like one. That made it easy for the

6'10" Mikan to plant himself just outside its borders, catch any pass, and instantly loft sweeping hook shots over shorter defenders.

This was not the game James Naismith envisioned in 1892, and it certainly wasn't the game the fledgling NBA believed could capture a large audience. They did not want their sport to be decided by the biggest guy standing underneath the basket and dropping the ball in over powerless shorter defenders. They doubled the width of the "key" to 12 feet in 1951, and then to 16 feet in 1964 to counteract the growing dominance of Wilt Chamberlain, who was much more physically imposing and skilled than Mikan.

In a stroke of irony, Mikan went on to become the commissioner of the American Basketball Association, a formidable competitor to the NBA for a decade that featured a more open style of play. Despite earning a cult following and wooing many talented players from their more established counterpart, the ABA could not stay financially solvent. It merged with the NBA in 1976 in a complicated deal that enabled its four most profitable teams (New York Nets, Denver Nuggets, San Antonio Spurs, and Indiana Pacers) to join the revamped pro league.

The ABA's most significant export wasn't a team, or even any of their superstar players like Julius Erving, George Gervin, and others. It was the three-point line. Though seldom used by today's standards, the innovation was popular enough in the ABA to increase scoring, open the game up, and limit wrestling matches under the basket that giants were bound to win.

Contrary to popular belief, the ABA was not the first professional league to include a three-point line. Abe Saperstein's short-lived American Basketball League of the early 1960s also featured one, and he was inspired by an experiment former Oregon basketball coach Howard Hobson conducted during a scrimmage between Columbia University and Fordham University in 1945. But the ABA was the first league to provide proof of concept over an extended period of time.

NBA lifers had long resisted calls to add the three-point line to its game. "What is it but an admission that you are dealing with inferior players who can't do anything but throw up long shots?" Eddie Gottlieb, the legendary Philadelphia Warriors coach who headed the NBA rules committee for 25 years, told *Sports Illustrated* in 1967. "You encourage mediocrity when you give extra credit to this sort of thing."

June 1, 1994 — Pacers at Knicks — ECF Game 5 (Tied 2-2)
Pacers 81, Knicks 79 — 3:31 left in fourth quarter

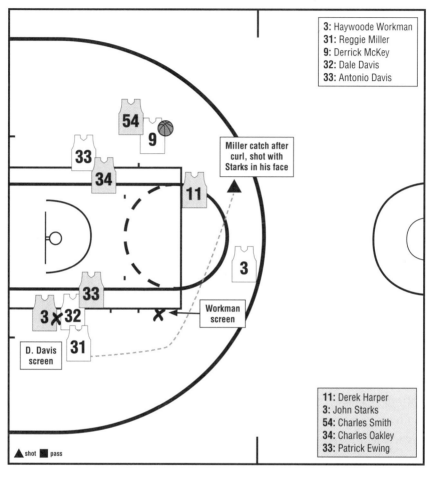

3: Haywoode Workman
31: Reggie Miller
9: Derrick McKey
32: Dale Davis
33: Antonio Davis

Miller catch after curl, shot with Starks in his face

Workman screen

D. Davis screen

▲ shot ■ pass

11: Derek Harper
3: John Starks
54: Charles Smith
34: Charles Oakley
33: Patrick Ewing

But momentum began to swing in those post-merger years. The mid-to-late 1970s featured overly physical play and no flagship team, especially once a budding Trail Blazers dynasty crumbled under the weight of Bill Walton's fragile feet. Back-to-back NBA Finals series between the Bullets and SuperSonics in 1978 and 1979 were physical slugfests that generated low TV ratings and spooked many of the league's most experienced basketball minds.

"That series was awful. I was ashamed," Al Bianchi, then a Phoenix Suns assistant coach who went on to be the general manager of the New York Knicks, told the *Arizona Republic* in 1978, right after the first Bullets–Sonics series ended. "I've been a part of the game for 21 years. It was brute force, and we never saw any real basketball because of the holding and grabbing."

The league was still reeling from the events of December 9, 1977, when Los Angeles Lakers big man Kermit Washington punched Houston Rockets forward Rudy Tomjanovich so hard that he fell unconscious within a pool of blood leaking from his jaw. Washington had not intended to hit Tomjanovich, who was rushing in to break up a fight between Washington and Rockets big man Kevin Kunnert. But the combined momentum of Washington's fist coming from one direction and Tomjanovich's face racing from the other was so powerful that the impact permanently damaged Tomjanovich's jaw and nearly killed him. The incident was replayed on national newscasts and on *Saturday Night Live*. It kick-started a crackdown on fighting that persists to this day.

Hobson, who had retired from coaching at this point, wrote a letter to then-commissioner Larry O'Brien urging him to adopt the three-point line during regular-season and playoff games. Hobson insisted that the three-point line was the key to eliminating the violence that increasingly endangered the sport. "Except for interceptions and fast-break goals, the game is played within a radius of about 23 feet from the basket," Hopson wrote in 1978. "Players are bigger now and when 10 of them get into such a small area, bodily contact leading to violence is bound to occur. It's like putting two heavyweight boxers in a telephone booth and telling them not to flinch. The three-point plan would draw the defense out, decrease the use of the zone, relieve congestion near the basket, add spectacular play for the fans, and give the team behind a better chance to catch up."

The list of dissenters was long. Legendary Boston Celtics coach and executive Red Auerbach dismissed the three-point shot as a carnival act the league put in place to kowtow to the whims of television ratings. Title-winning Trail Blazers coach Jack Ramsay called the three-point shot a "gimmick," and many of his colleagues agreed. Phoenix Suns coach John MacLeod said running plays to shoot three-pointers is "very boring basketball." Bullets head coach Dick Motta claimed the league pushed the three-point line through without consulting its coaches and refused to let his players practice it.[2]

That debate climaxed on one pivotal day in June 1979, when the 22 members of the NBA Board of Governors gathered in Florida to vote on adopting the three-point line on a trial basis for the upcoming season. Any rule change this significant required a two-thirds majority to pass.

The final tally: 15 in favor, seven against. It had cleared the two-thirds majority requirement … by a single vote. That's how narrowly the three-point line, now an NBA staple, snuck into the league.

One of those seven dissenters was Frank Mieuli, then the owner of the same Golden State Warriors franchise that shattered three-point records 35 years later. Mieuli, according to multiple accounts, was so incensed that he instantly resigned from the Board of Governors and vowed to never attend another owner's meeting. While Mieuli was wary of making any substantive change to the sport based on a short-term drop in attendance or TV ratings, he especially hated *this* specific change. Even something as radical as raising the rim to 12 feet, he said, made more sense than a three-point shot.

"Changing the two-point basket is immoral," Mieuli said. "The ABA had it and folded. What have we done except hurt ourselves? We have separated ourselves from the main body of basketball by tampering with a game that has lasted for 90 years. We have paid too high a price."

A reporter followed up on Mieuli's reference to the NBA's decade-long battle to ward off the insurgent ABA, which had embraced the three-point line with open arms.

"This has nothing to do with the ABA," Mieuli began. Then, as if deliberately trying to betray his own premise, he continued. "I thought it was carnival basketball when the ABA did it," he said. "It'll be carnival basketball when we do it."

Though Mieuli's opposition to the three-point line was, ahem, extreme, his point of view illuminated the two most powerful psychological forces that blinded teams and players to its potential.

---

2. This claim is inconsistent with reports from the Board of Governors meeting, which suggest the owners conducted an informal poll among 20 of the 22 coaches, finding 15 in favor of the three-point line and five against.

One is that awarding an additional point for a long shot felt unnatural. Every field goal had always been worth two points, no matter the distance or the difficulty. Because of that, coaches had little reason to design plays to shoot from farther away, which meant players had less incentive to learn how to shoot from farther away. Perimeter play still existed; teams still had to reach the basket and defenses weren't going to let them do that easily. But as long as short and long shots were worth the same, the need to get the ball inside was hardwired into every strategy. It'd take a lot more than painting a curved line on the court to overcome that cultural bias.

Then there was the simple reality that Mieuli accidentally (or deliberately) acknowledged: the three-point line was *an ABA thing*. It was one thing for an anti-establishment start-up league like the ABA to resort to "carnival basketball" to achieve a slice of relevancy. But the NBA *was* the establishment! It had just proved its supremacy by using its financial might to swipe the best parts of the ABA and let the rest wither away. It was hard for many NBA traditionalists to buy the idea that an artificial gameplay instrument from the failed start-up league the NBA squashed like a bug was now their salvation.

That group of people included some of the most respected coaches, players, and front office executives of the time. They were the tastemakers from whom others took their cues. The cool crowd bashing the new fad created a chilling effect that slowed the three-point line's mainstream acceptance.

This context is crucial to understand how it took the NBA more than three decades to fully appreciate the simple, mathematical truth that 3 > 2. Though the three-point line had (barely) enough support to sneak through that crucial 1979 Board of Governors meeting, it was the furthest thing from a (pardon the pun) slam dunk addition to the league. More importantly, its critics were louder than its proponents.

The impact of their opposition was felt most clearly during those early days of the three-point line. Remarkably, teams averaged *fewer* three-point attempts in 1981–82 than they did in 1979–80. The 1981–82 Los Angeles Lakers, anchored by Magic Johnson and Kareem Abdul-Jabbar, won the championship while making a total of 13 threes *all season*. That's one fewer than Klay Thompson made all by himself in an early-season 2018–19 game against the Bulls.

That year was the nadir of the grand three-point experiment. Over the next few seasons, the teams realized the line was here to stay and they may as well try using it. But even that progress was incremental. The league didn't average more than 10 three-point attempts per game until the 1993–94 season. Those numbers spiked when the league briefly moved the three-point arc closer to the hoop for the next three seasons, then fell off again once it was moved back before the 1997–98 season.

A new millennium brought another marginal increase in three-point attempts, but that growth plateaued by the end of the decade. In the 2007–08 season, 22.2 percent of the league's field goal attempts were threes. In 2010–11, when LeBron James played his first season in Miami and the Dallas Mavericks ended Kobe Bryant's quest for a sixth championship, 22.2 percent of the league's field goal attempts were threes.

By then, the contentious debates about adopting the ABA's gimmick had long faded from memory. Most players and coaches had grown up with the three-point line. Why were the events of three decades ago *still* limiting the widespread use of jump shots worth one more point than jump shots from slightly closer?

The answer to that question is obvious only in hindsight. It took long enough for the NBA to *use* the three-point line. It took even longer to see its larger purpose.

BEFORE IT SLIPPED through the tight grip of its many NBA detractors, the three-point line was often described with an evocative cross-sport metaphor.

"We called it the home run, because the three-pointer was exactly that," Mikan told Terry Pluto in *Loose Balls: The Short, Wild Life of the American Basketball Association.* "It brought the fans out of their seats."

The "we" in that statement is intentional, for Mikan did not invent the concept. In 1961, Abe Saperstein, the founder of the Harlem Globetrotters, haphazardly formed an eight-team pro league known as the American Basketball League. As part of his pitch to lure retired Boston Celtics star Bill Sharman to coach one of the teams, Saperstein proposed the idea of a "home run" shot taken from more than 25 feet away that could be worth an additional point. Sharman told him that distance was too far and the terminology wasn't "appropriate for basketball," but otherwise approved of the concept. Saperstein converted the idea into the three-point arc and included it in his league rules. The ABL failed after a year and a half, but Saperstein's ingenuity inspired Mikan's ABA to popularize the concept and co-opt the terminology.

The association between three-pointers and home runs was embedded deeply into the ABA's psyche. ABA arenas set off sirens, banged gongs, and created other local customs to commemorate three-pointers, much like a baseball stadium does for home runs.[3] Television commentators regularly reinforced the cross-sport analogy when calling games. Whether done intentionally or subconsciously, this was how league figures emphasized one of its unique attributes while simultaneously familiarizing novice fans with the concept that long shots could be worth more points.

The flip side is that doing so branded three-pointers as special events, meant to occur infrequently. Very infrequently, in fact. In 2019, the Arizona Diamondbacks and Philadelphia Phillies set an MLB record with 13 home runs in a single game. Combined, the two teams threw a total of 364 pitches (188 for Philadelphia's hurlers, 176 for Arizona's). That means that *in the most prolific long ball game in baseball history*, only 3.5 percent of the game's sequences ended in home runs.

Suppose that a basketball team attempted a three-pointer only 3.5 percent of the time they brought the ball down the floor. For the sake of clarity, let's pretend each team got exactly 100 possessions. If the three-pointer was literally a "home run shot," as Saperstein and Mikan analogized, fans would only see a total of *seven three-point attempts* that entire game. Seven! For both teams! And that's if they replicated the rate of the *most home run–heavy baseball game of all time*.

Saperstein, Mikan, and anyone else referring to three-pointers as "home run shots" were speaking metaphorically, not literally. But in those early days, the analogy hit close to home. The average number of three-point attempts per game in the ABA fell from a peak of 12.64 in the 1969–70 season to just 7.4 in 1974–75. NBA teams took the home run imagery even more literally: games from 1979 to 1982 featured just 4.71 three-point attempts on average. While those figures rose exponentially well before the

---

3. Public address announcers still carry on that tradition. Cue Madison Square Garden's longtime public address announcer Mike Walczewski's famous "THREEEEEEEEEEEEEEE POINTER" call.

more recent three-point explosion, the anchoring effect of the "home run shot" descriptor helps explain why the league took so long to fully leverage the shot's power.

The association between home runs and three-pointers artificially diminished the shot's capability to space the game out. In theory, the threat of the three-point shot opens up the floor and thus makes two-point shots easier to generate. That much was evident from the start. "The defense will have to be honest now," legendary New York Knicks coach Red Holzman said in 1979. "That will definitely open things down low for the big man."

But if offenses weren't willing to attempt three-pointers at a rate that far exceeded the rate of home runs in baseball, then defenses had little reason to fear the shot. One has to pose the threat of a three-point barrage to profit off it. That's why few coaches saw the point of changing their team's defensive shape to prevent such rare events. Better to fortify areas that teams used more frequently, such as the paint and the pivot.

In fact, most coaches and players took the opposite approach to *encourage* their opponents to shoot threes. They saw the shot as fool's gold and counterproductive to the urgent need to get the ball closer to the basket for more high-percentage shots. Some lured their opponents to make a few early three-pointers so they'd take more later and engage in self sabotage. The logic mirrored baseball's long-standing attitude that actively trying to hit a home run can mess up your swing and dramatically limit your ability to make contact at all. Those combined forces created a closed feedback loop that took players and coaches a long time to reverse.

"You have to tell your players to remember who the shooters are, and when those guys are 25 feet from the basket, get in their jocks and guard them. Don't give them the 25-footer, which is something players had been conditioned to do all their lives," legendary coach Hubie Brown told Pluto in *Loose Balls.* "And as a coach, if you have a shooter with range, you have to give him the freedom to take the 25-footer, which is a philosophy that goes against what you learned as a young coach—namely, pound the ball inside."

That conditioning left its mark for generations to come. Even as the three-point shot became mainstream by the 1990s and early 2000s, it was still seen as a special element of the game reserved only for the select few who made enough shots to earn it. To use another baseball analogy, you had your *home run hitters* and then you had everyone else.

"We didn't even talk about the three-point shot that much," Sam Mitchell, who spent three of his 13 NBA playing seasons with Larry Brown's Indiana Pacers before going on to be a coach and analyst, once said during an NBA TV pregame show. "Larry told Byron Scott and Reggie [Miller], in certain situations in the fourth quarter if we're down three, or if the score's tied and we have numbers and we had an opportunity to cover the glass if they missed, that was fine. But he didn't want us taking threes like that. It had to be a special situation, and it was only two guys that were allowed to shoot them."

Allowed is the operative word. It conveys an element of control that coaches did not give away easily. Many NBA-native coaches and players dismissed the three-point shot because of its ABA origins. They saw the ABA as "carnival basketball" and naturally resisted any of its innovations. But even former ABA coaches, like Larry and Hubie Brown, limited the use of the three-point shot on their future NBA teams. The idea that closer shots were always better was thoroughly hardwired into their brains, as was the idea that the three-pointer was as rare as a home run.

Because of that, they and everyone else were conditioned to view the three-pointer as a shot that didn't go in as often, not one worth an additional point when it did. Missed shots have many more potential outcomes and downstream effects, many of which are negative and none of which coaches could easily control. They couldn't stop *all* their players from shooting threes, but they could at least bestow the privilege only to the select few who made them often.

That approach may have calmed their psyches, but it was self-defeating. The less coaches allowed their players to pose the threat of a three-point shot, the less reason they gave their opponent to guard the three-point line and risk opening even easier shots up.

For a long time, only a few teams and coaches fought against that inertia. The list of players capable of making threes in games grew faster than the degree of threat their coaches allowed them to pose. Even higher-volume three-point shooting teams, like Hakeem Olajuwon's mid-1990s Rockets, Rick Pitino's late-1980s Knicks, or Stan Van Gundy's late-2000s Magic, used the three-pointer as a counter to the attention their centers caused in the paint.

But that was about to change, thanks to one team whose tentacles still reverberate today.

THE 2003–04 SEASON was supposed to be the Phoenix Suns' year. Their 25-and-under young core of Stephon Marbury, Shawn Marion, and rookie phenom Amar'e Stoudemire had pushed the eventual champion Spurs to six games in the first round of the 2003 playoffs. The backlash from 2001's trade of in-prime star Jason Kidd to New Jersey for the younger, more mercurial Marbury was fading. Expectations were high.

It instead turned into a disaster. A rocky start cost coach Frank Johnson his job, and new coach Mike D'Antoni hadn't improved their fortunes. By the time the calendar year changed, the Suns' playoff hopes were fading fast.

So the Suns hit the reset button. On January 5, they traded Marbury and veteran guard Penny Hardaway to the New York Knicks for a package of unremarkable players and future draft picks. The real prize for Phoenix: the deal cleared long-term salary, positioning them to make a big splash in that summer's free agency period.

They also had an ace in the hole. Outgoing longtime owner Jerry Colangelo was also the head of a special rules committee that was about to implement its boldest reform yet.[4] The league didn't announce its intention to police all forms of hand-checking until just before the 2004–05 season, but the Suns knew the edict was coming. "We knew from the very beginning what was likely to come about. So we were able to plan for longer than everybody else," David Griffin, the Suns vice president of basketball operations at the time, told The Ringer in 2018.

That advanced knowledge informed the decision that planted the first seeds of the three-point revolution. On July 1, 2004, the first day of free agency, the Suns offered 30-year-old point guard Steve Nash a six-year contract for a guaranteed $65 million.

The sweet-shooting Canadian point guard originally drafted by the Suns in 1996 had grown into a two-time All-Star after being traded to the Dallas Mavericks. With Dirk Nowitzki and Michael Finley as running mates and

---

4. Colangelo sold his majority stake in the franchise to Robert Sarver in April 2004, but the terms of the agreement enabled him to retain his title of chairman for another eight years. Also, his son Bryan was the team's general manager.

mad scientist coach Don Nelson egging them on, Nash quarterbacked a Mavericks team that emerged as a prototype for the high-octane era to come.

But after nearly reaching the Finals in 2002–03, Dallas took a step back in 2003–04, losing emphatically to rival Sacramento in the first round of the playoffs as Nash's production and health waned. Fearing Nash's creaky back and motivated to fix his team's loosey-goosey reputation, Mavericks owner Mark Cuban chose not to match the Suns' offer. (Dallas instead signed former Warriors center Erick Dampier to a seven-year, $73 million contract. Whoops!)

The Suns' decision to augment their young core with a defensively challenged 30-year-old with long-term health concerns was not without risk. But it was part of a larger bet that the upcoming hand-checking restrictions would reward speed over size and enhance the value of players like Nash.

That bet included retaining their interim coach, despite a less-than-stellar 21–40 record to close the 2003–04 season. D'Antoni, who starred as a player and coach in the more up-tempo style of European professional basketball, was already planning to shift Stoudemire to center, slide Marion to power forward, and play a fast-paced, pick-and-roll heavy style. Nash's combination of passing, shooting, and ball-handling skill just so happened to be an ideal fit.

The general public was less convinced. The Suns' preseason over/under win projection was 10th best in the West, and they were tied with the mediocre Knicks for the sixth longest title odds. A $1 preseason bet on them to win the 2005 championship would've yielded a $10,000 payout.

But they would become convinced quickly.

The Suns won 31 of their first 35 games and ended up with 62 victories total, the most in the league. Nash edged Shaquille O'Neal to win the league's MVP, while D'Antoni took home Coach of the Year honors. Phoenix tallied an average of 97.35 possessions per game, the most since the 1999–2000 Sacramento Kings, and lapped the league in three-pointers attempted (nearly 25 a contest) and percentage (39.3 percent).[5] That pace and those threes

---

5. According to the wonderful stats site pbpstats.com, only five teams since the 2000–01 season have used an average of less than 16 seconds on offensive possessions that came immediately after their opponent made a field goal: the four D'Antoni/Nash Suns teams (2004–05, '05–06, '06–07, and '07–08) and the 2019–20 New Orleans Pelicans, coached by D'Antoni's former lead assistant Alvin Gentry.

combined with Nash's slick passing and Stoudemire's rim-rattling dunks to overwhelm opponents with non-stop scoring barrages.

But those numbers only scratch the surface of the Suns' revolutionary approach. The more significant keys were who took those threes, when they took them, and the chaos the threat of those three-point shots was designed to cause.

Unlike previous teams, the Suns did not have "three-point specialists." Eight different Suns players attempted at least two three-pointers a game, which is common now but was far from common then. Any coach would've wanted Nash launching from downtown, and most coaches would have granted Joe Johnson similar liberties as long as he continued to drain nearly half of his triples. It took an innovator like D'Antoni to beg above-average marksman Quentin Richardson to launch eight threes a game or encourage Shawn Marion to consistently show off his ugly shooting form. That confidence improved both players' performances while presenting the defense with four willing shooters to honor at all times.

That was critical to the Suns' success for a few reasons. The simplest one is that, well, three *is* worth more than two. Players already took plenty of catch-and-shoot jumpers inside the three-point line, shots most coaches tolerated and even encouraged assuming proper ball movement and/or play design. Is a 23-foot jumper that much harder for an NBA player to make than a 19-foot one? May as well take a couple steps back and get the extra point.

Beyond that mathematical truth, the Suns' collective three-point embrace combined with their fast-paced style to create a dizzying effect for defenders. If any player on the court is liable to catch and shoot from any distance at any time, how could a defense get any sort of read on their tendencies? It was challenging enough for all five members of a defensive unit to break their normal habits to get into the jock of one proficient long-range shooter. Now they had to do that to four proficient long-range shooters, each of whom were willing to fire at any point in the shot clock. That's a lot of threats to address.

That leads to the real reason the Suns were innovators: they finally cracked the code on using the three-point line to generate even better shots. As D'Antoni told ESPN years later, all he really wanted to do was get more layups. The best way to do that in a post-hand-check, post–illegal defense world was to open the lane so drivers saw fewer bodies while attacking the basket.

D'Antoni and the Suns intuitively understood that the only way to consistently draw the defense out was to deploy as many able three-point shooters as possible *and* give them the freedom to fire at will. That ethos forced five defensive players to cover significantly more space than they had to against any other opponent. It was as if they played with a different set of court dimensions than the rest of the league. More space meant more potential threats for Nash to leverage, as well as clearer lanes to slip passes through.

That effect manifested in a delightfully simple setup: a pick-and-roll between Nash and Stoudemire with the other three players behind the three-point line. Sink too far off the shooters to stop the roll, and Nash found them for open triples. Hang too close, and Nash either pulled up with his sweet stroke or (more often) found Stoudemire surging down the lane for a dunk.

The system would've helped any point guard, but Nash's skill set was tailor made for it. Nash was patient enough to wait until the opportune moment to make his choice to pass. He relished resetting the initial pick-and-roll at will until the defense inevitably opened up one of those three devastating scoring options. He was also adept at keeping his dribble alive even as he circled underneath the basket, a move coaches began describing with a proper noun: "Nashing."

Much of the criticism to the Suns' style of play resembled that of anti-ABA traditionalists when the three-point line first entered the NBA. The Suns' run-and-gun style was a fine enough gimmick for the regular season, but it wouldn't work in the playoffs when things got serious.[6] The language was more politically correct than Frank Mieuli's "carnival basketball" quip in 1979, but it carried the same fearful undercurrent of a chaotic unknown that needed to be properly controlled. This was the exact orthodoxy D'Antoni and the Suns aspired to break. At one point during the 2004–05 season, they discovered an opponent's scouting report that described the Suns' offense

---

6. One of the most prominent of those voices was TNT commentator—and former Suns great—Charles Barkley, who repeatedly harped on the Suns' defensive and rebounding issues during the D'Antoni era. Sound familiar, Warriors fans?

May 22, 2005 — Spurs at Suns — WCF Game 1
Spurs 51, Suns 45 — 1:28 left in second quarter

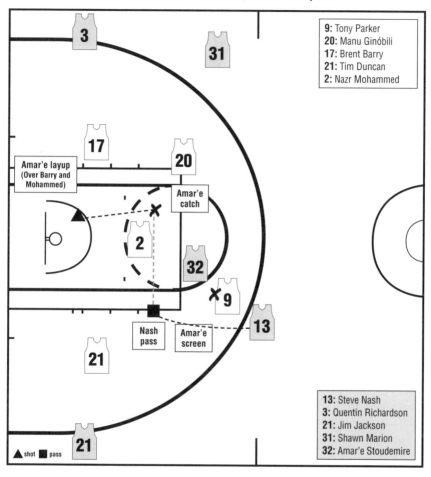

9: Tony Parker
20: Manu Ginóbili
17: Brent Barry
21: Tim Duncan
2: Nazr Mohammed

Amar'e layup
(Over Barry and
Mohammed)

Amar'e
catch

Nash
pass

Amar'e
screen

▲ shot ■ pass

13: Steve Nash
3: Quentin Richardson
21: Jim Jackson
31: Shawn Marion
32: Amar'e Stoudemire

as one where "literally nothing is frowned upon." Whoever wrote that line meant it derisively, but D'Antoni took it as a source of pride and often referenced it after Suns victories.

Unlike most teams of that era, the Suns offense didn't have many set plays. More traditional coaches believed that illustrated the Suns' lack of discipline. At the very least, it transferred direct control away from the coaches, which was seen as anarchic. But to D'Antoni and the Suns, that was the beauty of the system. They were the first to conceive of the three-pointer not as a longer shot that went in less often, but rather as a deadly weapon they could use to sow chaos.

Phoenix never did win the championship, falling to the San Antonio Spurs three times and the Dallas Mavericks once. They also received some rotten luck in the form of Johnson's face injury during the 2005 playoffs, Stoudemire's microfracture knee surgery that held him out of the next season, and multiple suspensions for leaving the bench during an altercation in their 2007 six-game series loss to San Antonio. Maybe the game's three-point revolution would've commenced sooner had they won it all.

Still, they were already rubbing off on their peers. Their tough battles with the Spurs helped convince Gregg Popovich to shift from a low-post offense centered around Tim Duncan to one built around whiplash ball movement, catch-and-shoot threes, and incisive dribble penetration from Tony Parker and Manu Ginóbili.[7] Years later, the Suns' success inspired Heat coach Erik Spoelstra's spread offensive system around LeBron James and Dwyane Wade that won back-to-back titles in 2012 and 2013.

Still, it took another decade for the 2004–05 Suns' lessons to fully sink in league wide. That was when two franchises took the roots D'Antoni's Suns laid down and sprouted revolutionary styles of play that soon became the NBA's new normal.

Both had direct ties to those Suns teams. Both agreed the league was only scratching the surface of the three-point line's true power. But their methods for shattering that glass ceiling could not have been more different. Like two sects of the same religion, they competed as bitter rivals while passing down the same larger lessons to the rest of the league.

---

7. San Antonio had already inspired a three-point revolution of its own: the use of the corner three. Knowing that it was a far shorter distance than the rest of the arc, the Spurs stationed their weakest offensive threat there and drilled them into becoming proficient with that shot. That practice continued as their offense transformed, and was eventually adopted by the rest of the league. They even pioneered the use of a set play known as "Baseline Hammer," which called for a guard to deliver a pass along the baseline to a shooter coming off a big man's screen to get open in the opposite corner. It's an after-timeout favorite to this day.

Chapter 2
The Holy War

Golden State, Houston, and the rivalry that forced
the rest of the league to level up.

It's February 5, 2013. The 26–23 Houston Rockets are polishing off a blowout home win over the 30–17 Golden State Warriors. Four minutes remain in a fourth quarter dominated by garbage time.

Reserve Rockets guard Daequan Cook catches a kickout pass at the top of the key. Eluding Golden State wing Kent Bazemore's long closeout, Cook takes two dribbles to his right and casts his eyes to the corner. That's where lefty power forward Donatas Motiejūnas stood, having backpedaled beyond the three-point line as defender Draymond Green helps on Cook's drive. Motiejūnas receives Cook's pass, steps in with his left foot, and drains the Rockets' 23rd three-point basket of the game, tying an NBA record.

That is the last three-pointer the Rockets make that night. The Warriors use any means necessary to ensure that.

With 15,453 fans egging them on, the Rockets squander three chances to set the record on the next three possessions. A fourth opportunity falls by the wayside when Green fouls point guard Patrick Beverley to stop a fast break. A fifth try ends when Green surrenders an open driving lane to Beverley, which the feisty Rockets point guard uses to throw down a righty tomahawk jam and shout in Green's face.

As the Rockets advance down the court for their sixth try at the single-game record, the Houston crowd rises to its feet. "You'd think this is the seventh game," longtime Rockets announcer Bill Worrell says wryly on the Houston broadcast.

That's when the Warriors' "any means necessary" kicked in.

Upon seeing Beverley pop open in the deep left corner, Green surges off his own man. He dives at Beverley, right arm raised in a desperate attempt to stop the shot. Beverley appears to elude him, but as he winds up for another three, he's greeted by Green's open left palm slapping him hard across the face.

Green is tossed for his antics, but he accomplished his goal. Beverley didn't shoot another three. Neither did any of the other Rockets after the melee ended.

By then, Warriors coach Mark Jackson had instructed his players to intentionally foul, as if they were trailing by just a few points. The crowd roared in protest, to no avail. The final score was Houston 140, Golden State 109, but the only number anyone cared about was the "23" in Houston's three-point column, which never became "24."

That moment planted the first seeds of the modern game's most important rivalry. The faces changed over the years, and the two franchises rarely fought as bluntly again. But the battle lines drawn that night kick-started a seven-year arms race between two innovative franchises who followed vastly different ideologies to achieve the same larger purpose. Though one claims victory on the scoreboard, both were equally instrumental in creating the NBA we see today.

Each was the offspring of the original Seven Seconds or Less Suns family tree. The Rockets employed D'Antoni himself during the height of their run. The Warriors countered with Steve Kerr, the Suns' general manager from 2007 to 2010, and assistant coach Alvin Gentry, who was D'Antoni's lead assistant in Phoenix before succeeding him in 2009.[8]

Most importantly, they had Stephen Curry, a slick-shooting lead playmaker who led mid-major Davidson to an improbable Elite Eight run

---

8. Gentry took over on an interim basis when Terry Porter was fired midway through a disappointing 2008–09 season. Porter tried and failed to change the Suns into a more traditional team. Gentry, on the other hand, largely restored D'Antoni's style.

and drew comparisons to Nash as soon as he entered the league. Kerr had tried desperately to acquire Curry while still running the Suns, orchestrating a trade that would have sent star Amar'e Stoudemire to Golden State for a package that included the Warriors' 2009 No. 7 pick. But the Warriors pulled out at the last minute, deciding to keep Curry for themselves.[9]

Five years later, Kerr finally got his chance to work up close with Curry when he took the Warriors coaching job over a similar offer from Phil Jackson's Knicks. Curry had overcome a string of ankle injuries to reach All-Star status, but there was still a sense that he had another gear to reach. A 54-point, 11-three night to lead the undermanned Warriors to a near-upset road win against the Knicks in 2013 teased Curry's potential to turn the sport inside out if given freedom to fire threes at will. When Curry followed that up with a breathtaking shooting display to lead the Warriors to the second round of the 2013 playoffs despite an injury to All-Star forward David Lee, many started to wonder if Curry could be that prolific from downtown *all the time* instead of just in emergencies?

That couldn't happen under Jackson. Hired to lead the Warriors out of the NBA's wilderness, Jackson built a hard-edged defensive spine that brought the franchise some much-needed respectability. But management increasingly believed his offensive rigidity, top-down leadership style, and constant in-fighting with his assistant coaches was capping their players' ceilings. They fired him after a narrow first-round loss in 2014 and hired Kerr, who had never been on an NBA coaching staff. As a token of their faith in their existing core, the Warriors refused to include young guard Klay Thompson in a proposed trade package for Minnesota Timberwolves All-Star Kevin Love. They trusted Kerr to install a system that'd transform both members of their beloved Splash Brothers backcourt.[10]

That system was a blend of several older ones. It incorporated alignments similar to the 1990s Bulls' Triangle offense, the designated off-ball cuts

---

9. The proposed deal was far enough down the line that the Suns drafted Louisville swingman Earl Clark with their own No. 14 pick instead of UCLA point guard Jrue Holiday, who they also liked but didn't believe they needed because they were about to acquire Curry to be Nash's heir apparent.

10. Some members of the front office were in favor of the trade, but two powerful people were against it. Kerr was one. The other was Jerry West, the legendary player and executive who had been wooed out of retirement to be owner Joe Lacob's special consultant. West threatened to quit if the trade for Love went through.

of former Jazz coach Jerry Sloan's Flex system, and the spacing prized by D'Antoni's Suns. Those elements were tied together by the consistent ball and player movement of the new-age Spurs. Gentry described it as a "melting pot" that reflected Kerr's career as a player and executive.

But the system's diversity, while impressive, was only revolutionary because of the way the Warriors executed it. Kerr saw up close how D'Antoni's Suns used the three-point line to whip defenses into a frenzy. He understood that the three-point arc wasn't just a way to score more points. It was even more valuable as a way to cause defensive chaos and indecision. The more freely the Suns shot from out there, the less prepared defenses felt to stop them and the more they feared the threat.

Kerr's system aimed to turbocharge that defensive confusion. The Suns hunted three-pointers, but most of them were spot-up attempts. They were generally unpredictable outcomes from more predictable entry points, most of which involved Nash handling the ball.

Kerr's mishmash, whirling dervish system added another layer of complexity to each sequence. It made the entry points of each play as impossible to predict as the end product. What was a defense supposed to do with elite three-point shooters firing from anywhere on the floor, off any sort of prior sequence, with any combination of players springing them open via any combination of screens, cuts, and passes? It was a question no other team in NBA history had ever dared to pose.

Curry's unique skill set made him the ideal fulcrum of the Warriors' bold gambit. He used an unconventional shooting motion growing up, releasing the ball by his chest as if firing a slingshot. The trick traded launch height for release speed, enabling him to get shots off against taller defenders.

Stephen's father, former NBA sharpshooter Dell Curry, was not as impressed. He insisted his son spend the summer between his sophomore and junior years of high school reconstructing his jump shot so it could hold up against stronger competition. They worked in painstaking detail to move Steph's release point up to his head while still maintaining the speed of the original slingshot-like motion. The work was tedious. It was "the most frustrating summer for me," the younger Curry admitted years later. But it resulted in a deadly, speedy, incredibly accurate jump shot that Curry could uncork from anywhere, at any point, and off any sort of prior sequence.

June 14, 2015 — Cavaliers at Warriors — NBA Finals Game 5 (Tied 2-2)
Warriors 85, Cavaliers 84 — 4:19 left in fourth quarter

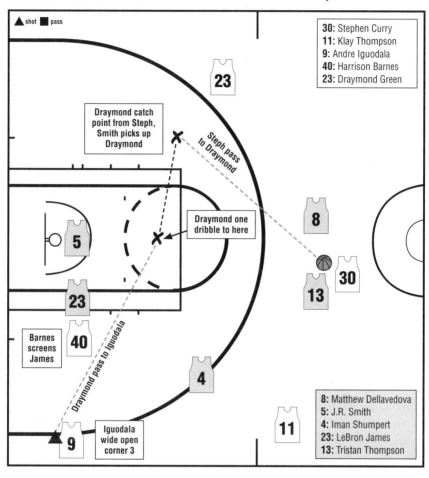

▲ shot ■ pass

30: Stephen Curry
11: Klay Thompson
9: Andre Iguodala
40: Harrison Barnes
23: Draymond Green

Draymond catch point from Steph, Smith picks up Draymond

Steph pass to Draymond

Draymond one dribble to here

Barnes screens James

Draymond pass to Iguodala

Iguodala wide open corner 3

8: Matthew Dellavedova
5: J.R. Smith
4: Iman Shumpert
23: LeBron James
13: Tristan Thompson

Under Jackson, Curry became an elite off-the-dribble long-range shooter that broke even the most disciplined pick-and-roll defensive schemes. But Kerr's system took Curry's long-range threat a quantum leap further. The flexibility of the system enabled Curry to fire with impunity off the dribble, curling off screens, stepping back, sprinting to any spot outside the line in transition, receiving dribble handoffs from his big man, or just running around a lot until his defender inevitably lost him. He was the cheese, and his opponents were mice running through an endless maze.

Curry's teammates were well-suited to maximize and capitalize on the terror he inspired. As the Warriors suspected, the system's constant movement enhanced Thompson's size, long-range shooting touch, and speedy release while hiding his still-developing handle and court vision. It enabled the Splash Brothers to better complement a cadre of average-at-best shooting wing players with different specialized skill sets. It was an ideal fit for their big men, who preferred high-post passes, well-timed dribble handoffs, and bone-crushing screens to post-ups or hard rolls to the basket.

The secret ingredient that made the Warriors' style as revolutionary as it was effective was a happy accident. Kerr planned to augment the Splash Brothers' shooting with the high-post passing and screening skill of big man duo Andrew Bogut and David Lee. But when Lee suffered a hamstring injury in the 2014–15 preseason finale, Kerr had little choice but to turn to Green, a former second-round pick who had wedged his way into Jackson's rotation. Kerr respected Green's toughness and defensive versatility, but wasn't sure he had a signature skill. Green didn't help matters by playing poorly in Kerr's first training camp while trying too hard to showcase skills he didn't have.

Green ended up being everything Kerr envisioned of Lee and a whole lot more. Green possessed the ball-handling to initiate any sequence, the physicality to spring the Splash Brothers with effective screens, the court sense to slide into the right openings, the vision to make the extra pass in odd-man situations, and the manic energy to trigger constant fast breaks that transformed the Warriors' brand of chaos into a never-ending storm.

More importantly, Green's defensive versatility allowed the Warriors to layer an innovative switch-everything defensive philosophy on top of Jackson's more traditional principles. Green could guard any position at any time, vaporizing mismatches that other teams yielded when they switched screens. That effect was especially devastating when Kerr deployed Green at center alongside Curry, Thompson, Andre Iguodala, and Harrison Barnes in what became known as the "Death Lineup." With Green as a roaming defensive anchor, that unit absorbed bigger teams' attempts to pound them inside, then ran them ragged on the other end.

With Curry and Green as their two hubs, the Warriors reimagined the purpose of the three-point line. It wasn't merely the Warriors' scariest threat. It had also become their line of scrimmage, enabling them to play outside-in when every other team played inside out. In effect, they inverted the very fabric of the game itself. They transformed what was merely a key component of the mid-aughts Suns' system into the very foundation of theirs. The switch-heavy defensive scheme that grew from Green's emergence was an added bonus that ensured opponents couldn't use the same offensive strategy against them.

The Warriors' breakthrough was overwhelming and swift. They won 36 of their first 42 games in Kerr's first season and polished that off with a championship trophy. Fueled by their remaining skeptics, they won their first 24 games of the 2015–16 season and broke the NBA's single-season win record, though they famously blew a 3–1 lead to LeBron James' Cavaliers in the 2016 Finals. After using a one-time salary-cap spike to sign Kevin Durant in free agency, the Warriors won the 2017 and 2018 titles and might've three-peated had Durant and Thompson not suffered devastating injuries in the 2019 Finals. Curry broke the single-season record for three-pointers with 286 in 2014–15, then shattered his own record with 402 the following year while earning the league's first ever unanimous MVP.

It seemed like the run was over following Durant's departure to Brooklyn, Curry's hand injury in 2020, and Thompson's torn Achilles on top of 2019's torn ACL. Their place in history was long assured. Instead, the Warriors re-emerged as the class of the NBA in 2022. Curry returned better than ever, a revitalized Green anchored one of the league's best defenses, and newcomers like Andrew Wiggins, Jordan Poole, and Gary Payton II breathed new life into the setup. The Warriors tore through the West playoffs, then rode an incandescent Curry performance to beat the bruising Boston Celtics in six games for their fourth title in eight years. As this NBA era enters its next chapter, the Warriors are once again poised to be its main character.

Curry, Green, and the Warriors undoubtedly are the spiritual leaders of the movement that reversed the NBA's decades-long three-point stigma. Yet their ideal blend of players, coaches, systems, timing, and luck also makes them difficult to emulate. No matter how much other teams tried, they couldn't recreate Curry, Green, Kerr, or any of the Warriors' team-building steps.

That's why the Warriors' primary adversary is just as influential to the modern game despite being less successful—and far less aesthetically pleasing.

THE HOUSTON ROCKETS viewed the three-point line differently than the Warriors. To them, its appeal was simple: it was a way to score more points on fewer shots.

That philosophy was largely personified by two men: general manager Daryl Morey and superstar guard James Harden.

In 2006, Morey was a 35-year-old unknown with no NBA playing background and less than four years of experience in a front office. But he *was* a pioneer in an important burgeoning field: sports analytics. That intrigued Rockets owner Leslie Alexander, a former bond trader who had made his fortune starting his own investment firm.

When general manager Carroll Dawson conveyed his desire to retire after nearly three decades with the organization, Alexander took it upon himself to find a replacement. Most believed he'd take the traditional route of promoting from within or plucking a basketball lifer from another franchise to run the front office.[11] Instead, Alexander tapped Morey to serve a one-year apprenticeship under Dawson and then take over the following summer.

Morey's first signature move was to trade the Rockets' 2006 No. 8 draft pick to the Memphis Grizzlies for Shane Battier, a 27-year-old forward who averaged just 10 points and five rebounds per game the previous year.[12] Lottery picks tended to yield much higher returns than that when dealt. Yet Morey's detailed statistical analysis showed that Battier was a plus-minus superstar. He figured Battier's knack for lifting the Grizzlies' overall performance without contributing individual statistics would carry over to Houston.

Morey was right. The Rockets regained their place as a Western Conference contender, and renowned *Moneyball* author Michael Lewis christened Battier as the on-court avatar of the burgeoning analytics movement. But the resurgence was short-lived, crumbling under the weight of Yao Ming and Tracy McGrady's brittle bodies. Morey needed a new statistical edge.

The one he found seems simple in hindsight: teams weren't shooting enough three-pointers. Specifically, they shot too many long two-point jump shots that went in about as often as threes without the reward of an extra point. Each game only provided teams a finite number of chances to score, so these shots were a waste. The Rockets could gain a leg up by converting as many of those shots as possible into threes.

---

11. Dawson's No. 2 at the time was Dennis Lindsey, who spent nine years as executive vice president of basketball operations for the Utah Jazz before resigning in 2021.

12. Morey was still the assistant general manager at this time, but he was the driving force behind the deal.

Morey built his team's roster and offensive system around generating as many layups or three-pointers as possible. (This philosophy came to be known as "Moreyball," a play on Billy Beane's strategy that revolutionized baseball a decade earlier.) He found several diamonds in the rough to keep the Rockets competitive and directed his coaching staff to retrain their players' habits. He used the team's D-League affiliate as a laboratory, hiring a former Division III coach to play at breakneck speeds, shoot tons of threes, and treat mid-range jumpers as cardinal sins.

Still, Morey needed a star—multiple stars, really—to break through the NBA's orthodoxy. Alexander would not allow the Rockets to stink and "earn" a high draft pick, so Morey needed to acquire one from another team. He embarked on a flurry of transactions that slowly built up a war chest of future draft picks and young players that might be enticing as a trade package. Those moves kept his present roster in constant flux and created the perception that Morey treated players like penny stocks instead of actual human beings. But those moves put him in position to get his superstar: James Harden.

The bearded left-handed playmaker quickly became the ideal prophet to spread Morey's gospel. The third of three future perimeter superstars selected by the Oklahoma City Thunder from 2007 to 2009, Harden thrived in a Sixth Man role while teaming with Durant and Russell Westbrook to lead the Thunder to the 2012 Finals. Despite losing to Miami, the Thunder appeared to be a budding dynasty. But with Harden's rookie contract about to expire, the small-market Thunder did not want to trigger punitive luxury-tax penalties that the league's owners insisted on strengthening during testy 2011 CBA negotiations. With Durant and Westbrook already locked up on maximum contracts, Harden was deemed a luxury the Thunder couldn't afford.

The Thunder surreptitiously shopped Harden around the league in the summer of 2012, and Morey flashed his well-earned arsenal of future draft picks and young players. When Harden turned down an extension for less than the maximum salary, the Thunder traded him to the Rockets for Kevin Martin, Jeremy Lamb, and future draft picks that became Steven Adams, Mitch McGary, and Alex Abrines.

As a Sixth Man extraordinaire in Oklahoma City, Harden had demonstrated a remarkable knack for generating the holy grails of Moreyball:

layups, threes, and free throws. Many doubted his ability to do the same as the centerpiece of his own team. Morey, though, was a true believer, and he was emphatically proven right. Harden immediately matched the exploits of his former Thunder teammates in 2013–14, then teamed with free-agent signing Dwight Howard to lead the Rockets to back-to-back 50-win seasons in 2013–14 and 2014–15.

The second of those two seasons was Harden's most prominent to date. It was also his first year in the Warriors' long shadow. He finished a distant second to Curry in MVP voting, and Golden State defeated the Rockets in five games in the Western Conference Finals.

Harden's style of play didn't exactly have a universal approval rating. Whereas Curry and the Warriors flew around the court like a beautiful symphony, the Rockets centralized their offense around Harden himself. He wasn't an explosive leaper, but he could change speeds at will and weave around defenders on his way to the hoop. He was remarkably adept at dissecting the second line of defense and kicking out to open shooters. He also used every trick possible to draw fouls, which annoyed opponents and non-Rockets fans.

These skills made him a one-man Moreyball shot generator, so the Rockets figured their best strategy was to give him the ball as often as possible. The more they did, the more he developed a reputation for being a devious hacker who cheaply exploited the game's loopholes. The fact that it worked was beside the point. To many, Harden and the Rockets were gaming the sport and fulfilling the worst fears of the three-point line's earliest critics.

A disappointing eighth-place finish in 2015–16 gave the Rockets a chance to pivot off Moreyball, or at least moderate it. Instead, they doubled down, letting Howard leave in free agency and filling his cap space with oft-injured long-range snipers Eric Gordon and Ryan Anderson.

More importantly, they hired Mike D'Antoni to be their new head coach. The decade since the Suns' breakthrough had not been kind to their innovative coach. D'Antoni's methods didn't work with the Knicks and Lakers due to clashes with their isolation-heavy superstars and some messy internal politics. But the Warriors' success reinvigorated him, providing validation for his philosophy and fuel to push it even further. D'Antoni made Harden the point guard, which put the ball in his hands *even more* than before, and instructed his long-range shooters to fire from well *beyond* the three-point line when open. "The line is there," D'Antoni said at one point during the season. "Doesn't mean you have to stand on it."

The latter directive seemed odd at the time, but D'Antoni knew the spacing benefits far outweighed the extra distance. These super-long threes required longer closeouts, making them even harder to contest than a triple on top of the line. If defenders flew by the shooters in an attempt to force a drive, they could still take one step in and launch a three-pointer. Above all else, the threat of a super long shot stretches the defense out even farther, giving Harden even more space to do his one-on-one thing.

The result was a shot chart that was impossible to imagine even five years earlier. The Rockets attempted 40 three-pointers a game in 2016–17, becoming the first team in NBA history to eclipse the 35-per-game mark (reminder: the league averaged more than 35 three-pointers a game five years later). They launched an average of 24 of those 40 from 25 feet or farther, and nearly half of their 7,152 field goal attempts were three-pointers.[13] They took just 579 mid-range jumpers all season, fewer than four individual players (DeMar DeRozan, Carmelo Anthony, Russell Westbrook, and Andrew Wiggins). It was Morey's D-League experiment in the big leagues.

But while Houston overachieved in winning 55 games, the San Antonio Spurs dispatched them in the second round before they could even face the reloaded Warriors. Harden made a series of critical errors in an overtime Game 5 defeat, then shot 2–11 with six turnovers as the Spurs ran the Rockets off their home floor in Game 6, despite missing fellow MVP candidate Kawhi Leonard.

The Spurs placed a big man deep in the paint while Harden's primary defender fought vigorously over the screen. They dared Harden to take mid-range jumpers and long floaters, the very shots Moreyball excised from Houston's diet. When Harden largely refused, the Spurs stayed in their defensive shape and denied his kickout passes to perimeter teammates.

This was proof to Houston's critics that no team could eschew mid-range jumpers entirely if they wanted to win in the postseason. Sometimes, that's all the defense gives you.

---

13. To be specific: 40.3 three-point attempts per game, 24.3 from 25 feet and beyond, and 46.2 percent of their shots as threes.

May 22, 2018 — Rockets at Warriors — WCF Game 4 (GSW leads 2-1)
Rockets 87, Warriors 86 — 4:16 left in fourth quarter

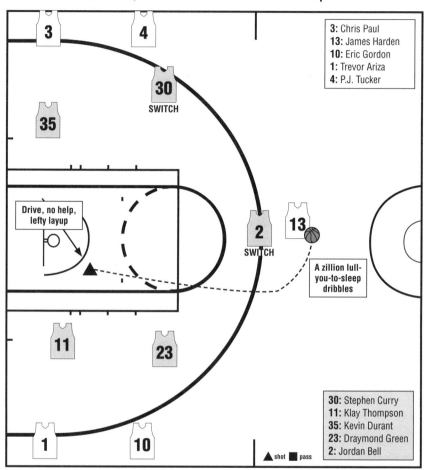

3: Chris Paul
13: James Harden
10: Eric Gordon
1: Trevor Ariza
4: P.J. Tucker

SWITCH

Drive, no help,
lefty layup

SWITCH

A zillion lull-
you-to-sleep
dribbles

30: Stephen Curry
11: Klay Thompson
35: Kevin Durant
23: Draymond Green
2: Jordan Bell

▲ shot ■ pass

The Rockets had a different interpretation for Harden's late-series collapse: their star was exhausted and needed a running mate. That summer, Morey swung a complicated sign-and-trade nine-time All-Star point guard Chris Paul. The talent upgrade to Paul was clear, but Paul's ball-dominant style seemed like a poor fit next to Harden's.

The Rockets didn't see it that way. D'Antoni was already deemphasizing the pick-and-roll, reasoning that the Rockets could create a numbers advantage even more effectively by spreading out and letting Harden beat his own man off the dribble. This seemed heretical to D'Antoni's philosophy, which had become intrinsically tied to Nash's pick-and-roll brilliance. But

Harden wasn't Nash. He was a far better and more willing scorer, especially in one-on-one situations. With more teams mimicking the Warriors' strategy of switching ball screens to avoid or at least delay a numbers disadvantage, it was often counterproductive to send a screener to Harden and risk pulling another defender in his way. This made Paul an ideal fit, since he could make enough plays one on one to lighten Harden's playmaking load when they shared the court and maintain the Rockets' isolation-based style of play when Harden sat on the bench.

The result was a your-turn, my-turn dynamic that worked like a charm, while also violating every basketball aesthetic. Fewer pick-and-rolls meant more time with Harden and Paul dribbling while teammates stood still. It was a throwback to the tactics the NBA tried to eliminate years before, and it certainly didn't make Houston any less predictable. But it was incredibly effective. Houston led the NBA in points scored per 100 possessions while winning a league-high 65 games, seven more than the Warriors. Harden earned his first MVP Award, and no Warriors even made the top five.

The Rockets had brought the purpose of the three-point line full circle. Rule changes had disincentivized the endless low-post backdowns and mid-post staring contests of prior eras, for reasons we'll discuss in Chapter 3. Yet Harden found a way to tilt the math back in his favor.

He helped himself by developing a shot few dared try in non-desperation situations before: the stepback three-pointer. Most scorers used a similar mechanism to create space inside the arc when defenders cut off their drives. Some players, most notably Curry and Thompson, were taking one dribble to the side when defenders closed out wildly so they could stay behind the three-point arc. (Writer Ethan Strauss who authored a 2020 book chronicling the Warriors' rise, dubbed this move the "Side Steph" at some point during the 2015 season.)

Yet Harden deployed the stepback move for a single purpose: to leap behind the three-point line and get an extra point for his trouble. The distance of the shot, a powerful deterrent in the past, was of little concern to Harden. Defenders who lunged to contest the shot tumbled into Harden, leading to loads of three-shot fouls and four-point plays that furthered Harden's foul-baiting reputation.

The inevitable showdown between the Warriors and Rockets took on even higher stakes as a test of the two teams' divergent philosophies. This was not just a de facto championship series. It was a collision between the two splinter groups of the game's original three-point revolution.

The series devolved into a slugfest. The two teams were so in tune with each other's strengths and weaknesses that they often brought out the worst in each other. The Rockets edged Golden State in Game 5 to take a 3–2 series lead, but lost Paul to a hamstring injury in the closing minute. The Warriors won Game 6 at home, then took Game 7 in Houston in the cruelest way possible. The Rockets' early double-digit lead evaporated when they missed 27 consecutive three-pointers between the middle of the second and fourth quarters. Their greatest weapon deserted them at the worst possible time.

The Warriors went on to win the 2018 title and didn't hesitate to rub salt in Houston's wound. They believed that series victory—and especially that seventh game—proved their interpretation of the three-point line's purpose was the correct one in high-leverage playoff series. The best way to use it was in tandem with the rest of the floor, not as a means to replace it. Warriors general manager Bob Myers used the platform of the annual MIT Sloan Sports Analytics Conference that Morey founded in 2006 to convey this point.

"Take Game 7 against the Rockets," Myers mused during a panel. "They took a ton of threes and didn't make them. Were they bad shots? Should they not have taken them? There are times when you shoot the three and it's working. We're seeing now that no 20-point lead is safe because of the three-point shot. But I think what we're missing a little bit is … there are certain guys who go down in a possession and say, 'We're down 10 and we HAVE to get points.' Down 10, a stepback three? Okay, I guess. But what about … 'Let's get to the free throw line, let's cut 10 to eight, and let's not let 10 get to be 13, 15. And let's set our defense.' So I think we get a little loose with the three. Is it bad? No, that doesn't mean it's bad. But in a playoff game, sometimes you just have to score."

The Warriors punctuated that point in the ensuing postseason, beating Houston in six games even after Durant injured his calf in Game 5. By then, Houston's window was closing. Tension between Harden and Paul bubbled to the surface, causing Morey to make an ill-fated decision to trade Paul and multiple draft picks to the Thunder for Westbrook. Harden's reunion with his former Thunder teammate was awkward at best, even after Morey dealt center Clint Capela to commit to a small lineup. D'Antoni left after a second-round defeat to the Lakers, and Morey followed him out the door a year after a seemingly innocuous pro–Hong Kong tweet caused a bizarre standoff with the Chinese government. Harden pushed for and received a trade to the Brooklyn Nets, reuniting him with Durant for a year until he pushed for and received a trade to the Philadelphia 76ers, Morey's new team. While Golden State experiences a revival, Houston is beginning what promises to be a long rebuilding process.

But the ripple effects of their rivalry will be felt for years to come. *Every team* copied them in some form or another. Some, like the 2020 Miami Heat team that reached the NBA Finals in the post-COVID-19 bubble, lean more toward the whiplash movement of the Warriors. Others, like Luka Dončić's Mavericks and the 2018–20 iteration of Giannis Antetokounmpo's Milwaukee Bucks, more closely align with the Rockets' superstar + space approach. Still others, like Nikola Jokić's Nuggets or Joel Embiid's 76ers, merged the principles of both rivals to build hybrid structures around uber-skilled centers. At a minimum, the Warriors and Rockets forced the league's big men to develop three-point range and/or lateral quickness to avoid extinction.

The space beyond the three-point line is now essential territory within any team's offensive strategy, even those who try not to overdo the long ball. Myers' 2019 criticism of the Rockets' overreliance on the three-pointer was the perfect illustration of the movement's starting speed. It took just four years for the ultimate disruptors to transform into the old guard.

In the 2015–16 season, the 73-win Warriors attempted a league-high 31.6 three-pointers per game. Only nine teams had even cracked the 20-threes-a-game mark in the previous five years. Only two did in the five years before *that*. None did five years before *that*. In fact, only eight teams shot more than 20 threes a game in the 20 years after the three-point line was added in 1979, and six of those came when it was temporarily moved in for three years between 1995 and 1997.

Six years later, 29 of the league's 30 NBA teams launched at least 30 three-pointers a game in the 2021–22 season. The Warriors' 31.6 mark that led the league five years earlier would've ranked 28th. Twenty-eighth! That's how thoroughly the three-point revolution inspired by the mid-aughts Suns and accelerated by the late-2010s Rockets-Warriors holy war upended the sport.

Everything you've read so far is just the tip of the iceberg. The rest of the book will dive into the ways the three-point revolution upended strategies, tactics, skill sets, floor geometry, learning methods, and even the bodies of the players themselves.

Since this is the NBA, there's only one place to start.

Chapter 3
Schrödinger's Superstar

The rule change that allowed the game's best players
to do less and more at the same time.

In the late 1800s and early 1900s, an Italian economist named Vilfredo Pareto was obsessed with wealth distribution. He poured over data from his native Italy, England, Paris, several German states, and far-flung locales like Peru, studying both the present and the past. An avid gardener, he applied the same vigor to track which of his pea pods harvested the most peas.

Wherever he looked, he found the same general pattern: inequality.

Lots of it, in fact. In each case, a small percentage of people (or pea pods) held most of the resources. The ratio of imbalance between the top earners and the total wealth held by that population was consistent. It persisted across time and space despite significant differences in size, culture, and social norms.

Using a complicated formula and logarithmic charts, Pareto published a series of graphs that revealed similarly shaped slopes. He then shifted his focus to sociology, found his ideas co-opted by the Italian fascist movement, and was largely forgotten.

Half a century later, a Romanian-born American consultant named Joseph Juran set out to write the ultimate quality control guide for managers. Seeking a simple way to stress the distinction between a "vital few" that determine the bulk of a product's success and the rest of the "trivial majority," he thought back to a trip he took to General Motors' headquarters a decade earlier, when one of the company's managers showed him a graph of the company's executive salaries alongside one of Pareto's charts on wealth distribution. Each showed the same ratio: roughly 80 percent of the output (wealth or salary) went to 20 percent of the relevant population (GM executives or Italian landowners).

With the parallel fresh in his mind, Juran described the phenomenon of a select few inputs producing the vast majority of outputs as "Pareto's principle." It was a logical leap, since Pareto focused exclusively on wealth distribution and never simplified his models to reach an 80/20 ratio precisely—or even to ensure the two numbers added up to 100.[14] But the combination of its qualitative basis and the elegant 80/20 quantitative shorthand transformed Juran's "Pareto principle" into one of the most powerful concepts in modern human history.

Since Juran codified Pareto's principle in 1951, many have demonstrated its broad application across a wide variety of fields, organizations, and institutions. Anyone with a business background is familiar with the parable that 20 percent of customers account for 80 percent of sales. But the ratio, or something close to it, has also been observed in software bugs, healthcare spending, income tax returns, COVID-19 deaths, and much more. It has spawned a self-help cottage industry, in which business leaders and other gurus stress "the 80/20 rule" as motivation for you to focus your attention on what's important.

Squint hard enough, and you can apply the Pareto principle to anything. For example: 20 percent of the NBA's 30 franchises (Celtics, Lakers, Bulls, Warriors, Spurs, and 76ers) account for 73.33 percent of the total number of championships won.[15]

In the 125 years since Pareto published his first wealth distribution charts, his discovery has been rebranded to become a universal truth despite lacking empirical precision. As Austrian economist Josef Steindl put it in 1965: the Pareto law (his words), is "an empirical law which nobody can explain." It just *exists,* everywhere you look, in some shape or form, despite anyone's best efforts to defy it.

---

14. Juran apologized for creating the misperception about Pareto's work in a 1974 paper titled "The Non-Pareto Principle; Mea Culpa."

15. As of 2022.

The NBA is no exception. It, too, has a golden rule that everyone accepts without knowing its origin story. It's best embodied by a 1996 NBC promo for a Bulls-Knicks playoff game. "The concept may be team," reads legendary broadcaster Marv Albert as a blurry figure dribbles inside a gated cage. "In reality, it's the individual." You can probably guess which two faces appear next.[16]

One can quibble with the merits of the point or the partiality of its narrator and his employer. But much like Pareto's principle, it is a widely accepted and often unspoken universal truth. You know these players as "stars" or, if your team is lucky, "superstars." They rule the league, have always ruled the league, and will always rule the league.

That is why our journey through this new age of basketball—which we'll dub the Spaced Out Era for simplicity's sake—begins with them.

On a basic level, the ubiquity of the Pareto principle's "80/20" ratio is a snug fit with a sport that requires each team to field five players at once. To state the obvious: 20 percent of five players is one player, i.e., the star. Every team, even the most egalitarian on the surface, needs a foundation from which to build. It's a lot simpler when that foundation is a single person.

Drilling down on each possession reveals a similar 80/20 distribution of labor. Though basketball is a continuous and interdependent game, each sequence involves three separate stages, which we'll call **setup, advantage creation, and advantage exploitation**. First, each team aligns their five players to maximize (or minimize) the scoring threat they aim to pose (or limit). Then, the offense will try to turn five on five into a numbers advantage—ideally one on zero, but two on one, three on two, four on three, five on four, or anything in between will do. If successful, they'll attempt to turn that numbers advantage into the best scoring opportunity possible.

One or more of those three stages can be resolved before the offensive team gets the ball. Fast breaks skip right to Stage 3, and every turnover or defensive rebound within the game's run of play has the potential to do the same depending on the offense's resolve and defense's floor balance. The whole point of "pushing the pace" or "seeking early offense" is to bypass Stage 1 and, if possible, Stage 2 to advance straight to Stage 3. (We'll talk more about the new concept of pace in Chapter 5.)

---

16. *whispers* Michael Jordan and Patrick Ewing.

On the flip side, half-court possessions feature all three stages, sometimes multiple times if the defense is particularly effective. This is true whether they climax in an isolation, pick-and-roll, or any other multiplayer action like an off-ball screen. Those stages can be simple (clear out for star, star creates his own shot, star shoots), or elaborate (many quick passes, scorer sneaks away off one screen after pretending to screen for a third player, rapid ball movement that turns a good shot into a great shot), but they *always exist*.

On some level, then, the success and failure of each sequence rests primarily (but not exclusively) on a single person. A well-designed setup in Stage 1 improves their odds. An unselfish team can function as one in Stage 3 to amplify the damage. But *someone* needs to push the first domino over in Stage 2, and life is a lot easier when a team has a single person capable of being that someone most of the time. The old coaching adage states that someone must be open when you draw a double team, yet it's the inverse of that statement that encapsulates the overwhelming impact of star players. If nobody draws a double team, then nobody is open.

The most important skill in the sport, then, is the ability to create an advantage for your team to exploit. The players who can do that will always matter more than advantage exploiters, probably by a ratio resembling 80/20. And the players who are best at creating advantages for themselves and teammates are exceedingly likely to be ones you know as superstars—again, by something resembling a 4-to-1 ratio.

That's an oversimplification, even if perhaps a helpful one. The beauty of basketball, especially at the highest levels, is that its style contains multitudes and its players need to collaborate to become more than the sum of their parts. One plus one doesn't always equal two. Sometimes, it equals less, and sometimes it equals much, much more. Just ask any team who has paired multiple superstars.

Yet the empirical squishiness that allows Praeto's principle to endure also resolves the apparent contradiction of a team sport decided disproportionately by a select few individuals known as stars. Credit or blame for a possession's output never adds up to 100 precisely. There are too many interdependent factors to consider between the shooter, the primary defender, the passer, the screener, the help defenders, the timing, the environment, and myriad others. But just as we know Pareto principle's "80/20 rule" is more of a rough guide, we can say definitively that the star (the 20 percent) has an outsized impact on their team's per-possession and overall output without pinning a specific figure down.

That's worth remembering as we dive into the ways modern basketball has transformed the role of the select few essential players who rule it.

It's undoubtedly true that the Spaced Out Era requires more ball and player movement, well-rounded skill sets, collaborative coordination, and several other proxies for team play than prior eras. The three-point line has democratized offenses by forcing them to deploy more players who can threaten the defense when they don't have the ball.

At the same time, stars are in many ways responsible for *more* of their team's production than ever before. In 1991, only four players posted usage rates above 30 percent. In 2020, 15 players eclipsed that mark.[17] That stat arguably undersells the modern superstar's ball dominance, since many are also their team's primary playmaker and thus dribble a lot before setting up open teammates to shoot. This phenomenon is colloquially known as "NBA Heliocentrisim" because it invoked the visual of planets (the team) all orbiting around a single sun (the superstar).[18]

So are superstars more or less important in the Spaced Out Era? The answer is both … at the same time. Schrödinger's Superstar, so to speak. But what appears to be a paradox instead reflects the subtle misunderstanding left unspoken in Vilfredo Pareto's original discovery. Credit or blame is doled out unequally, but it need not add up to 100.

It especially doesn't these days. Why? Because of a six-decade proxy war over a specific tactic that became a rule change that transformed the sport forever.

ON JUNE 6, 1946, a group of businessmen gathered at the Commodore Hotel in New York City. They owned large indoor stadiums in big American cities, used primarily to host professional hockey games. The problem? How to fill their cavernous sporting venues when hockey wasn't on the schedule.

---

17. "Usage rate" is a statistic that measures how often a player ends a possession with a shot, drawn foul, or turnover while on the floor. Theoretically, 20 percent is average, since that would mean each of the five players are sharing equally in the output of a game's possessions.

18. The term was first coined by Seth Partnow, the former Milwaukee Bucks executive and author of 2021's *The Midrange Theory: Basketball's Evolution in the Age of Analytics.*

The solution? A professional basketball league they dubbed the Basketball Association of America.[19]

Once they got down to brass tacks, these men granted franchises to 12 cities (one of which, Buffalo, never played a game) and deputized then–American Hockey League president Maurice Podoloff to pull double duty as the fledgling hoops league's commissioner. Later, they drew up a series of rules that included a 48-minute game instead of college's 40-minute standard.

Six months later, many of those same men reconvened at a different New York City hotel. The BAA's inaugural season, which began on November 1, 1946, featured lagging attendance and media indifference. Something needed to be done to generate more interest in the league, even if it meant tinkering with the rules.

That something was to eliminate zone defense.

"The move was made because it slowed down the game, kept scoring down, and bored the customers," BAA publicity director and future NBA commissioner Walter Kennedy told assembled writers. "And after all, the fans pay the freight."

The ban wasn't exactly precise. It outlawed "stationary" zones, but permitted switching man-to-man schemes and what was then known as a "sliding" zone defense. Kennedy insisted that only three of the 11 teams even violated the new rule in the past, and only for short periods of time. The only mechanism to enforce the ban was a verbal pledge from each of the 11 franchise owners.

But though the ban didn't alter gameplay or fix the poor attendance numbers that season, it defined cultural ethos that persisted for decades. Beyond creating an enduring association between zones and boring basketball, it branded the tactic as one that stifled the talent and artistry of the best individual players. Anything that might prevent fans from witnessing their athleticism and individual skill was assumed to be bad for business.

---

19. The league we now know as the NBA was the result of a 1949 merger between the BAA and the National Basketball League (NBL), which began in 1935 and was renamed in 1937. The NBL's six remaining teams joined with 11 of the 12 existing BAA teams, and the two league names were combined into the National Basketball Association. Yet the NBA, curiously, considers the inaugural 1946–47 BAA season to be its first season as well, saying the six NBL teams were "absorbed" into the existing league before it was "renamed."

Fifty-five years later, that decision came full circle. By the spring of 2001, league-wide scores had dropped to their lowest levels in decades, causing television ratings to tumble from the highs of the previous decade. The league's stakeholders were desperate enough to view their onetime nemesis as a potential radical solution. That's why they agreed to allow zone defense back into the NBA, with the caveat that it required a defensive version of the long-accepted three-second violation.

Though it was sold as a way to give defenses more freedom, the real purpose of welcoming zone back into the fold was to juice scoring. Proponents hoped it'd disincentivize stodgy offensive strategies built around one-on-one play with four spectators and instead nudge more teams into a faster, more open style that'd provide more players an opportunity to showcase their athleticism and skill. "Allowing defensive freedom will take away the standstill part of the game," Dr. Jack Ramsay, former NBA title winning coach and member of an 11-person advisory committee that endorsed the need for rule changes, wrote in an ESPN.com column.

Many players and coaches vehemently opposed the change. Michael Jordan, who once referred to one-on-one basketball as "the flagship of creativity," insisted he would not have become the acrobatic, high-flying GOAT[20] if zone defense was allowed during his prime. Sweet-shooting forward Glen Rice feared scoring would drop to the 50s and 60s. Legendary coach Pat Riley warned that zone defense would further clog the paint and close off the very things it was designed to open up.

But it was two-time title-winning Houston Rockets coach Rudy Tomjanovich who said the quiet part out loud for his peers.

"We should create a situation where great players get a chance to excel because they can do so many great things. That's the direction we should be going instead of trying to take things away," he told the *Washington Post*. "Zones neutralize great athletic ability. I don't think it would be good for the league, as far as entertainment. People want to see the guys who can soar to the basket soar to the basket."

Hindsight has proven his argument to be absurd. Most current detractors of the modern NBA believe it's too *easy* for superstars, not too hard. At

---

20. Greatest of All Time, a status most believe Jordan retains despite stiff recent competition from LeBron James.

the time, though, Tomjanovich and his fellow skeptics were mirroring the same logic used by those 11 BAA owners in 1946. Stifling superstars was the reason the NBA had shunned zone defense for decades. Why was it suddenly the league's salvation?

What they didn't realize—or perhaps knew while lacking the imagination or incentive to address—was that the longtime zone defense ban had gradually incentivized coaching strategies that inadvertently neutralized the stylistic brilliance and artistry of very stars they believed they were enhancing. Put another way: the job of a superstar was becoming simpler every season. They needed more of a challenge.

The original ban on zone defense became more specific over time. In 1966, the league stipulated that "a defensive player may not station himself in the key area longer than three seconds if it is apparent he is making no effort to play an opponent." (This was adapted into today's defensive three-second violation.) A further clarification before the 1981–82 season required defenders to be positioned outside the paint if their man stood beyond the three-point line. More importantly, it explicitly prohibited off-ball double-teaming, limiting the other four defenders' choices to "follow the cutter, switch, or double-team the ball." That was, more or less, the measure used to define an illegal zone defense until 2001.

Defenses had just two ways to guard the game's best offensive players. They could check them one on one, or they could double-team when they had the ball. They may as well have shouted, "HEY GUESS WHAT WE'RE DOUBLE-TEAMING YOU" as they came. Some teams, including Riley's Lakers of the 1980s and George Karl's SuperSonics teams in the 1990s, found ways to hide quasi-zone defenses in plain sight. But most weren't so clever.

Over time, ingenious coaches realized they could give the ball to their superstar and move their other four players to the other side of the court until the superstar either shot the ball or got double-teamed. In a perverse way, they helped their superstar teammate *more* by being a spectator instead of an active participant. They didn't even need to be an offensive threat! The rules still required their defensive man to either guard them anyway or travel a long way to outright double-team the guy with the ball. The farther away these non-threats stood from the guy with the ball, the better.

This caused teams to treat the three stages of each offensive sequence like a static checklist instead of a free-flowing set of parameters. They set

May 24, 1995 — Rockets at Spurs — WCF Game 5 (Tied 2-2)
Rockets 66, Spurs 58 — 2:56 left in third quarter

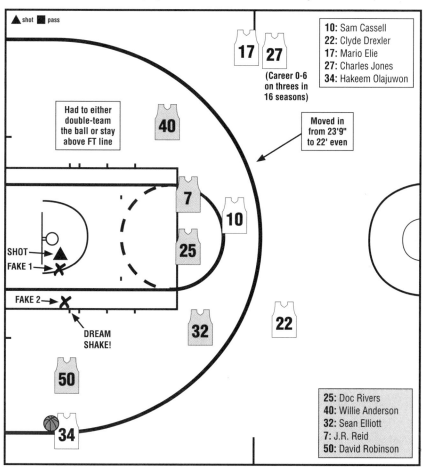

up in a rigid formation to isolate the star at a specific spot on the court, the star worked to create an advantage while everyone else waited, and then he exploited that advantage in the form of a shot or a pass to the double-teamers' man. More "progressive" teams of those times still followed that station-to-station descriptor. The Showtime Lakers' half-court offense was essentially "Give the ball to Kareem Abdul-Jabbar (and later Magic Johnson or James Worthy as Kareem aged) in the post and wait for him to do something." Tomjanovich's Rockets won two titles by posting up Hakeem Olajuwon, dotting three or four shooters along the perimeter, and making defenses pick their form of death.

Even the Triangle offense created by Tex Winter and implemented by Phil Jackson to the tune of 11 champ;ipnsikp[ringhs[21] was designed to simplify the superstar's job. Players shuffle between specific points on the court, collectively drawing the outline of a triangle. Because each of the five players could theoretically occupy any of the key zones, they needed to learn how to go off script and read the defense. The triangle (lowercase "t") thus changed places during each play.

But the whole point of making triangles was to provide a simple framework to give the star the ball—usually in the post—and then space the floor to more easily take advantage if he got double-teamed. Once Jordan embraced the system, he realized it made it *easier* for him to focus on what he did best: score. The concept was equal opportunity. In reality, Jordan led the NBA in usage rate in six of his eight seasons under Jackson.[22]

What began as a smart tactical approach given the rules of the sport was bastardizing the "flagship of creativity" that Jordan held so dear. As long as it was illegal for defenses to do anything other than single-cover or actively double-team the ball, superstars only needed to be deployed as one-man scoring battering rams that beat defenses into submission. While that centralized superstars' power, it also neutered their artistry. Maybe they *could* do so many different great things, as Tomjanovich said, but they no longer *needed* to for their teams to succeed.

Coaches, in other words, had become too good at exploiting the illegal defense rule. The whole point of removing it was to lay down a platform for innovation that would open up the game.

Eventually, it did just that. Today, it's clear Jack Ramsay was right and Rudy Tomjanovich was wrong. Allowing defenses the freedom to position their five players wherever they chose did more than give stars a *chance* to excel because they could do so many great things. It *required* them to be that multifaceted to even be considered stars at all.

The key word is "eventually."

---

21. This is a nod to a famous 2013 Jackson tweet in which he (purposely, we think?) misspelled "championship rings."

22. The exceptions: 1990–91 (Chicago's first title) and 1994–95 (the year Jordan returned from baseball).

AT FIRST, IT was just as Rudy T. feared. Allowing zone defense initially made it easier for defenses to shackle superstars.

That wasn't because teams actually deployed more zones. Most of the league's early flirtations with them were situational and often ineffective. (Minnesota, which placed long-limbed superstar Kevin Garnett atop its 2–3 zone, was a notable exception).

Instead, loosening off-ball defensive restrictions empowered teams to finally ignore offensive non-threats and clog the lane with multiple bodies. This turned many games into ugly wrestling matches. In fact, the four lowest-scoring playoff games of the shot clock era happened during the first three years after 2001's rule changes. All four featured a single common thread: the Detroit Pistons.[23]

Powered by a stifling defense that overcame the absence of a classic offensive superstar, the Pistons came to define this transitional era of the sport. Detroit won just 32 games in 2000–01, the year before zone defense was allowed. They won 50 in 2001–02, traded leading scorer and one-on-one savant Jerry Stackhouse in the offseason, and still earned the East's No. 1 seed while reaching the Eastern Conference Finals in 2002–03. Dismayed by a four-game sweep at the hands of Jason Kidd's New Jersey Nets, Detroit fired successful coach Rick Carlisle and replaced him with Larry Brown.

A well-traveled, but highly successful college and pro coach, Brown was known for two things: his exacting attention to detail and the short shelf life his demands imposed on his players. He had just completed a successful, but exhausting, six-year tenure with the Philadelphia 76ers, during which he frequently clashed with superstar Allen Iverson. Detroit provided a fresh start, along with a gritty, star-less roster that fit his philosophy.

Brown was also a traditionalist that disdained the idea of zone defense. He once claimed a single possession of zone cost UCLA the 1980 NCAA title, even though the Bruins fell by five points to Louisville in the championship game. "We might have lost the national championship my first year because we went zone that one trip against Louisville," Brown told reporters in 2001, when he was still coaching the 76ers. "That kind of busted our bubble a little bit."

---

23. The four: Game 3 of the 2002 Eastern Conference Semifinals vs. Boston (66–64 win); Games 2 (72–67 win) and 6 of the 2004 Eastern Conference Finals vs. Indiana (69–65 win); and Game 1 of the 2004 Eastern Conference Semifinals vs. New Jersey (78–56 win).

But Brown embraced any way to make a stingy man-to-man defense even stingier. He inherited a Pistons team with two-time reigning Defensive Player of the Year Ben Wallace in the middle, a tough lead guard in Chauncey Billups, and a lanky young wing in Tayshaun Prince who showed promise in the 2003 postseason. A midseason trade for Rasheed Wallace, an imposing power forward whose emotional outbursts belied his remarkable on-court intelligence, provided the final piece. With the Wallaces patrolling the backline, Prince locking down top wing scorers, and the combination of Billups and pitbull backups Lindsey Hunter and Mike James hounding ball-handlers, Brown could play his beloved man-to-man defense while also exploiting the looser zone rules that allowed his other four defenders to clog up space.

Layering off-ball zone principles on top of a physical man-to-man defense provided the antidote to the "superstar as one-on-one battering ram" game plan. Those Pistons teams loaded up to the ball while actively ignoring non-shooting threats off it. If said players cut to the basket, one or both of the Wallaces were already in position to wall off the basket.

"Loading up" is different from outright double-teaming superstars when their coaches isolated them on one side of the floor. The Pistons used the NBA's new zone defense rules to make great one-on-one scorers feel like they had to navigate an endless maze of defenders to shoot or pass. This blurred the advantage creation and advantage exploitation stages in ways superstars were ill-equipped to process at the time.

Brown's first season in Detroit ended in an unlikely championship. After upsetting the top-seeded Pacers in a six-game Eastern Conference Finals in which no team topped the 85-point mark in a single game, the Pistons faced a star-studded Los Angeles Laker team finally gelling after a season dominated by on- and off-court drama.[24] The Lakers had the two best players in the series and were thus heavy favorites to win.[25]

Instead, they crumbled against the Pistons "man-to-man plus" defense. Detroit swarmed Shaquille O'Neal and Kobe Bryant without outright

---

24. Ranging from issues as trivial as Gary Payton's struggles with the Triangle offense to ones as serious as Kobe Bryant's sexual assault trial.

25. The Lakers' pre-series betting line was listed as -700, which means you needed to bet $700 to win $100. The only time the favorite's odds have been shorter since was in 2018, when the Golden State Warriors' line to beat the Cleveland Cavaliers was -1075.

June 10, 2004 — Lakers at Pistons — NBA Finals Game 3 (Tied 1-1)
Pistons 16, Lakers 13 — 3:27 left in first quarter

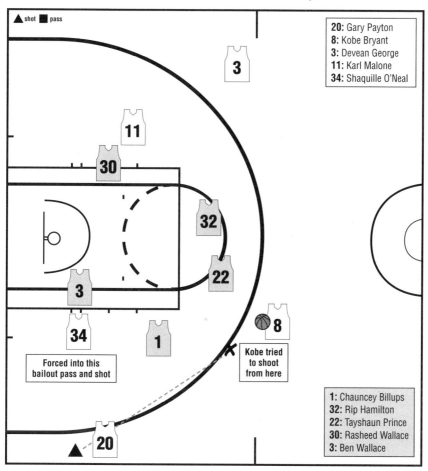

double-teaming them, sending multiple bodies to muck up their one-on-one space while ignoring Gary Payton, Derek Fisher, Devean George, and Slava Medvedenko.[26] Bryant shot just 38 percent from the field in the series, flinging contested shots and missing potential open teammates. O'Neal scored efficiently when he got the ball, but Detroit's roaming and Bryant's shot-jacking limited his touches.

---

26. Medvedenko became a more prominent figure than expected because Karl Malone was laboring through a knee injury. Malone was a shell of himself in the first four games of the series and sat out Game 5 entirely. His ailments made Detroit's strategy even more effective.

Though the Pistons had not employed a classic zone defense, their 2004 title reflected the fears of Tomjanovich and other detractors of the 2001's rule changes. The Pistons' strategy, aided by looser defensive restrictions that allowed off-ball defenders to ignore their men and clog the superstar's space to go one on one, stifled the individual talent of the Lakers' marquee players. Pistons fans and the Lakers' many detractors were happy with their triumph, but this was the exact opposite of the wide-open game the league envisioned three years ago.

Yet this became the nadir from which a new kind of superstar rose. The Pistons' triumph doubled as a warning for the league's best players and their coaches. Evolve into something more than a one-on-one scoring machine or condemn yourself to a lifetime of overloading defenses. The NBA had its desired platform for innovation.

That made it the perfect time to enforce the now-famous 2004 crackdown on all forms of perimeter hand-checking. The chain reaction from the merging of that measure and 2001's loosening of zone defense restrictions created the conditions that the Spaced Out Era exploited a decade later.

In the short term, these measures enhanced superstar perimeter players. With perimeter contact severely curtailed, teams realized the best way to empower their superstar was to keep the ball in his hands from the jump. Posting them up close to the basket and/or deputizing other players to get them the ball in specific spots on the floor lost much of its appeal.

The incumbent players who possessed the well-rounded offensive skill to pass and dribble around overloaded defenses tended to be point guards or smaller perimeter scorers forced into the position due to their height. Their status skyrocketed overnight. Nash rose from fringe All-Star to two-time MVP. Youngsters Chris Paul and Deron Williams forged a rivalry while leading emerging West contenders. Baron Davis, whose career had stalled after a promising start in Charlotte, led the 2007 Golden State Warriors over the 67-win Mavericks in one of the great first-round upsets in NBA history.[27] Combo guards like Washington's Gilbert Arenas and Portland's Brandon Roy briefly rose to prominence before succumbing to injury. Tony Parker, a 6'2" penetrator playing alongside a slimmer Tim Duncan, became one of the NBA's most prolific paint scorers.

---

27. More on the significance of this series in Chapter 4.

The new rules began to affect draft decisions for the better. In 2008, the Chicago Bulls selected high-flying Memphis guard Derrick Rose with the No. 1 pick over a much more productive college player in Kansas State forward Michael Beasley.[28] Rose blossomed into the NBA's youngest MVP three years later, while Beasley's most noteworthy role was as cap fodder in Miami's successful quest to sign LeBron James.

In that same draft, the soon-to-be Oklahoma City Thunder used the No. 4 pick on Russell Westbrook, a slashing off guard who the Thunder envisioned as a dynamic lead ball-handler, even though he finished third on his college team in scoring. After seven seasons quarterbacking a (mostly) devastating Thunder offensive attack alongside Kevin Durant, Westbrook won MVP in 2016–17, becoming the first player to average a triple double since Oscar Robertson in 1962. He achieved the feat in each of the next two seasons, and then again with the Washington Wizards in 2020–21.

Though superstar lead guards benefited most from the 2001 and 2004 rule changes, the three most influential players of the ensuing era defied positional convention. One was Bryant, who took on more ball-handling responsibility after O'Neal's departure in 2004 and won titles in 2009 and 2010 as the head of a looser version of Phil Jackson's Triangle offense. The other two were LeBron James and Dwyane Wade. Before teaming up in Miami in 2010, these two friends and 2003 draft class phenoms showed the next generation of superstars how to dominate games in a post-zone, post-hand-check era. Detroit's 2004 title represented a cohesive five-man defensive unit triumphing over the one-on-one superstars of the pre-zone era. Wade and James willing their unbalanced teams past those same Pistons in consecutive years was the superstar's counterpunch.

Neither's player's game fits neatly into any sort of box. Wade was listed as a shooting guard, but he played more like a blend of the two backcourt spots, soaring through defenders and slithering around them in equal measure. James was pegged as a phenom who combined Karl Malone's physique, Bryant's athleticism, Magic Johnson's passing, and Michael Jordan's scoring. Both possessed excellent court vision—more than excellent in James' case—

---

28. Beasley averaged 26.2 points and 12.4 rebounds per game at Kansas State while generating 10.7 win shares. Rose's numbers for Memphis: 14.9 points, 4.5 rebounds, 4.7 assists, and just 6.6 win shares.

that allowed them to simultaneously scan the floor and make the right decision while driving. They could manipulate the court well enough to deter defenses from loading up on them in ways 2001's rule change allowed.

Each represented a much harder puzzle for the Pistons' vaunted "man-to-man plus" to solve. After sneaking past Miami in seven games in 2005 with Wade limited by an injured rib, Detroit seemingly fortified their favorite status by winning an NBA-high 64 games in 2005–06 under new coach Flip Saunders. That was 12 more games than Wade's Heat, which made Detroit a significant favorite in their playoff rematch.

But this time, Wade danced around and through the flummoxed Pistons in a six-game upset. Miami deployed Wade farther away from the hoop, providing him more space to exploit the Pistons' overloading defense with precise drives and passes to open teammates. The Pistons' efforts to limit Wade's scoring only made things worse. Wade shot just 6–15 from the field in Game 6, but took advantage of Detroit's defensive attention to dish out 10 assists and create countless more buckets indirectly in Miami's 17-point victory.

Wade then torched the Dallas Mavericks in the 2006 Finals, rallying Miami from a 2–0 deficit with one of the most prolific scoring series of all time. Mavericks fans claim that Wade benefited from soft officiating, citing the NBA-record 97 free throws he shot in the six-game series. But their failure to contain Wade had more to do with the rule changes enhancing a new kind of superstar. Wade's combination of sharp movement and court sense was tailor-made for a strategy that opened the floor for him to create for himself and teammates. That way, Wade could use his quickness to zip by the first line of defense and his court vision to manipulate the second.

Yet Wade's ball dominance paled in comparison to James' in Cleveland's run to the 2007 Finals. Handicapped by a severe deficiency in supplementary scoring, the Cavaliers rode their defense and an overwhelmingly James-centric offense to grind out a second consecutive 50-win season and advance to the Eastern Conference Finals. Those same Pistons, other than the departed Ben Wallace, awaited them. The two teams split the first four games, with James drawing (stupid) criticism for passing to open three-point shooter Donyell Marshall with Cleveland trailing by two points in the closing seconds of a Game 1 defeat.

That sequence, while unsuccessful, revealed the crack that brought the Pistons' hybrid zone/man-to-man scheme down for good. Detroit's strategy paralyzed great one-on-one scorers and clogged an offense's usual supply lines to and from them. The new zone defense rules made it possible to perform both of those jobs. But the scheme assumed those tasks were entirely separate, which doomed them against opponents who could centralize the two around a single player like James. He could be trying to score at will on his primary defender, or he could be manipulating the other four to find the right open teammate. The Pistons never knew which. They had to pick their poison and hope for good fortune. Like, say, an excellent three-point shooter bricking a wide-open, game-winning corner three.

In the long run, LeBron's decision to kick out to Marshall at the end of Game 1 informed the historic events of Game 5. With the series tied at two, James stunned Detroit by scoring 48 points in a double-overtime Game 5 victory, including the Cavaliers' last 25 by himself.

Cleveland's late-game, half-court offense didn't exactly embody Ramsay's hope to eliminate the standstill part of the game. They ran no plays, kept their other players still as floor spacers, and let LeBron dribble as much as necessary at the top of the key. They practically begged the Pistons to lock all 10 eyes on LeBron. Yet this time, the superstar paralyzed the Pistons, not the other way around.

James used his combined scoring and passing threat to lull all five Pistons defenders to sleep, attacked his primary defender, then accelerated past the other four before they could slide in position to cut him off. His final two points came when he drove to his left to get inside of Chauncey Billups, slowed down at the free-throw line to make it seem like Detroit's overloading help defense was making him hesitate, then took one large step to the middle of the lane to split Tayshaun Prince and Jason Maxiell for the game-winning, double-clutch layup. To use Tomjanovich's words, a great player succeeded precisely *because* he could do so many things at once.

That remarkable stretch shook the Pistons to their core. In Game 6, the Pistons sent even more defenders James' way, repeating the mistake they made with Wade the previous season. James scored just 20 points on 3–11 shooting, but leveraged Detroit's defensive attention to supply former second-round pick Daniel Gibson with a barrage of threes that put the Pistons away for good.

May 13, 2010 — Cavaliers at Celtics — ECSF Game 6 (BOS leads 3-2)
Celtics 78, Cavaliers 74 — 8:43 left in fourth quarter

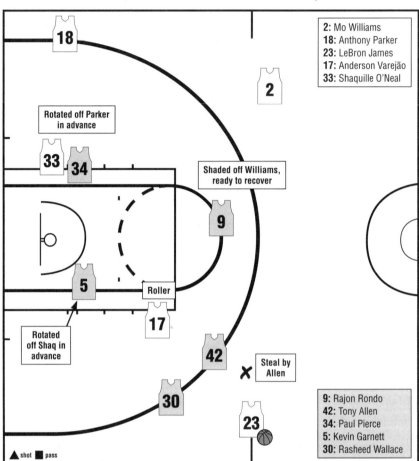

The re-emergence of Bryant's Lakers and the formation of Boston's Big 3—Kevin Garnett, Paul Pierce, and Ray Allen—temporarily delayed the coronation of this new kind of superstar. James in particular struggled against the Celtics' revolutionary defensive scheme. Devised by assistant coach Tom Thibodeau, Boston's system called for the two players involved in any pick-and-roll to swarm the ball-handler while the other three defenders worked together to account for the other four offensive players. It was often called a "strong side zone" because the combination of the on-ball trap and the three-man off-ball shell was designed to pin the ball on one side of the floor. By sending extra defenders to that side to run interference, the Celtics hoped to make it impossible for the new-age, ball-dominant superstar to even see potential open teammates.

This tweak, enhanced by the maniacal Garnett and the Celtics' blue-collar culture, temporarily solved the design flaw that James and Wade exploited against Detroit. The Celtics did not allow James to easily take the ball in space and patiently read their five-man defensive coverage like an elite quarterback. They instead pressured him on the ball while preying on his teammates' limitations off it. James fell just short against the Celtics as an underdog in 2008, crumbled as a favorite in 2010, and only defeated them in 2011 and 2012 after teaming up with Wade in Miami.

Their union was supposed to allow both stars to conquer these five-man overloading defenses once and for all. It sure seemed like they would when Miami zipped past the vaunted Celtics and Thibodeau's new-and-improved Bulls to reach the 2011 NBA Finals. But their ultimate triumph required one more failure.

This time, it was against a veteran Mavericks team who cleverly shifted between man-to-man and outright zone to upset Miami in six games. Using a combination of Shawn Marion, Jason Kidd, and longtime James nemesis DeShawn Stevenson, Dallas successfully concealed their defense's intentions while funneling the Heat's stars into the waiting arms of rim-protecting center Tyson Chandler. James averaged just 17.8 points per game in the series, including a baffling eight-point performance in Game 4, and finished third on the Heat in field goal attempts behind Wade and Chris Bosh. He had been paralyzed into indecision. Again.

James spent that offseason deep in what we now see as necessary soul-searching. Years later, having won four championships with three different franchises, James credited the scheme's designer, then-Mavericks assistant and current Pistons head man Dwane Casey, with ushering in a turning point for his career. There's no question that the 2011 Finals failure inspired James to conquer the final obstacle in his hero's journey.

But James wasn't the only member of the Heat who used that Finals failure as a turning point. Erik Spoelstra, the 40-year-old Pat Riley protégé who survived an early-season firestorm to earn James' trust, was also about to make a much-needed change that would forever transform the sport.

And just as James' evolution personified the ongoing shift in the ever-present reality of superstar's influence, Spoelstra's decision represented the final step of another long-brewing movement.

Chapter 4
The Positional Revolution

Size no longer dictates a player's position—in either direction.

Billy Knight saw the future. And he wanted to make damn sure his Atlanta Hawks were at its forefront.

He owed the Hawks that much. Atlanta brought him into its front office in 2002 after his unsuccessful short stint as the Vancouver Grizzlies GM, then handed him the keys a year later. The franchise knew its long-term situation was bleak, so Knight had plenty of runway to slowly implement his vision.

That vision: a team of versatile, do-everything, multi-position players who could shapeshift on the fly. Forget point guards, shooting guards, small forwards, power forwards, and centers. Knight's team would transcend such basic designations.

"The NBA is too stuck on saying you've got to have a small forward and a power forward," Knight said in the summer of 2005. "What's wrong with being a basketball player? What's wrong with being just a forward?"

Today, the answer to Knight's rhetorical questions is obvious. Once upon a time, being a jack of all trades and master of none doomed NBA careers. Nowadays, versatility is arguably the most prized commodity in the sport. Superstars, as established in the last chapter, must possess all-around games to be considered superstars. Role players must be proficient outside shooters, capable defenders against all sizes of opponents, and competent off-the-dribble playmakers to counteract aggressive closeouts.

Clearly, the days of pigeonholing players into a distinct position are long gone. Point guards don't have to look like floor generals, centers cannot just play like big men, and the three positions in between increasingly blend core elements from all five. That's convinced many to declare this the era of "positionless basketball," embracing Knight's theory that there's nothing wrong—and in fact everything right—with "being a basketball player."

So yes, Billy Knight saw the NBA's future.

There's just one teensy, tiny problem.

That Knight quote from 2005? The one that now seems so ahead of its time? He said it to justify one of the worst draft decisions in NBA history: selecting 6'9" North Carolina sixth man Marvin Williams with the No. 2 pick instead of All-American point guards Chris Paul or Deron Williams.

How did a seemingly clairvoyant NBA figure make such a terrible decision? For that matter, how did Knight make so many others like it during his unpopular, six-year tenure as Hawks GM?[29] Was the NBA simply not ready for a man who said that 6'8" was the ideal height for a basketball player? Was he in fact *too* far ahead of his time?

That's an easy conclusion to reach. It's also the wrong one.

Knight was correct that versatility was about to become the name of the game. But he was wrong—more wrong than most traditionalists, in fact—in anticipating *how* that movement would redefine the in-game application of NBA positions.

Yes, the five positions hardwired into every basketball fan's brain are outdated. Yes, players are being used in ways that require a more fluid positional spectrum. But that does not mean that the positions themselves are obsolete.

In truth, the Spaced Out Era has transformed the concept and application of basketball positions in far more drastic ways than Knight and most of his

---

29. To sum up Knight's proto-positionless swingman fetish: He chose Josh Childress over Luol Deng and Andre Iguodala in 2004, picked Marvin Williams in 2005 despite needing a point guard, selected *another* forward in Shelden Williams over Brandon Roy in 2006, and passed up Mike Conley in 2007 to use his third pick on *yet another forward* in Al Horford—which worked out well in the end, but happened in part because Knight had another point guard lined up in No. 11 pick Acie Law IV, which … yeah.

peers could comprehend. Though the oft-cited "positionless basketball" trope isn't *wrong*, it is a form of shorthand that obscures as much as it illuminates.

Instead, the Spaced Out Era is the culmination of a far more powerful force: a *positional revolution*.

This phrase, coined in 2006 by Nathaniel Friedman—pen name Bethlehem Shoals, creator of the cult favorite Free Darko blog—[30], better reflects the scope of the NBA's new reality. Teams no longer choose players to fill positional roles. They now choose positional roles to most appropriately fit their players. That means creating customized designations that are firm enough to provide a top-down hierarchy, yet flexible enough to rearrange on each possession. Positions, in short, are no longer two-dimensional.

That may seem like a vague description to you, so let's cut to the chase. What are the different NBA positions today if not "point guard," "shooting guard," "small forward," "power forward," and "center"? How many are there, anyway? Five? More than five? Less than five? How do we make sense of today's "centers" playing like yesterday's guards, and vice versa?

These are fair questions, but they also illustrate why the sport underwent an all-out positional revolution and why Knight's approach was doomed to fail. It's time to unlearn what our previous basketball education taught us.

And we'll start by going back to the beginning. The *very, very beginning*.

SPRINGFIELD COLLEGE, 1891: James Naismith, the inventor of the sport we love, organizes the first Basket Ball[31] game in human history. It features two teams self-organized into three positions: guards, forwards, and centers. There are three players for each, in fact, since Naismith's 18 students all needed to play.

Though Naismith's original 13 rules of basketball did not specify these three positions, it was only natural for the players to align themselves this way and use that terminology. Each score reset the action with a "center jump" that resembles the one we use today to start a game. The players positioned in the middle of the floor were, of course, the "centers." That left the remaining six players to line up on opposite sides. The ones defending

---

30. As in Darko Miličić, the Serbian big man who the Pistons infamously took in the 2003 NBA Draft over Carmelo Anthony, Chris Bosh, and Dwyane Wade.

31. That's how he wrote his new sport.

their own basket were "guards" while the ones positioned to attack their opponents' goal were—you guessed it—"forwards."

The game quickly shrunk to five players per side, but the terminology still fit. Teams featured one "center" to do the center jumps, two "guards" to protect their own hoop, and two "forwards" to attack their opponents'. Early summaries differentiated the guards and forwards only by the side they occupied: "right forward," "left forward," "right guard," and "left guard." The game's positions were so named because the players were, quite literally, occupying those positions on the court.

The nomenclature used by Naismith's 18 gym students still persists 130 years later. All-NBA teams feature exactly two guards, two forwards, and one center.[32] All-Star teams were voted on in the same way until 2013, when the center requirement was replaced by an additional "frontcourt player" who could be a forward or center. Television starting lineup graphics still list two guards, two forwards, and a center, even when the players don't look the part. The first five lines of a box score still read: F, F, C, G, G. The sport has advanced quantum leaps since Naismith's first experimental game, yet the naming convention for the players' positions somehow endured.

Isn't that ... strange? Today's guards don't just guard their own basket. Today's forwards don't cherry pick like lazy pick-up players. Today's centers don't line up for hundreds of center jumps à game. They didn't even do those things 70 years ago! It's been a long time since the game's positional lexicon fit the on-court roles of those players.

The purpose of this lesson is threefold. One: there's no reason to cling to the actual naming convention of basketball positions. Two: the on-court responsibilities we may associate with specific positions are constantly evolving with the game's rules and strategies. Three: the specific language of basketball positions always oversimplifies and often obscures their inherent fluidity and actual purpose.

In broad strokes, the game's positional structure evolved in three distinct stages. The first 60 or so years of the sport established a direct link between a player's height and which of the three positions they played. The next half

---

32. The NBA has always made a handful of players eligible at multiple positions, but they significantly loosened the restrictions in 2021. Most notably, they made Nikola Jokić and Joel Embiid eligible at both forward and center.

century expanded those three roles to five more specific ones to reflect the game's increasing tactical complexity. Finally, just as the five distinct positions became ironclad, the last 20 or so years have broken them back down again. That's how we reached the seminal moment of the sport reimagining the very purpose of positions.

Let's rewind back to 1891. With a cold New England winter rapidly approaching, Naismith needed to invent an indoor game that could provide physical exertion for his class of large, aggressive boys. His number one goal was to avoid violence, which ruled out any game that could be won by barreling through opponents to reach a destination. He needed to reward speed and finesse, not brute strength.

"The way smaller kids play is closer to what he intended," Luther Halsey Gulick III[33] told the *Boston Globe* in 1991. "If he saw it now, he might have tried to figure out a game that would fit his theory."

Naismith knew his new game would prohibit players from running with the ball, which is how they learned to bounce it and thus invent dribbling. But his eureka moment came while recalling a childhood game known as "Duck on a Rock." Each player received a small stone to use to dislodge a medium-sized stone (the duck) perched atop a larger stone or tree stump (the rock). That convinced him to perch his new game's goal in the air.

"I thought that if the goal were horizontal instead of vertical, the players would be compelled to throw the ball in an arc," Naismith wrote in his notes. "Force, which made for roughness, would be of no value."

Naismith taped peach baskets atop a pole, settling on 10 feet as the proper distance above the ground. That way, he thought, the relative height difference between the players was immaterial; since none were 10 feet tall, they all needed to throw the ball *upward* to score. That should have freed the players to organize their teams by on-court position and function, not height.

There's just one problem with that logic. Sure, no human being is 10 feet tall. But it sure helps to be closer to it.

It didn't take long for the game's earliest figures to figure that out. By the early 1900s, taller players were regularly steered into playing the new game. This, naturally, intensified the search for even taller players that could stop

---

33. Gulick was the nephew of Dr. Luther Gulick, the physical education superintendent under whom Naismith served at Springfield College.

them. Larger players meant more collisions, especially under the basket, and the rough play that Naismith's invention hoped to avoid. Unsurprisingly, Naismith publicly railed against the state of the game in the years preceding his death in 1939.

Though the long arms race affected all three positions, it radically transformed centers. With the center jump persisting after every made basket until the 1930s, teams could theoretically score once, deploy their tallest player to win the ensuing center jump, and hold the ball until the clock ran out. The taller, the better. Height became synonymous with a center's value, even as Naismith produced several self-conducted studies showing that smaller players were as likely to win these "center jumps" assuming the referee tossed the ball high enough.

That held true even after troubled coaches and members of various rule committees eliminated the center jump after each basket in the mid-1930s. That's because coaches and teams had discovered another reason bigger centers made for better centers.

By the early 1930s, most teams scored by patiently working the ball until they could get close to the basket. There was no shot clock, and the jumper hadn't been invented yet. The easiest way for a team to score was to position its tallest player to shoot over opponents from as close to the hoop as possible. The incumbent tall people were, of course, "centers," and being taller than their peers dramatically improved their performance in their new role.

The more creative teams of that era used their center's size as the pivot point of their entire attack. They threw the ball to him early so he could peer over shorter defenders and decide to shoot *or* pass to open teammates. Two barnstorming pro teams in particular popularized that approach: the all-White Original Celtics with 6'1" "Dutch" Dehnert and 6'5" Joe Lapchick in the 1920s, and the all-Black New York Renaissance (colloquially the "Rens") with 6'4" Tarzan Cooper in the late 1920s and early 1930s.[34] You can trace

---

34. The Original Celtics and Rens were both inducted into the Hall of Fame as full teams. But while the Celtics earned their spot in 1959, the Rens needed to wait another 20 years before they got the call. Basketball history often downplays the Rens' accomplishments because the racism they faced in their heyday too often left them out of sight and mind. Many potential opponents refused to play them, and those who did made them play in front of all-White crowds. Legendary UCLA coach John Wooden, who played against both the Celtics and Rens, once said the Rens "were definitely better" than the Original Celtics.

the legacy of the Original Celtics and Rens to today's brilliant passing big men like Nikola Jokić.

The centers kept growing over the next decade and a half. Lumbering 6'10" giant George Mikan dominated the early NBA years, leading the Minneapolis Lakers to five championships in six seasons. He was so unstoppable that the league doubled the width of the paint from six to 12 feet before the 1951–52 season, forcing Mikan to post up from twice as far away.

By then, there was an additional premium on perimeter size that clarified the differences between guards and forwards. Before the jump shot was invented sometime in the mid-1930s,[35] the other four players' jobs were to control the ball, pass to the center, and patiently repeat ad infinitum until a close shot presented itself. They had two ways to perform that job: passing and dribbling. The jump shot gave offenses a third option: fire it in from the perimeter. The best jump shooters possessed the right combination of size and leaping ability to get their shot off, plus the touch to make it consistently.

As the jump shot rose in prominence, dribbling evolved in ways Naismith never intended. Naismith had mixed feelings about the dribble, which did not feature in his original 13 rules. He admired the players' ingenuity to use it and believed it could be a spectacular feature of the game. Yet he envisioned the dribble as a high bounce to get around defenders, not a low one that enabled offensive players to plow through them.

"When the original 13 rules were drawn up, the dribble was put in there to be an intrinsically defensive action. Its purpose was to enable the man who was cornered to get away from close guarding. The old dribble was waist-high and the guard had a chance to snatch the ball away," Naismith said just before his death in 1939. "But nowadays the dribbling is so close to the ground that it becomes an offensive action, and time and time again I have seen dribblers deliberately crash into a defensive man. The whistle blows and the officials penalize the defense instead of the [player] who brought about the contact."

---

35. The origins of the jump shot remain murky, with upward of 10 different players credited with being the first to attempt one in a game. But everyone agrees the first jump shot occurred sometime in the 1930s and spread in the decades to come.

Naismith's objections did little to change players' habits. There was no rule that regulated dribble height, so why would any dribbler give a defender the chance to snatch the ball away? The lower the dribble, the better, especially when advancing forward. This naturally gave shorter players an inherent dribbling advantage for a simple reason: they were the closest to the ground.

This is how basketball's early days created the height-based division of labor that anchors our current perception of positions. Size mattered for everyone,[36] but it mattered more for some positions than others thanks to a combination of rule changes and innovative figures. Guards dribbled, a skill that incentivized *not* being tall. Forwards shot jumpers, which incentivized a tall and lean physique. Centers performed the dual roles of inside scorer and pivot man, which required them to be both tall and wide so they could carve out space close to the basket. Mikan's Lakers dynasty fit these requirements to a T. Their guards were short dribblers, their forwards were lean perimeter scorers, and their center was Mikan, the biggest giant of all.

It wasn't until the *next* half century that the game's evolution necessitated more specific titles *within* those three positions. The five positions so many hold dear are themselves a more recent invention.

It's hard to pinpoint exactly when basketball shifted from three positions to five. The specific language to demarcate each was not widely cited until the mid-1970s. But as the game became more popular, coaches slowly exerted more influence on their teams' tactics and alignment. They needed to label each player on the court when designing plays and strategies, and the simplest way was to count off 1–5. From their perspective, those numbers became each players' "position."

By the late 1970s, the concept of five positions rather than three went mainstream. The "1" was the "point guard" because they operated at the point of the five-player structure. That made the "2" the "off guard" or "shooting guard," "3" the "small forward," "4" the "power forward," and "5" the center. As more coaches publicly labeled their players with one of those five distinct names and numbers, the public co-opted the terminology on a wider scale.

Naming convention aside, the functional evolution of each of these five positions occurred at different speeds. Much like the previous half century,

---

36. A 1952 *New York Times* headline, for example, called basketball "A Real Goon Game."

a combination of rule changes, innovators, and practical realities slowly cemented their differences.

This decades-long process began in a Syracuse bowling alley in the spring of 1954. Danny Biasone, the owner of the establishment and, more importantly, the NBA's Syracuse Nationals (who moved to Philadelphia and became the 76ers in 1963), summoned general manager Leo Ferris and head scout Emil Barboni to brainstorm ways to eliminate the NBA's worst new tactic. Teams who took the lead were starting to hold the ball for as long as possible, forcing their opponent to foul them to get it back. "Stall ball" was slowing games to a crawl and causing fans to flee in droves.

One of the three took out a napkin and doodled a simple calculation. The trio theorized that the previous season's most entertaining games featured at least 60 shot attempts per team, or 120 shots total. One hundred and twenty shots, divided by 48 minutes, equaled 2.5 shots per minute, or one every 24 seconds. Why not mandate teams reach that elusive shot threshold?

The 24-second shot clock was the most significant invention in basketball history. It turned the sport into the back-and-forth spectacle we now take for granted. There was only one purpose to having the ball: to score points with it. No more possession for possession's sake.

The shot clock also required players to tap into an extra layer of decision-making. Twenty-four seconds was a long time—longer than many players realized, in fact. But it was not infinite. Players had to make split-second choices they never needed to consider in the past. Is this our best chance to score, or do we have enough time left on the shot clock to seek out a better one? If I don't take this shot, will we get a better one before the buzzer sounds?

Like any fledgling start-up, basketball teams were in need of an on-court organizational chart to guide those split-second decisions. Step 1 was to appoint a leader to run the show. This floor general, if you will, got the rest of the team organized, distributed the ball to the right players, spotted quick-scoring opportunities (i.e., "fast breaks"), and applied his coach's strategic directives to the battlefield. Hence, "point guard."

Those best suited to the task at the time were almost exclusively guards, and usually the shorter of the two. Smaller players were better dribblers and thus able to dictate the pace of play. They were also generally faster than bigger players, which comes in handy when leading "fast" breaks. More broadly, smaller players tended to have exceptional on-court intelligence, since they needed to use their brains to overcome their lack of size.

Boston's Bob Cousy became the platonic ideal of this new position. Celtics coach Red Auerbach was not initially a fan of Cousy's game, dismissing the Holy Cross star as a "local yokel" who was all flash and no substance. He passed on Cousy in the 1950 NBA Draft, refusing to yield amid pressure to select the local guy. But Cousy's new team, the Chicago Stags, folded a month before the season. The league placed Cousy and two more established Stags veterans in a dispersal draft, and Boston got stuck with the short end of the stick.

Cousy quickly proved Auerbach wrong, immediately becoming the Celtics' best player and the game's biggest star. His passing and dribbling exploits earned him the nickname "Houdini of the Hardwood" while turning Boston into the league's most effective fast-breaking team. Bill Russell arrived six years later, teaming with Cousy to form a devastating one-two punch that overwhelmed the league. With Russell's defense triggering Cousy's fast-break rushes, the Celtics won six of the next seven titles before tacking on five more after Cousy retired in 1963.

Cousy represented the more deferential interpretation of the new point guard position. His pre-shot clock experience nurtured him to think pass-first, and his post-1956 teams didn't require him to seek his own offense because they were loaded with top-notch scorers.

Meanwhile, Celtics rival Oscar Robertson became the founding father of a more aggressive sect of the position. The original triple double king was taller than most point guards, but the lowly Cincinnati Royals deployed him as a floor general *and* primary scorer to mask their shallow roster. Robertson compiled outrageous numbers in the role and led the Royals to competency, but could never get past the deeper Celtics and Philadelphia 76ers. Robertson's only championship came with the Bucks at the tail end of his career, when he teamed with a young Lew Alcindor.[37]

Robertson's subversion of the position briefly inspired a golden age for "score-first" point guards. The late 1960s and early 1970s featured Walt Frazier thriving in New York, Earl Monroe reinventing style with the Bullets, and Nate Archibald leading the NBA in points *and* assists per game in

---

37. This was before he legally changed his name to Kareem Abdul-Jabbar.

1972–73 with the Kansas City Kings. Dual point guard setups like Frazier–Monroe in New York and Jerry West–Gail Goodrich with the Lakers had a brief moment in the sun.

Yet each score-first success story had at least one counterpart whose prolific numbers did not translate to much team success. Archibald's points/assist feat came while his Kings finished 36–46 and missed the playoffs, with nobody else on the team averaging more than 14 points per game. Pete Maravich's ball-handling wizardry was matched only by the losses his Atlanta Hawks and New Orleans Jazz teams accrued. That conveyed the idea that scoring point guards were doomed to reach a low glass ceiling, tilting the positional archetype back to the Cousy mode.

Codifying the point guard position began to clarify the jobs of the other four. With the point guard coordinating the attack, centers had less reason to develop all-around offensive skills. As long as they could hold down a spot as near to the basket as the rules allowed, their point guards could feed them, or at least direct teammates to do so. Their relationship worked in reverse on defense. The center directed traffic, walled off the basket, and grabbed rebounds that facilitated fast breaks led by the point guard.

The point guard and center became the most common pillars of teams in the 1960s and early 1970s. Examples include Cousy and Russell in Boston, Chamberlain and Hal Greer in Philadelphia, Chamberlain and West in Los Angeles, Frazier and Willis Reed in New York, late-career Robertson and a young Alcindor in Milwaukee, Monroe and Wes Unseld with the Baltimore (and later Washington) Bullets, and more.

The other three positions were initially more interchangeable. But that began to change in the mid-'70s, thanks to two separate forces that collided with 1976's NBA/ABA merger.

While the NBA coalesced around point guards and centers, the renegade ABA incubated lean gliders like Julius Erving, David Thompson, and George Gervin. These players were taller than any guard, but possessed far more athleticism and skill than typical forwards. They were the descendants of Elgin Baylor, the former Los Angeles Lakers high-flier who starred in the early and mid-1960s before knee injuries took their toll. The open ABA style allowed them more space to experiment.

At the same time, both leagues grew more physical as players kept getting bigger and taller. With no three-point line in place in the NBA, the action resembled a wrestling match, much like it did in the 1930s and 1940s. Teams had a need for wide-body enforcers who could do the dirty work and deter opponents from messing with the taller centers or sleeker forwards. Bill Walton had Maurice Lucas. Dave Cowens had Paul Silas. Kareem Abdul-Jabbar had Kermit Washington. The Bullets followed the same principle while inverting the two positions with the more physical center Unseld pairing with sleeker forward Elvin Hayes.

The awkward stylistic marriage between the NBA's point guard/center orthodoxy and the ABA's high-flying ethos split the forward spot into two distinct positions. The multi-skilled gliders became "small forwards," while the blue-collar enforcers were, appropriately, "power forwards." Their relationship was symbiotic: the small forward's all-around skill simplified the power forward's job, while the power forward's grunt work freed the small forward to glide on the perimeter.

The last spot of the five to take on universal characteristics of its own was shooting guard. This position's patron saint is well known. He wore No. 23 and led the Chicago Bulls to six championships in eight years.

Michael Jordan's impact is well known to even the most casual basketball fan. He combined the athletic flair of the post-merger small forward with the scoring capabilities of the pre-merger off guard. The result, combined with his incredible marketing success, turned shooting guard into the game's glamour position. It meant you were 6'6" or so, more than adequate as a shooter, creative as a scorer, majestic yet powerful as a leaper, and a Type A alpha that demanded the ball in big moments. The league spent years searching for Jordan's successor, elevating many false kings before they carved out their own niche or wilted under MJ's shadow.[38]

Jordan's rise was the last domino that expanded three positional archetypes into five. Point guards were small floor generals, shooting guards were mid-sized scorers, small forwards were athletic all-around players, power forwards were the tough guys, and centers were giants. The few exceptions to these descriptors weren't significant enough to alter the norms themselves. This labeling of basketball positions, 110 or so years in the making, persists to this very day.

---

38. Call it the "Harold Miner to Kobe Bryant" spectrum.

Now, it's dying, if not dead already. And the tipping point of its ongoing execution occurred in the spring of 2007, thanks to a downtrodden franchise and a unique set of players who refused to be pigeonholed.

And no, they weren't Billy Knight's Atlanta Hawks.

THE GOLDEN STATE Warriors will forever be the franchise that symbolizes the Spaced Out Era. The overwhelming success of Stephen Curry, Klay Thompson, Steve Kerr, Kevin Durant, Draymond Green, and the other members of squads in the 2010s ushered in many of the modern NBA's distinct features. They certainly played their part in this modern era of positional fluidity.

But those Warriors did not strike the first significant blow against the game's five-position orthodoxy. That honor belongs to the cult favorite team that preceded them by a decade.

With the 2001 zone defense rule and the 2004 crackdown on hand-checking firmly in the rearview mirror, something big was about to happen. It had already begun with several ingenious superstars. In Philadelphia, Allen Iverson scaled the microwave scorer role up to an MVP level. Tracy McGrady and Kobe Bryant were merging the skill sets of all three perimeter positions into an amorphous "giant wing" role. Kevin Garnett and Dirk Nowitzki glued the forward positions back together with their combination of power and finesse. The Suns pierced through the Tao of the dominant big man with sleek dunking machine Amar'e Stoudemire, then pierced it again with point center Boris Diaw. LeBron James was just beginning to break the entire system in Cleveland.

By the fall of 2006, it was only a matter of time before positional ingenuity trickled down to the team level. Non-traditional superstars required non-traditional systems, which required non-traditional pieces to make them, well, non-traditional. Days before the 2006–07 season began, Free Darko's Nathaniel Friedman coined a new term that would foreshadow the modern game.

The NBA, Friedman posited, was poised for the "March of the Positional Revolution." It wouldn't just be individual *players* defying the five-position structure. Soon, it'd be entire teams and organizations.

"The Positional Revolution has flourished only because it has seen its future reflected in an Organizational Revolution. This is perhaps the next great evolutionary leap—never could there be multiple Garnetts or Nowitzkis roaming the court, but teams could very well conceive of themselves as if liberated by their example. Maybe only one or two players in the league are truly beyond positionality; this does not mean, however, that coaches cannot organize a team as if their entire roster were. Creative combinations and unorthodox dynamics require discarding the anonymity of the Old Basketball Order for a deeper, more personal understanding of a player's capabilities. What matters most is not finding omnipotent individuals but most effectively distributing the finite resources of those available."

Friedman predicted that one team would emerge that season to disrupt the game's positional structure. He was wrong about the specific team,[39] but right on the point itself.

That team was the "We Believe" Golden State Warriors. Their peak was brief. Their divorce was messy. But the game is still feeling the ripple effects of their run today.

They were the culmination of Don Nelson's three-decade war against the game's five-position structure. He fired his first salvo in 1984 while coaching the Milwaukee Bucks, an East powerhouse overshadowed by Larry Bird's Celtics and Julius Erving's 76ers.[40] He built his team around 6'7" combo forward Marques Johnson and 6'3" off guard Sidney Moncrief, each of whom became perennial All-Stars and 20-point scorers while playing bigger than their height.

When the Bucks lost to the Celtics in the 1984 Eastern Conference Finals—the fourth straight time either Boston or Philadelphia ended their season—Nelson appeared to push the reset button. With training camp for the 1984–85 season just one day away, Nelson traded Johnson and 30-year-old small forward partner Junior Bridgeman to the Los Angeles Clippers for young power forward Terry Cummings, sharp-shooting guard Craig Hodges, and third-year swingman Ricky Pierce. The Bucks were expected to take a step backward after the deal, with good reason. It seemed to dramatically thin out their strongest position (small forward) without addressing their

---

39. He thought it'd be the Washington Wizards, which breaks my heart as a Wizards fan.
40. The Bucks had been in the Western Conference before 1980, but the league moved them to the East to make room for the expansion Dallas Mavericks.

weakest (point guard, which had become a revolving door since Quinn Buckner left in 1982).

But Nelson solved both of those problems in a single stroke, inspired, ironically, by an experiment involving Johnson the previous season. With the Bucks' already-thin backcourt battered by injuries, Nelson asked Johnson to take on more ball-handling responsibilities during their second-round series against the New Jersey Nets. Confused, Johnson asked if that meant he was a "point forward." Nelson hadn't heard the term before, but he liked it. With Johnson performing ably, if not always artfully, the Bucks slipped by the pesky Nets in six games before losing to Boston in the next round.[41]

Johnson was gone, but the Bucks had another player with the potential skill set to fit this new position even more effectively. That player was Paul Pressey, a sturdy 6'5" former first-round pick who had carved out a utility role behind Moncrief, Johnson, and Bridgeman. With two of those three gone, Pressey needed to play.

The question was where to put him. Nelson initially envisioned Pressey as a sixth man, but changed his mind after talking with Del Harris, the former Houston Rockets coach who was between jobs at the time. Harris recalled using big guard Robert Reid as a "point forward" earlier in the decade. He suggested Nelson do the same with Pressey.

Nelson agreed, immediately labeling Pressey as his starting "point forward" in multiple interviews that preseason. With Pressey flanking Hodges and Moncrief on the wings and Cummings up front, the Bucks won 59 games and finished second behind the Celtics in the East. Pressey was a revelation, doubling his scoring average from eight to 16 points while contributing seven assists and more than five rebounds per game.

Pressey wasn't the first tall point guard, nor was he even the first player to perform like a "point forward." But unlike Robertson or even Magic Johnson, who unambiguously played like *point guards* despite their height, Pressey's position changed within each game. On offense, Pressey was as

---

41. Johnson didn't start at point guard, as the Bucks normally listed veteran shooter Mike Dunleavy as Moncrief's backcourt partner. But Johnson did regularly initiate the offense, especially during the Bucks' closeout win on the road in Game 6. Johnson only had two assists to go along with his 25 points and 13 rebounds, but he brought the ball up on nearly every possession from the middle of the third quarter on.

liable to post his own man up as he was to throw a teammate a post entry pass. On defense, he defended multiple positions, not just small forwards.

More importantly, his interchangeability freed Nelson to deploy him alongside teammates who also possessed uncommon skills for their size. Pressey's playmaking made the 6'2" Hodges a viable starting shooting guard, channeled Pierce into the sixth man role he loved, and enabled top options Moncrief and Cummings to shoulder the bulk of the scoring instead of worrying about positionally appropriate duties like passing or rebounding. Those players, in turn, covered up Pressey's errant perimeter shooting and scoring reluctance.

Taken separately, each lacked the prototypical skill set for their position. Together—and *only* together—they filled every on-court job necessary to succeed. They, in a sense, represented the original Positional Revolution.

Nelson's experiments continued after he left the Bucks in 1987. His high-powered trio of Tim Hardaway, Chris Mullin, and Mitch Richmond, codename Run TMC, upset Larry Brown's more traditional Spurs in the first round of the 1991 playoffs. Nelson used a strategy that mocked the illegal defense rule discussed in Chapter 3. Knowing Spurs superstar center David Robinson was best when close to the hoop, Nelson instructed his three centers—journeyman Jim Petersen, former Bulls cast-off Tom Tolbert, and rookie Tyrone Hill—to stand as far away from the basket as possible on every offensive possession. The rules forced Robinson to go with them, leaving him unable to help San Antonio's weaker perimeter defenders combat the post-ups and/or isolations involving the Warriors' three deadly perimeter weapons.

After a half-season failed attempt to remake the defensive-oriented Knicks in his image, Nelson moved to Dallas in 1997. There, he incubated an offense-first, defend-later title contender, building around prolific scoring trio Steve Nash, Dirk Nowitzki, and Michael Finley. The Mavericks won 53 games in Nelson's third full season in 2000–01, jumped to 57 and 60 wins the next two years, and might've broken through if Nowitzki didn't injure his knee in the Western Conference Finals against the Spurs.

By now, Nelson's tenures were following the same pattern: surprising initial success followed by some sort of internal drama that prevented his ideas from earning enough staying power to go from renegade to mainstream.

Nelson seemed to relish being a maverick, pun intended. Most of his peers admired him from afar without adopting his ideas up close.

By 2006, though, the Warriors were such a laughingstock that another Nellieball merry-go-round appealed to them. Mullin, now Warriors' general manager, wooed Nelson for weeks, finally convincing him to return as head coach at the end of August. The Warriors initially floundered, but a midseason trade with the Pacers for Stephen Jackson and Al Harrington spurred a 16–5 finish that snuck them into the playoffs for the first time since Nelson last coached the team in 1994.

As fate would have it, Nelson's most recent former team awaited as their first-round opponent. Avery Johnson, a feisty former point guard who succeeded Nelson at the end of the 2004–05 season, had transformed Mavericks into a snarling, half-court, defense-first unit. It was hard to argue with the results: Dallas reached the NBA Finals in 2006 and responded to their collapse against Miami with a 67–15 season in 2006–07. Nowitzki, the last holdover of Nelson's Big 3, largely ditched three-pointers to focus on dominating in the high post and mid-range areas. This more "traditional" version of Dirk ascended to become the league's first European-born MVP.[42]

Nelson's Warriors, fittingly, were the antithesis of "traditional." Their eight-man rotation featured one oversized point guard (Baron Davis), a point-guard-sized shooting guard (Monta Ellis), a classic post-Jordan 6'6" shooting guard (Jason Richardson), three small forwards with different odd skill sets (Jackson, Matt Barnes, and Mickaël Piétrus), a shooting power forward (Harrington), and an undersized center (Andris Biedriņš). Most referred to the Warriors as a "small-ball" team, or even an anarchic one with no positions or structure whatsoever.

They misunderstood the method to the Warriors' madness. Zoom out, and Golden State had all the elements of a normal team. They paired a superstar (Davis) with a collection of role players who each brought something different to the table. They teamed scorers (Davis, Ellis, Richardson) with role-playing specialists (Barnes, Piétrus, Biedriņš). They had shooters (Richardson, Harrington, Jackson, and Piétrus), playmakers (Davis and Jackson), lockdown defenders (Jackson, Piétrus, and Barnes to a lesser

---

42. Hakeem Olajuwon, born in Nigeria, was the first non-American-born player to win the award in 1993–94.

April 22, 2007 — Warriors at Mavericks — WCQF Game 1
Warriors 72, Mavericks 68 — 10:48 left in fourth quarter

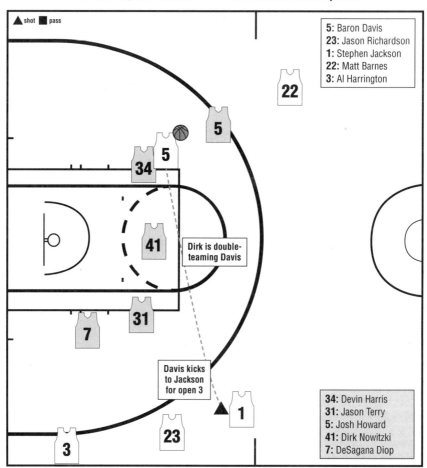

extent), slashers (Davis, Ellis, Barnes), and rebounders (Davis, Biedriņš). They didn't have a towering big man, but they had tough defenders inside and out (basically everyone except Ellis). They had play-starters (Davis, Jackson) and play-finishers (everyone else). They had microwave scorers (Ellis) and dirty-work specialists (Barnes and Biedriņš). The players who filled those roles just didn't play the positions typically associated with them.

That meant the Warriors could structure different team hierarchies on each possession. As TNT's Kenny Smith bellowed at halftime of Golden State's Game 1 victory in Dallas, "Everything you would want to have, they have, and it works well for them. … They are everything opposite." As

Friedman predicted, the Warriors embodied the Positional Revolution on a team scale. That made them the perfect foil for a Mavericks team trying desperately to embody the exact opposite.

Many expected the Warriors to challenge Dallas, since they had Nelson and handed the Mavericks three of their 15 regular-season losses. But few expected them to decisively pull off one the greatest upsets in NBA playoff history. After Dallas rallied late in Game 5 to avoid elimination, Golden State ran the No. 1 seed off the floor to win in six games.

The Warriors swarmed Nowitzki on the block, ran the ball down Dallas' throats, and bypassed the Mavericks' rugged interior defense with long-range bombs. Their unconventional alignment glitched the Mavericks' well-drilled system. Johnson tinkered with starting lineups, initially benching his centers for an extra wing player, then reinserting them when that failed. Either way, the Warriors scored easily in transition, collectively shut Nowitzki down, and spread the Mavericks defense out so Davis could break down their slower defenders at will.

Even by Nellie's standards, the "We Believe" Warriors had a short peak. By the fall of 2008, Davis was a Clipper, Richardson was a Charlotte Bobcat, and Ellis was a franchise pariah after seriously injuring his ankle in an unsanctioned moped accident. But their 2007 run foreshadowed the fundamental reshaping of basketball positions that loomed on the horizon.

Though Nellie lacked the players or temperament to finish the Revolution, he understood three key points before others adopted them as gospel.

First, skill determines one's position, not size. Just because most shorter players are better dribblers and passers than taller players doesn't mean that *all* shorter players are better dribblers and passers than *all* taller players. Similarly, just because taller players were usually better rebounders, shot blockers, and interior scorers than shorter players doesn't mean every tall guy is automatically better at those tasks. Size can help guide a coach's lineup choices and a player's developmental focus, but it cannot make those decisions for them.

Second, each player's position must be determined by specific contextual factors like team composition, style of play, and the unique shape of each possession. Positional labels have always been shorthand to some degree. It takes less time to call Michael Jordan a "shooting guard" than a "point guard when he brings the ball up, a small forward when he cuts to the corner, a shooting guard when he faces the basket, and a center when he posts up." But the growing three-point awakening, 2001's elimination of illegal defense, and league-wide crackdown on hand-checking has freed (or forced, depending on your point of view) all kinds of players into different spots on the floor. The wider the court, the less a five-pronged labeling convention simplifies.

The third point explains why Nelson's Warriors, and not Knight's Hawks, inspired the Positional Revolution that followed. Individual player versatility was indeed essential, but successful teams and players manifested that versatility by *changing* positions within games and sequences. The Warriors didn't overwhelm the Mavericks because they used five generalists of similar height and weight. They did it with five-man *units* that arranged the necessary basketball skills in different patterns than their predecessors. They had a versatile *team*, not just a bunch of versatile players. Knight's team of 6'8" guys, by contrast, proved to be as inflexible as one neatly stratified by height.

That distinction is important to understanding the 2007 Warriors' decisive defeat in the next round. If "small ball" (or simply "not normal-sized ball") drove the Warriors' first-round triumph over the bigger Mavericks, it should have been even more effective against their second-round opponent: the bigger, worse, and even more traditional Utah Jazz. Instead, Utah dispatched Golden State in five games by staying committed to *their* positional arrangement instead of altering it to match the Warriors'. Even now, "big ball" can work just as well as small ball when performed by the right combination of players.

Nellie's ideas found their mainstream vessel in the Miami version of LeBron James. Though the King's individual positional fluidity was obvious from an early age, the Cavaliers teams from his first stint in town squandered it by deploying burly, non-shooting power forwards and centers alongside their star. That didn't matter in the regular season, but it neutered James' best qualities against top playoff opponents.

The same problem torpedoed James' first season in Miami. Whether by choice or necessity,[43] the Heat retrofitted two of the game's most versatile stars in James and Dwyane Wade into a size-based positional arrangement.

---

43. The Heat didn't have much money to build an optimal roster around their three new near-maximum salaried players, especially after mid-level exception signing Mike Miller struggled through an injury-plagued 2010–11 season.

Chris Bosh, the third star in the Heat's new Big 3, played a scaled-down version of his Raptors power forward role alongside plodding centers and shorter, floor general point guards. That arrangement treated Wade and James like most 6'4" and 6'8" guys in NBA history instead of maximizing their ball-dominant, attacking games with effective spot-up shooters.

That's why the Mavericks' hybrid defensive scheme neutralized James in the 2011 NBA Finals. Dallas could roam off Miami's non-perimeter threats without actively double-teaming James to the point of activating his pinpoint passing. They made James play passively by closing off driving lanes and shrinking the space he could manipulate with his playmaking.

It wasn't until the next season that the key lesson of the Positional Revolution sunk in. James was an unstoppable freight train, supernatural passer, physical marvel, and arguably the most multi-dimensional superstar in NBA history. The Heat, to use Friedman's words, needed to be liberated by his example. The failure of the 2011 Finals had convinced the Heat that *their* structure needed to prioritize shooters and play-finishers at all positions, not just the ones typically associated with shooting and play-finishing.

James' two titles in Miami were the product of that lesson. Coach Erik Spoelstra spent the summer of 2011 drawing inspiration from an unlikely source: then-Oregon football coach Chip Kelly's spread offense. Pat Riley, now the Heat's president of basketball operations, used a precious salary-cap exception on Shane Battier, betting that the skill set that made him a terrific off-ball player complemented their stars even though he played the same traditional position (small forward) as James. Bosh accepted fewer touches, increased his shooting range, and anchored Miami's manic defensive scheme.

Their efforts culminated in the 2012 playoffs, when Spoelstra moved Battier into the starting lineup and made Bosh the unit's "biggest" player.[44] That

---

44. While Bosh and Battier only started together in the final four games of that season's NBA Finals, the spirit of Spoelstra's decision to downsize and reimagine their positions began earlier. First, Bosh suffered an injury in Game 1 of their second-round series against Indiana. Miami started little-used big men Ronny Turiaf and Dexter Pittman in his place for the next two games, both losses. Down 2–1, Spoelstra chose to start Battier in Game 4 and make Udonis Haslem a super-sub. The Heat won the next three games, then split the first four games with Boston in the next round. Bosh returned in a limited role in a Game 5 loss, then played starter's minutes while coming off the bench in the Heat's next three games (wins over Boston in Games 6 and 7, followed by a loss to the Thunder in Game 1 of the NBA Finals). At that point, the Heat decided Bosh had sufficiently healed from his injury and moved him back into the starting lineup in place of Haslem.

June 7, 2012 — Heat at Celtics — ECF Game 6 (BOS leads 3-2)
Heat 19, Celtics 12 — 2:47 left in first quarter

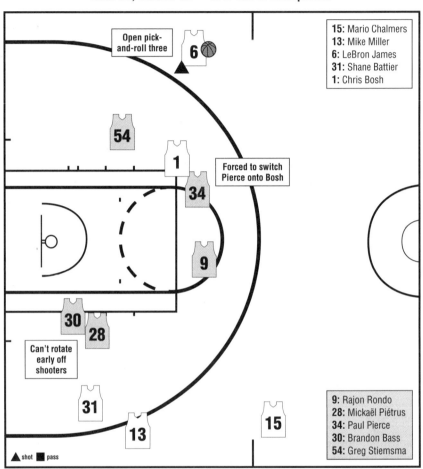

Open pick-and-roll three

6

15: Mario Chalmers
13: Mike Miller
6: LeBron James
31: Shane Battier
1: Chris Bosh

54

1

Forced to switch
Pierce onto Bosh

34

9

30

28

Can't rotate
early off
shooters

31

13

15

9: Rajon Rondo
28: Mickaël Piétrus
34: Paul Pierce
30: Brandon Bass
54: Greg Stiemsma

▲ shot ■ pass

move spurred playoff victories over the ferocious Pacers, seasoned Celtics, and precocious Oklahoma City Thunder to earn James his first championship.

Spoelstra often refers to his teams as "positionless," which is true to a point. The shortest guy didn't run the offense. The best spot-up shooter defended the opponent's strongest post-up player. The tallest guy shot more threes and stepped out furthest when defending pick-and-rolls. The second-shortest guy refused to shoot threes and anchored the back line of their defense. Each of those positional inversions served a superstar small forward who kind of functioned as a point guard, except when he posted up like a big man or went one on one like a Jordan-esque off guard.

But the Heat's setup did not upend positional roles, it reorganized them around context-specific qualities. They had players who fulfilled the *jobs* designed for point guards, shooting guards, small forwards, power forwards, and centers. They just weren't the players who *looked* like point guards, shooting guards, small forwards, power forwards, or centers—or even the same five players each time down the floor. That's how Miami built a system that was firm enough to maximize their roster's strengths, but fluid enough to adapt to any circumstance. It is only "positionless" in comparison to the size-based, five-position norm.

It also wasn't "small ball," another catch-all term that falls short of capturing the power of the Positional Revolution. Like Nellie's Warriors, the Heat were considered a "small-ball" team for superficial reasons. They didn't have a tall big man playing center, shot lots of three-pointers, and scored most often via perimeter drives to the basket. That meant they played "smaller" in practice than their 2012 opponents. But that was only because the rest of the league remained anchored to an outdated five-position structure.

In truth, the Heat weren't a small team at every position, or even most positions. They had the same goal as any team built around a post-up center: to enhance the advantage their biggest/strongest/quickest guys had on their defenders. The difference is the Heat's biggest/strongest/quickest guys were James and Wade, two freaks of nature who looked like a shooting guard and small forward, respectively. The wider their driving lanes, the more easily their two stars could use their physical advantages to attack the basket. Given the rise in three-point attempts, elimination of hand-checking, and relaxation of zone defense rules, their stars' greatest physical advantages were deadliest when farther from the hoop, not closer to it.

That's not "small ball." It's more like taking size from positions associated with inside play (power forward and center) and redistributing it to positions associated with perimeter play (shooting guard and small forward, in this case).

The term "small ball" has become even more misleading during the Warriors' post-2014 run of dominance. Like the Heat, the Light Years Warriors[45] of Stephen Curry and co. superficially played "small ball." Their

---

45. A nod to owner Joe Lacob boasting to *The New York Times* in 2016 that his franchise was "light-years ahead of probably every other team in structure, in planning, in how we're going to go about things."

shortest starter was their best player, and he inspired more terror the farther he moved from the basket. He and his teammates shot the type of audacious threes that nobody else dared try before them. Their defensive strategy of switching screens kept their opponent on the perimeter. They became the best version of themselves whenever they used 6'7" (at best) Draymond Green as their nominal center.

In reality, the Warriors were much *bigger* than their opponents at most positions. Klay Thompson, Andre Iguodala, Harrison Barnes, Shaun Livingston, and, of course, Kevin Durant were all oversized perimeter players. Green isn't tall, but he has long arms and a thick chest. Even Curry is listed at 6'3", which is above-average height for a point guard.

"People say Golden State downsizes. They don't downsize. They're huge," longtime NBA coach Steve Clifford once said. "They play Draymond Green at the '5' and people say they downsize. Try to play against them. They're bigger than you at every single position. Someone will throw up one of these clichés, and they don't study the issue. It's crazy."

The Warriors' genius was they made *other teams* go small to match up with them. Green could cosplay a traditional big man on one end, then run them out of the gym on the other. Thompson, Durant, and Iguodala played like smaller players on offense while blinding the best shooters or dribblers with their length. Curry was quicker than most pint-sized perimeter defenders and far too elusive to fall victim to the physical play of more rugged ones. Defeating them with an old-school lineup arranged by size was a fool's errand. Downsizing just meant playing their game with smaller players. Damned if you do, damned if you didn't.

The positionally fluid sport we see now is a direct result of those Warriors forcing the rest of the league to quickly get on their level. Many traditionalists feared the Warriors driving tall players into extinction. But the tall players didn't die, nor did smaller players stage a violent coup. Instead, they learned to think about positions more holistically and co-opted each other's skills.

Their success dramatically accelerated the Positional Revolution to the point where it's barely a revolution anymore. It's weird to find a tall player who *isn't* capable of playing on the perimeter, whether they're skinny or stout. We expect small guys to finish around and through big men at the rim, whether they look like skinny twigs or powerful bowling balls. We expect each set of players to sometimes occupy spaces on the floor once reserved for the other. It no longer makes sense to categorize a player's on-court function using five terms based primarily on physical characteristics.

Yet it's equally misleading to suggest that the Spaced Out Era has done away with positions entirely. Yes, many taller players play like shorter ones and vice versa, an upheaval that has largely resulted in more well-rounded players of all sizes. But there is a big difference between "this guy does not exclusively play this single position" and "this guy does not *have* a position at all." Today's players move freely *between* different positions on the court, shifting from task to task between and within possessions in conjunction with their teammates. Basketball positionality is multidimensional, not obsolete.

That's why flat positional designations are fundamentally flawed even with more specific parameters. In 2012, a Stanford University senior named Muthu Alagappan conducted a multi-regression analysis of seven per-minute statistical categories to come up with 13 positions. One of them was dubbed "One of a Kind" because none of the other 12 slots fit their games. Two of the "One of a Kind" players were Derrick Rose and Dwight Howard, who just so happened to fill the top two slots in 2011 MVP voting.

In 2020, a Sloan Sports Analytics Conference paper used 23 different inputs—height plus 22 per-minute individual statistics—to plot NBA players along a spectrum featuring nine positions. The authors then reclassified the players from every lineup that appeared in a game from 2009 to 2018 to determine the most optimal combination of the nine positions. Their model predicted that the ideal lineup "consists of 1.25 Ball Dominant Scorers, 2.25 Versatile Role Players, 1 Traditional Center, and 0.5 Stretch Forwards."

Both of these studies are interesting and rigorous, but they suffer from the same problems. They are each anchored to the classic positional framework that itself evolved over time. As we've outlined in this chapter, the bundling of skills that now makes a center "traditional" was not always so. Each labels players retroactively based on their production in prior contexts, which downplays the reality that the game's constant evolution reshapes necessary player skills in unpredictable ways.

Most importantly, they both assume a linear relationship between a player's statistical outputs within the lineups they have played in and the positions they'd fill within *any* five-man lineup they'll play in the future.

This ignores the most powerful lesson of the Positional Revolution: the two variables are inherently symbiotic.

The five players on the court are best enhanced when they have complementary skill sets, but those skill sets also change based on the specific combinations of players on the court. James Harden, Kyrie Irving, and Kevin Durant didn't suddenly turn into "versatile role players" upon teaming up with the Brooklyn Nets, but they also didn't produce exactly like "ball-dominant scorers" (on the rare occasions they shared the court). There's more than one way to skin the lineup cat in the modern NBA. A universal positional naming system must reflect that fluidity.

The post-COVID-19 pandemic seasons reveal the dangers of replacing one rigid positional structure with another. Take the 2019–20 Los Angeles Lakers, who brought James his fourth title with his third organization. James' success in Miami and Cleveland came when he was surrounded with one other perimeter scorer and pristine floor spacing at every position, which made it easier for him to attack the basket via drives or post-ups.

By that standard, the Lakers' mix was about to fail him. Few doubted Anthony Davis' capability to be James' co-star, but he wasn't a second perimeter scorer, was far too talented to fill a Bosh/Kevin Love-esque tall spot-up shooter position, and preferred playing alongside physical, big centers who rarely possess three-point range.

With few funds at their disposal after trading every key young player not named Kyle Kuzma for Davis, the Lakers were forced to fill out their roster with many of the select few non-shooters still left in the sport. The ensuing roster was top heavy, anchored in the past, and devoid of the qualities that James supposedly required, especially in a post-Warriors era.

Yet it worked like a charm—for that season at least. While the rest of the league downsized to match Golden State, the Lakers doubled down on physical defense while maintaining enough agility and length to cover the game's increasingly wide court. Instead of maximizing space to help James succeed, they used his precise passing, pristine decision-making, and opportunistic fast breaking to prop up defensive-oriented lineups. They used Davis alongside traditional centers for most of the game and season, then unleashed a rested version as their center to finish teams off.

While the Lakers' built their counterintuitive roster after a shotgun wedding, another budding West power is spreading the Positional Revolution gospel on a longer timeline.

The Denver Nuggets are built around former second-round pick Nikola Jokić, who appeared to be a chubby seven-footer going out of style in an NBA that required mobility from its big men. Even as he emerged—first as a rotation player, then a starter, then an All-Star—he and his team seemed doomed to hit a glass ceiling. He looked like a center, and centers, no matter their unique qualities, were seen as being on the road to extinction.

So is Jokić a center? Well, yes and no. He certainly can play like one, using his, ahem, wide base to ward off opponents like a camp counselor playing keep away. He regularly bullies defenders in the post, scoring countless hoops or picking out passes from the swirl of cutters around him.

But Jokić also dribbles the ball up the floor and orchestrates the Nuggets offense from beyond the three-point arc, making him more like the goofiest point guard in NBA history. He certainly passes like a point guard—hell, he's one of the best passers of all time, period, no matter the position. Jokić is also an improving three-point shooter and creative finisher on the move, skills once prized in traditional shooting guards and small forwards. When he's not doing all that, he's wedging opponents under the basket for rebounds in much the same way enforcer power forwards once did.

So what position does Jokić play? Any and all of them ... often within *the same sequence*. He's not just a center, despite his size, but he also doesn't play like he has no position in practice. He *can* play like a center. He just also *switches* between that and the other four positional roles, often instantaneously and unpredictably. That combination of positionally rigid size and positionally fluid skill made him a two-time MVP and a perennial matchup nightmare.

Jokić's unique talent might have been squandered if not for the Nuggets' creative front office and coaching staff. They've surrounded Jokić's one-of-a-kind combination of size and skills with idiosyncratic teammates who also operate outside height-based positional norms. Jokić certainly props up players like combo guard Jamal Murray, oversized wing shooter Michael Porter Jr., and jack-of-all-trades-and-master-of-none forward Aaron Gordon, to name a few. Injuries have prevented us from seeing their roster at full flight, but they've remained an able West contender despite key absences.

**September 11, 2020 — Nuggets vs Clippers — WCSF Game 5 (LAC leads 3-1)
Nuggets 94, Clippers 91 — 5:11 left in fourth quarter**

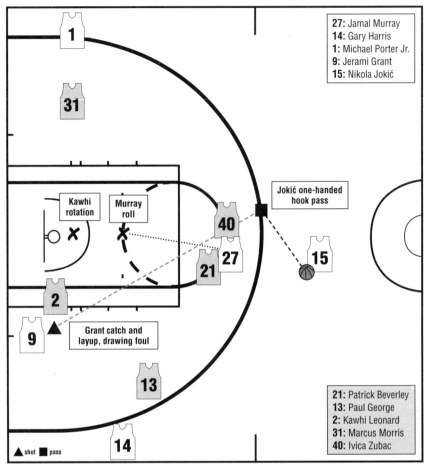

Those Nuggets also help Jokić by providing off-the-dribble shooting, defense, and one-on-one perimeter scoring. Freeze a typical Nuggets possession at different times, and it's hard to pinpoint each individual player's position. If you didn't know anything about their heights, you'd have no clue how to classify them. But their overall structure can still be constant no matter how Jokić is being deployed any given time. The Nuggets find a way to cover all five positions, just not by the same people at the same time.

Jokić's 2021 and 2022 NBA MVP honors, along with fellow tall-guy-with-absurd-small-skills Joel Embiid's emergence as his equal, is often interpreted as a sign of the big man's resurgence. But that perspective is as narrow-minded as "small ball" or Billy Knight's 6'8" fetish.

The modern NBA is height agnostic. Teams instead embrace exceptionally skilled players at any height, seek out players of all sizes to find the complementary skills *their best player(s)* need, and retrofit the positions after the fact. That's how we get a league in which players who look as different as Curry, Jokić, Embiid, Durant, Giannis Antetokounmpo, and James can each thrive.

That may be inelegant for winning an argument with friends or picking All-NBA teams. Its complexity makes the term "positionless basketball" tempting shorthand. But it's the only way to fully understand how the Spaced Out Era transformed the very concept of basketball positionality.

Chapter 5
Our Best Play Is "Random"

The rise of "pace and space" and the merging
of fast break and half-court play.

In 2007, Jeff Van Gundy and first-year assistant general manager Daryl Morey collaborated on a joint project to mold Morey's data-driven approach with Van Gundy's seasoned pragmatism. The task was simple and the implications were obvious. They wanted to know which Van Gundy play calls performed the best.

Two-thirds of the way through the project, Morey took a peek and discovered that the play at the top of the list was unfamiliar to him. Confused, he asked Van Gundy what it was called.

"[He said] 'It's called random. That's when the play breaks down, and we just set a random screen.'" Morey recalled during a 2014 Sloan Sports Analytics panel. "So I was like, 'Well, that might tell us something right there.' Our best play is 'Random.'"

Neither man believed that "something" was to have no offensive structure at all. Still, the data was sending a powerful message with wide-ranging implications that few grasped in 2007, more understood in 2014, and almost everyone in the game takes for granted in 2022. The best way to score isn't to diagram an elaborate sequence that beats a set defense. It's to sew and exploit chaos. To play instead of calling a play. To be "random."

That discovery has become the ethos that defines every single modern NBA team. Instead of stopping to script a path through a set defense, they keep the game moving in an attempt to bypass it entirely. The goal is to run Van Gundy's deadly "Random" play as often as possible.

Every team has jumped aboard the speed revolution with startling, uh, speed. The 2004–05 Phoenix Suns, who revolutionized the sport with their "Seven Seconds or Less," "pace and space" style, averaged what was then a league-leading 97.35 possessions per game. That same figure would've ranked them 28th in 2020–21. Look down at your phone for a split second, and you'll miss teams zipping up the court and getting multiple shots off. Television crews now pan to player close-ups at their own peril.

The game's loudest critics decry this as undisciplined basketball. Too many bad shots. Too many turnovers. Too little structure. But there is a method to the fastness. Speed creates chaos, and it's easier to score by exploiting chaos than trying to control it. After decades of resistance, the league's coaches and players learned to welcome chaos' benefits instead of fearing its costs.

The in-universe jargon to describe this widespread movement is distilled into a single word: pace. Yet pace is far more than a catch-all term to describe the many different ways teams play fast. It is also a mindset that binds those strategic methods and historic developments to a team's overall strategy. "Pace" is the spark that lights the fire of the mushroom cloud that is the Spaced Out NBA.

So before we dive into pick-and-rolls, off-ball screens, split cuts, or any of the elaborate tactics used to defend all those fun things, we must explore how and why teams go to great lengths to avoid doing any of that stuff in the first place.

Since the advent of the shot clock in 1955, basketball possessions have historically taken one of two forms. Most fall into the category of half-court play: five offensive players against five defensive players, all of whom stand beyond the mid-court line. The rest come when the offense rushes the ball up the floor in an attempt to score before the five defenders can get set. In these situations, the word "transition" is used interchangeably with "fast break" because the team with the ball is "breaking" out as "fast" as possible while both sides "transition" from one end to the other.

All things being equal, it's easier to score against fewer defenders than all five. The numbers support this no-duh observation. According to the website Cleaning the Glass (an indispensable subscription service created by former league executive Ben Falk), the league averaged 119.2 points per 100 possessions in transition and just 83.1 points per 100 possessions in half-court situations in 2003–04, the first season tracked by that database.[46] Both numbers steadily rose as the league got three-point religion, but the difference between the two has remained consistent. By that logic, every team in NBA history should run way more fast breaks.

All things, of course, are not equal. Defenses hope to avoid fast breaks as much as offenses yearn to create them. Fast breaks mean lots of running, and running makes players tired. The numbers also reflect a selection bias, since teams only try fast breaks after spotting an easy scoring opportunity. There are a whole host of other factors.

But the biggest reason teams haven't forced more fast breaks is psychological rather than tactical. They arise from in-game circumstances that require players to act immediately rather than stopping to think. A botched fast break is considered undisciplined. Cartoonish. Amateur. Thoughtless. A failed half-court set? The plan made sense, it just didn't work out. You *blow* fast-break opportunities. You *don't convert* half-court sets. As the great behavioral psychologists Daniel Kahneman and Amos Tversky famously wrote, "Losses loom larger than gains."

A fast break, by design, is something coaches can't stop to diagram for their players. They arise when players choose to surge ahead rather than taking a beat to consider every possible option. Chances are, they're doing it for a good reason: to beat the defense down the court. But they might also rush into it and end up doing something stupid. The fear that it might go wrong is more intense than the hope that it might go right. There are few things human beings crave in life more than control, and there are few people on this planet who crave control more than NBA coaches.

This sounds like a diss, but it's only natural for coaches to want to be in control considering how little they naturally possess. They are middle managers within their organizations, neither picking the players (in most cases) or actually playing the game. Their salaries are closer to the team's role players than their stars. They manage up to their front office, down

---

46. Falk defines a transition sequence as "Anything that occurs as the teams are switching sides of the court and all five defenders are not back and set in a normal guarding position."

to their assistants, and sideways to their players, trainers, and other team personnel. They are paid in part to serve as personifications of their entire team's performance, so getting judged harshly for someone else's actions is an occupational hazard. You'd grasp for some semblance of control, too, if you faced their predicament.

Drawing up plays is one obvious way for a coach to assume direct responsibility for what happens in a game.[47] The more plays a coach draws up and calls, the more directly they control their own fates. This also allows them to substitute a challenging question—*How many minutes does Player X's overall performance justify*—with a simpler one—*Is Player X running my plays?*

No team, of course, eschews fast breaks entirely. Even the most controlling coach wants players to take easy scoring opportunities when they arise. But a coach's desire to call set plays tends to neuter players' natural running instincts. The time it takes for the coach to decide which play to call and transmit his instruction to the players is time not spent galloping up the floor quickly to explore easy scoring opportunities. It is called a fast break, not a (stop and think for a second before you) fast break.

Each coach in NBA history lands somewhere between the two poles of the fast-break risk/reward spectrum, with some calling more set plays and others tolerating more quick shots. Every Mike D'Antoni has a counterpart Mike Fratello. The coaches themselves alter their philosophies as they learn from their peers, experiences, and players. Franchise mainstays like Gregg Popovich coach differently now than they did when they first entered the league. Frankly, everyone does to varying degrees given the massive changes in the sport.

Different eras of the sport weighed fast breaks differently. The slowdown 1950s gave way to the run-and-gun 1960s, which backlashed into the slower 1970s[48] until the success of the Showtime Lakers and other lesser-known speedster teams picked up the pace in the 1980s, which then sparked a slowdown revival led by the Bad Boys Pistons and Pat Riley's flagrant-fouling Knicks, whose overt physicality inspired the rule changes that incubated the Seven Seconds or Less Suns, etc.

---

47. The other is to decide which five players take the court at any given time.
48. In the NBA, at least. The ABA was where the fast break thrived.

Each of those eras demarcated a clear line between fast breaks and half-court set plays (or sets, for short). Teams either generated what they considered to be easy shots quickly—layups, dunks, sometimes open two-point jumpers, maybe three-pointers if they were wiiiiiiiiiiide open—or they pulled the ball out to run a set. Pushing the pace was seen as a means to an end, not a worthy goal in and of itself. Offenses got better at forcing fast breaks, defenses responded with more effective tactics to stop them, offenses pushed the envelope further, defenses responded in kind, and so on.

But the Spaced Out Era's emphasis on pace is an entirely new concept that has broken the usual cycle of transition innovation. Contrary to popular belief, teams aren't scoring more on fast breaks now. In the 1996–97 season, which occurred at the height of one of the NBA's lowest-possession eras, the average NBA team scored 14.2 fast break points a game. In 2020–21, despite scoring and possession figures skyrocketing, the average NBA team scored just 11.4 fast break points per game. That discrepancy likely overstates the fast break's decline, since there's no clear definition for a "fast break" that every single in-arena statistician uses.

But that possibility further explains what makes this era so distinct historically. The line between a fast break and a half-court set has never been blurrier. The league is just playing *faster*, period, at all times.

Every factor behind this new approach to pace flows from the Rockets' 2007 epiphany. If a team's best "play" is ad-libbed—what Van Gundy called "Random"—how important is it to call a set play when it probably won't be as effective as the quick thinking the players do once it fails?

This was an uncomfortable question the league had avoided for a long time. For a variety of reasons, the Spaced Out Era forced them to finally reckon with it.

Once they did, they realized something powerful. They were wasting a lot of goddamn time.

SOMEWHERE IN THE cosmos, a certain basketball innovator is wondering what took the NBA so long to figure all this out. His name is John McLendon, born April 5, 1915, deceased October 8, 1999.

The son of an Black college professor and a Delaware Indian student, McLendon loved basketball growing up in Kansas City. After one year at junior college, McLendon transferred to the University of Kansas to be close to James Naismith. As legend has it, McLendon declared himself the basketball inventor's newest mentee the first time he ever walked into his office. Impressed by McLendon's boldness, Naismith agreed to take him under his wing.

The two quickly struck up a lifelong friendship. McLendon couldn't play because Kansas's team was still segregated, but Naismith taught him the intricacies of the sport and provided whatever opportunities he could amid the harsh racial climate. McLendon's main basketball takeaway from that relationship: the game was *supposed* to move quickly.

"[Dr. Naismith] said the ultimate game is to attack wherever the ball is, and let your offense begin wherever you get the ball," he told biographer Milton Katz. "He told me the game is patterned to be played with a full-court offense and full-court defense. I patterned my whole game after that philosophy."

"That philosophy" is how McLendon "invented" the fast break during the slowdown era of the 1940s. He insisted his teams shoot within eight seconds of receiving the ball, even without a shot clock. Creating a numbers advantage was so important to him that he pioneered the concept of players running the wing after changes in possession. He later instituted a "four second rule," which required all five players to advance past the mid-court line within four seconds. He ran his players ragged in practice, then watched them dominate slower opponents in the games.

McLendon's devotion to the fast break went far deeper than Xs and Os. He didn't just see it as the best way to win or even the path to attracting new fans. He knew it was the type of game its inventor had always intended. Deploying a fast-break style was McLendon's way of honoring his mentor's legacy and spreading his gospel.

McLendon codified his ideas in a landmark 1965 tactical book that reads like a present-day text shoved into a time machine. Using more than 200 pages of painstaking detail to support his point, McLendon explained that the fast break was a "planned attack with multiple applications" rather than "an 'aimless,' 'helter-skelter,' 'run and shoot,' 'fire horse' game." He laid out 15 reasons to use a fast-paced system, which range from philosophical to tactical. But his most crucial point was that the sport needed a mindset change. It was time to "break away from the stereotyped game of 'set offense first and fast break when you can,' to 'fast break first and set offense when you have to.'"

That line—published way back in 1965—best describes the crucial difference between the modern Spaced Out NBA and prior eras.

Sadly, McLendon's transformative influence on the sport is largely forgotten due to the racial segregation of his time. His teams at what is now North Carolina Central University won eight Central Intercollegiate Athletic Association titles in 13 years, but were barred from the NCAA and NIT tournaments and were almost never allowed to play all-White schools.

One of the lone exceptions occurred in 1944, when McLendon helped organize a covert scrimmage between his North Carolina Central team and Duke University, who had won the Southern Conference championship the previous season. The details of the game were kept secret for 52 years, becoming public in a 1996 *New York Times* magazine story. McLendon secured an official game clock and found accredited referees, but did not tell the Duke administration, barred spectators, and convinced a reporter from one of Duke's weekly papers to refrain from publishing any details. Duke's players waited until most of Durham's inhabitants and police force went to church, then took a winding road to NC Central's gym while pulling jackets over their heads.

The ensuing game wasn't even a contest. The final score: North Carolina Central 88, Duke 44.

After winning three straight NAIA titles with Tennessee A&I (now Tennessee State) from 1957 to 1959,[49] McLendon moved on to the Cleveland Pipers of Abe Saperstein's short-lived start-up American Basketball League. It was a landmark moment, since McLendon was the first Black coach of any integrated pro team. But he lasted just half a season after repeatedly clashing with meddling owner George Steinbrenner (yes, that George Steinbrenner) and his only other pro coaching gig ended after just 28 games with the ABA's Denver Rockets in 1969.

Despite his success and innovations, the Hall of Fame enshrined him in 1979 as a "contributor" rather than a coach. (It re-enshrined him as a coach in 2016, albeit posthumously.)

---

49. The NAIA began inviting HBCU schools to participate in its tournament in 1953. McLendon's Tennessee A&I team was the first HBCU to win the title.

Whether by coincidence or direct influence, "McLendonball" has taken over the modern NBA. In coachspeak terms, the sport is played most often through principles and flow rather than diagramed sets. Teams still run plays when they must, but they look to score quickly first. They have all adopted McLendon's mindset for how the sport should be played.

It used to be common to see NBA teams grab rebounds, slowly toss the ball to a guard in the backcourt, and walk up the court as the coach transmitted his play call from the bench. Today, that rarely happens outside of the end of quarters and (fewer) critical crunch-time possessions. Teams rush the ball up court after *made* shots rather than waiting to call a play, especially when their opponent just made a driving layup. "Half-court possessions" are beginning and ending earlier than they once did.

These developments have fine-tuned McLendon's "fast break" offensive mindset into a slightly different application known as "playing with pace." Anyone who has listened to a basketball coach talk has heard this term.

But what do they actually want their teams to do? The answer is surprisingly hard to reverse-engineer. We know when a team is playing with pace, but nailing down the specifics of how they're doing it or what they need to do to "play with more pace" is more challenging.

This remains the case even with some of the more formal methods available to track the speed of a game. The simplest is known as "Pace Factor," which estimates how many offensive possessions each team gets.[50] The more they can squeeze into a 48-minute game, the faster their "Pace Factor," or "Pace" for short. Unsurprisingly, the typical NBA team today generates more possessions than its predecessors. In 2003–04 (the year before the league-wide crackdown on hand-checking) the Denver Nuggets were the "fastest-paced" team in the league with an average of 94.64 possessions per game. Seventeen years later, the New York Knicks were the league's "slowest-paced" team at 96.32 possessions per game.

But despite its name, the stat is best understood as a *reflection* of playing with more pace rather than the *prescription* for how to do it. It measures how quickly a team shoots, which strongly correlates with pace of play, but isn't exactly the same thing.

---

50. It's not quite as simple as just counting possessions, because different forms of the stat consider offensive rebounds and free throws to be something less than a full possession.

"Playing with pace" doesn't merely refer to generating more fast breaks, shooting quicker, or running more. It's a call to carry out a philosophy that requires players to make quick decisions with the ball, not waste time, and move themselves and the ball continuously between actions so the defense doesn't get any time to get comfortable. Often, that results in better shots opening up faster, thereby upping possession counts.

But it's possible to shoot quickly without playing with pace, and it's possible to play with pace without shooting quickly. The speed of *play* matters more than the speed of *the play*.

Ultimately, "playing with pace" is a way to take John McLendon's fast-break emphasis and reimagine it as a much faster form of half-court offense. And, as with many Spaced Out Era concepts, one influential man and team brought its tipping point into the mainstream.

MIKE D'ANTONI'S PHOENIX Suns were often described as a fast-breaking powerhouse. Their motto—"Seven Seconds or Less," immortalized by Jack McCallum's seminal book chronicling the 2005–06 season—harkened back to John McLendon's fast-break system. They lapped the field in Pace Factor in 2004–05 and 2005–06 before other teams started to catch up.

But for a team that supposedly embodied a fast-breaking style, the Suns sure broke a lot of up-tempo conventions.

They didn't force many turnovers via a full-court pressure defense. They weren't a deep team—D'Antoni, in fact, preferred a *short* playing rotation. They lacked a shot-blocking big man to start their fast breaks, and they didn't have one who fired pinpoint outlet passes. The engine of their attack, Steve Nash, was nobody's idea of a speed demon. To quote McCallum: "The central dichotomy about the NBA's fastest offense, then, is that it is quarterbacked by someone who's not all that fast."

The Suns undoubtedly *played* fast. They clearly shot fast. But their revolutionary approach was built on two simple observations that could be applied equally to fast breaks *and* half-court sets. One is that offenses score more easily before the defense is set. The other is that they score more easily when defenses must account for all five players at the same time.

Hence the phrase that those Suns made famous: "pace and space."

Combining both pieces into a single overarching philosophy broke through the long-running stylistic war between fast breaks and controlled half-court sets. D'Antoni never understood the appeal of a deliberate half-court offense. Instead of breaking a defense's structure with a prolonged series of coordinated dribbles, screens, passes, cuts, and drives, wouldn't it be easier if the defense didn't form its structure in the first place? Advancing the ball up the court quickly wasn't a means to an end. It was a means to open up as many desirable ends as possible, forcing the defense into their equivalent of a Sophie's Choice.

D'Antoni's Suns showed that "playing with pace" is about engaging the defense quickly in all situations, not shooting quicker shots. The best in-rhythm shot is likely to occur sooner rather than later, especially after a defensive stop. But it may take a few passes, drives, and/or moves to materialize once a team's fast pace creates the initial advantage. The objective is fulfilled by getting the defense moving and reacting right away. It's using the same tools as any half-court set play, just sooner.

"Sooner" refers to both time on the clock and space on the floor. Though the Suns players all ran plenty, they weren't all sprinting the full length of the floor on every possession. They just needed to run fast enough to reach certain spots that left the paint open, from which they could flow into a typical action like a pick-and-roll. They got into *something resembling their offensive structure* quickly, without zipping around chaotically. Mistaking the latter for the former is why the NBA often devolved into slowdown ball in the past.

The "pace and space" offense the Suns introduced is more like executing half-court possessions over the full 94 feet of the court than running fast breaks. It includes pick-and-rolls, off-ball screens, designed cuts, curls in from the side, pitch-ahead passes, dribble hand-offs, and all the other building blocks of half-court play. The only differences are that the "half-court set" begins as soon as the offense receives the ball and extends along the entire surface area of the court. With proper teamwork, it forces opponents to cover as much of the court's space as possible before their defense can get set.

Many of the modern NBA's most common offensive alignments, actions, and plays flow from D'Antoni-ball's twist on McLendon's fast-break ethos. One of D'Antoni's most frequent sets is called "21," because it involves some

May 8, 2007 — Spurs at Suns — WCSF Game 2 (SA leads 1-0)
Suns 28, Spurs 27 — 7:17 left in second quarter

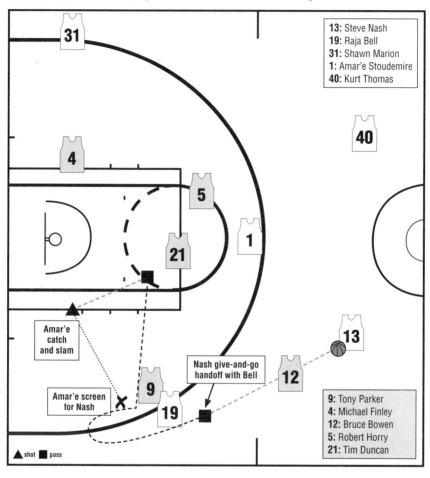

sort of interaction between the off guard (2) and point guard (1).[51] The "2" and "3" players race to the corner, the "4" trots to the opposite wing, and the "5" trails the play at the top of the key. As all four get into position, the "1" quickly dribbles up the same side as the "2" while the opponent is changing ends of the floor. Nobody goes inside the three-point line until the actual sequence begins.

---

51. Others refer to it as "Pistol," still others use the term "Delay," and your team might call it something else entirely.

This setup could lead to anything. That initial action between the "1" and "2" could be a pass, dribble handoff, screen, give-and-go, or just two players running past each other in opposite directions. It could trigger a pass back to the "5" man to swing the ball to the opposite side, a side pick-and-roll between either guard and the "5," or a double screen for the guard in the corner. That movement immediately flows into any combination of possible actions that would take entire books to chronicle.

But charting this alignment on a static clipboard only scratches the surface of its power. With each player moving to and from their positions in different lanes at different speeds starting the instant the offense takes the ball from out of bounds, there's little time for the defense to differentiate decoy from threat. Better yet, all that setup is happening beyond the three-point line, which forces the defense to make a difficult choice without much time to do so informatively. If they scramble back in a defensive shell, they allow the offense to run the 21 set unimpeded and potentially give up open three-pointers. If they press up to disrupt the play's rhythm, they'll leave the entire lane open for a backdoor cut.

This is why "pace and space" requires a willingness to take three-pointers early in the shot clock. For years, teams and players were told that fast breaks needed to end with layups or dunks. Anything else wasn't worth the risk. To quote the old coaching cliché, "We can get that shot anytime."

D'Antoni-ball flipped that saying on its head. If a team is willing and able to take that perimeter shot anytime, the defense must always remain in "pick your poison" mode.

Instead of fearing the negative outcome of missing long jumpers and wasted possessions, "pace and space" embraces the positive chaotic effects of a demoralizing dagger three. The extra point of a made three-pointer doesn't fully explain its value. The larger goal was to plant another seed of danger into the already-scrambling defenders' heads that, crucially, was located far from the site of the other deadliest threats at the front of the rim. It's hard enough for a defense to stop both when it has time to align itself. It's even harder when it doesn't.

Though D'Antoni was not an "advanced stat" guy, the Rockets' study of Jeff Van Gundy's set plays provided "pace and space" with much-needed empirical proof. The reason the Rockets scored more efficiently on "Random" than any of their set plays was simple: no opponent can scout chaos. The primary purpose of "pace and space" is to induce chaos as often as possible.

Putting those two findings together eventually convinced number-crunching idealists and pragmatic old heads alike that early three-pointers were powerful drivers of efficient offense. In this respect, D'Antoni, unlike McLendon, was in the right place at the right time.

The combination of the zone defense relaxation and the crackdown on hand-checking had already incentivized the perimeter play required to execute "pace and space" effectively. The rising basketball analytics movement—personified by Morey's Rockets, but not driven exclusively by them—became the ultimate "pace and space" hype man by providing numerical proof that it worked.

Those two forces exploded to create the modern Spaced Out style of play. While D'Antoni's Suns (and Rockets) never won it all, they inspired each of the sport's champions from 2010 on and nudged all 30 teams to embrace their own versions of playing "random." That chain reaction continues to leave countless aftershocks, some of which have been covered and many more that we'll get to throughout the rest of this book.

But its most significant impact would have been near and dear to John McLendon's heart. It ascended his beloved fast break into the sport's very essence.

SINCE THE EARLY days of the Boston Celtics dynasty in the late 1950s and 1960s, NBA teams have conceived of fast breaks as a well-oiled assembly line. The defense gets a stop, the center cements it by getting the rebound, the center finds the point guard, the point guard sprints in the middle of the court with teammates flanking him on either wing, and he finds the open man before the opponent knows what hits them. The platonic ideal of a fast break occurred when each player did their job and handed off to the next guy to do theirs.

In such a setup, big men had an essential, yet limited role. With so much of the game action clustering around the basket, teams had an immense need for centers who could clog the middle, corral rebounds in traffic, and bypass several retreating defenders in one fell swoop with a quick outlet pass. Bill Russell perfected this job in the 1960s, but he was a one-of-one athlete and on-court genius whose blocked shots served a dual purpose. It was hard to emulate him.

To the naked eye, Wes Unseld represented a more attainable archetype. The Hall of Fame Washington Bullets center of the 1970s was short for his position, couldn't jump high, and didn't run particularly fast. He lacked elite low-post moves, feared high-pressure free throws, and certainly couldn't weave around obstacles while dribbling. But he was unmatched in one area that turned his Bullets teams into one of the best of their era.

He was the world's best fast-break generator.

Nobody in Unseld's time—perhaps nobody in NBA history—was better at clogging space in the middle. He ran nightly post defense and rebounding positioning clinics, plowing through smaller players with his wide chest while wedging out taller opponents with his strong-as-steel base to prevent them from out-leaping him. Whenever the opponent missed a shot, Unseld made sure he or another Bullet grabbed the ensuing carom.

Once he got the rebound, he made sure to *always* get rid of it quickly and accurately so his guards could run a fast break. His long chest passes to hit streaking teammates in strides were the stuff of legend, but Unseld was equally proficient at shorter kickouts that led his guards into odd-man situations. Unseld's signature skill became known as an "outlet pass." His ability to collect the ball amid the most congested crowds and spray it out to faster teammates before the crowd dispersed was worth far more than the individual numbers Unseld produced. Coaches and purists alike worship at his altar while hoping their favorite big man can embody his example.

In that respect, they have been left wanting. The half century since the 1970s has seen many great big men, but none quite like Wes Unseld. I'm not sure we'll ever see another player like him. You cannot tell the story of the NBA without him.

But without detracting too much from Unseld's greatness, there's another reason nobody has assumed his outlet passing mantle. That reason holds the key to understanding how "pace and space" has transformed the NBA fast break from situational basketball to, well, basketball.

The utility of an outlet pass is inversely proportional to the size of the crowd from which it emerges. Crashing the glass can, of course, be worth it to preserve possession and/or get an easy putback. But there's a built-in cost that Unseld was incredibly adept at exploiting. The more people go for offensive rebounds, the farther they need to travel to get back on defense. The more distance they have to travel to get back on defense, the more vulnerable they are to fast breaks.

The risk/reward calculation for crashing the offensive glass is one of those eternal strategic questions with no fixed answer. Still, it didn't take long for coaches to realize the balance in Unseld's era was way off. They started requiring several players to forego crashing the glass and instead get back on defense in advance. What good is an outlet pass if it no longer bypasses as many retreating defenders?

This realization birthed the institution of transition defense. Once upon a time, transition defense was simply "bust your ass back or I'll sub you out." But starting in the mid-1980s, teams began using more sophisticated alignments that anticipated fast breaks before they could even start. The 76ers designed a strategy against the Showtime Lakers' fast break that involved dropping their guards back on jump shots, using Maurice Cheeks to face-guard Magic Johnson, and letting Moses Malone handle all the offensive rebounding. Other coaches, like the meticulous Hubie Brown and Mike Fratello, installed specific rules governing when to pick up ball-handlers and how to match up in scramble situations. But it was Chuck Daly's Bad Boys Pistons who inspired the most imitators.

"Detroit has created a defensive mindset around the league, and teams copy success," Pat Riley said in 1990. "In the early '80s, transition defense was non-existent. When a team was running, a coach would say, 'Just get back.' Now there's sophistication to defense."

Detroit's success inspired the now-familiar concept of "building a wall," which called for teams to contain the ball-handler with multiple bodies first and resolve any matchup confusion later. Where big men once found open space to find their guards to trigger fast breaks, they now saw a block of defenders back to shrink potential windows for outlet passes. What good is an outlet pass if it doesn't expose *any* retreating defenders?

"Pace and space" provided the answer to this problem. In doing so, it fundamentally reconfigured the look and feel of fast-break basketball.

Those transition three-pointers that old-school commentators often lament serve an essential purpose. The transition defense strategy of "building a wall" is an effective way to stop layups and dunks. Tossing in the threat of threes, though, loosens those walls up considerably. Defenses now have to worry about the perimeter, too, all while scrambling to match up. The Suns and their descendants capitalized on that confusion to get open looks from downtown, then drove for layups and dunks when opponents stretched too far. This is why the 2017 and 2018 Finals were symbolized by the Cavaliers allowing uncontested Kevin Durant fast-break dunks instead of open Stephen Curry threes.

One way to address this growing threat is to build walls that never surrendered a numbers disadvantage. Several coaches, most notably the Van Gundy brothers and Doc Rivers, instructed their teams to punt the offensive glass entirely in the name of getting everyone back on defense. They reasoned that the dual threat of threes and layups was so intense in a "pace and space" world that even a split second of matchup confusion could potentially lead to an uncontested shot. The reward of a single offensive rebound was not worth risking *anyone* getting stuck behind the ball.

But while these measures contributed to a historic league-wide drop in offensive rebounding, they did little to stem the speed revolution. That's because "pace and space" was designed to convert half-court sets into quick-hitting, free-flowing, full-court sequences, not to generate more fast breaks. The league's historical conception of the latter required passing over and/or running past retreating defenses that were now retreating in advance. "Pace and space" on the other hand, taught teams to respond by flowing seamlessly into "random" plays that used the whole court and the full breadth of their players' expanded offensive skill sets. Instead of coming to them, make them come to us.

This was one way the early-2010s San Antonio Spurs and the Light Years Warriors built on the base of D'Antoni's Suns teams. The Suns pioneered a number of full-court tricks to get their players open shots against set defenses. The most significant was known as a "drag" screen, which is when the screener trailing the play abruptly stops his run up the court so the guard can drive off him in a sort of ad-libbed pick-and-roll. (We'll dive deeper into the drag screen and its sibling, the "step up screen," in Chapter 9.)

The Spurs and Warriors expanded on the drag screen concept to punish those opponents who punted the offensive glass. Spurs coach Gregg Popovich was not naturally drawn to D'Antoni's style, preferring instead to win with defense and the structure of the league's thickest offensive playbook. But his

June 10, 2014 — Spurs at Heat — NBA Finals Game 3 (Tied 1-1)
Spurs 29, Heat 20 — 2:31 left in first quarter

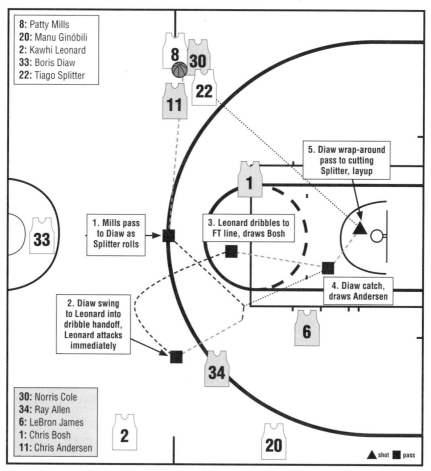

8: Patty Mills
20: Manu Ginóbili
2: Kawhi Leonard
33: Boris Diaw
22: Tiago Splitter

5. Diaw wrap-around pass to cutting Splitter, layup

1. Mills pass to Diaw as Splitter rolls

3. Leonard dribbles to FT line, draws Bosh

4. Diaw catch, draws Andersen

2. Diaw swing to Leonard into dribble handoff, Leonard attacks immediately

30: Norris Cole
34: Ray Allen
6: LeBron James
1: Chris Bosh
11: Chris Andersen

▲ shot ■ pass

battles with the Suns were key in successfully merging his philosophy with the "pace and space" ethos to extend San Antonio's title window.

Popovich's Spurs pushed the pace as a way to enhance their half-court offense. The faster they got the ball up the floor, the more stuff they could pack into each half-court possession. They deployed drag screens, baseline picks, passes in and out of the post, dribble handoffs, and plenty of other stuff as they marched up the floor, all of which flowed naturally into their detailed playbook. All that movement made defenses dizzy, which the Spurs further exploited by decoying one action on one side while simultaneously running their real play on the other. They used "pace and space" to become masters of misdirection.

The Warriors co-opted many of those same tricks while carrying out the Suns' zest for scoring quickly. No team in NBA history was deadlier attacking off missed shots. They built their transition game around Stephen Curry and Klay Thompson's revolutionary combination of three-point range, accuracy, release speed, and shot versatility, all of which made them deadly threats from any spot off any type of prior action. Those drag screens, ad-libbed pindowns, dribble hand-offs, give-and-gos, flare screens, etc. left defenders bewildered, and got their stars open threes. Curry mastered the art of giving the ball up and immediately sprinting to get it back along the three-point line when his defender relaxed. They never gave opponents time to breathe.

The Warriors also extended "pace and space" to all positions rather than just guards, thereby shattering the Unseld-ian platonic ideal. Before they came along, the idea of a big man grabbing a rebound and dribbling the ball up the floor himself was considered radical. Even D'Antoni preferred his big men set drag screens and lag at the top of the key to swing the ball to the other side or hit a cutter with a backdoor pass.

The Warriors, on the other hand, empowered their big men to skip the outlet pass and just go. If the goal is to push the pace to score quickly, why waste time finding a guard or peering through an air-tight transition defense wall for a pass that may not exist?

Eschewing the outlet pass dramatically amped up the unpredictability of the Warriors' transition game. Anyone could start it, anyone could finish it, and opponents had no way to prepare for any possibility. Draymond Green emerged as the modern-day Unseld equivalent, combining point guard skills, a big man's base, a wing player's height, a superstar's relent-lessness, and a role player's unselfishness to trigger countless early scoring opportunities.

His success has inspired a new generation of "grab and go" players who aim to convert every rebound into a coast-to-coast chance for themselves or teammates. Some, like Russell Westbrook, are considered guards. Others, like Miami's Bam Adebayo, are new-age "big men" who use their speed and playmaking to refashion the center position. Still others, like Brooklyn's Ben Simmons (when he's actually playing), combine point guard skills with a

September 17, 2020 — Heat vs Celtics — ECF Game 2 (MIA leads 1-0)
Celtics 64, Heat 49 — 10:09 left in third quarter

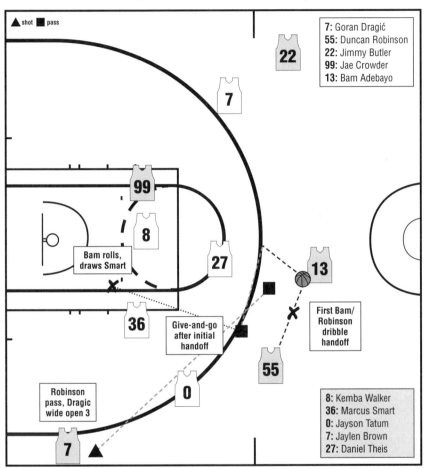

bigger man's body. Freakishly athletic wing players like Antetokounmpo, big men like Jokić and Joel Embiid, and original transition freight train LeBron James are all regular grab-and-go masters.

The net effect of these dramatic shifts has merged the fast break and the half-court set into a free-flowing, "random" transition game that only a whistle can stop. It has become nearly impossible to delineate between the two. A better method is to instead split possessions into those that occur off missed shots and those that occur off dead balls.[52]

---

52. Something that the wonderful website pbpstats.com already does in painstaking detail.

Increasingly, though, even that breakdown is insufficient. Every change of possession—even those following a made shot—is an opportunity to flow into a quick-hitting attack that beats even the most prepared defensive wall down the floor.

There are many ways teams create numbers advantages early that pay off later in the possession. Chris Paul, historically known to prefer a half-court style, now often darts in front or directly behind a retreating player and then makes his move when they turn around. James and Jokić are inspiring an outlet pass revival to hit bigger players ducking into quick post-ups that punish smaller players for switching onto them. Some teams even position their biggest guy on the block in advance during opponent free throws. When the shot goes in, they race the ball up the floor before the opponents lined up on the opposite free-throw line can come to double team.

These methods and many more are examples of teams *playing with more pace*. The fact that possession counts and point totals have dramatically risen during the Spaced Out Era is a byproduct of the fast break and half-court set merging together. The cause of that trend is a widespread mindset shift that conceives of every second of the game and every inch of the court as an opportunity to advance a scoring chance.

That is the idea that binds Bill Russell's Celtics to Mike D'Antoni's Suns, the old-school fast break to "pace and space," John McLendon to Daryl Morey, and the Wes Unseld–style outlet pass to Draymond Green's grab and go.

It's also why one timeless action has replaced another as the modern game's dominant weapon—and why it may be time to rename it.

Chapter 6
The Legal Pyramid Scheme

The pick-and-roll's journey from set play to basketball's way of life.

On July 12, 2018, one half of arguably the best pick-and-roll partnership in NBA history blessed (or cursed) NBA TV viewers with an entertainingly awkward rendition of a grumpy old-timer.

Sporting a thick silver beard and his trademark Louisiana drawl, Karl Malone played all the hits during the third quarter of a Summer League game between his beloved Utah Jazz and the Orlando Magic. The 14-time All-Star bemoaned the game's lack of structure ("Tell me, when are they gonna run a play?"), the players' lean physiques ("When's someone gonna lift some weights around this place?"), youth development ("I am so tired of all these AAU things going around"), analytics, the three-point shot, and more.

But he saved his best (or worst) for the broadcast's return from a commercial break. As the screen showed a replay of a well-executed Magic pick-and-roll between former Cincinnati guard Troy Caupain and onetime UNLV big man Khem Birch, play-by-play announcer Kristen Ledlow turned to Malone.

"That's got to make you at least a little happy, Karl, right?" she said.

Malone paused, a quizzical look on his face. He turned to stare at Ledlow while pointing to the court.

"Did ... did you just call that a pick-and-roll?" Malone responded.

Ledlow's face curled into a sheepish look. "I thought that would make you happy!" she said.

"I guess it would've if they put a body on somebody, my goodness." Malone responded. "That's a pick-and-roll? Set a screen first. You're gonna get the ball back!"

The environment wasn't exactly conducive to serious basketball discussion, and Malone is hardly the only past legend to dismiss the Spaced Out NBA. But this wasn't the first time Malone drew a hard line between *his pick-and-roll* and the modern twist on one of basketball's most timeless concepts.

"So many guys say, 'We're running the pick-and-roll.' No you're not!" he said during a February 2009 *Inside the NBA* segment with Kenny Smith. "Let it happen!"

Three years later, NBA TV invited Malone to do an on-court demonstration. "What are they, out at the three-point line?" he began. "That's not pick-and-roll. I don't know what that is."

Malone's longtime pick-and-roll partner has conveyed a similar attitude, though with far less bluntness.

"There's no resemblance, how the pick-and-rolls changed," John Stockton said during a rare media appearance in 2017. "It's nearly impossible to guard now with the rules."

Taken literally, their argument is beyond absurd. The pick-and-roll is, of course, the very core of the modern game and has been for two decades. During the heyday of the Stockton-Malone union, the post-up reigned supreme with the pick-and-roll as an alternative. Nowadays, the ratio has more than flipped.

Truth be told, the pick-and-roll *is* today's game all by itself.

No stat does the pick-and-roll's modern omnipotence justice. The league-wide percentage of plays finished via a pick-and-roll jumped from around 15 percent in 2004–05 to more than 33 percent in 2016–17, according to Synergy Sports Technology, a video service used by most NBA teams.[53] But even that figure dramatically understates the pick-and-roll's impact because

---

53. Synergy Sports started tracking play types in the 2004–05 season, at least on its main product. So it's exceedingly likely the 15 percent league-wide average in 2004–05 was itself much higher than it was in Stockton and Malone's primes in the 1990s. It's also worth noting that the 15 percent figure was buttressed by the D'Antoni-Nash Suns, who were one of just two teams (Seattle being the other) to crack the 20 percent mark.

it only measures the pick-and-rolls that directly lead to shots, fouls, or turnovers.[54] It doesn't include dribble handoffs, which function like pick-and-rolls with a different entry point, nor does it include spot-up jumpers and/or cuts that occur as a result of a pick-and-roll creating a numbers advantage.

It also undercounts pick-and-rolls that set up other pick-and-rolls, whether by the same two players or others on the opposite side of the floor. During the 2020–21 season, three players (Atlanta's Trae Young, Dallas' Luka Dončić, and Portland's Damian Lillard) received more than 2,800 screens while dribbling *beyond the three-point line.*

In the Spaced Out Era, the pick-and-roll is the bedrock of every offensive and defensive strategy. If you want to identify a defensive scheme, figure out how it defends the pick-and-roll. That gets you most of the way there.

It would therefore be easy to dismiss Malone as a bitter, uninformed curmudgeon. He certainly wouldn't be the first retired athlete—or retired person in general—to believe the game stopped changing when his own playing career ended.

Still: Why would one of the game's premier pick-and-roll practitioners argue that the thing that dominates the modern game no longer exists? He can't be that dense, right?

Imagine, for a second, that you're tasked with renaming the broad category of plays we currently call "pick-and-rolls." You're told to zap all prior convictions from your brain, then given a playlist featuring a select few of those 2,800 screens Young, Dončić, and Lillard each received while dribbling.

Does that phrase "pick-and-roll" broadly encompass those sequences? How many such plays actually feature a hard "pick" and a "roll" to the basket? How many include one, but not the other? How many include neither? Is there another all-encompassing term that fits better than "pick-and-roll"? Perhaps "two-man game" or "ball screen"? If so, would "pick-and-roll" become a subcategory of that more general label? How do we differentiate between each of those subcategories? Do we even have to?

---

54. Data from Second Spectrum, the NBA's official play-tracking provider, includes some of the plays that a pick-and-roll sets up, but even those probably undercount the actual number of pick-and-rolls in a game.

Asking these questions paints Malone's comments in a new light. The modern game features endless varieties of two-man on-ball interactions that we've labeled "pick-and-rolls" largely because we lack a better term. They are as different from the Stockton-to-Malone prototype as they are *from each other*. When Malone dismisses the variations as not being *real* pick-and-rolls, he's really saying they don't look like the pick-and-rolls of his day. That point of view is more understandable.

Yet even that framing obscures the strong underlying connection between the pick-and-rolls of past eras and whatever term you choose to use to describe today's ubiquitous ball screen interactions.

Over the course of the Spaced Out Era, the league took a question that was inconceivable in the late 1990s and turned it into one that's become too basic to even ask today. If something as simple as a ball-handler rubbing off at least one screener can produce so many different positive outcomes, why not just slam them together as much as possible?

In doing so, it revealed a deeper truth that binds Stockton-to-Malone to today's two-man interactions.

THE QUESTION LINGERED on the tips of everyone's tongues throughout Stockton and Malone's two-decade partnership. You knew exactly what they wanted to do, how they wanted to do it, and where they did it on the floor.

So how did their pick-and-roll keep working?

"I finally came up with a way to stop it," Lakers guard Nick Van Exel once told reporters. "Bring a bat to the game and kill one of them."

Others expressed similar bewilderment, albeit without Van Exel's dark humor. They weren't spouting off clichés publicly while protecting a master plan behind the scenes. They were honestly stumped. How could a basic action that everyone knew was coming work so well?

The answer begins with a cross-sport analogy.

In American football, every play begins at a fixed yard marker known as the line of scrimmage. Before either side can advance some combination of their 11 players past this force field, they need to line up on opposite sides and stare each other down. Only when the quarterback yells "HIKE" can all hell break loose.

Basketball doesn't explicitly work this way. Sequences can begin from anywhere on the court, and there is no imaginary barrier that separates the five offensive players from the five defensive players. The goal is to launch a ball through a spherical ring 10 feet in the air, not to advance it through an "end zone."

But basketball *does* have something that functions like football's line of scrimmage. There may not be a fixed line that places the two teams on opposite sides until a starting gun sounds, but there is always a spot on the floor from which an offensive team endeavors to create an advantage. A "point of scrimmage," so to speak. Or, to use a basketball term, a "point of attack."

While no two points of attacks are the same between or within possessions, they're the place to start when determining how teams scored or prevented a score on each sequence. You've heard the adage that the best football teams "win the battle at the line of scrimmage?" The best NBA teams win the battle at the point of attack.

They do so with mechanisms known as "actions," the building blocks of the sport's Xs and Os. Offensive possessions usually feature multiple actions, with a series of "actions" adding up to a "play." All plays have actions, but actions can also occur outside of planned plays, especially with the pace and space revolution shrinking the time teams spend transitioning between offense and defense. The initial player alignment from which actions combine into plays is known as a "set." Dead-ball situations give coaches a chance to call a "set play," and extended stoppages enable them to diagram a subset of this category that goes by the acronym ATO for "after timeout."[55] A "system," then, is a series of broad principles that define the philosophy that binds a team's actions, sets, set plays, and ATOs together.

Just as football teams throughout history choose between running and passing, basketball teams will always use two broad categories of actions to score. One is to *isolate* one of their players in a prime scoring position against a single defender. The other is to have one or more teammates set a *pick* on the on-ball defender and, if necessary, *roll* into open space to receive a pass or at least draw a reaction that opens up a scoring opportunity elsewhere.

---

55. Technically, coaches call "ATO plays" or "set plays after timeouts," but "ATO" is a simpler catch-all term. It's akin to using the shorthand phrase "write off" instead of "tax write-off." That one's for my fellow *Schitt's Creek* fans.

Though we use the terms "isolation" and "pick-and-roll" to describe more specific actions, they convey the two broad ways basketball teams battle at various points of attack. Post-ups are isolations with the offensive player's back turned to their defender. Dribble handoffs are pick-and-rolls in which the screener hands the ball off as they set their pick. Off-ball screens are pick-and-rolls for someone who doesn't have the ball (yet). Spot-up shots or cuts come after an initial isolation or pick-and-roll creates a numbers advantage. In basketball, all squares are rectangles, but not all rectangles are squares.

Using a football analogy to describe "isolations" and "pick-and-rolls" allows us to see how one of those two family trees usurped the other as the NBA's preferred action. When prime scoring opportunities arose from winning one-on-one duels, the isolation was the sport's tool of choice. But in a league that allows zone defense, tightly enforces perimeter contact, and has finally embraced the power of the three-point line, the pick-and-roll's inherent flexibility makes it the ideal multi-use tool to stress a defense's overall shape.

That same quality explains why the Stockton/Malone version flummoxed the teams of their era. The league wasn't ready to defend an action that yielded so many possible outcomes.

The exact number has ballooned over time. "Two guys who know what they're doing can make the simple little screen roll look like about half a dozen different plays," longtime assistant coach Johnny Bach told *Sports Illustrated* in 1995. Malone pegged the number at 11, "off just the action of me setting the pick" in 1998. However, in a 2020 appearance on Barstool Sports' Pardon My Take podcast, he claimed the Jazz "probably had 30 counters off our pick-and-roll." But even that last lofty figure vastly undersells the true effect of the Stockton/Malone duo and those that followed it.

It doesn't take long to see why. Either player could shoot from the perimeter[56] or drive to the basket. Stockton could drive right or left, into or away from Malone's screen, and then finish either scenario with a wide variety of layups. Malone could make contact with Stockton's man on his

---

56. In those days, that meant long two-point jumpers. Today? Stockton unquestionably possessed three-point range despite his shooting reluctance. Malone never quite got there, but if he could master the 20-footer, surely he could've been a knockdown 23-foot shooter if he wanted to be.

screen and hold his position, or he could roll for a layup, dunk, or to get deeper post position. He could also pop out to the elbow or corner, either to take the jumper or fake it and drive the closeout. He could also slip to any of those locations before his screen contacted Stockton's defender and perform any of those tasks. Then, there's all the ways either player could pass to teammates, set up reruns of the action, and....

You get the picture. A well-executed pick-and-roll can theoretically scale into an infinite number of potential outcomes depending on the ingenuity and tenacity of its practitioners. It is basketball's version of a legal pyramid scheme. Which makes Stockton and Malone the NBA's Amway.[57]

They weren't the first two players in NBA history to run the pick-and-roll or even innovate on its design. Detroit's Isiah Thomas and Bill Laimbeer had already discovered ways to wield the pick-and-pop to power other elements within the Pistons' sets. But Stockton and Malone were the first pair of teammates to scale the pick-and-roll into an offensive system on its own. Their pick-and-roll had no obvious tendency and could arise from any number of alignments. As long as the action gave the Jazz a numbers advantage, however fleeting, Stockton and Malone would find a way to pounce on it.

The best way to stop it was to avoid yielding a numbers advantage in the first place. But with illegal defense still prohibiting off-ball zones, opponents couldn't easily align their forces in advance. Utah often bunched three players, including giant centers Mark Eaton and (later) Greg Ostertag, on the opposite wing so Malone and Stockton could play two-on-two with an entire side of the floor cleared. Good luck stopping two players that skilled and in-sync with only two defenders.

The most the rules allowed opponents to do was place additional defenders slightly above the free-throw line, but that was rarely close enough to deter the Jazz stars or get a head start on the defensive rotations they inevitably caused. While off-ball defenders were restricted in their movements, off-ball offensive players could go wherever they wanted.[58] Utah spent nearly two decades exploiting the asymmetry.

---

57. I realize this analogy is awkward given that Amway's co-founder owns the Orlando Magic.
58. Provided the officials didn't notice them standing in the paint for more than three seconds at a time.

That brings us to 1998 and the second of the two Jazz defeats to Michael Jordan's Bulls. While the back-to-back Finals series took on similar tones, the rematch was the one that foreshadowed the evolution of pick-and-roll defensive schemes once the illegal defense rule was abolished.

Chicago's defense deployed an early preview of what is now known as ICE coverage.[59] The goal was to force Stockton to the baseline and make Malone pop to the outside, thereby cutting off many of those seemingly infinite counters. While the two primary defenders on Stockton and Malone played key roles, the strategy's success hinged on a third player sliding in advance to the "nail," a spot in the middle of the free-throw line from which they could deter Malone's rim rolls or open jumpers.[60]

That early rotation is not easy to pull off with the current defense rules, much less 1998's more restrictive illegal defense provision. This player needed to be quick enough to cover lots of ground, long enough to make the brilliant Malone hesitate, aware enough to keep track of his own man while also watching the ball, and intelligent enough to time his movements to confuse Stockton, Malone, *and* the officials enforcing illegal defense violations.

Luckily, the Bulls had the one player in NBA history most suited for this very task. They had Scottie Pippen.

The Bulls used Pippen's versatility to smother Mark Jackson in their seven-game war with Indiana in the previous round. But instead of repeating that strategy in the Finals, they tasked Pippen with "guarding" Utah's motley crew of centers[61] while actually playing a proto one-man zone on the Stockton/Malone pick-and-roll.[62] The move worked like a charm. Chicago held Utah, the NBA's most efficient offense during the regular season, to just

---

59. Some teams call it "Down," "Blue," "Push," or any host of other team-specific terms used to disguise their intentions.

60. It's called the "nail" because builders tie a string to a literal nail to precisely measure the court's dimensions before painting on the various lines. Once they're done, they take the nail out, leaving a small hollow spot that sits in the exact middle of the free-throw line: 15 feet from the hoop, eight feet from the edge of each side of the paint.

61. Ostertag, Greg Foster, Adam Keefe, and Antoine Carr.

62. This wasn't the first time the Bulls deployed Pippen on the opposing team's center. They used Pippen to guard Laimbeer and switch his vaunted pick-and-pop with Thomas in 1991's four-game sweep of their hated rivals from Detroit.

June 10, 1998 — Jazz at Bulls — NBA Finals Game 4 (CHI leads 2-1)
Bulls 8, Jazz 8 — 7:22 left in first quarter

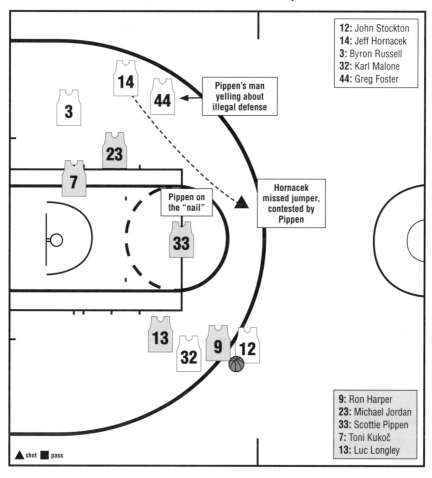

96.1 points per 100 possessions in the series, including a 54-point Game 3 showing that remains the lowest point total in any NBA Finals game.

Pippen's role in solving the seemingly unsolvable Stockton/Malone pick-and-roll became the model for years to come. Once the illegal defense rule was abolished in 2001, teams could divert players far less exceptional than Scottie Pippen to help pin pick-and-rolls on one side of the floor. Today's generation is well-schooled in the art of properly positioning themselves on the nail, no matter the scheme their team runs.

The rise of the "nail defender" gradually forced teams to initiate their pick-and-roll actions in more sophisticated ways. The Stockton/Malone version was deadly because the rules allowed it to function more like a football play. Stockton surveyed on the left wing, Malone rooted himself into perfect screening position, and the other three players clustered in stationary positions on the opposite wing. The illegal defense provision rewarded the Jazz's slow and steady approach in manipulating the floor's geometry to their benefit.

But time became the defense's ally after 2001's rule changes. Time allows opponents to set up zone-like off-ball structures to defend pick-and-roll actions with all five players instead of two or fewer. To more easily access that endless cascade of pick-and-roll outcomes, offenses needed to develop a similarly infinite supply of pick-and-roll *preludes* to keep defenses from loading those shells up in advance.

That necessity became the mother of the inventiveness that broadened the pick-and-roll's usage. The pick-and-rolls of the Spaced Out Era occur within a never-ending stream of continuous action. Anything can build to one, and every and any domino that falls thereafter can be tied back to one. That is why today's pick-and-roll actions do not look and feel like Karl Malone's even though they share the same name.

Yet despite their superficial differences, the many complexities that made the modern pick-and-roll so all-encompassing reflect an underlying philosophy that should warm the Jazz legends' hearts.

THE PHOENIX SUNS had the Denver Nuggets on the ropes. They held a 3–0 advantage in their 2021 second-round playoff series, led by six points with three-and-a-half minutes left in Game 4, and were facing an opponent down both of its stars with Nikola Jokić's ejection and Jamal Murray's knee injury.

Chris Paul caught Jae Crowder's inbound pass from the left sideline and drifted toward one edge of the giant Nuggets logo at half court. Deandre Ayton and Devin Booker stood at the left and right elbows, respectively, while Mikal Bridges parked himself deep in the right corner. As Paul turned his body, Ayton screened for Booker to slice out to the left wing in what's known as an "Iverson cut," named because it was the former 76ers great's bread and butter.

Booker pivoted toward the baseline once he caught the ball and saw Crowder cutting in his direction. Though Denver's Aaron Gordon stayed closely attached to the Suns' star, teammate Michael Porter Jr. was glued to

June 13, 2021 — Suns at Nuggets — WCSF Game 4 (PHX leads 3-0)
Suns 109, Nuggets 103 — 3:24 left in fourth quarter

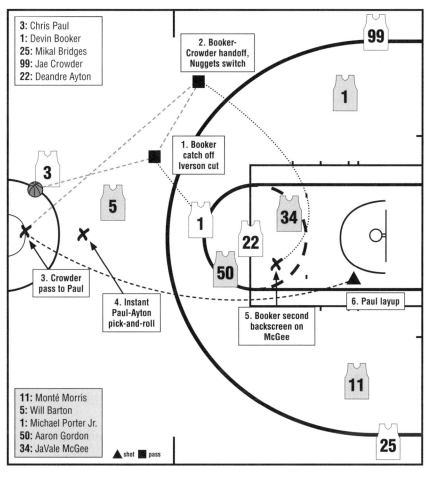

3: Chris Paul
1: Devin Booker
25: Mikal Bridges
99: Jae Crowder
22: Deandre Ayton

2. Booker-Crowder handoff, Nuggets switch

1. Booker catch off Iverson cut

3. Crowder pass to Paul

4. Instant Paul-Ayton pick-and-roll

5. Booker second backscreen on McGee

6. Paul layup

11: Monté Morris
5: Will Barton
1: Michael Porter Jr.
50: Aaron Gordon
34: JaVale McGee

▲ shot ■ pass

the corner, having taken a beat too long to react to Crowder's movement. Booker handed the ball off to Crowder and continued running toward the baseline, forcing Gordon and Porter Jr. to switch assignments.

Before they could execute their switch, Crowder immediately passed *back* to Paul near the logo. At the same time the Booker-Crowder handoff occupied the Nuggets' attention, Ayton was drifting well beyond the three-point line to screen for Paul. Bridges, meanwhile, never moved an inch from his spot in the corner, occupying Nuggets defender Monté Morris' attention.

That left Denver's other four defenders to handle a pick-and-roll that snuck up on them amid Phoenix's decoy movement. Paul used Ayton's screen to flatten his own man, which cued Denver big man JaVale McGee to step up to contain the ball. It would be tough, but not impossible, for McGee to cut off Paul's drive, stop Ayton's roll, and deter Paul's deadly mid-range jumper. But just as McGee got low to engage Paul, he recoiled from a brick wall in his back. Instead of sprinting in the corner after his handoff with Crowder, Booker curled back to the free-throw line to set a second on-ball screen for Paul.

That left Porter Jr., already processing the action a beat too slowly, in a horrible spot. He hadn't started the possession defending Booker, yet Phoenix had arranged a pick-and-roll setup that thrust three perilous threats—Paul's drive, Ayton's roll, and Booker's potential fade out for an open jumper—in his face simultaneously with no time to process them. It's little wonder Porter Jr. watched Paul surge around McGee, before fouling him in a foolish last-ditch attempt to block his layup. Two points for the Suns, plus one more at the line.

What would you call this sequence that took six paragraphs to describe?

If you're a coach, you'd respond with technical jargon that sounds like gibberish to the layperson. Something like "SLOB Horns Rub Entry Iverson DHO into Middle Spain Action,"[63] or some more manageable shorthand. If you work for the Suns, you'd use a codename and/or hand gesture to disguise it from your opponent. You may have even changed it mid-series because you suspected a Nuggets player, coach, and/or video coordinator was onto the initial call.

If you're like the rest of us, though, you'd use a more universal term to sum up that Suns play: pick-and-roll. Specifically: a cool/good/super-dope/whatever-kids-say-today pick-and-roll.

You wouldn't be wrong. The Suns did score via a pick-and-roll action, or at least incorporated one as the culmination of their after-timeout set play. Its outcome was a driving Paul layup, but it could have easily ended with a Paul mid-range jumper, a Paul pull-up three, a Paul pass to the rolling

---

63. "SLOB" is an acronym for "sideline out of bounds." Horns is a set that places one guy at the top, two players at each elbow, and two in each corner. "Rub Entry" refers to Paul's initial cut before catching the inbound pass. "Iverson," as noted, refers to Booker's cut. "DHO" is an acronym for "dribble handoff." "Spain Action" is a type of pick-and-roll involving a second on-ball back-screen by a different offensive player on the screener's defender. "Middle" is, well, the middle of the court.

Ayton, a Paul pass to the popping Booker, a Paul pass to Bridges for a corner three, or something else entirely. It had infinite potential outcomes involving any combination of the five Suns players, just like each Stockton/Malone pick-and-roll.

Yet the setup and design of the Suns' finishing blow to the Nuggets was quantum leaps ahead of the Utah prototype. Each element of that Suns pick-and-roll setup was a mutation of the many methods the league developed to force all five defenders to make stressful split-second decisions that threatened to shatter their team's entire defensive shape.

The 2001 rule change to allow zone institutionalized pick-and-roll defense as a five-man operation. The five offensive players could already go wherever they wanted. Now, so could the five defensive players. That didn't give defenses the power to address *every* pick-and-roll possibility, but it did enable them to align their five players to address the greatest threat, especially if that meant ignoring one or more of the other offensive players deemed to be unthreatening.

Suddenly, the three players not directly involved in the pick-and-roll action became wayyyyy more important to its success. They had to present a *constant* off-ball threat to prevent or at least slow off-ball defenders from loading up to the ball. Once offensive teams internalized that reality, the pick-and-roll morphed into the increasingly complex multi-front basketball war we see today.

The ways those other offensive players do that fall into two categories: spacing and movement.

It is impossible to overstate the impact of an off-ball player with a halfway decent jump shot standing beyond the three-point line instead of inside the arc. To state the obvious, it's a lot harder for one defender to cover man and ball when one is farther away from the other.

The simple adjustment on pick-and-roll actions was a crucial step in allowing offenses to reclaim the asymmetry they once exploited with the now-abolished illegal defense rule. The penalty for loading up to the ball now cost defenses an extra point, especially since the additional length of the closeout either enabled that three-point shot to be less contested or provided the shooter more space to elude it and drive.

The same spacing adjustment also works to the offense's advantage in the other direction. More threatening off-ball three-point shooters forced their defender to follow them farther from the ball, which in turn gave the two players directly involved in the pick-and-roll more space to operate. A great shooter can act like a gravitational pull that sucks up defensive attention. Hence the new-age term "gravity."[64]

This double-edged sword powered the deadly Steve Nash/Amar'e Stoudemire tandem in Phoenix. The Suns spread shooters along the perimeter in their pick-and-roll actions, paralyzing all five defenders by playing multiple threats off each other. Hanging too close to the shooters gave Stoudemire more room to roll unimpeded down the lane. Roaming too far *off* the three shooters risked easy kickout passes, open three-point shots, and more room to drive past overeager closeouts. Prioritizing those two immediate passing options gave Nash room to shoot his deadly pull-up jumper or probe with the dribble until he found another opening. One slow reaction from any of the five defenders, and the Suns had multiple built-in ways to pounce.

While there were mechanical differences between the Nash/Amar'e two-man game and the Stockton/Malone pick-and-roll, they were far more alike than different. Both were deadly advantage-creation mechanisms that scaled up into entire offensive systems. Both maximized their bread-and-butter by positioning the other three players in spots that forced the defense to pick its poison. The difference was that the 2005 rules incentivized the Suns to place their three off-ball players along the three-point line, whereas the Jazz's approach to cluster theirs on the opposite side took advantage of the old illegal defense rule.

As a related byproduct, removing the illegal defense rule shifted the pick-and-roll's preferred point of attack. The Stockton/Malone duo mostly worked the wing because that was where the most open space existed given the restrictions the illegal defense rule placed on off-ball defenders.[65] Nash and Stoudemire preferred working the "high" pick-and-roll because that was where they had the most open space to do their thing with illegal defense restrictions lifted. Now that teams could load up to the pick-and-roll's point

---

64. I'm not sure where I first heard this term, but whoever invented it deserves a ton of credit. Talk about an evocative metaphor!

65. The left side, specifically, in large part because it allowed Stockton to dribble into the middle of the floor with his strong hand. This was another reason the Bulls' strategy to force Stockton to the baseline worked effectively.

of attack with all five players, pick-and-roll practitioners needed to read and leverage all five of those guys at once. It's a lot easier for the ball-handler to do that when he can see them.

The geometric structure of a pick-and-roll action, and, by extension, offense itself, was rapidly changing. The rule changes that inspired the Suns' success elevated the importance of drilling and maintaining proper floor spacing. The corner three-pointer became especially prime real estate because it was both closer to the basket than an above-the-break three *and* farther away from a high pick-and-roll's point of attack. The San Antonio Spurs were the first to realize the corner three-pointer's potential to squeeze offensive value out of elite perimeter defenders like Bruce Bowen and Danny Green. Over the course of the Spaced Out Era, creating the basic shape of three shooting threats—two in each corner if possible—alongside an ace ball-handler and a deadly rim roller became the most obvious way to maintain an effective pick-and-roll attack.

As more offenses spread out to stretch off-ball defenders thin into the early 2010s, defenses largely became more risk-averse to limit the need to make long rotations at all. Though some teams still deployed aggressive on-ball traps at the point of attack, most took a page from the Bulls' strategy against Stockton and Malone. They dropped their big man into the paint to contain drives, tasked the on-ball defender with getting through the screen, and slid a third guy onto the nail and no farther while instructing the other two defenders to stay with their assignments. Allowing an open jump shot from the ball-handler or screener was preferable to yielding a layup or open three from whiplash ball movement.

Though many teams adopted this strategy, the Indiana Pacers were the team that perfected the art of defending the pick-and-roll two-on-two at all costs. Under young head coach Frank Vogel and ace defensive coordinator Dan Burke, the Pacers deployed 7'2" center Roy Hibbert as a one-man wall around the basket and tasked everyone else with funneling pick-and-rolls into Hibbert's giant (straight-up) arms. Their stifling defense, along with the emergence of young star Paul George and the 2012 addition of hard-nosed power forward David West, transformed the Pacers into the LeBron-era Heat's primary adversary and briefly shot them to the top of the league. (We'll talk more about the Pacers when we dive into pick-and-roll defense in Chapter 7.)

The initial success of the Pacers-style "drop" defense ushered in a second pick-and-roll spacing revolution. The Pacers and their fellow drop enthusiasts correctly deduced that conceding easier pull-up two-point jumpers and floaters was an acceptable price to pay for shutting off the rim and spot-up three pointers. But that trade-off became a lot harder to accept once ball-handlers and screeners turned more of those pull-up twos into threes. The marginal efficiency difference between off-the-dribble twos and off-the-dribble threes is significant enough to threaten the wisdom of a conservative defensive approach.

Offenses further enhanced the threat of off-the-dribble or pick-and-pop threes by setting the screen's point of attack beyond the three-point line. That gave the ball-handler more space to use, either to step into open threes or build up speed for drives, and allowed screeners to get pick-and-pop threes without retreating.

This second on-court spread combined with the initial three-point revolution to create what became known as "five-out offense," so named because all five players need to be honored when standing or moving beyond the three-point line. It was harder to justify using rim protection specialists like Hibbert at all, much less centering entire defensive schemes around them. At age 27, Hibbert was the game's premier pick-and-roll defender. Three years later, he wasn't even on an NBA roster.

Of course, spreading the floor with stationary long-range shooting threats is not the only way to engage off-ball defenders during a pick-and-roll action. The other obvious tactic is to have those players move around, especially with well-timed cuts that defenders cannot easily anticipate. While these off-ball tactics co-evolved with the growing value of spread-out floor spacing, they became far more essential in the second half of the 2010s in response to a novel defensive approach to contain the ball at the point of attack without being forced into long off-ball rotations.

The Golden State Warriors did not invent the concept of switching pick-and-rolls, nor were they even the first team to weave switching into their larger defensive philosophy. But they were the first team to understand that the NBA's shift into a pick-and-roll heavy game was heightening the value of defenders who could credibly guard multiple positions. To use a simple formula: more on-ball screens + more space to collectively cover = more opportunities to switch. If a team could repeatedly execute the maneuver without surrendering clear mismatches, they could achieve what drop coverage couldn't and neuter the pick-and-roll's core function as an advantage creation mechanism.

The Warriors' system and personnel came as close to fulfilling that lofty promise as any team had before them. Golden State built on the principles of the solid drop pick-and-roll defense they used prior to Steve Kerr's arrival in 2014 and cranked it to another level by switching those screens instead. They built the system around Draymond Green, a physical rim protector, one-on-one defender, off-ball roamer, agile closeout artist, and defensive quarterback all in one, and supplemented him with multiple long perimeter defenders who could credibly shut off the basket and the perimeter points of attack. At their best, the Warriors made setting screens—the fundamental bedrock of any offensive system, especially those based around the pick-and-roll—seem pointless. Why bother when the Warriors easily switched them without surrendering a mismatch?

The allure of the Warriors' strategy was obvious. If a team had enough players of similar size and quickness, they theoretically could switch every on-ball screen and never have to rotate to all those spread-out off-ball players at all. That promise, of course, obscured the massive "if" at the start of that sentence. The Warriors' many imitators soon realized that finding their equivalent of Draymond Green, Klay Thompson, Andre Iguodala, Shaun Livingston, Kevin Durant, etc. was a lot harder than it looked.

The team that came closest was the Warriors' chief rival from Houston. The Rockets didn't possess Golden State's length, but they had many players with wide torsos that played far bigger than their height—"middle linebackers," as Kerr once called them. They spent the entire 2017–18 season perfecting their version of the Warriors' switch-everything scheme, an effort that culminated in the two teams' seven-game 2018 Western Conference Finals showdown.

That series, won by Golden State, was more than just a showdown between rivals. It also represented another significant pivot point in the pick-and-roll's rise to offensive action supremacy.

THE UNDERLYING FACTORS that pushed Kevin Durant to leave the Warriors after two championships in three years are too numerous and interwoven to list here. Still, one factor was clear, in hindsight if not at the time. There was a growing divide between Durant's one-on-one scoring genius and Kerr's collaborative offensive system.

"The motion offense we run in Golden State, it only works to a certain point," Durant told the *Wall Street Journal* two months after signing with the Brooklyn Nets in the summer of 2019. "We can totally rely on our system for maybe the first two rounds. Then the next two rounds we're going to have to mix in individual play."

It's difficult to pin down exactly when Durant fell out of love with the system that drew him to Golden State in the first place in 2016. But in retrospect, that 2018 seven-game war with Houston was a pivotal inflection point. While the Warriors survived to win in seven games,[66] the series seemed to foreshadow the isolation's resurgence after a decade-plus decline. With both teams perfecting defensive schemes that switched each pick-and-roll and off-ball screen, games were often decided by brilliant one-on-one play against perceived mismatches—the very antithesis of the Warriors' ethos.

That placed a ton of stress on Durant and Kerr, who needed to properly balance their team's greatest advantage against the league as a whole (their free-flowing style) with their greatest advantage against this particular opponent (Durant's one-on-one scoring as the ultimate switching kryptonite). During Game 5, TNT's cameras caught Kerr telling his star to trust his teammates and not get sucked into playing Houston's game. "When [Michael Jordan] was with the Bulls, we had a playoff game and he kept trying to score," Kerr told Durant. "And he was scoring, but we weren't getting anything going."

Their struggle was a microcosm of the rising threat effective switching defenses were causing for a league increasingly built around pick-and-roll actions. The most obvious downside to switching pick-and-rolls is yielding a mismatch of some kind, and the simplest way to punish a mismatch is to isolate that player against the weaker defender in a threatening position. The Warriors knew the power of that approach well, having witnessed LeBron James relentlessly target Stephen Curry for switches during the team's two Finals battles with Cleveland in 2015 and 2016. One reason they pursued

---

66. The Rockets might have won the series had Chris Paul not suffered a series-ending hamstring injury at the end of Game 5. Yet it is only fair to point out that the Warriors missed Iguodala for the last four games of the series due to a leg injury that was later diagnosed as a "spider fracture."

May 31, 2018 — Cavaliers at Warriors — NBA Finals Game 1
Warriors 100, Cavaliers 96 — 3:01 left in fourth quarter

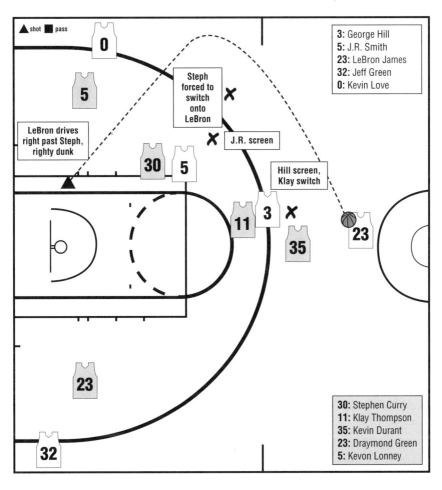

Durant so aggressively after that second series was so he could add that trick to their own repertoire.

Kerr, however, had long believed that the best way to punish a switch was to run their offense even more to take advantage of defenders being placed in unusual off-ball situations. "Offensively, our team, we don't really try to pick on anyone. Our whole philosophy is, 'Let it come out in the wash,'" he told ESPN's Ethan Sherwood Strauss in November 2015, before Durant joined the team. "We just push the ball and move it, pass and cut, movement, all that stuff."

The stylistic tension between Kerr and Durant, first heightened by the Rockets' strategy to push the Warriors to the brink in 2018, was bad for Golden State and their relationship. The league as a whole, though, saw that both men were right to a point. Each had found an effective way to combat the growing trend of pick-and-roll switching. Why not adopt both tactics and even merge them together?

That's exactly what's happened in the intervening four years. The game's best perimeter scorers began mimicking James, Durant, and the Rockets' strategy of inducing weak defenders to switch an initial pick-and-roll as a prelude to a more favorable isolation action. Today, the practice of running a pick-and-roll as a means of "hunting" a mismatch is so ingrained that both sides have developed more complex screening tactics to force the switch (offense) or avoid it (defense). Each of those, of course, carry their own trade-offs that either side can exploit.

But Kerr was also right that the usual cutting, ball movement, screening, etc. that occurs after pick-and-roll actions against more traditional defensive schemes can be as effective, if not *more* effective, against switches.

It's easy to forget that defenders are performing an active maneuver every time they switch a screen. Just because defenders *know* to switch a screen in advance doesn't mean they will coordinate their switch properly in real time. While each individual switch is simpler than the multi-layered help-and-recover tactics other pick-and-roll defensive strategies require, a scheme built around switching every screen requires more of those coordinated maneuvers in total. That means more chances for communication breakdowns, mistimed movements, improper effort, and other forms of human error that even highly trained professional athletes can't avoid.

That's especially true when teams continue to run their motion offense after their opponent switches the initial pick-and-roll action. As Hubie Brown famously preaches, the main purpose of setting screens is to make defenders think. The more they're thinking, the slower they're reacting. Hunting a mismatch after the defense switches the initial pick-and-roll action may yield a higher-leverage isolation, but it also removes the possibility of a more damaging botched switch later on. The more off-ball offensive players move, the more stuff they make defenders think about.

Off-ball movement designed to distract off-ball defenders is known as misdirection. This can take the form of two simultaneous scripted actions that force defenders to make multiple decisions or decide which is the real threat. It can occur organically with multiple off-ball screens or cuts *after* a pick-and-roll switch. The San Antonio Spurs turned misdirection into an art form during their two Finals runs in 2013 and 2014. It was common to see San Antonio run a pick-and-roll between Tony Parker and Tim Duncan on one side at the same time Manu Ginóbili or Kawhi Leonard curled off a screen on the other. The Iverson cut by Booker in that Suns-Nuggets example was a form of misdirection because it distracted McGee while Ayton crept into position to screen for Paul.

Teams also increasingly began using an initial pick-and-roll action as misdirection to give a second pick-and-roll a head start. This tactic can take a variety of forms. One involves screening the screener's man before they come to the ball for the pick-and-roll. Another is to screen the screener's defender after the initial pick-and-roll, a maneuver colloquially known as the Spain pick-and-roll because the Spanish national team was the first to use it frequently.[67] It's what Booker did to McGee in the Suns' example, and it can be an especially effective way of surprising the switching defender before they are ready to cover their new assignment.

Yet an emphasis on "letting the switch come out in the wash" need not be so complicated. The Mike D'Antoni 21 set from Chapter 5 offers a starting point to execute a pick-and-pop that then flows into a second pick-and-roll or a dribble handoff with a different ball-handler on the opposite side. The Milwaukee Bucks go-to offensive set on their march to the 2021 title involved Jrue Holiday running a pick-and-pop with Giannis Antetokounmpo on the right side, who then drifted directly into a wide dribble hand-off at the top of the key for Khris Middleton curling in from the left corner. The simple act of using one pick-and-roll action on one side to set up a second one on the other worked wonders for an occasionally stagnant Bucks half-court offense.

Durant-style on-ball targeting and Kerr-championed off-ball movement can both feature several more specific on- and off-ball methods that are effective counters to pick-and-roll switches. By the 1990s, smart big men like Malone had mastered the art of "slipping out of the screen," which is

---

67. The concept of a high pick-and-roll with a second back-screen has been used overseas since the early 2000s, but it really emerged on NBA radars after the Spanish national team used it frequently in earning a bronze medal at the 2016 Olympics. Some call it a "stack" pick-and-roll. Nowadays, it's one of the league's most popular pick-and-roll actions.

when they roll before their teammate uses the pick. Stockton, meanwhile, created the same effect by darting the opposite direction of the screen he planned to use, a practice known as "declining" or "rejecting" the screen. Both tactics emerged as ways to beat the on-ball traps that were common in their era.

But the same principle that makes either an effective way to bypass a trap can also be applied to anticipate a switch. There is always a specific window when the two main pick-and-roll defenders are actively swapping assignments, so a well-timed slip or rejection of the screen can short-circuit that process in multiple ways.

Best-case scenario, a slip or reject makes a planned switch look like a cartoonish failed trap. But the mere threat of either tactic can paralyze both defenders enough to pry open that switching window a bit longer. Players have even learned to time their pull-up three-point jumpers to the precise instant their opponents begin to execute a pick-and-roll switch, catching both off balance so neither can contest the shot. (This is a Middleton specialty, though he's hardly alone.)

Ultimately, the tension between Kerr and Durant was rooted in a false choice. Isolation actions could be *a* tool to combat pick-and-roll switching without having to be *the* tool. The rise of switching did not foreshadow the decline of the pick-and-roll's power. Instead, it reinvigorated old methods to punish the defense (i.e., isolations) while also spurring additional movement innovation that further enhanced its ability to force defenders into difficult split-second decisions. The modern pick-and-roll remains an uncanny instrument of chaos against any defensive strategy. On-ball switching is certainly another tactic defenses can use to neutralize the pick-and-roll's power, but it did not turn out to be its Kryptonite.

That is why the modern pick-and-roll is spiritually aligned with the Stockton/Malone prototype despite so many aesthetic differences. At its core, the Stockton/Malone pick-and-roll was a tool to force and then exploit a cascade of defensive reactions. Its predictable unpredictability defined the Jazz's entire offensive system. That is the same quality that powers the increasingly complex and ubiquitous pick-and-rolls of the Spaced Out Era.

Today's pick-and-roll actions may feature more spread out points of attack and spacing alignments. They may have traded precision for speed, structure for flow, physicality for finesse, directness for trickery, and reliability for misdirection. They may have many different potential ball-handlers and screeners rather than just guards and big men, respectively. They may be vehicles for isolations, additional pick-and-rolls, or other actions rather than individual play calls within a set. They may be defended differently based on the rules and strategic norms of the times. They may not feature an actual "pick" or a clear "roll" to the basket.

But those differences are far less significant than the beautiful read-and-react sympatico they share with the Stockton/Malone combination that baffled opponents for two decades. If it looks too easy for today's players to run pick-and-roll, it's because they all have a little bit of Stockton and Malone in them.

Chapter 7
No Wrong Answers

The Milwaukee Bucks title journey and why the best pick-
and-roll defensive scheme is many schemes.

The first seed of the Milwaukee Bucks' 2021 NBA championship was planted on April 9, 2012. That was when a different group of Bucks players were embarrassed in a way that defined the franchise's response in the decade to come.

The 2011–12 Milwaukee Bucks were desperate to make the playoffs, which they had only done twice in the previous seven seasons. Achieving this modest goal had become an unspoken requirement for then-owner Herb Kohl.

That helped explain the controversial trade-deadline deal that yielded high-scoring Warriors guard Monta Ellis in exchange for injured franchise center Andrew Bogut.[68] The trade paired Ellis with fellow jitterbug Brandon Jennings in a backcourt that critics deemed too small and defensively challenged to succeed beyond a doomed race to mediocrity.

---

68. We could write a whole book on this trade, which sent Ellis, Ekpe Udoh, and Kwame Brown to Milwaukee for Bogut and Stephen Jackson. Early versions of the deal included future two-time MVP Stephen Curry, but the Bucks, wary of Curry's history of ankle injuries, did the deal for Ellis instead. (Then-Warriors general manager Larry Riley has repeatedly insisted that Curry was only involved in trade talks as a negotiating ploy. However, current Bucks owner Marc Lasry and Bogut himself both said the Bucks preferred Ellis because of his clean bill of health at the time.)

UNDER ONE/UNDER TWO

ONE-SENTENCE DESCRIPTION: When the on-ball defender ducks under the pick. "Under one" is when they go under the screen, but over the screener's defender. "Under two" is when they go under both.

MOST COMMONLY USED: Against non-shooters and/or athletic drivers, though either tactic—particularly "under two"—can be used in a softer trap or switch.

SYNONYMS: "Under two" is often interchangeable with "push" or "jam," which is featured later.

ADVANTAGES
• Baits pull-up jumpers from below-average shooters.
• Helps slower defenders beat quick drivers to a spot.
• Can stagnate the offense as the ball-handler decides how to use the space they're given.

DISADVANTAGES
• Even the NBA's worst pull-up shooters can make an uncontested jumper.
• Strong drivers are able to build up speed, making it even harder to stay in front of them.
• Incentivizes a passive defensive mentality that can morph into a culture of laziness.

EXAMPLE TEAMS: Spurs against LeBron James in the 2013 and 2014 NBA Finals, lots of teams against Rajon Rondo or Russell Westbrook, Anthony Davis (and later Giannis Antetokounmpo) against Jimmy Butler.

The Bucks won 10 of their first 14 games after the trade, albeit against a weak schedule, to move to within one game of the No. 8 spot. Game No. 15 offered stiffer opposition. The young Oklahoma City Thunder, led by Kevin Durant, Russell Westbrook, James Harden, and Serge Ibaka, were coming to town. This was a key test for the new-look Bucks.

They failed. Spectacularly.

Using their overwhelming combination of size, speed, and length, the Thunder amped up their defensive pressure to block out the Bucks' offense. They were particularly cruel to Ellis, who shot just 3–12 from the field with long-armed Thabo Sefolosha swarming him at the point of attack. The Thunder surged to a 33–12 first-quarter lead and cruised to a 20-point victory.

As the Bucks' front office watched their small-market comrades reinforce their own minor league status, they made a vow to never get beat up again.

"That night, Bucks management peered into the future and imagined a team that would be all arms, legs, and hops," *ESPN The Magazine*'s Kevin

Arnovitz wrote in 2017. "The Bucks might never attract a superstar in free agency, but they vowed to never be outlengthed and outathleticized again."

A decade later, the Milwaukee Bucks won their first title in half a century with a stifling defense that doled out their own form of punishment to high-scoring offenses. Their journey doesn't fit neatly into a hoops textbook. It required the improbable draft selection and rise of a seven-foot Nigerian-born Greek refugee, featured many coaching and personnel missteps, and survived multiple ownership groups and front-office squabbles. Yet the Bucks never wavered on the promise they made to themselves on that brisk early-spring night in 2012. They were never outlengthed and outathleticized again.

The manner in which the Bucks *applied* that length and athleticism toward the pick-and-roll defense that became their signature, though, ran the full gauntlet.

Over the course of the decade, Milwaukee shifted from Jason Kidd's aggressive trapping style to Mike Budenholzer's hyper-conservative drop coverage. The league adjusted to shred the former after initially getting caught off guard, while the latter's often-historic regular-season effectiveness was undone by its inflexibility in high-level playoff series against hot pull-up shooting and/or deadly isolation scorers. It was only by blending the two together and adding a touch of on-ball switching that the Bucks overcame their postseason demons and won the title.[69]

The Bucks' journey offers a window into the rapidly evolving task of stopping the action that increasingly defined offenses in the Spaced Out Era. In particular, the Bucks illustrate three fundamental truths of defending the modern pick-and-roll.

- There is no single "right way" to do it.
- Every team must decide which outcomes they most want to avoid and which they can accept as occupational hazards.
- Perfecting one scheme is good. Being capable enough to perform more than one scheme is better. Merging the best elements of each scheme into a strong, yet flexible philosophy is best.

---

69. The Bucks slipped to 10th in defensive efficiency during the regular season, but had the best playoff defensive rating by far among the 16 teams who made the postseason.

Though the database of pick-and-roll defensive coverages swells every year, it's hard to find universally agreed-upon language to delineate them. Teams use different naming conventions on the practice court, which their players translate into different shorthand to ease on-court communication. Neutrals fluent in retroactive film study often define the same team's coverage differently because it's hard to precisely know if each player's positioning is the product of his team's game plan, their own instincts, or the offense's actions.

All that said, most NBA pick-and-roll defensive schemes fall into one of three general categories. Focus less on the naming convention and more on the general descriptions.

TRAP: Two players on the ball, three rotating early to anticipate the ensuing passes.

DROP: The on-ball defender fights over the top, the screener's man hangs back to protect against a drive or roll to the basket, and the other three players stay on their individual assignments.

SWITCH: The on-ball defender and the screener's man swap assignments.

Think of the first two categories as the opposite ends of a spectrum, with the trap occupying the far left (aggressive) pole and drop occupying the far right (conservative). The many variations of each—described in various sidebars throughout this chapter—fall somewhere between those two extremes. Switching, meanwhile, can be aggressive or conservative depending on how it's executed. The same is true of various zone defenses, which are experiencing a revival in the NBA,[70] and any approach that involves the on-ball defender ducking under the screen—a strategy by itself in lower levels, but more of a situational tactic that can be used to trap, drop, or switch in the NBA.

Though coaches, executives, players, writers, and fans will forever debate the relative merits of all three, there is no one-size-fits-all approach. The three strategies have opposite strengths and weaknesses that can be mitigated or exacerbated by each team's personnel. In choosing which to use as their base strategy, a coach is really asking themselves which potential outcomes they most want their teams to eliminate and which they're willing to live with as a trade-off. (They'd put it slightly differently to their players, of course.)

---

70. More on this trend in Chapter 12.

ICE

ONE-SENTENCE DESCRIPTION: The on-ball defender forces the ball to the screener on the baseline, while a third defender drifts toward the "nail" to deter the screener from rolling to the basket.

MOST COMMONLY USED: On side pick-and-rolls, especially on the ball-handler's weak hand.

SYNONYMS: Down, blue, black, or your team's color of choice.

ADVANTAGES
• Cuts the court in half by pinning the ball on one side of the floor
• Keeps the ball away from the middle, limiting the ball-handler's passing options.
• Can be converted into a baseline trap or a deep drop.
• Dictates the offensive player's move.

DISADVANTAGES
• Vulnerable against quality pick-and-pop players who can shoot and/or quickly rotate the ball to the other side of the floor.
• Dead to rights if the ball-handler gets to the middle of the floor before using the screen.
• Opens up an easy roll to the basket if the third defender is too slow to help.
• Short-circuited by "snake dribble" popularized by Chris Paul that crosses in front of trailing on-ball defender to get back to the middle after using the screen.

EXAMPLE TEAMS: The 1997–98 Bulls against Utah, Tom Thibodeau's teams. In truth, most teams use ICE situationally in some form.

Nevertheless, as the sport's transformation yielded new pick-and-roll dimensions, the NBA of the Spaced Out Era became a copycat league in desperate search of a winning formula to copy. As defenses struggled to address the growing challenge of covering an increasingly large amount of territory with the same number of defenders, each of the three general pick-and-roll defensive strategies had moments of mainstream dominance.

But in the end, the league as a whole learned the same lesson the Bucks did over the same time period. The best way to defend the pick-and-roll is the way that works best for your specific mix of players.

Scratch that. Not "the way"—"the ways," plural.

FOR BETTER OR worse, team media days exist primarily to stage viral moments that excite diehard, Internet-savvy fans. That is how a single photo turned the 2013 Milwaukee Bucks' edition into a smashing success.

Starting center Larry Sanders stood in the middle of the paint, with backup John Henson on his right and a rookie named Giannis Antetokounmpo

SHOW

ONE-SENTENCE DESCRIPTION: The screener's defender jumps into the ball-handler's path with his chest facing the sideline, but only to temporarily slow the ball-handler while the on-ball defender recovers.

MOST COMMONLY USED: Against elite pick-and-pop players, or (increasingly) like-sized or inverted pick-and-rolls (smaller player screens for a bigger one) that try to get a weak defender to switch.

SYNONYMS: Soft hedge, show and recover.

ADVANTAGES
- Deters the ball-handler from turning the corner without putting two men on the ball for too long.
- More proactive than dropping or switching, yet less risky in theory than blitzing or hedging.
- Easier to execute repeatedly in the same possession than similar coverages like a hedge or blitz.

DISADVANTAGES
- Less effective at throwing off the ball-handler's timing than a blitz or hedge, especially on inverted or like-sized pick-and-rolls.
- Easier for the ball-handler to turn the corner and bypass both defenders than other trapping pick-and-roll schemes.
- Vulnerable to the screener slipping or "ghosting" the pick, which is when they run through the ball instead of stopping to screen.

EXAMPLE TEAMS: Warriors when Stephen Curry's man screens for an elite ball-handler, most teams before 2005, many teams before 2012 on all screens involving non-centers.

positioned to his left. The three players each extended their arms straight to their sides, the edge of their fingers touching to form a straight line that extended way out to the short corner. The length of that line: 22 feet. *The sum of those three players' wingspan was 22 feet.*

The message was clear. The Bucks may be young, but they would more than make up for that with freakish length. And while their absurd wingspans didn't save them from sinking to a league-worst 15–67 record that season, it inspired their next coach, Jason Kidd, to deploy the era's boldest experiment.

When Kidd took over the Bucks in 2014 after a messy separation with the aging Brooklyn Nets, the league was tilting toward conservative pick-and-roll defensive schemes. Offenses were just discovering the joys of the drive-and-kick and corner three, both of which opened up once defenses were forced to scramble. Deep drops, perfected by teams like the Pacers, Bulls, and Spurs, cut off access to those juicy shots by limiting the need for defensive rotations in the first place.

The exception to the trend was the team that dominated the era. It never made sense for the Miami Heat to deploy a conservative pick-and-roll defense given their superstars' athletic gifts and their lack of interior size. But their seminal decision to spread the floor with shooters and forego traditional centers rendered even the more aggressive strategies of years past as half measures. They decided to send a *hard* double-team to every pick-and-roll's point of attack, even if that meant leaving themselves vulnerable behind it.

This pick-and-roll coverage, which became known as "blitzing," is the most offensive of all defensive pick-and-roll coverages. It is a bet that the on-ball pressure of the trap will cause turnovers, hesitation, fear, and slow-moving passes, all of which allow the Heat to defy the cliché that the ball moves faster than the man. When it works, the blitz does more than stop the offense's pick-and-roll game. It also crushes their spirit.

That last quality separates the blitz from less insane trapping schemes like "showing" and "hedging." Those two strategies, which share the same philosophy despite subtle differences,[71] involve a temporary on-ball trap that buys time for each defender to recover to their assignments before yielding an opening. Both originated during the illegal defense era, when the rules forced the other three players to guard their own man, and evolved into the mid-2000s Pistons' and Celtics' strong side zones that featured off-ball defenders loading up to the ball in advance. Each of those approaches are designed to preempt the ball movement that forces defenses to rotate.

The Heat's blitzing scheme, on the other hand, welcomed those scramble situations. Like the show and hedge, the blitz requires the other three defenders to load up to the ball and anticipate the obvious passes out of the trap. But the Heat didn't stop there. They trapped the next pass, and the next, and the next, until they won or the traps were spent.[72] The third player

---

71. The main difference between the two involves the body position of the screener's man when they leap out. In a "show," their chest is perpendicular to the ball and parallel to the direction the player is headed. In a "hedge," the opposite is true: the chest faces the backcourt in a more normal defensive stance.

72. That's a *Star Wars* reference. Shoutout Jyn Erso and *Rogue One,* an excellent movie.

in the trap moved one pass ahead of the ball, trusting that a teammate would do the same behind them.

While stopping the pick-and-roll had become a team-wide task after 2001's rule changes, the Heat's blitzing scheme was the first that required all five men to constantly function as a single unit. They popularized the evocative "on a string" metaphor, often cited by coaches to illustrate how any one player's movement should cause the other four to shift in tandem.

When all five players locked in, the Heat's blitzing scheme pulled off the seemingly impossible task of pressuring the ball and blanketing the other four offensive players despite a man disadvantage. The frightening sight of James or Wade buzzing behind play unnerved opponents, especially once the third Heatle, Chris Bosh, embraced the often-thankless role of trapping the ball to force the passes his fellow star teammates deflected or stole. The Heat's defense could reach the highest of highs, like when they put the breaks on Linsanity in a marquee 2012 regular-season matchup[73] or when rallying to win high-stakes playoff series against the Pacers, Celtics, and Spurs.

The challenge was the "locked in" part. Every scheme requires peak effort, but blitzing necessitates something more than that. Trapping the ball is *hard*. Bumping the roller and then sprinting back to close out to the perimeter is *hard*. Doing both over and over again, multiple times a possession, over multiple seasons … you're exhausted just thinking about it. Because the blitz is such a high-risk scheme, it is especially vulnerable once players' reservoirs of mental and physical energy naturally run out.

That's exactly what happened by the end of the Heat's run in 2014. Their core players were wearing down, their roster was aging, and their opponents were increasingly devising ways to facilitate quicker pick-and-roll passes that beat the Heat's on-ball traps and backside rotations. Those developments came to a head when the Spurs' whiplash ball movement lit up Miami in the 2014 Finals, ushering James back to Cleveland in free agency.

But when Kidd studied his new team that summer, he decided its roster was well-equipped to build on Miami's example. The Bucks could

---

73. President Barack Obama, a known NBA junkie, referenced the Heat's dominating defense when describing his 2012 re-election campaign strategy against Mitt Romney. "We're the Miami Heat, and he's Jeremy Lin," Obama told an aide, according to *The New York Times*. Lin went 1–11 from the field with eight turnovers in the 102–88 defeat.

HEDGE

ONE-SENTENCE DESCRIPTION: The screener's man jumps into the ball-handler's path with his chest facing the ball, then actively diverts the ball-handler backwards until the on-ball defender can recover.

MOST COMMONLY USED: Against slashing ball-handlers who use the pick-and-roll to attack the basket.

SYNONYMS: Hard show, hedge and recover.

ADVANTAGES
- Can stop the ball-handler instead of just deterring them without ceding a mismatch.
- Gives the other three defenders more time to get into ideal help positions.
- Forces the offense to retreat instead of attack.
- Better against slips, quick passes to the wing, hesitation dribbles, boomerang action (ball-handler passes and immediately receives a pass back so they can attack on the catch with more space), and other delay tactics that help teams beat a show.

DISADVANTAGES
- Much riskier than a show. If the ball-handler does turn the corner, the defense is severely compromised.
- (Usually) forces a less mobile defender to slide laterally against (usually) a quicker ball-handler.
- Slightly mistimed hedges lead to ticky-tack blocking fouls, especially as more ball-handlers mastered the art of ~~exaggerating contact~~ flopping.
- Becomes a mistimed trap if the two primary defenders don't coordinate their recoveries.

EXAMPLE TEAMS: Denver Nuggets with Nikola Jokić, Grit 'and Grind Grizzlies (sometimes), Kevin Garnett's Celtics, early Durant/Westbrook Thunder.

trot out lineups that included some combination of the gravity-defying Antetokounmpo, a center combination of 6'11" shot-blocking sensation Sanders and 6'10" skyscraper Henson, oversized 6'8" wing Khris Middleton, and 6'8" jumping jack rookie Jabari Parker. Eventually, it also included 6'5" lanky point guard Michael Carter-Williams—acquired in a midseason trade for shorter lead guard Brandon Knight—and tantalizing 7'0" guard/forward/center prospect Thon Maker, the Bucks' surprising 2016 NBA Draft No. 10 pick. Those long arms, immortalized in that viral 2013 media day photo, were bound to cause turnovers and panicked passes while shrinking the space the backside defenders needed to cover to contest shots.

Though Kidd repeatedly cited the Bucks' collective length as the main reason he installed a Miami-esque blitzing defense, his own recently concluded playing career was also fresh in his mind. As one of the best playmakers in NBA history, Kidd intuitively understood the danger of letting superstar ball-handlers get comfortable. "Great players, if they only see two bodies, they think, 'Maybe I can still beat 'em,'" he told Grantland early in his first season in Milwaukee. "But if they see three bodies, they think, 'Maybe I need to get off of it.'"

One objective of the Bucks' blitzing scheme was to force the ball away from the superstar and toward players who are more susceptible to pressure. Whereas drop coverage invites those master manipulators to slowly dissect the pick-and-roll coverage, a trap forces them to read it immediately. Theoretically, that's far sooner than they want and even sooner than their teammates can react to them. A blitz thus functions like an obstacle in a relay race in that it disrupts the timing of each leg, not just the first one.

Kidd's Bucks were *really* committed to disrupting their opponents' timing. He instructed staffers to measure the arc of their opponents' passes. (He often used the dual cross-sport metaphor of no "fastballs" or "strikes" to underline his message.) Intercepting or deflecting those passes out of the initial trap was ideal, but even slowing them down helped significantly. Less velocity, plus a non-superstar with subpar court vision receiving the ball in an unfamiliar spot, multiplied by the Bucks' length, would hopefully equal lots of turnovers and panicked offensive possessions.

Initially, it did. Milwaukee's blitzing scheme caught the league off guard in Kidd's first season, converting countless fastballs into off-target offspeed pitches. The Bucks posted the NBA's fourth-best defense, earned a surprising playoff berth, and challenged the Bulls in the first round before losing in six games.

But that defensive success did not hold up in the ensuing seasons. Milwaukee tumbled to 23rd in points allowed per 100 possessions in 2015–16, 19th in 2016–17, and were near the bottom of the league when Kidd got fired midway through the 2017–18 campaign. He never came up with an effective Plan B.

Why did the sticker shock of the Bucks' blitzing scheme wear off so quickly? One reason is that length alone doesn't make a hyper-aggressive pick-and-roll strategy work. Proper positioning is essential—perhaps *more* essential when trapping on the ball instead of dropping back or switching. What good are a player's long arms when the lower body doesn't move into the right position to use them?

April 18, 2015 — Bucks at Bulls — ECQF Game 1
Bulls 62, Bucks 55 — 9:50 left in third quarter

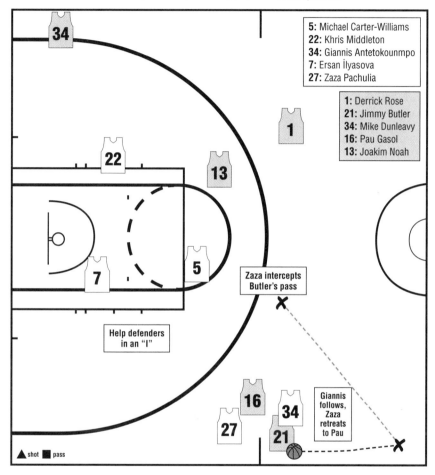

The Bucks had a series of rules that guided the other three defenders before and during the on-ball trap. The two farthest away from the ball were instructed to line up in an "I" along the center of the floor: one at the nail[74] discouraging the immediate pass to the screener and the other protecting the hoop on the baseline to act as what's now known as the "low man." Both players needed to read the situation quickly to reach those spots before the ball-handler passed out of the trap.

---

74. Refer back to Chapter 5 for this definition.

Veterans have more experience navigating that balance, even if they lack the wingspan to cover as much of the ensuing ground. The Bucks' successful 2014–15 unit benefited greatly from two such players in combo forward Jared Dudley and sturdy big man Zaza Pachulia. The Bucks' defense was never the same after they let both go to sign high-scoring free-agent center Greg Monroe, whose slow feet, shaky defensive instincts, and short arms made him an especially poor fit for Kidd's scheme.

On top of that, the league's spacing revolution was stretching the blitz beyond its breaking point. When Kidd first introduced it in 2014, teams were still regularly deploying lineups with two non-three-point-shooting big men. The Bucks' 2015 first-round playoff opponent started Pau Gasol and Joakim Noah together along with Derrick Rose, who was not much of a three-point marksman at the time. Chicago had enough talent to win the series, but did not have a standout offensive performance until top shooter Mike Dunleavy got loose in the Game 6 clincher.[75]

Two years later, the Bucks' initial 2–1 series lead over the Raptors disintegrated once Toronto coach Dwane Casey started wing Norman Powell over lumbering center Jonas Valančiūnas to provide more breathing room to move the ball against the Bucks' pressure. After scoring a ghastly 86.3 points per 100 possessions in Game 3, Toronto averaged nearly 110 points per 100 possessions over the next three games to win the series in six.

That development was exacerbated by the concurrent rise of the "short roll." Theoretically, the on-ball trap swarms the ball-handler too quickly for the screener to complete the "roll" part of a pick-and-roll. The "short roll," however, shattered that assumption. Instead of rolling all the way to the rim, screeners learned to stop near the top of the key, quickly receive the ball-handler's pass, and make the correct next pass to punish the ensuing four-on-three situation. Draymond Green set the standard for this maneuver, inspiring fellow big men to slim down and embrace their inner guard. When combined with wider floor spacing, the short roll morphed into the blitz's kryptonite.

---

75. Dunleavy's, shall we say, *shenanigans* also caused Antetokounmpo to lose his cool and shove him in the back with two hands, thereby getting ejected. But the Bulls were already up big when that happened.

BLITZ

ONE-SENTENCE DESCRIPTION: An aggressive double team on the ball combined with early backside rotations to anticipate the likeliest pass out of the trap.

MOST COMMONLY USED: To force turnovers and/or make anyone other than the superstar beat you.

SYNONYMS: Trap, hard trap, really hard trap, etc.

ADVANTAGES
- Converts defense from an inherently reactive activity to an *active* one that constantly pressures the offense.
- The best way to force live-ball turnovers that lead to easy buckets the other way.
- Forces stars out of their rhythm and makes their teammates do stuff they don't usually do.
- Builds into a cumulative effect over time that causes players to hesitate, hear footsteps, and lose their poise.

DISADVANTAGES
- The riskiest scheme of all because it does the pick-and-roll's main job: creating a numbers advantage for the offense.
- Requires coordinated, precise defensive rotations that are hard to time once, much less repeatedly.
- Yields a high volume of open spot-up three-pointers and offensive rebounds.
- Takes a *lot* of effort to execute over the long haul, which is why the LeBron-era Heat were so worn down by the end of their run.

EXAMPLE TEAMS: The 2010–14 Miami Heat, Jason Kidd's Bucks, 2021–22 Minnesota Timberwolves.

These two trends warped the primary purpose of a trapping pick-and-roll scheme, especially hyper-aggressive ones like the blitz. Congratulations, you prevented the superstar from beating you! Except, in preventing that superstar from scoring at will or picking out an open teammate with an incisive pass, you've given him even more power as a decoy that creates a constant four-on-three advantage for his team, one buttressed by wider spacing, better three-point shooting, and more developed supplementary playmaking. Talk about a pyrrhic victory!

(This is why Stephen Curry's greatest superpower isn't his long-range shooting or handle. It's his ability to constantly draw two defenders to him 35 feet from the hoop and thereby enable his team to be on a never-ending power play, to use a hockey term.)

PUSH

ONE-SENTENCE DESCRIPTION: The screener's man wedges into the pick to "push" it forward, while the on-ball defender goes under both players to meet the ball-handler on the other side.

MOST COMMONLY USED: At lower levels. In the NBA, you see it against non-shooting ball-handlers, elite pick-and-pop big men, or to avoid switching into a mismatch.

SYNONYMS: Under two, jam, squeeze.

ADVANTAGES
• Prevents a mismatch without the screener's man having to double-team.
• Negates the initial threat of a pick-and-pop without switching into a size mismatch.
• Forces the ball-handler to take a circuitous route when using the screen.

DISADVANTAGES
• Sometimes the two defenders end up screening each other. The technical term for that is "bad."
• Can expose the on-ball defender, since the screener's man isn't helping beyond the initial jam.
• The screener often occupies defensive attention without moving.
• Yields dribble penetration to the middle, which forces the help to sink off shooters.

EXAMPLE TEAMS: Dallas' opponents during the late Dirk Nowitzki era, Mike Woodson's Knicks, LeBron James' opponents in crunch time.

Trapping (almost) everyone, as Kidd's scheme required, began to have the same effect. Opponents baited Milwaukee traps, then gleefully accepted the four-on-three gifts they provided. The Bucks' length, already dwindled by the end of Kidd's tenure,[76] had little effect on lineups featuring more capable three-point shooters and intelligent short-rolling screeners. Kidd himself was the last to realize this, much to Bucks fans' chagrin. The Bucks briefly used more conservative pick-and-roll schemes in 2017–18 during an early-season road trip, only for Kidd to switch back to blitzing in a double-digit loss to rival Boston. He was fired a month later.

That summer, the Bucks made two pivotal decisions that foreshadowed a sharp left turn from Kidd's defensive ethos. The first was hiring Mike Budenholzer, the former Hawks coach and longtime Gregg Popovich

---

76. Though Antetokounmpo and Middleton developed into franchise cornerstones, other hopeful "long ball" core members like Sanders, Carter-Williams, Parker, Maker, Henson, and Tony Snell failed to develop. The list of Bucks players who logged more than 1,000 minutes in 2016–17 included undersized and/or short-armed players like Matthew Dellavedova (3rd in total minutes), Monroe (5th), Jason Terry (7th), and Mirza Teletović (8th).

apprentice who preferred strategies that contained pick-and-rolls rather than disrupting them. The second was to take a chance on a veteran center whose style of play teetered on the edge of extinction.

BROOK LOPEZ NEARLY joined the Milwaukee Bucks in 2014. Okay, "nearly" is a stretch. But it might have happened if Jason Kidd got his way.

Before Kidd coached the Bucks, he spent a dramatic year coaching a veteran, star-laden Brooklyn Nets team with absurd expectations. After a rocky start, the Nets turned their season around when Lopez went down with a season-ending foot injury in December, forcing Kidd to pivot to a small lineup that powered a 34–17 finish after a 10–21 start. "The injury is something that changed the whole landscape of who we were trying to be," Kidd said that April.

Nevertheless, Kidd coveted Lopez after orchestrating his exit to Milwaukee later that spring.[77] The Bucks had lots of cap room and Lopez was a high-scoring young big man reaching restricted free agency.

In the end, Lopez chose to re-sign with the Nets, but he admitted to considering Milwaukee's offer. "I heard from J-Kidd, we talked a little bit," Lopez told reporters after inking a three-year, $64 million maximum contract. "But at the end of the day, I'm here right now. This is where I wanted to be."

The Brook Lopez that arrived in Milwaukee four years later was not nearly as coveted. He toiled on increasingly barren Nets rosters for three seasons, then slogged through a difficult season with the rebuilding Lakers. Though L.A. initially acquired Lopez to be a stop-gap starting center, coach Luke Walton regularly benched him in favor of smaller, quicker lineups featuring the 6'8" Julius Randle at center.

Many interpreted that as another sign that lumbering, slow centers like Lopez were becoming dinosaurs in a game defined by speed and space. That included the Lakers, who didn't even offer Lopez a contract to stay once they signed LeBron James. With his options limited, Lopez was forced to settle for a one-year, $3.3 million deal with the Bucks.

77. Possibly before as well. There are reports that Kidd suggested the Nets trade Lopez in a package for Bucks center Larry Sanders, both in-season and after the year ended. The latter occurred just weeks before he orchestrated his departure to Milwaukee, which raised eyebrows in hindsight.

Milwaukee's brass saw Lopez as a low-risk acquisition and hoped Budenholzer's system was a better fit for his game. They instead found the anchor of what would become the league's most stifling pick-and-roll defense.

Instead of lamenting Lopez's supposed lack of mobility, Budenholzer used his size, strength, and long arms as centerpieces of a hyper-conservative drop pick-and-roll scheme. With Lopez turning the rim into a no-fly zone, Milwaukee bucked the league-wide trend toward switching[78] and revived an approach that seemed out of date after the Pacers' swift fall in 2015. The Bucks ranked No. 1 in points allowed per 100 possessions by a wide margin in 2018–19, then *improved* by nearly two and a half points per 100 possessions in 2019–20 to finish first again. They planted a giant roadblock around the basket, finishing No. 1 in opponent shot frequency and percentage on restricted-area shots.

Milwaukee's drop pick-and-roll defensive scheme shared the core attributes of past versions like the early-2010s Pacers. With Lopez playing Roy Hibbert's role, the Bucks eliminated shots at the rim and spot-up three-pointers from the three players not involved in the main action. They did whatever possible to keep the pick-and-roll in front of them and avoid the vulnerable scramble situations of a numbers disadvantage. The Bucks also didn't fear the off-the-dribble and pick-and-pop threes that were largely replacing the pull-up two-point jumpers that prior drop coverages happily yielded. They believed the cure to that problem was worse than the disease.

To protect Lopez's lack of mobility, the Bucks upgraded many of the tactics Indiana used with Hibbert. Though they covered pick-and-pop threes less aggressively, they tasked their on-ball defenders with pursuing the play from behind and, if necessary, switching only after the ball-handler reached Lopez in the paint. They also ducked under quick-hitting pick-and-rolls, preventing ball-handlers from using the extra space to build up speed attacking the slower Lopez. Budenholzer repurposed Antetokounmpo as an off-ball roamer that lurked ominously as the last line of defense if the opponent somehow pierced Milwaukee's shell. Those tactics freed Lopez to do what he (now) did best: turn the rim into a no-fly zone.

---

78. Pun intended.

DEEP DROP

ONE-SENTENCE DESCRIPTION: The screener's man stays back in the paint while the on-ball defender fights over the pick.

MOST COMMONLY USED: With slower big men, though it helps to have physical perimeter defenders who are difficult to screen.

SYNONYMS: Zone up, or just "drop."

ADVANTAGES
- Barricades the rim, the most valuable space on the court.
- Induces less efficient off-the-dribble jumpers, especially when they're two-pointers.
- Limits ball movement and the need to make defensive rotations.
- Clear structure and simple rules make it easier to master during the regular season.

DISADVANTAGES
- Gives ball-handler carte blanche to read and manipulate the defense coming off the pick.
- Yields too much space for elite pull-up three-point shooters, pick-and-pop threats, and creative drivers.
- Generates few turnovers.
- Often ineffective in the postseason due to its inflexibility and vulnerability against high-level offensive players.

EXAMPLE TEAMS: 2005–09 Houston Rockets (Yao Ming era), 2012–15 Indiana Pacers (Roy Hibbert era), 2018–present Milwaukee Bucks (Brook Lopez era).

In the process, the Bucks uncovered some hidden benefits to drop coverage that escaped their predecessors. The simplicity of the scheme allowed the Bucks to master it quickly and apply it broadly in the regular season, even though it represented a 180-degree shift from their old coaches' philosophy. Limiting stressful rotations eased defensive rebounding responsibilities, which triggered *more* Antetokounmpo open-floor, fast-break drives. Though their scheme differed from Golden State's switch-heavy approach, the Bucks duplicated the Warriors' ability to push tempo while preventing opponents from doing the same to them.

Most importantly, reducing the pick-and-roll to a two-on-two game ruined offenses' flow by making the other three offensive players feel like spectators. The Bucks, in effect, induced many ball-handlers to freeze out their teammates.

That last quality was especially evident when the Bucks went back to their drop coverage roots to defeat the Suns in the 2021 Finals. After two difficult defeats in Phoenix to start the series, the Bucks realized the Suns' pick-and-roll attack was most dangerous when it sucked in multiple defenders to then kick the ball out and force rotations. They instructed their other three players to stay glued to Phoenix's shooters, dropped Lopez and Bobby Portis back slightly at the point of attack, and trusted tenacious Jrue Holiday and P.J. Tucker to fight through screens involving Chris Paul or Devin Booker. Paul's effectiveness waned over the course of the series, and while Booker put together some big scoring games—42 in Game 4, 40 in Game 5—the Bucks successfully cut him off from his teammates. Booker had 28 "potential assists" in the first two games and just 22 in the last four combined.[79]

But while it'd be ridiculous to say Budenholzer's conservative pick-and-roll strategy *failed* given the Bucks' regular-season defensive success, it did not fully address the fundamental flaw that drove Kidd to a trapping scheme in the first place. To gain the benefit of rim protection and even numbers, drop coverage surrenders one crucial element to ball-handlers: control. And control is exactly what the game's best playmakers and perimeter scorers crave most.

"That one [drop coverage] is easy to pick apart because it's like they're at your mercy," Damian Lillard told ESPN in 2021. "You can kind of have what you want."

To superstars, drop coverage is an open invitation to take over. Their ability to manipulate, dissect, and break defenses is precisely what separates them from their peers. When they see the screener's defender hang back in a pick-and-roll instead of pressuring them at the point of attack, they know they have more time and space to do what makes them special.

Specifically, drop coverage is vulnerable to two moves that separate superstars from the rank and file.

One is the pull-up jumper, especially the three-point variety and *especially* those deep ones from "the logo."[80] While pull-up jump shots are less efficient on average than layups or spot-up threes, the ball-handlers who run the most pick-and-rolls—the Lillards and Stephen Currys of the world—get that privilege *because* they are the exceptions to the rule. The same holds true for elite mid-range shooters—e.g., Booker, Paul, Kawhi Leonard, Kevin

---

79. "Potential assists" includes passes that would've been scored as assists if their teammate made the shot. Booker's potential assists by game in the 2021 Finals: 16, 12, 5, 5, 4, 8. The Suns' potential assists as a team by game: 53, 44, 41, 38, 29, 41.

80. This refers to the outline of the half-court logo, which generally stretches 30 feet and beyond.

CENTERFIELD

ONE-SENTENCE DESCRIPTION: The screener's man jabs their body out to deter a pull-up jumper, then retreats to the paint to contain the ball-handler's drive and the screener's roll to the rim.

MOST COMMONLY USED: Against the classic pick-and-roll combination of a skilled pull-up shooter and a dangerous roller.

SYNONYMS: "Up to touch."

ADVANTAGES
- All the same as a deep drop.
- Addresses the deep drop's biggest weakness (the pull-up jumper) without opening up a roll behind the screener's man.
- Can cause hesitation coming off the screen that gives the on-ball defender time to recover.

DISADVANTAGES
- Requires the screener's defender to be intelligent, agile, and able to anticipate tricky ball-handlers' intentions. It's hard to retreat while maintaining proper balance, cover two offensive players at once, and protect the rim without fouling.
- Struggles against lob threats (i.e., "vertical spacers"), especially when paired with elite passers.

EXAMPLE TEAMS: Gregg Popovich's San Antonio Spurs.

Durant, DeMar DeRozan, and Khris Middleton—and those with trademark "giant killer" floaters like Trae Young and Ja Morant.

The threat of that elite pull-up jumper sets up the second superstar attribute that breaks drop coverage: the ability to hold multiple defenders' attention while the other offensive puzzle pieces slide into place.

In theory, the screener's man is positioned to stop drives and rolls to the basket. In practice, his job is difficult. He must honor the threat of a pull-up jumper or floater without lunging so far that he opens up the drives and rolls he's supposed to prevent. Superstars are adept at using hesitations, ball fakes, body gyrations, crossovers, in-and-out dribbles, and countless other forms of manipulation to exploit this gray area. (More on these in Chapter 8.) The same challenges apply to expert long-range pick-and-pop marksmen and three-point snipers who need just a sliver of daylight when curling off screens or dribble handoffs. There aren't many of those players in the league either, but they tend to be the ones involved in the most on- and off-ball screening actions.

STRONG/WEAK

ONE-SENTENCE DESCRIPTION: A type of drop defense on high pick-and-rolls that funnels the ball-handler to their strong (right) or weak (left) hand. (To avoid confusion, most teams use this terminology even if the ball-handler is left-handed.)

MOST COMMONLY USED: When facing a right- or left-hand-dominant dribbler, but not necessarily for the reasons you'd expect. Teams may force the ball-handler to their strong hand to take away their pull-up jumper, funnel them toward or away from help, or because they have data indicating he's a worse passer when driving that way.

SYNONYMS: N/A

ADVANTAGES
- Regains some defensive control on a type of pick-and-roll that otherwise offers a wide range of options to ball-handlers.
- Can be tweaked to negate a specific ball-handler's strength, whether that's driving, snake dribbling, pull-up shooting, passing, or manipulating the second line of the defense.

DISADVANTAGES
- Hard to force a ball-handler one way from the middle of the floor.
- Requires pinpoint communication between the on-ball defender and the screener's man.

EXAMPLE TEAMS: Utah Jazz with Rudy Gobert, many teams against James Harden.

All this explains why drop coverage is often viewed as a regular-season strategy that doesn't work against better opponents deep in the playoffs. This point is often applied too broadly, as if stingy regular-season performances are utterly meaningless or the playoffs are a completely different sport (see Gobert, Rudy). But the underlying logic makes sense. The same qualities that make conservative pick-and-roll schemes dominate average opponents make them vulnerable to exceptional ones. Even if one man can't bust drop coverage on his own over the long haul, can a coach really afford to take that chance in a short playoff series?

The Bucks became case studies of those oft-cited downsides during Budenholzer's first two seasons. The Raptors scored a solid 108.2 points per 100 possessions in their six-game Eastern Conference Finals victory in 2019, while the Heat surged to a 112.8 mark in their five-game second-round upset in 2020. Neither rating was *spectacular,* but each was much higher than the Buck's defense regular-season average that season. Both opponents were elite perimeter shooting teams that exploited the Bucks' religious devotion to rim protection.

Their methods for doing so were slightly different. Toronto ran pick-and-pops well beyond the three-point line, generating space for Kyle Lowry and Fred VanVleet to step into threes and Leonard to wiggle for his trademark mid-range jumper. Miami, on the other hand, wound Milwaukee up with quick-hitting dribble handoffs, off-ball screens, and constant ball movement funneled through star Jimmy Butler and big man Bam Adebayo, all of which forced Lopez to move and negated Antetokounmpo's impact.

But the common denominator between them was that they were *exceptional* shooting teams, not just average ones. The closer a team gets to a title, the more exceptional their opponents get.

And the more exceptional the opponent gets, the more Budenholzer's drop became a liability. It provided a far sturdier foundation than Kidd's blitz, which counts for a lot. But when it came time to pass the toughest tests in a title run, the Bucks needed the same thing Kidd never developed.

They needed a Plan B.

"DID YOU ASK Bud to take Jimmy late?"

The question, posed by The Athletic Bucks writer Eric Nehm during Giannis Antetokounmpo's postgame press conference, hung in the air for an uncomfortable beat following the Bucks' 2020 Game 1 second-round defeat to the Miami Heat.

The Bucks' star had just watched counterpart Jimmy Butler cap off his 40-point performance with a dominating crunch-time display that turned a one-point Heat deficit into an 11-point victory. As in, Antetokounmpo *watched* it happen, over and over again, standing next to defensive assignment Jae Crowder in the opposite corner. While Antetokounmpo lurked for drives that never came, Butler patiently targeted Milwaukee's smaller defenders and shot over them in one-on-one situations. The 2020 Defensive Player of the Year may as well have been a courtside fan.

"To guard him?" Antetokounmpo asked back. Then, his answer to the original question shot out the instant Nehm confirmed. "No," Antetokounmpo said. He raised his eyes toward Nehm on the Zoom projector. "Why would you ask that?"

August 31, 2020 — Heat vs Bucks — ECSF Game 1
Heat 104, Bucks 98 — 2:27 left in fourth quarter

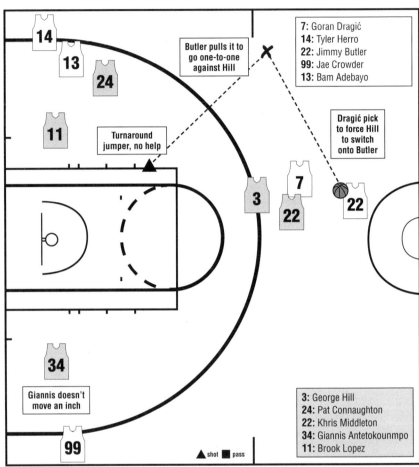

Nehm, of all reporters present, knew the significance of his question. He had covered the team since 2014 and had developed a close relationship with the Bucks' star, a rarity given Antetokounmpo's history of keeping reporters at arm's length. A month earlier, he published an in-depth feature breaking down Brook Lopez's role in Milwaukee's defensive scheme and Antetokounmpo's central job as a roamer playing off him. But Nehm didn't back down.

"Is that something you want to do going forward," he followed up.

"No. I do whatever Coach tells me to do," Antetokounmpo replied.

LEVEL

ONE-SENTENCE DESCRIPTION: The screener's man surges up to the pick-and-roll's point of attack, then retreats once the on-ball defender recovers.

MOST COMMONLY USED: Against great long-range shooters who pull up from well beyond the three-point line.

SYNONYMS: Leveling off, up to the level, any form of the word "level."

ADVANTAGES
- Theoretically contests the pull-up jumper while also stopping the ball-handler from building up speed to drive. *Theoretically.*
- Puts pressure on the ball without needing to trap and then rotate.
- Can be converted into a switch if necessary.

DISADVANTAGES
- Is by far the hardest scheme to execute properly.
- Requires the screener's man to cover a ton of ground and the rest of the team to time their rotations precisely.
- The split second between the screener getting level to the point of attack and the on-ball defender recovering is exactly when most star playmakers make their move to shoot, pass, or drive.

EXAMPLE TEAMS: Lob City Clippers, the 2020 Lakers when Anthony Davis played center, the 2019 Toronto Raptors.

That curt exchange set off a firestorm that dominated talk shows for the next 48 hours. Fans, pundits, and even some fellow players lambasted Antetokounmpo for not demanding the assignment.[81] "As a competitor and DPOY that's your job to take that assignment," high-scoring guard Isaiah Thomas tweeted. "I know Marcus Smart, Avery Bradley, Kawhi woulda been like FOH[82] I'm guarding him."

Antetokounmpo's critics resurfaced a month later between Games 3 and 4 of the NBA Finals. After Butler torched the Lakers for 40 points in a Game 3 victory, Anthony Davis, the Lakers' star big man and Antetokounmpo's main competitor in that season's Defensive Player of the Year race, did exactly what Antetokounmpo refused to do: demand to guard Butler. The

---

81. Antetokounmpo's best defense came from an unlikely source: Jimmy Butler himself. "He is one of the best help-side defenders that there is in the league. And that's what he's been doing all year long," Butler told The Athletic's Sam Amick before Game 2. " And I think you can't get stuck on what we do. I think you've really just got to focus on what you do—you've been doing it all year. Nah, I'm not surprised."

82. Short for [expletive that looks like "Fork"] Outta Here.

Lakers made the switch, held Butler to 22 points in a crucial Game 4 victory, and won the series in six games. Though Davis did not finish the series as Butler's primary defender, his peers noticed how he took on the marquee one-on-one matchup when Antetokounmpo wouldn't.

Beneath the bravado of the individual comparison, it was clear the Bucks' pick-and-roll defense needed to become more flexible against top playoff opponents. Flexibility means more switching, the ever-more-popular third pick-and-roll defensive strategy the Bucks had largely shunned the previous two years. In theory, switching could strike the ideal balance between Budenholzer's drop and Kidd's trapping.

Yet the Bucks did not adopt the switch-everything-all-the-time approach popularized by the Warriors and Rockets. Instead, they noticed how the Lakers *added* switching to a strong base scheme that blended drop principles on the ball with the aggressive off-ball roaming normally associated with trapping.[83] The Bucks needed to pull off the same feat if they wanted to put Antetokounmpo in position to duplicate Davis' defensive excellence.

Davis and Antetokounmpo each possessed the bona fides of a third type of elite defender incubated by the Spaced Out Era. Once upon a time, the league's best defenders were either intimidating shot blockers or lockdown one-on-one stoppers. While those players still exist and are exceedingly valuable, neither fully describes Davis or Antetokounmpo. They are instead omnipotent help defenders, each possessing enough size, speed, and length to cover the modern pick-and-roll's vast vertical and horizontal space.

LeBron James and Chris Bosh pioneered the role with the Heat. Draymond Green turned it into an art form with the Warriors. Kevin Durant held it in reserve until his teams desperately needed it. Davis fulfilled his promise with the Lakers in 2020 after showcasing it in flashes during his New Orleans Pelicans stunt.

Antetokounmpo's combined experiences with Kidd and Budenholzer brought him to the doorstep of this exclusive defensive club. Kidd's trapping scheme sped up his off-ball recognition, while Budenholzer's drop put him in position to be an off-ball deterrent without needing to rotate. The last step

---

83. The Lakers' head coach was Frank Vogel, who presided over those great Pacers drop defenses in the mid-2010s. Their lead assistant coach? None other than Jason Kidd.

SOFT SWITCH

ONE-SENTENCE DESCRIPTION: The on-ball defender goes behind the screener, while the screener's man yields space to the ball-handler while executing the switch.

MOST COMMONLY USED: In crunch time and/or against great passers who can exploit the small windows of the more aggressive contact switch.

SYNONYMS: Switch under.

ADVANTAGES
- Keeps the ball in front of all five defenders.
- Maintains two-on-two coverage against the pick-and-roll.
- Protects against slips and other "ghost" screens that effectively counter more aggressive contact switches.
- Baits stagnant isolation play without spreading the five-man defensive shape thin.

DISADVANTAGES
- Often fosters lazy habits and unwarranted switches.
- Risky against elite pull-up shooters and ball-handlers adept at using extra space to their advantage.
- Less effective against pick-and-pops.
- Creates mismatches on the backside that can compromise future defensive rotations.

EXAMPLE TEAMS: The Bucks in the 2021 Finals, the Lakers when Anthony Davis plays center, current L.A. Clippers in their non-center lineups.

in his rise required applying those same principles of intimidation to on-ball defense. And that required his coach to embrace switching screens.

Perfecting an air-tight switching pick-and-roll scheme in the NBA is much more complicated than shouting "Switch!" in a pick-up game. While switching is often seen as a way to combine the strengths of the other two pick-and-roll schemes, it also takes on each of their weaknesses. Not only does switching screens require players of a certain size, it also forces each player to make *more* quick decisions, not fewer. More decisions means more chances for players to mess up, especially as the complexity of the modern pick-and-roll threatens to overload players' working memory.

What the Warriors made to appear instinctual was in fact honed through a series of on- and off-ball rules they practiced repeatedly and grounded in a culture that embraced positional fluidity. The Bucks, like every NBA team that tried to mimic the Warriors, learned that lesson when they dropped to 10th in points allowed per 100 possessions in the 2020–21 season, despite adding elite perimeter defenders Jrue Holiday and P.J. Tucker. They had to

CONTACT SWITCH

ONE-SENTENCE DESCRIPTION: The on-ball defender and the screener's man jump to the *outside shoulder* of their new assignments, bumping them (or at least maintaining contact) as they execute their switch.

MOST COMMONLY USED: To deny the ball—or at least delay the catch—on dribble handoffs, rolls to the basket, and other critical offensive timing maneuvers.

SYNONYMS: Switch over, hard switch.

ADVANTAGES
- Stops the screener from slipping unimpeded to the basket.
- Delays the ball-handler's initial surge, which can cause stagnant isolation play.
- Limits the time any single player is "unguarded," ideally down to zero.
- Forces pinpoint passes to take advantage of mismatches while also applying more pressure to the passer.

DISADVANTAGES
- Cedes inside position to the screener, opening up lobs over the top, backdoor passes, and easier post-ups against smaller defenders.
- A well-timed split or other aggressive drive by the ball-handler beats both defenders at once.
- Needs the other three defenders to collectively sink in or even execute a scram switch to deter the roller, opening other ways to pass through the defensive shape.
- Requires precise timing, so any brief communication breakdown is especially damaging.

EXAMPLE TEAMS: 2017–20 Houston Rockets, Light Years Warriors, current Miami Heat with Bam Adebayo, current Boston Celtics (though they also do a fair bit of soft switching).

suffer some short-term consequences to achieve the long-term benefits that put their defense over the top.

Though pick-and-roll switching is currently *an emerging field of study,* to use social science parlance, teams increasingly need to master three different ways to switch screens. One is the "soft switch," which has a negative reputation despite retaining some strategic value. In a soft switch, the two defenders duck *underneath* the two offensive players while trading assignments. They don't need to make contact with their original man, their new assignment, or each other. All they need to do is keep the ball-handler and the screener in front of them. The cardinal sin of a soft switch is allowing either offensive player to get behind their new defender. It's the drop coverage of switching, in a sense.

The upside of a soft switch is that it is seamless. The on-ball defender only needs to get behind the screener, while the screener's defender only needs to stop the ball-handler from turning the corner or dribbling into an uncontested jumper. If one defines good defense as "avoid a massive screw-up," the soft switch works like a charm. It is an effective way to throw off the flow of a multi-action, well-oiled offensive machine, especially in crunch time, when a mistimed defensive rotation is more damaging.

The downside of the soft switch is that it's, well, *too* seamless. Coaches often believe, with some justification, that players default to soft switching out of laziness rather than necessity or proactivity. This criticism applies within the context of a single soft switch decision (*You didn't need to switch and concede that mismatch*) or to its repeated usage over time (*You're developing bad defensive habits that will come back to bite you*). Basketball rewards aggression, and the soft switch is the opposite of aggressive. That's why it has developed an increasingly pejorative reputation league-wide.

The "contact switch," on the other hand, requires that the two defenders swap assignments *at the level of the pick-and-roll* rather than beneath it. The "contact" portion of the term applies on two levels. Instead of dropping below the screener, as in a soft switch, the on-ball defender must slide parallel or directly underneath him and maintain *contact* with their body to stop them from rolling into open space. It should look like they're playing low-post defense on a perimeter screen.

But the "contact" term also conveys the need for the two defenders to maintain contact *with each other* while executing the switch. That way, the on-ball defender can bump the screener's man toward the ball while taking his place to cover the roll. Any delay in that little relay race opens up space for the two offensive players to sneak behind the play. "[The two defenders] have to come together," Robert Covington told Bleacher Report in 2017. "If you don't, the screener can slip, or the guard can split it."

While that logic makes sense, it also creates a layer of coordination that switching was supposed to eliminate. The upside of a well-executed contact switch is higher than that of a soft switch, but the downside of a mistake is costlier as well. There's also no guarantee a contact switch creates enough, well, *contact* to stop a drive or roll to open space. The screener can overpower a smaller on-ball defender, sprint through the pick against a slower one, or pin the switching defender on his back for a lob pass or post duck-in.

PEEL SWITCH

ONE-SENTENCE DESCRIPTION: The on-ball defender chases his man from behind until a teammate picks him up, then "peels" off to switch onto the screener or a third player.

MOST COMMONLY USED: Against traditional ball-handler/rim-roller pick-and-roll combinations, or to contain dribble-handoffs in the middle of the floor.

SYNONYMS: Veer-back, scram.

ADVANTAGES
• Prevents a numbers disadvantage while limiting the time spent in a mismatch.
• Can be easily disguised because it looks like other coverages until the last second.
• Especially effective at deflecting or stealing pick-and-roll pocket passes.
• Can involve any two players anywhere on the floor in theory, even if they're not directly involved in the pick-and-roll.

DISADVANTAGES
• Requires pinpoint coordination and trust that is hard to build and easy to lose.
• Inevitably causes a size mismatch somewhere, even if the initial switch shuts down the most obvious pass.
• May encourage lazy switches that allow a weaker defender to cop out of an assignment
• Yields unpredictable backside rotations that can lead to future breakdowns and awkward movements for certain types of players (i.e., big men making long closeouts and/or guards jostling for rebounds position).

EXAMPLE TEAMS: 2014–present Golden State Warriors, 2019–21 Toronto Raptors, Brad Stevens' Celtics (and current Celtics), current Phoenix Suns, many European teams.

That takes us to the "peel switch," an increasingly popular maneuver that appeals to coaches who want their players to keep the ball in front, but don't want to incentivize lazy habits. In a peel switch, the on-ball defender tracks his own man into the nearest help defender, then "peels off" to pick up a different player, whether the helper's man or a third teammates'. The defense is still switching the pick-and-roll, but only *after* exhausting other options to contain it. When executed correctly, the peel switch is versatile enough to be used at any levels of the pick-and-roll.

The peel switch originated from a similar tactic that defenses started using to mitigate post-switch size mismatches in the low post.[84] Instead of leaving the smaller pick-and-roll defender to cover a post-up, teams instructed a (bigger) third player to rotate from the opposite side and boot the smaller on-ball defender back out to the perimeter. The second off-ball switch is

---

84. Or to use one of my favorite forms of basketball slang, "MOUSE IN THE HOUSE."

May 13, 2018 — Cavaliers at Celtics — ECF Game 1
Celtics 61, Cavaliers 35 — 11:42 left in third quarter

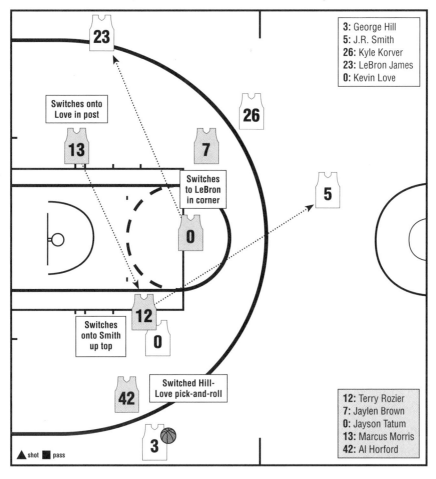

known as a "scram" or "kickout" switch. The Warriors made this a critical component of their revolutionary scheme, and others began to notice after observing Brad Stevens' Boston Celtics use the tactic to slow Joel Embiid, Ben Simmons, and Kevin Love in the 2018 playoffs.

The peel switch broadened the concept to other spots on the floor. It can be executed by the two main pick-and-roll defenders, or by the on-ball man and a third teammate guarding a perimeter shooter or a baseline cutter. The Bucks quickly adopted one type of peel switch known as a "veer back," which is when the on-ball defender trails over the top of a pick-and-roll as if he's in drop coverage, waits for the screener's man to contain the ball, then

NEXT

ONE-SENTENCE DESCRIPTION: The perimeter defender on the opposite wing cheats off their man to pick up the ball-handler, allowing the screener's man to stay in the lane.

MOST COMMONLY USED: Overseas, particularly against off-ball screens. But more NBA teams are dabbling with it.

SYNONYMS: TBD.

ADVANTAGES
- Protects slower big men who lack the lateral quickness to defend in space.
- Limits the need for additional defensive rotations.
- More likely to switch a similarly sized player onto the ball and thus minimize a mismatch.
- Stops drive-and-kick opportunities at their source: the free-throw line extended.

DISADVANTAGES
- Sends the pick-and-roll to the middle of the floor, yielding more passing options.
- Works best when one of the wing players is a poor perimeter shooter, which is more common overseas than in the NBA.
- The more space an offensive team uses, the longer the "nexter's" rotation.

EXAMPLE TEAMS: Mostly European teams for now, though teams like Miami, Utah, Toronto, and Dallas deploy similar concepts when playing zone.

abruptly veers into the screener's path on a late switch. The veer back was an effective way to maximize Holiday's defensive versatility and protect Lopez from switching too far out on the perimeter.

While the peel switch requires even more coordination than the soft and contact switches, it also offers the most upside. Some overseas teams have begun using the peel switch as their base pick-and-roll coverage. Will Voigt, who coaches for German club Telekom Baskets Bonn and the Angolan national team, instructs his players to peel switch in almost every possible situation that may involve dribble penetration, with different specific rules for different specific scenarios. "You're going one over like the minutes on a clock," he said during a 2021 appearance on the *Slappin' Glass* podcast. "If you think about it in a traditional defense, everybody would be doing that off the ball anyway."

The Bucks didn't need to do anything that radical. They just needed another tool in their pick-and-roll arsenal that could transfer Antetokounmpo's backside intimidation to anywhere else on the floor. Switching more pick-and-rolls was the solution, but it required a mindset shift from Budenholzer, more versatile personnel alongside Antetokounmpo, and a full season of behind-the-hood tweaks to properly blend it into the Bucks' existing base.

The fruits of that labor were evident from the opening tip of the Bucks' first playoff game against those dreaded Miami Heat. To outsiders, the first-round rematch was the last thing Milwaukee needed. Many were surprised when the Bucks did not rest key players against Miami on the final weekend of the regular season when a loss would have vaulted the Heat to the No. 5 seed and out of the Bucks' playoff path. But the Bucks knew they were not the same team the Heat easily took down the previous season.

To prove it, they made the very move they refused to make then. They had Giannis Antetokounmpo guard Jimmy Butler.

Using a strategy straight out of the Lakers' playbook with Davis, Antetokounmpo ducked under pick-and-rolls and kept Butler out of the paint. The Heat couldn't avoid him without parking their best player in the corner, which was of course unthinkable. They couldn't even use Butler as the hub of their off-ball screens because Antetokounmpo was happy to switch out to deter Miami's shooters.

"It changes it quite a bit actually," second-year Heat guard Tyler Herro said after Butler shot 4–22 in a Game 1 defeat. "Giannis usually is roaming around and being in the help-defender position."

It sure did. The Bucks ground Miami's offense to a halt in a dominating four-game sweep. Butler averaged just 14.5 points per game on less than 30 percent shooting in the series and scored just nine points on 3–16 shooting when matched up with Antetokounmpo, according to NBA.com's player tracking data. While many interpreted these numbers as proof the Bucks messed up the previous season, they were as much a product of Antetokounmpo and Budenholzer venturing out of their defensive comfort zones during the 2020–21 regular season.

Antetokounmpo and Budenholzer continued to showcase their defensive evolution in leading the Bucks to the title. After surviving a seven-game war with the increasingly shorthanded Brooklyn Nets in the second round,[85] the Bucks piloted a new strategy to limit Hawks star Trae Young.

In response to Young dominating their base drop coverage in Game 1, the Bucks tasked Antetokounmpo with soft-switching any on-ball screen while Holiday picked up Young full court. The move vaporized Atlanta's signature "double drag" pick-and-roll set, which involves Young coming off two sequential staggered ball screens involving power forward John Collins and center Clint Capela. Fearful of Antetokounmpo pursuing from behind, Young hesitated when attacking the second ball screen, making it harder for him to manipulate Brook Lopez in his usual drop coverage. If Lopez exited the game, Antetokounmpo shifted to center, soft-switched any pick-and-roll, and induced Young to shoot from way downtown. Young hit some long-range bombs, but Antetokounmpo prevented him from getting in the paint and breaking the Bucks' defensive shell.

While injuries to both stars abbreviated that chess match, the Bucks adopted the same strategy to limit Phoenix's pick-and-roll game in the NBA Finals.

The Suns, like the Hawks, loved to use multiple screeners in their pick-and-rolls—though theirs were more elaborate. Milwaukee again tasked Holiday and Tucker with pursuing Phoenix's guards full court, while Antetokounmpo again switched the first screen to slow the Suns' rhythm attacking Lopez in the second. When Lopez went to the bench, Antetokounmpo shifted to center and switched every pick-and-roll outright. Together, Antetokounmpo and Holiday made Chris Paul's life a living hell, cut Devin Booker off from his teammates, and took away the Suns' pristine ball movement.

Switching more pick-and-rolls freed Antetokounmpo to perform his own version of Davis' 2020 act. His unique combination of length, speed, size, and intelligence shines in any of the three main pick-and-roll defensive philosophies, but switching is the only strategy that fully weaponizes his

---

85. Antetokounmpo didn't guard Kevin Durant much in the series, which briefly rekindled the previous season's criticism when Durant torched the Bucks for 49 points in a Game 5 victory. But Durant's pull-up shooting made him an entirely different beast than Butler and prevented Antetokounmpo from ducking under pick-and-rolls. Durant scored at will against Antetokounmpo when Milwaukee briefly switched the matchup in that Game 5 win, but (barely) ran out of steam when Milwaukee went back to the more traditional P.J. Tucker/Jrue Holiday combination in Games 6 and 7.

July 14, 2021 — Suns at Bucks — NBA Finals Game 4 (PHX leads 2-1)
Suns 95, Bucks 94 — 3:24 left in fourth quarter

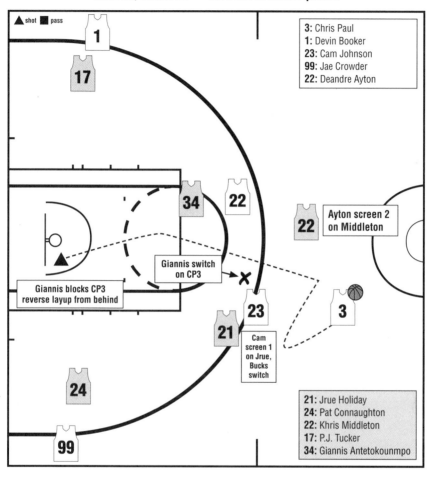

power in any situation. It turns players like Antetokounmpo from high-speed desktops into equally high-speed smartphones.

That's different than saying switching is a panacea that replaces all other forms of pick-and-roll defense. For one, unless you're a Bucks, Warriors, or Lakers fan, your favorite team doesn't have Davis, Green, or Antetokounmpo. Exceptions never prove the rule.

It's also important to remember that switching takes on the vulnerabilities of both alternate schemes in addition to their strengths. While switching pick-and-rolls can alleviate both of their kryptonites (short roll for trap, pull-up three for drop), offenses deploy both of those tactics to great effect in the middle of a planned switch. Ball-handlers have learned to pull up and shoot right as the defense switches, and screeners are increasingly adept at timing their slip into short-roll position at that exact same moment.

But the larger lesson of the Lakers and Bucks titles is that they *added* switching to the menu of pick-and-roll defensive tactics they already mastered. They did not change their entire restaurant's cuisine.

As the NBA advances into the 2020s, never forget the golden rule for guarding the game's most crucial action. The modern pick-and-roll is far too complicated to address with just one scheme. The only way the defense can stop it is to use multiple ways. Plural.

Chapter 8
Subatomic Shifts

The three simultaneous battlegrounds on every pick-and-roll.

The pick-and-roll is so dominant in the Spaced Out NBA that we often forget it's performed by exceptional human beings moving against other exceptional human beings. This *no duh* point applies to any professional activity, sports or otherwise. But, it's especially relevant with one that is this fluid.

The only way to fully understand the modern pick-and-roll is to accept that its components *always* link together in dynamic ways. Why do some NBA pick-and-rolls work while others don't? The difference is often determined by tiny, context-specific cues that pros have learned to process in less than a split second. Perhaps it's something they saw, or heard, or felt with their body movement, or just sensed in a way they can't explain. But when everyone is a pick-and-roll master, those microscopic environmental differences add up.

This, to some degree, is how the pick-and-roll has always worked. Indeed, it's how any skill that can be mastered works, athletic or otherwise.

Still, the pick-and-rolls of the Spaced Out Era are unique in that they require players to make more of those microscopic reads in motion while simultaneously zooming out to account for all their potential effects. Not only is there more room for either side to apply a slight change in the angle, tempo, or distance of each pick-and-roll element, but the downstream impacts of that shift are now spread over more space. The more the pick-and-roll becomes a five-player act, the more ways either side can execute it slightly differently each time.

This is why the most significant in-game and playoff series "adjustments" are microscopic shifts within an existing strategy or tactic rather than dramatic changes in either. Informed fans and media are quick to propose more radical changes. *Stop switching Star X's pick-and-rolls! Run more with these two guys instead of those two guys! Go after this bad defender more!* This causes many coaches to pooh-pooh the need to adjust at all, beyond imploring their players to play harder, smarter, better. "Writers always love to say, 'They made an adjustment,'" then-Hornets coach Steve Clifford said during the 2016 playoffs, quoting mentor Jeff Van Gundy. "Usually the adjustment is some guy that went 1-for-8 [now went] 6-for-8."

The modern pick-and-roll is far too complex for either answer to be sufficient.

Clifford's humility is admirable, but coaches and players are too smart to *not* make adjustments every play, game, and series. Those shifts became exponentially more numerous, creative, and narrow in just the last decade and a half, and it'd take three times as many pages as this book to describe them all. They're all occurring for the same reasons: to create, maintain, and exploit the numbers advantage the pick-and-roll is designed to provide.

But it's also true that they are occurring at more subatomic levels than the general public often sees, even among those who know basketball. I do not claim to possess the X-ray vision and knowledge to process every single tiny pick-and-roll adjustment in real time. Nobody can with a straight face.

But the purpose of this chapter is to at least identify some of the more common ones that determine a pick-and-roll's success or failure. You may not see them all at once because they happen simultaneously in different places on the court. You may not be able to weigh their relative importance to a pick-and-roll's outcome because they are interconnected, to say nothing of the myriad external factors that statisticians call "noise" or "randomness." But hopefully you'll be better equipped to spot them as they hide in plain sight on your screen.

These mini-adjustments are implemented at three different levels of the pick-and-roll: before the screen, after the screen, and when the ball-handler makes their shoot-or-pass decision. The screener's role is most pivotal in the first, the off-ball players are most crucial in the third, and while the ball-handler is essential to all three, the second is where they make their biggest mark.

So let's dive deeper into the three components of the pick-and-roll, and how players can tweak their technique within each.

THE SCREEN

Tim Duncan's Hall of Fame career splits neatly into two equally impressive parts. In the first, Duncan is the Spurs' dominant low-post force. In the second, he's their unselfish cultural pillar who embraces less glamorous jobs while ceding some direct control to enhance his teammates.

The moment that separates these two eras occurred just before 9:00 PM local time in Athens, Greece, on August 27, 2004. That was when Tim Duncan got called for an illegal screen.

It was the semifinals of the 2004 Olympic basketball tournament. Team USA, who had shockingly lost two group stage games for the first time since NBA pros were allowed to compete, trailed upstart Argentina by 11 points with five minutes to go. Duncan set a screen for Allen Iverson, extending his right leg out slightly when Argentina guard Alejandro Montecchia tried to dodge him.

Montecchia slammed into Iverson. The whistle blew. Foul … on Duncan, for a moving screen. It was his fifth of the game, disqualifying him.

NBC commentator Doug Collins was at a loss for words as the replay rolled. "Wow," he managed after a long pause. "That's what I talked about, knowing how to play with fouls. Tim Duncan has struggled with what is a foul and what isn't. He's really gotten a tough whistle into the Olympics."

"Now, he did move into him," play-by-play man Mike Breen offered. "But that's a play they have not called. Moving screens are a part of international basketball. There's the inconsistency."

Two days and four more fouls later—taking him to 30 in 207 minutes through the tournament—Duncan abruptly retired from international play. "I'm about 95 percent certain my FIBA career is over," Duncan told reporters in Athens. "FIBA sucks."

The moment was emblematic of the screening revolution that instantly traveled stateside to the NBA's waters. There was a league-wide reawakening to the legality *and* technique of an effective screen, especially in the pick-and-roll. It diversified the art of setting a screen, transformed the way to judge it, and enhanced its impact on any given sequence. In an amusing stroke of irony, Duncan rebounded from his foul Olympic experience to become one of the best new-age screen setters in the sport, to the point that opponents complained that *he* constantly got away with moving screens.

It also resulted in a convoluted illegal screen rule that is easily misinterpreted. If you're confused by the NBA's increasingly liberal interpretation of moving screens, you're not alone. You, and me, and the 2004 version of Mike Breen, and countless others had been told our whole lives that the screener must stay still on every kind of pick. "Moving screens" are just "illegal screens" by a different name.

But when you turn on a modern NBA game, you easily spot screeners moving into defenders without a whistle. To the naked eye, *every* screen kinda looks like a moving screen now. You don't understand why officials only penalize a small handful of them—always, it seems, when they involve anonymous role players and *never* more prominent stars. They must be deliberately ignoring them.

If only the answer were so simple.

In truth, the phrase "moving screen" is an extreme shorthand for a more detailed regulation that is increasingly harder to define in the Spaced Out Era. There *is* a specific point when the screener must be stationary, just as we were all told. But that instant depends on many contextual factors, occurs for an infinitesimally short amount of time, and features a number of exceptions that are occurring more often as the game spreads out.

Rule No. 4, Section X of the 2021–22 NBA rulebook defines a screen as "the legal action of a player who, without causing undue contact, delays or prevents an opponent from reaching a desired position." Rule 12, Section III explains what constitutes "undue contact":

A player who sets a screen shall not (1) assume a position nearer than a normal step from an opponent, if that opponent is stationary and unaware of the screener's position, or (2) make illegal contact with an opponent when he assumes a position at the side or front of an opponent, or (3) assume a position so near to a moving opponent that he is not given an opportunity to avoid contact[86] before making illegal contact, or (4) move laterally or toward an opponent being screened, after having assumed a legal position. The screener may move in the same direction and path of the opponent being screened. In (3) above, the speed of the opponent being screened will determine what the screener's stationary position may be. This position will vary and may be one to two normal steps or strides from his opponent.

There is further clarification, if you can call it that, in an additional comment on the rules under "Contact Situations":

When a player screens in front of or at the side of a stationary opponent, he may be as close as he desires providing he does not make contact. His opponent can see him and, therefore, is expected to detour around the screen.

If he screens behind a stationary opponent, the opponent must be able to take a normal step backward without contact. Because the opponent is not expected to see a screener behind him, the player screened is given latitude of movement. The defender must be given an opportunity to change direction and avoid contact with the screener.

To screen a moving opponent, the player must stop soon enough to permit his opponent the opportunity to avoid contact.[87] The distance between the player screening and his opponent will depend upon the speed at which the players are moving.

If two opponents are moving in the same direction and path, the player who is behind is responsible for contact. The player in front may stop or slow his pace, but he may not move backward or sideward into his opponent. The player in front may or may not have the ball. This situation assumes the two players have been moving in identically the same direction and path before contact.

---

86. Prior to 2016–17, this line prohibited screens that did not provide the defense a chance to "*stop and/or change direction before making illegal contact.*" Now, it reads "an opportunity to avoid contact before making illegal contact." That change to make the wording even more vague is the only alteration to this rule since 2010.

87. This, too, was changed from "to stop or change direction" to "the opportunity to avoid contact" in 2016–17.

So the screener cannot move after establishing position … except when the defender is also moving along the same path … as long as they are given enough space to reasonably avoid contact … except the screener can also slow down without stopping as long as they're not backing up or jutting sideways … but only *after* they establish position. Also, the position a screener must establish is defined by where their defender is relative to them: one normal step in some stationary situations, zero steps in others, and any number of steps if the defender is also moving, which is most of the time these days. That means it's okay for the screener to move, but only if they're moving along the same path as the defender. Right?

And you thought the NFL's catch rule was confusing!

Crucially, the rule does not specify any body parts that are off limits, even if, in practice, screeners cannot jut out their hips, stick their legs beyond shoulder width, or extend their arms to shove opponents. The league periodically releases video examples of those infractions alongside legal counterparts in which the screener absorbs the defender's weight in the chest. Every so often—most recently in 2013 and 2016—curbing these extraneous movements becomes an officiating point of emphasis for the season.[88]

Yet that never seems to stop players—and certain players in particular—from getting away with leg kicks, hip checks, and two-handed shoves on their screens. Why?

The common explanation is that these illegal movements are impossible to enforce. There is some truth to that. Joe Borgia, a former official who served in the NBA's referee operations department from 1999 to 2020, most recently as the NBA's senior vice president of referee operations, once said a typical NBA game features at least 200 screens. Even the most highly trained official is bound to miss on some of those. A 95 percent success rate still means there are 10 screens per game that are incorrectly allowed or prohibited.

But the rulebook's conspicuous omission of body parts presents its own set of challenges. Without any specific language that prohibits or even regulates their use, screeners can theoretically move as much and as unnaturally as they want, as long as they don't "cause undue contact." A screen only becomes illegal if it actually causes the specific type of harm that an illegal screen theoretically would cause.

---

88. These memos are now called "points of education."

This circular logic may be necessary to preserve a free-flowing game that isn't bogged down by too many whistles and/or excessive player caution as they try to avoid illegal screens. But the logic is still, well, circular. I can see why you're annoyed by it!

Regardless, the upshot is that the letter of the NBA's screening law has always permitted players to move in certain circumstances. Duncan's 2004 Olympics foul fest was only partially caused by his unfamiliarity with his teammates and the international game. The unspoken, yet critical factor was that the non-American players in that tournament had spent much more time perfecting techniques for when and how they could legally move on their screens. It was a lesson Duncan took back to the States in the years to come.

The "moving screen" myth, if you want to call it that, led to a more subtle one that has been laid bare during the Spaced Out Era.

The idea that screens should "lay the wood" on defenders is well-meaning, but it obscures the real purpose of a screen. It's *not* to contact the defender and bump them. It's to divert their path by any means necessary to make it easier for the ball-handler to beat them. Setting a bone-crushing screen that slams the defender to the ground is one way to divert their path, of course, but it's hardly the only way.

It's not always the most effective way, either. With the rise of the pick-and-roll, stricter perimeter hand-checking enforcement, and the ongoing three-point revolution, ball-handlers have more space and freedom to dance. The timing of a screen is more crucial than it was on a more constrained playing surface. Since a screen only becomes illegal when it makes "undue contact" with the defender, it's often counterproductive to seek it out when the screener still does their job by being an obstacle that makes the defender take the long way to get around them.

The wider floor gives the screeners that extra room to dance as well. Remember: they only need to be stationary at a precise instant that's defined by their *relative* position from the defender, not a fixed distance. That gives them more space to shift ever so slightly and still avoid improper contact with the defender at the moment of impact. A deadly modern screen is not a display of brute strength. It's performing a choreographed two-man dance routine with the ball-handler. Illegal screens result from failing to sync those mini-movements, not because either side was wrong to move in the first place.

The best modern screens, particularly those on the ball, hinge on those subtle body shifts in tight quarters. A good screener works in tandem with their teammate to set the on-ball defender up properly. We're easily mesmerized by the crossovers, in-and-outs, hesitations, spins, behind the backs, between the legs, reverse pivots, "tween crosses,"[89] etc. that ball-handlers use to fool defenders.

But because our eyes are drawn to the ball, we miss the screeners simultaneously sliding a tiny bit here, twisting slightly there, and hopping around the on-ball defender to lure them into the same trap. Sometimes, the screener's goal is to smush the defender in the chest. Sometimes, the goal is to make them jump early and allow the ball-handler to dribble away from the pick. Either way, they are equal partners in a two-person routine, whether the screener touches the ball or not.

If contact doesn't differentiate a good modern screen from a bad one, what does? There are four key components of an effective modern screen: speed, direction, entry angle, and exit angles.

It is essential that a screener *change* speeds during the setup process. Just as great ball-handlers shift gears to keep their defender off balance, so too do great screeners. The days of walking slowly into position, getting big, and waiting for the ball-handler to act are long gone. Instead, today's coaches want their players to run into the pick and then abruptly slow down just before the desired point of attack.

Sprinting the first 95 percent of the journey allows the screener to hide their intentions and read the on-ball defender's body positioning before delivering the decisive blow over the final five percent. That's when the screener conspires with the ball-handler with a series of subtle body shifts designed to divert the defender as far off their recovery path as possible. That two-man dance is so quick that it's easy to miss in real time. Watch the best screens closely, though, and you'll see they result from the screener swiveling from the waist down to face the defender at the moment of desired impact, then pivoting their entire body in one direction with their legs and arms shoulder width apart before they roll or pop.

---

89. Think of it as a mutant version of Tim Hardaway's famous killer crossover. It's when a ball-handler crosses the ball and both feet in one direction before pulling the ball behind their back or between their legs while hopping both feet back the other way.

The deadly pattern of instant acceleration followed by equally abrupt deceleration is critical to two of the most popular types of modern on-ball picks: step-ups and drags. Both began as transition tactics before featuring in all situations as the fast break and half-court set merged. The screener's initial positioning is the main difference between the two: it's a "step-up" when they come up behind the defender to meet the ball-handler and a "drag" when they run ahead or parallel to them and *then* stop so the ball-handler uses them.

Neither are possible if you assume "moving pick" means "don't move at all at any point." Drags and step-ups occur in the open floor as defenders are moving their fastest. It's impossible to set one by standing still, yet it's equally difficult to pull off without causing improper contact in plain view of the officials. The only way to strike the right balance is to accelerate, then decelerate, then shift ever so slightly before stopping for just an instant at the point of impact. If it looks like the ball-handler did all the work, the screener did their job.

The second, related key to a modern screen is to change *directions* when running into it. Sprinting in a perfectly straight line makes it too easy for the defense to anticipate the direction the ball-handler wants to go. By taking a series of detours instead, the screener can hide their intentions and trick the defense into jumping the wrong way on impact. This is why today's screeners must master the "flat screen," which is when they stop directly behind the defender, wait for the ball-handler to pick their direction, and execute a last-second body twist to catch the on-ball defender off guard. Flat screens only work if the screener is willing and able to shift their body in tight spaces.

That takes us directly into the third indicator of a good screen: its angle at the point of attack. Eventually, the ball-handler will use the screen in some capacity. When they do—and only at the precise instant they do—the screener must become a (mostly) stationary obstacle. This is when they must choose the ideal angle to best divert the defender off their path.

In practice, screeners are subconsciously asking and answering a laundry list of questions. Where should they stand? How tall and wide to make an impact without forcing undue contact? How far away should they be from their teammate? From the defender? What spot is most likely to achieve a desired outcome? The answers to these questions and more depend on the players involved, the game situation, and the cues the pre-screen motion uncovered. They are also altered game-to-game, especially within a playoff series. There is no single correct one.

Once the screener chooses the angle of their screen, they must live with whatever happens next. It can be tempting to stick the leg, hip, or arm out to hit the defender *as they're eluding the screen*, but that triggers the "undue contact" of an offensive foul.

Most illegal screens result from mistimed or poorly positioned entry angles. Duncan's fifth foul in that 2004 Olympic semifinal is a classic example. While Duncan was punished for the infraction, Iverson shares equal blame for starting his drive too soon. Had he waited a beat, Montecchia would've been unable to jump in front of the pick and Duncan wouldn't have been tempted to kick his leg out at the last moment. That would not have happened with a more in-sync duo, like, say, Duncan and Argentinian Spurs star Manu Ginóbili.

While bad entry angles often trigger the criteria for an illegal screen, great ones exploit the rule's "undue contact" loophole. Many of the game's best screeners, Duncan included, stick body parts out unnaturally and get away with it. The reason is that they deploy those tricks *just before* their screen's entry angle instead of afterwards. The hope, usually warranted, is that the defender follows their natural instinct to dodge them, thereby ensuring they won't trigger the "undue contact" provision of the rule. Theoretically, a screener can do almost anything so long as they don't contact the defender.

That's why the screen's entry angle is essential. It is the very thin line of demarcation that separates an underhanded-but-effective screening scare tactic from an obvious offensive foul.

There are ways to shift the angle of a screen that are, shall we say, more on the up and up. One is known as "turning" or "twisting" the screen.[90] That's when a screener plants themselves on one side of the defender, then rotates their entire body to the other side at the last possible instant before committing to their entry angle. The ball-handler can actively use that first pick and turn into the second, or they could dart away from the turn/twist before the defender can do the same. Regardless, the move is only legal if

---

90. Many people use the verb form of "re-screen" interchangeably with either term. They're not exactly the same thing—the "turn" or "twist" is the movement itself, the "re-screen" is the product of that movement—but the difference is immaterial. Others use the more general "changing the angle" phrase. They all roughly mean the same thing.

the screener flips their entire body to keep their chest square to the ball-handler's desired driving angle while giving the defender a step to avoid them. Otherwise, they'll cause "undue contact."[91]

The last piece of the puzzle is the screener's exit path. How does the screener know how to time their roll or pop? Short answer: it depends. Longer answer: it depends on a lot of different factors. Even longer answer: it depends on several different factors the screener senses as the pick happens. No two exit paths are ever the same.

The first decision is whether to roll (or pop) at all. Sometimes, the screener's best decision is to stay put. If the screen opens a lane for the ball-handler to attack the basket, it doesn't do much good for the screener to also roll into that space. If it creates a pull-up jumper against drop coverage, the screener will want to hold their ground, give or take a few small steps if a re-screen is necessary. If it flows into a second pick-and-roll on the opposite side of the floor, the screener may want to stay still to become an outlet to recycle possession.

If the screener does roll or pop, the next decision is when to start. The answer depends on the defense's pick-and-roll coverage. If the screener senses a trap, it pays to slip the pick, i.e., roll or pop before the ball-handler reaches them. While this tactic has existed for decades, the wider floor and faster pace allows for many more ways to slip screens effectively.

The Spaced Out Era has incubated a similar screening tactic known as the "ghost screen." This is when the screener runs up like he's going to set a pick, only to keep running through the point of attack without contacting the defender. (It's really just a fake screen, but it's a lot more fun to say "ghost screen.") Ghost screens can go away from the hoop (some call this a "peel action") or they can turn back toward the basket. Either way, the defense is caught flat-footed. They end up preparing for a screen that doesn't exist.

If, instead, the screener sees drop coverage, it pays to hang still for an extra beat and take their cues from their teammate. They may want to roll or pop once the ball-handler engages the second defender, or they may want to

---

91. A few players, like Ginóbili's Argentina teammate Luis Scola, discovered an ingenious way around this rule. Instead of flipping to square their chest to the defender, they turn the other way and square their back to them. This is technically legal as long as the screener holds his ground, absorbs the blow in the rear, and doesn't stick his leg or butt out.

wait for the ball-handler to distract them before abruptly zipping into open space.

If the screener senses a switch, all possibilities are on the table. Remember: switching takes on the strengths and weaknesses of the other two pick-and-roll coverages. The screener might want to slip as the switch is occurring, or they may want to roll into the on-ball defender to force the switch.

The official language permitting a screener to move "in the same direction and path of the opponent being screened" opens ingenious ways for screeners to maximize their exit path. You've all seen referees seemingly ignore screeners who move through on-ball defenders like lead blockers clearing a hole for a running back. No way that's legal, right? Because of that sentence in the rulebook, it is—or at least can be.

The best way to illustrate this is through a hypothetical situation. Suppose Screener X is setting a flat step-up screen on Defender Y. Screener X sprints in a jagged line before stopping directly behind Defender Y, tucks his body parts in to avoid initiating illegal contact, then shifts his angle ever so slightly to the right. Defender Y senses the last-minute change, but brushes Screener X while trying to duck under the screen. Offensive foul, right? Not necessarily. If Screener X twists his whole body in one motion so he keeps his chest square to Defender Y, he can technically roll directly into their path like a pulling offensive lineman. Believe it or not, that is a legal move, as long as the screener does not initiate "undue contact" by extending their legs, arms, or hips beyond shoulder width.

Hypothetical situations like that occur *all the time* in the modern NBA. As drop coverage spread across the league in the mid-2010s, some non-shooting big men learned how to screen the on-ball defender, twist their bodies to roll, and then set a *second* screen to clear out their own man. This double on-ball screen, known colloquially as a "Gortat,"[92] is legal as long as they move "in the same direction and path" of the help defender. Clever, right?

Ultimately, the Spaced Out NBA has allowed screen-setting to blossom into as much of an art as dribbling, passing, or shooting. It is no longer defined by brute strength and muscular men standing still like stone pillars. Instead, the game's wider playing surface has allowed screeners to diversify

---

92. In reference to Marcin Gortat, the Polish center who perfected the maneuver during a 12-year NBA career with the Magic, Suns, Wizards, and Clippers.

their speed, point of attack angle, and their entry and exit paths into the pick. Each element can be tinkered depending on the opponent and situation, making them ideal playoff adjustments in place of scrapping the entire scheme. The best screeners are master magicians who trick the defense into believing one story while performing another.

Tim Duncan figured that out after his 2004 Olympic experience. Today's screen-setters are indebted to his sacrifice and transformation.

THE BALL-HANDLER

Chris Paul is a basketball savant.

Some version of this line has been repeated by more people than anyone can count. "I think he's a child prodigy, like a concert pianist or a tremendous mathematician," Florida State coach Leonard Hamilton said in 2005, when Paul was a sophomore at Wake Forest.

Over the next 16 years, modern technology combined with Paul's longevity and success to reaffirm his prodigy status.

Geniuses like Paul tend to demand the same level of obsession from others who don't naturally match their mental processing skills. Their intensity can inspire others to reach their level, or it can demoralize them and wear thin. Paul has experienced both in his illustrious NBA career, though he appears to have found a happy medium spearheading the young Phoenix Suns.

Paul's history of inspiring reverence and annoyance in equal measure comes down to his other distinct genius quality. Through intelligence and sheer force of will, Paul has learned to reduce the complexity of the modern pick-and-roll down to a few simple if/then decisions.

"If you're tryin' to drive to your house, there's only so many different ways to get there. Right?" he told *Sports Illustrated* in 2017. "So I think about that on the basketball court. When I beat this guy, there's only a couple places where another defender can come from."

Sounds obvious when you put it that way! His ability to make a multi-layered sequence look and sound so easy is amazing and a bit aggravating.

It's fitting, then, that Paul discovered one of the most important moves of the modern NBA while messing around in practice early in his NBA career with the Hornets. Here's how he matter-of-factly described inventing what we now know as the "snake dribble."

"Everybody was trying to go under my screens," Paul said on former Clippers teammate J.J. Redick's *Old Man and the Three* podcast in December 2020. "So it was like 'Tyson [Chandler], come set it.' So then I'd snake or cut back. It forced the two-on-one every single time."

The "snake dribble" is a perfect name for the move given Paul's pathological need to outsmart opponents. It involves coming off the on-ball screen one way and crossing sharply back the other to get back in front of the on-ball defender, cutting off their recovery path. It's basketball's version of a driver veering into the fast lane, only to go the speed limit or slower while the cars behind them have no way of switching lanes. With that defender pinned on his back and out of the play, Paul could wait for Chandler to roll and create a two-on-one situation that was easy for him to manipulate.

These days, every ball-handler is well schooled in "snaking" the pick-and-roll. They know how to perform Paul's invention at varying speeds, angles, and paths, using different levels of space to set up different finishing moves. "Snaking" is so common in the modern NBA that we *expect* to see ball-handlers use it even when it's not necessary or practical. Still, few snake *quite* as sharply as Paul, who still manages to weave through defenders as if he's tracing a backwards "S" on the court.

The power of the snake dribble is so obvious that you wonder why nobody thought to perfect it before Paul. The whole point of running a pick-and-roll is to turn an even numbers situation into a man advantage for the offense. Once the offense achieves that numbers advantage, the defense must give something up. If the defense must give something up, the pick-and-roll has done its job. All the snake dribble does is keep that window pried open long enough for the ball-handler to locate the domino that will cause the most damage when toppled.

But the first step of that logical train of thought requires acknowledging the important lesson that Paul, in his genius way, intuitively understood.

Technically, the pick-and-roll is a race with a winner and a loser. But the offensive player's goal isn't to win. It's to make sure their defender loses. And the defender will always lose if the ball-handler is blocking their path to victory. That is why the snake dribble must be paired with a second Paul invention that became a pick-and-roll necessity: the hostage dribble, or, as most call it, "putting the defender in jail."

May 19, 2008 — Spurs at Hornets — WCSF Game 7 (Tied 3-3)
Spurs 71, Hornets 58 — 10:20 left in fourth quarter

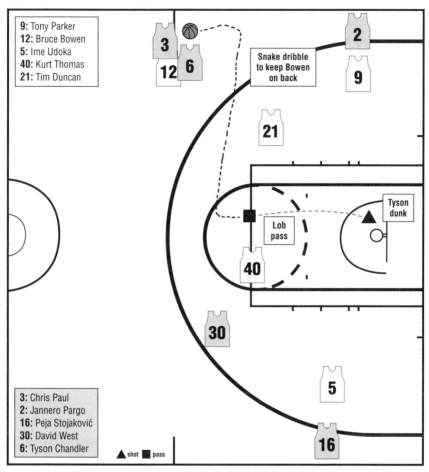

9: Tony Parker
12: Bruce Bowen
5: Ime Udoka
40: Kurt Thomas
21: Tim Duncan

Snake dribble
to keep Bowen
on back

Tyson
dunk

Lob
pass

3: Chris Paul
2: Jannero Pargo
16: Peja Stojaković
30: David West
6: Tyson Chandler

▲ shot ■ pass

That's when a ball-handler slows down after executing their snake dribbles, crouches extremely low to the ground, and dribbles in place way in front of his body while pinning his man on his back. It's like boxing out a rebounder, except with dribbling. The goal is to maintain the five-on-four advantage of the snake dribble long enough for the screener to roll and/or for the ball-handler to scan the rest of the floor to determine the best way to exploit his numbers advantage. The on-ball defender is considered to be in "jail" because they're being shut out of the play even as the ball-handler doesn't go anywhere. No defender wants to end up in jail.

Ideally, they wouldn't have allowed the ball-handler to cut in front of them in the first place. One way to beat the snake dribble is to stay glued to the ball-handler so they can't run them into the on-ball screen. Another way is to slip underneath the screen at the last second to beat the ball-handler to the "snaking spot," so to speak. That's a specialty of Milwaukee's Jrue Holiday and Boston's Marcus Smart, among others. If those methods fail, the on-ball defender must be patient when pursuing the snake dribble. They can't lose touch entirely, but they also can't get so close that the hostage dribble permanently pins them on the ball-handler's back. (We'll detail the new-age footwork of this and other ongoing defensive battles in Chapter 12.)

The power of the snake and hostage dribbles grew as the three-point revolution spread the game farther out. Both are tools ball-handlers use to ensure the pick-and-roll race stays rigged in their team's favor. Seeing as the average pick-and-roll race in the Spaced Out Era covers far more distance with more freedom of movement than ever before, that's a lot of room to deploy those dribble tactics.

It shouldn't be surprising that others like them have popped up in recent seasons. One close cousin of snaking is known as "Nashing"[93] in honor of the two-time Suns MVP. This is when the ball-handler keeps his dribble alive along the baseline, waits for the precise moment when the on-ball defender and screener relax thinking they've stopped the pick-and-roll, lets them feel safe enough to retreat to their original assignments, *then* exploits their confusion to create the man advantage. If snaking is like blocking your opponent's path to the race's finish line, Nashing is more like picking the finish line up, moving it farther and farther away, and then abruptly dropping it back on the floor when both defenders least expect it.

The same idea also applies to "dragging it out," which is when pick-and-roll ball-handlers slowly move backward or sideways when they see a blitz or hedge. The goal is to bait the two defenders to follow the ball, opening up more space to pass or drive around them. It's like using a fishing rod to reel the defenders away from the offense's intended finish line. (The forward version of the move is sometimes known as a "patient dribble.") "Dragging it out" is like a hostage dribble in reverse, with the ball-handler preserving a one-on-two situation rather than a two-on-one.

---

93. So named because Steve Nash was the first guard to regularly perform it.

Other tactics involve ball-handlers altering their body and step cadence when coming off the screen. (The fake spin move, colloquially known as the "Smitty," is a popular one,[94] though hardly alone.) Still others, such as well-timed in-and-outs, crossovers, behind-the-backs, or between-the-legs dribbles, alter the ball's direction. A whole host of others tinker with the ball's *vertical* plane, either via super-low dribbles or by bouncing the ball high enough to essentially reset the dribble in the middle of a move. (One personal favorite is the "throw ahead" dribble, an anti-drop coverage tactic in which the ball-handler tosses the ball far out invitingly to the screener's defender before yanking it back.)

Finally, there's a whole class of dribble fakes that defy categorization. One is known as a "cut" or "yo-yo dribble," which is when the ball-handler uses the same arm motion as a one-handed pocket bounce pass, but applies backspin so the ball goes back to them. Announcers often believe it to be a mistake, at least until they see a replay.

This move was popularized by … you guessed it, Chris Paul.

In 2006, the NBA introduced a new basketball made out of a special synthetic material. It proved to be a terrible decision. While manufacturers touted it as the future, players universally loathed it because the coarse material caused finger lacerations and bloody cuts. After less than two months, the league relented and went back to the older leather ball. Yet Paul, then in his second NBA season, noticed how the ball's new material allowed him to "actually throw it out away, really far from me and it can still come back," he said years later. That inspired him to start practicing the move, and he continued even after the old ball returned.

Paul did not exactly *invent* the "cut" or "yo-yo dribble." It's more accurate to credit And1 streetball legends like Grayson Boucher ("The Professor"), Rafer Alston (code name "Skip to My Lou"), or any of the other members of that tour.[95] His genius realization was that a move once used for entertainment purposes could be applied to perform the essential function of the game's most essential action. The backspin freezes the screener's man, thereby maintaining the offense's pick-and-roll's numbers advantage.

---

94. This move is known as the "Smitty" because it was the personal favorite of Steve Smith, a former NBA shooting guard and current Turner/NBA TV analyst.

95. Alston parlayed his And1 streetball fame into a 10-year NBA career, most notably with the Houston Rockets.

Is that a boring way to describe a cool move? Of course. Classic CP3. But that's also why it and so many others of its ilk are flourishing in the Spaced Out NBA.

THE FLOOR "SPACERS"

Mike Budenholzer knew exactly how the 2018–19 Milwaukee Bucks should play.

As coach of the Atlanta Hawks, Budenholzer relied on a dizzying motion offense to minimize the absence of a single dominant player. Now, Budenholzer faced the opposite problem in his new job. The Bucks had one dominant star, but he was stuck in a system that didn't maximize his talents. How would Budenholzer apply the principles of those overachieving Hawks teams to enhance a single player?

The answer began when he tasked five video coordinator staffers with a special pre-training camp project. They were sent to purchase rolls of blue tape and bring them to the Bucks' main practice court. Over the course of an hour and a half, they outlined five square boxes, each 1.5 feet by 1.5 feet, in five different locations beyond the three-point arc. Two went in the corners, each hugging the baseline and sideline. One was up top, near the front edge of the half-court logo. The other two were angled out to the wing, each well beyond the line and parallel horizontally to the box in the middle.

Together, the boxes were a visual illustration of Budenholzer's key coaching point that linked his new team to his old one. The Bucks needed to space the floor, largely (but not exclusively) to facilitate Giannis Antetokounmpo's downhill attacks.

Budenholzer's tale of the tape was one of several examples of NBA coaches "gamifying" their practice facilities to drill floor spacing.[96] In February 2017, then-76ers coach Brett Brown directed his staff to paint a gray four-point line on their practice court to encourage their shooters to let it fly from way downtown. The practice spread across the league, even among more reputed old-school coaches. One of Tom Thibodeau's first moves upon taking the Knicks' head coaching job in 2020 was to request his own four-point line at the team's Tarrytown facility.

---

96. Gamify is the phrase then-76ers coach Brett Brown used in multiple interviews.

"It also provides a good line for spacing so that when you do get movement and penetration, spray out, pass, pass that a guy can get rhythm into a shot and attempt or step into a three," he told The Athletic. "So his weight is going forward."

Other teams used visual aides to stress the corner three-point shot. Some, like the Chicago Bulls, drew the four lines of a box in the deep corner rather than using tape. Others, like the 76ers, painted the corner three-point area a darker color—red, in their case—so it would stand out against the light tan of a hardwood floor. In 2017, the Toronto Raptors even changed the points system during their offseason scrimmages. Players got four points for making a corner threes, three for any other long-range shot, two if they got a layup or dunk, and zero or sometimes even negative one for any jumper or floater inside the arc.

"Gamifying" clearly works. The Bucks jumped from 44 wins to 60 in Budenholzer's first season. The 76ers leapt from the depth of despair into a 50-plus-win East contender in 2018 and 2019. The Knicks surged from the NBA's basement to the No. 4 seed in Thibodeau's first season in charge. Toronto won an East-high 59 games in 2017–18 and the NBA title the next season. It's one thing to know the value of spreading the floor. It's another to stand inside of boxes, participate in wacky scrimmages, and draw your eyes to color-coded areas day after day.

At the same time, the NBA's gamifying craze has unintentionally painted (pun intended) an overly simplistic and often misleading picture of floor spacing to the public, and sometimes the players themselves. It's of course better to spread out on a pick-and-roll or isolation than crowd together. Drilling those precise locations is clearly worthwhile for an NBA team.

But the boxes and uniquely painted zones are just the tip of the spacing iceberg. There's so much more that goes into maintaining proper floor spacing than where a player stands.

Modern NBA spacing is dynamic, three-dimensional, and constantly in motion. It is a structure whose shape constantly changes. It moves in tune with the ball and the defense's reaction to its ever-changing location. The boxes and/or color-coded areas are meant to be starting points and key landmarks, not literal boxes that confine players at all times until (or if) their superstar teammate passes them the ball.

Yet the visual of a static painted or taped line on a fixed floor surface has nurtured the flawed idea that spacing and cutting are sworn enemies rather than equal partners in the game's increasingly sophisticated off-ball dance. "[Cutting] has been something that has really sort of died in the NBA," longtime NBA coach and current TNT analyst Stan Van Gundy told Bleacher Report before the 2020 bubble playoffs.

But that could not be further from the truth.

In fairness to Van Gundy, the immediate aftermath of the Warriors-Rockets rivalry enhanced this misperception. From afar, it appeared there was a league-wide split between teams who relied on static spread floors to aid superstars (think Houston, Milwaukee at first, Cleveland with LeBron James, Dallas with Luka Dončić, the Clippers with Kawhi Leonard, and Atlanta with Trae Young) and teams who championed sharp cutting and off-ball movement (Golden State, San Antonio, Miami, and Denver most prominently).

But the dichotomy occasionally perpetuated by the public and some old-school analysts never made sense to the coaches gamifying their practice courts. Each of them aimed to use those boxes to act as a form of offensive structure that would then *facilitate* the art and spontaneity of cutting. Some teams and players picked up on that immediately. It didn't take long for the rest to figure it out, too.

The result is a constant off-ball game within the game that hides in plain sight while most of us gaze at the ball. In this ever-evolving duel, cutting and spacing are two parts of a virtuous offensive cycle that turns non-openings into shot attempts, small advantages into greater ones, and good shots into great shots. The more teams drilled and systemized their initial floor positioning, the more easily players spotted prime cutting opportunities once obscured by congested floor spacing. The impact of those cuts grew as more teams spread the floor with shooters, just like the threat of deadly three-point shooters opened up space for drives to the basket.

Most of all, the repeated emphasis on maintaining a well-spaced collective offensive shape encourages the other four players to change their positioning—to *cut*—to alter or exploit the defense's shape. This dynamic shapeshifting process requires the right mix of moving and standing still. It is the essence of modern NBA floor spacing.

There are two different types of cuts in the modern NBA: those that create the initial floor spacing and those that exploit it.

While the first category can become easy scores if the defense doesn't track them, that is not their primary purpose. They instead function like receivers going in motion before a football snap, providing insight into the defense's coverage that can be exploited later in the play or game. Some coaches refer to these cuts as "automatics" because the players automatically know to run them, yet different sequences have different automatic cuts depending on the time of the game, the play call (if it is a set play), the side in which the ball-handler initiates the possession, the actual ball-handler themselves, the defense's initial shape, and myriad other factors.

The other function of automatics is to show the defense different looks. The goal is to temporarily confuse opponents so they react a beat slower to the pick-and-roll, off-ball screen, or isolation they've seen a thousand times on film. You often see "automatic" cuts when a big man dribbles to a side with two teammates in the wing and corner, an alignment that can yield many different kinds of pick-and-roll or dribble handoff actions.

One such example calls on the wing player to step toward the big man and then veer the other way for a sharp backdoor cut. The offense will take a layup if it's there, but the real purpose of the cut is to clear their defender from that side so the corner man can loop up for the actual dribble handoff. Not only does the initial "automatic" backdoor cut trigger a reaction that distracts the defense from preparing for the more dangerous threat, but it also provides more insight into the overall defensive game plan. The way the wing defender defends the automatic cut—overplaying to denying the ball (i.e., "top locking"), chasing from behind ("lock and trailing"), cheating underneath the pick ("shooting the gap"), switching, etc.—provides a clue for how they'll defend the main action and/or similar alignments in the future.

The beauty of this automatic cut is that it sets up the ideal floor spacing for the next part of the sequence. One of the hardest modern actions to defend is a pick-and-roll (or dribble-handoff) that sends the ball-handler from one wing (or corner) to the middle of the floor. This is known as an "empty" pick-and-roll because it leaves the entire side open with no help defenders in sight. If the ball-handler can create a two-on-one situation with the screen, there's little the defense can do to prevent an open shot.

You may think that decoy automatic cut to create the empty floor spacing is pointless when you could just clear that space from the start. But if the other three offensive players simply stood where they were supposed to stand for an empty pick-and-roll, the defense would know what was coming and change their five-man shape to anticipate it. They can't do that when one or more offensive players starts the sequence in one spot and "automatically" cuts to another. This is why pristine floor spacing is dynamic, not static.

"Automatics" are not a new concept in the NBA. If anything, they were *more* significant before the mid-2000s Suns popularized the modern "pace and space" ethos. This is one half of the reason for the persistent myth that cutting is a dying art in the Spaced Out Era. If you view the purpose of cutting exclusively as setup motion to guide half-court set plays, you'll find the speed of the modern game eliminates time to complete those slow-developing automatics. On the flip side, if you viewed cutting as *entirely* instinctual, you might view the presence of literal (small) taped boxes on a floor as a prison that neuters the spontaneity players need to cut effectively. Perhaps a lighter tape color would have been more inviting.

Both impressions are understandable, but misleading. Just as "automatics" aren't meant to be slow and rote, those "instinctual" cuts aren't entirely spontaneous.

Instead, they make up a second category of cuts that are designed to best *exploit* the floor spacing *after* the initial action creates a numbers advantage of some form for some time. The defense is in scramble mode, having altered its shape to anticipate and address what they deem to be the most dangerous potential outcomes. It's hard enough for the defense to mitigate the damage of a man disadvantage when the five offensive players are spread out over a wider space. It becomes even harder once the offense tacks on some well-timed cuts out of that initial spacing.

The post-advantage creation stage of possessions has grown much more elaborate in the last decade. When Steve Nash and Amar'e Stoudemire were spamming their deadly pick-and-roll at the start of the 2004–05 season, the other three Suns didn't need to do much more than stand along the three-point line. Most teams' defensive rotations were reactive rather than proactive, a relic of the illegal defense rule that was abolished only three years earlier. The three off-ball players could wait for Nash and Amar'e to draw an extra defender, prepare for a kickout pass, and then swing the ball until a good shot turned into a great shot. The ball moves faster than the man, as the old cliché goes.

Their success forced defenses to develop ways to muck up the wider off-ball space that incubates such lovely ball movement. Help defenders must display smarter initial positioning, take shorter recovery paths, close out at different speeds depending on the shooter, and master techniques like "stunting" or "gapping" between two well-spread shooters.

One of the most important tactical innovations of the Spaced Out Era is the "X-out," which is when defenders close out on the nearest open shooter rather than their initial man-to-man assignment. The off-ball defender closest to the three-point line will immediately leave their man to rush to the driver's first kickout pass, while the lowest help defender gets a head start on making the much longer rotation to the next shooter. Their closeout paths form an "X," hence "X-out." Once you see it for the first time, you won't be able to unsee it. (We'll return to the X-out in Chapter 12.)

Defeating these increasingly sophisticated scramble tactics requires a healthy marriage between regimented floor spacing and incisive cutting. The offspring of that union is this ever-growing second category of cuts that penetrate the defense's shape in much the same way as drives, passes, or rim-rolls.

It's crucial to understand that not every cut is supposed to go *toward* the basket. Many of the most effective ones move away from it, while several others move sideways rather than backward or forward. The direction of the cut is less important than its primary purpose: to create or increase the window to deliver a pass that will eventually lead to a better shot, whether it's a layup, open three, or something in between.

The two most prominent horizontal post-advantage cuts in the modern NBA are known as "lift" and "drift."[97] Both movements are subtle, yet essential ways to beat scrambling help defenders before they can deploy those sneaky scrambling tactics. And both *require* the ideal floor spacing structure those gamified practice courts are designed to reinforce.

Remember, the whole point of a five-man defensive scheme is to limit the numbers advantage the pick-and-roll naturally creates. The best way to

---

97. "Shake" is a common synonym for "lift." Similarly, coaches use several different terms to describe the cut in which a wing shooter "drifts" to the baseline corner.

do that, no matter the defensive strategy, is for any combination of the three help defenders to sink into the lane in advance to deter the ball-handler or roller, then close out back to the perimeter. This is known as "sink and recover," and almost every competitive team at any level practices it with the shell drill.[98]

The maneuver is never *easy*, especially when it must be performed over long distances to account for the abundance of long-range shooting in today's game. But it's a hell of a lot *easier* when those floor-spacing shooters stay in the same place throughout the sequence. At least the help defender can sink and recover in a straight line.

What are they supposed to do when those shooters are *also* moving to different spots while staying behind the three-point line? That's the impossible challenge the "lift" and "drift" cuts introduce.

Theoretically, shooters can and do relocate to any point along the arc at any time when presenting drive-and-kick passing options. They're rarely standing perfectly still even if they appear to be to the naked eye. But the "lift" and "drift" cuts are regimented rather than instinctual. They specifically task players with moving from one spacing hotspot to another. Corner-to-wing (or wing-to-middle)? "Lift." Wing-to-corner? "Drift."

Each is synced up with the main pick-and-roll action at the precise instant their help defender performs a sink-and-recover movement on the roller or driver. Talk about a two-on-one pickle! How is that help defender supposed to cover two players moving in opposite directions?

Though the lift and drift cuts operate on the same general principle, they tend to occur at different times. Lifts tend to occur before or during a sink-and-recovery move, often paralyzing the help defender into chasing the wrong threat. If they sink too far into the lane, the ball-handler has a clearer line of sight to feed the lifting shooter than if they stood in the corner. If the lift instead distracts the help defender, they risk giving up a layup or dunk to the driver or roller. Even average pick-and-roll playmakers know how to manipulate the threat of one to open up the other. The Heat were adept lifters in the mid-2010s before every team copied them.

---

98. There are many variations of the shell drill, but the basic idea involves a group of defenders practicing sinking in and closing out to a group of spot-up shooters in different ways, depending on which shooter receives the ball.

October 25, 2019 — Raptors at Celtics
Raptors 104, Celtics 104 — 3:30 left in fourth quarter

Drifts, on the other hand, tend to be more reactive. The goal is to arrive at the corner when the ball-handler (or roller, theoretically) runs out of room around the basket and needs an outlet along the baseline. They work best when the help defender is fully sunk into the lane, but hasn't started his recovery to the perimeter. The Spurs long deployed a set play known as "Baseline Hammer," which involves a ball-handler driving to the baseline on one side while a big man sets a screen to aid a shooter's drift cut on the other.

The modern drift cut is a pick-and-roll version of the same concept, though "Baseline Hammer" remains a popular league-wide after-timeout play.[99]

The lift and drift concepts are both the result of dynamic off-ball play that features a combination of spacing and cutting. They are timed cuts out of a spread pick-and-roll shape that force help defenders to address multiple offensive players moving in different directions at the same time.

The latter point is crucial whether your team positions all five players behind the three-point line (known as five-out) or not. The Spaced Out Era's most important discovery was that drawing defenders away from the highest-value area on the floor (the rim) is more effective than flooding it with offensive players. One guy charging the basket, combined with four teammates spreading out to give them room, is exceedingly difficult to defend. That task becomes nearly impossible if at least one of the other four guys also moves away from the rim or sideways in tandem with the charger.

Once the value of the pick-and-roll became self-evident, teams increasingly found new iterations of the general "one charger plus four spacers" infrastructure. One such tactic is known as "roll/replace," which is when one screener rolls to the basket and another player stationed inside the three-point line pops out to "replace" them on the perimeter. It looks like two cars driving past each other on a one-lane road. The Spain pick-and-roll described in Chapter 7 is a more elaborate version of the same concept.

Embracing the modern spacing/cutting marriage also opened teams up to the idea that the charger can be an off-ball cutter not directly involved in the main pick-and-roll action. Once help defenders began addressing lifts and drifts, offenses developed the natural counter of those shooters cutting to the basket instead. Pick-and-rolls now had their own category of backdoor cuts. When are those most effective? When the defense overplays the perimeter and vacates space behind them. The cutter thus became the charger.

One of the most common examples of this principle involves the wing off-ball shooter slicing to the middle of the lane during a pick-and-roll. This movement, known as a "45 cut," plunges one of the central tenants of pick-

---

99. In 2013, the Spurs began teaching shooters to cut from one corner to another in certain situations. This move, known as the "Danny Green cut" because he was (and still is, as of press time) its most common practitioner, was designed to beat Miami's blitzing pick-and-roll scheme.

and-roll defense—a third defender drifting to the nail to clog the lane—into a deep existential crisis.

The idea of the nail as essential to help defense assumed that the pick-and-roll itself was the offense's only downhill threat. Either the ball-handler would drive, or the screener would roll. The "45 cut," however, offers a third way to attack the hoop, which poses an uncomfortable question to any pick-and-roll scheme. Monty Williams' Phoenix Suns are the gold standards of the "45 cut," but they're hardly alone. Most teams drill it relentlessly, and several include it as an automatic in many of their half-court sets.

This is why the "45 cut" and others like it from different locations on the court are useful even if the cutter doesn't receive the pass. They give defenders something to cover, which makes it easier for someone else to get open, especially if they're also moving without the ball. (Mo Dakhil, a former video coordinator for the Spurs, Clippers, and Australian national team who now podcasts for The Athletic and elsewhere, dubbed this the "cut assist.") Cuts can topple the first domino of lovely ball movement in much the same way as the pick-and-roll itself.

This second category of post-pick-and-roll cuts explain why the taped boxes and shaded areas on so many practice courts are best understood as necessary *starting points and beacons* that guide a coordinated series of off-ball cuts, not, well, actual boxes. It's not ball movement that becomes contagious. It's the player movement that *triggers* the ball movement that becomes contagious. The on-court markers are there to connect the cuts, not eliminate them.

The full weight of that message did not come easily to Budenholzer's Bucks, despite their dramatic regular-season improvement. The mere emphasis on spread-out spacing took Antetokounmpo's game to a new level, made them deadly in transition, and was a major improvement on Jason Kidd's cramped half-court sets. But the Bucks still labored through bouts of half-court stagnation, especially against top defenses in the playoffs. Their players still interpreted the boxes too literally, standing still to spread the floor instead of deploying more dynamic spacing + cutting tactics. They lacked that cutting edge (pun intended) once the Raptors and Heat loaded up on Antetokounmpo in back-to-back postseasons.

In an attempt to change that, Budenholzer greeted Bucks players with a new set of taped boxes prior to the 2020–21 season. The most significant addition was a narrow rectangular one underneath the basket, stretching 15 feet long in each direction along the baseline and six feet wide while overlapping the out-of-bounds line.

This is known as the "dunker spot" because the player occupying it is located one step from, well, dunking.[100] NBA teams have stationed big men there for years, particularly those lob threats like Chris "Birdman" Andersen with the Miami Heat, Clint Capela with the Houston Rockets, and several members of the high-flying Thunder teams of Kevin Durant and Russell Westbrook. But the practice was waning as more teams adopted five-out spacing alignments, believing the upside of spreading the floor was better than cramping it with a tall guy near the basket.

Budenholzer was influential to that growing five-out movement, both with Atlanta and Milwaukee. So why did he reverse course?

The main reason was to topple the defensive walls that kept Antetokounmpo from the basket. Once opponents adjusted to the Bucks' five-out spacing, they realized that if they kept them out of transition—a difficult, but not impossible task—they could stall the Bucks' offense with aggressive sink-and-recover tactics to neuter Antetokounmpo *and* the stationary shooters. The Heat went a step further in their 2020 playoff victory, using a combination of a 2–3 zone and a stunt-heavy, man-to-man system to flood bodies to the area around the free-throw line, in essence building their wall *there* rather than closer to the rim. That was their way of short-circuiting Antetokounmpo's mad dashes to the rim by not letting him build momentum to get there in the first place. It was the basketball equivalent of a high defensive line in soccer that clogs space in the midfield.

Moving one of the off-ball players from beyond the three-point arc to the dunker spot was the Bucks' way of driving that wall back. It forced that player's man to step back and honor the threat of a lob or duck-in layup, thereby weakening the barrier at Antetokounmpo's pickup point. Even if they stepped up as Antetokounmpo drove, they'd be too deep in the paint to do much about it.

The tactic was inspired by George Karl. In 2011, the veteran NBA coach began directing one or more of his Nuggets players to stand out of bounds

---

100. Some people also call it the "short corner," but I prefer "dunker spot" because the goal is to finish at the rim, not shoot a short-corner jumper.

June 10, 2021 — Nets at Bucks — ECSF Game 3 (BKN leads 2-0)
Bucks 49, Nets 46 — 9:54 left in third quarter

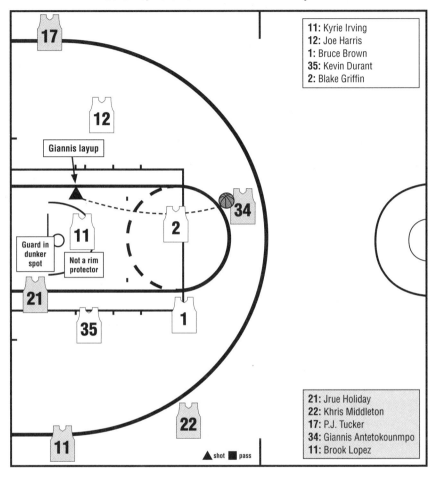

underneath the basket, even if they couldn't catch and score from there. The odd tactic of *removing* a player from the court improved his team's spacing because that players' defender would invariably follow them and hilariously pin themselves too far underneath the basket to help when a different Nugget drove to the hoop.[101] The Bucks' use of the dunker spot a decade later follows a similar logic.

---

101. Karl was too clever. Once the NBA spotted this tactic, they closed the loophole by adding an "out-of-bounds violation" to the 2013–14 rulebook.

The Bucks' added twist was to place a *guard* in the dunker spot rather than a big man. That way, the defender, who was already disadvantaged because he now had to step out from farther under the hoop, was the equivalent of a flea to Antetokounmpo. Offseason addition Jrue Holiday was an ideal fit for this role because he was sturdy enough to finish through contact, quick enough to shift from one side of the box to the other, athletic enough to sky for offensive rebounds, yet creative enough as a passer to kick the ball back out to shooters if need be.

Budenholzer's new spacing mandate worked after some early growing pains. The Bucks scored five more points per 100 possessions than they did the previous season,[102] while Antetokounmpo recovered from a mortal start to the regular season to dominate the 2021 NBA Playoffs and lead Milwaukee to a title.

The Bucks' dunker spot success illustrates two central truths about modern floor spacing. One is that "good spacing" is *not* the same thing as dotting the court with long-range bombers. Spreading the defense out is one way to generate good spacing, and undoubtedly the best way on a pick-and-roll. But it's not the *only* way. Sometimes, it can be useful to pin the defense in or to slice a cutter down the lane and then shift the other players off the defense's reaction.

The second is that good spacing requires the *combination* of a well-drilled structure and incisive off-ball movement. The Bucks' first gamified practice court featured five like-sized taped boxes, each 1.5 feet by 1.5 feet. Their second one featured two 1.5-by-1.5-feet spots at the top of the key, two longer rectangles in the corners, and a giant pillar that stretched 30 feet long and six feet wide on the baseline. The message to the players was clear: You have lots of room to move within these boxes, so use it.

Modern floor spacing is thus a blend of positioning *and* motion. Spreading out is necessary, but only to a point. Cutting helps, but only to a point. The only way to achieve the dynamic spacing necessary to run a modern pick-and-roll is by putting them together.

And that's when the playmaking magic happens.

---

102. They only jumped two spots in the rankings because offense as a whole was more efficient in 2020–21, for reasons we'll discuss in Chapter 12.

Chapter 9
Scan Less, See More

*The modern game is incubating a golden age
of passing and spatial awareness.*

It's the closing minutes of the first quarter of a critical, 2021, late-season contest between the Los Angeles Lakers and New York Knicks. The Lakers' primary ball-handler stops in the middle of the "STAPLES CENTER" logo on the right wing and uses an Anthony Davis on-ball screen to get a half step on his defender going right, slowing down with a high hesitation dribble that floats up around his head.

As he shields his body to protect the dangling ball, the Lakers' primary ball-handler tilts his head back to freeze Davis' man, crouches into an acceleration pose, returns his right hand to the ball, and clutches it while swinging both arms over his head. Three Knicks converge on him: his recovering primary defender from behind, Taj Gibson from the right corner, and Frank Ntilikina from the left.

The Lakers' primary ball-handler ignores them all while tilting his head to the opposite side. Two teammates flash through his line of sight: one (Kyle Kuzma) in no-man's land after cutting from the left wing to the basket, the other (Ben McLemore) spotted up in the left corner. A single help defender, R.J. Barrett, stands between them.

Barrett begins hatching a devious plan. He'll step in front of Kuzma, wait until the Lakers' ball-handler looks away, then sneak toward McLemore to pick off any pass along the baseline. It seems to work. Barrett rotates to Kuzma as his three teammates swarm the ball, forcing the Lakers' primary ball-handler to take a long leap underneath the basket. As Ntilikina blinds him with perfect verticality, Barrett rushes over to intercept the baseline pass that is sure to come.

It never comes.

Instead, the Lakers' primary ball-handler, with no clear line of sight and two feet that are a split second away from landing on the floor, whips a perfect one-handed fastball underneath Ntilikina's arms to McLemore, who is in the middle of executing a lift cut to the left wing. The pass could not have been timed any better, sliding directly into McLemore's shooting pocket. Instead of a turnover, the Lakers' primary ball-handler generated three points for his team. He didn't just throw McLemore open. He threw McLemore open while making Barrett, McLemore's man, think he couldn't.

The full sequence required complex pick-and-roll playmaking manipulation. The Lakers' primary ball-handler used a series of head fakes, hesitations, and fancy dribbles to create an advantage, then left his feet with no guarantee that he'd even *see* the payoff pass before he landed. He plotted several passes in advance while ignoring the three Knicks in his grill and focusing on a fourth that never came near him. Then he delivered a perfect one-handed crosscourt fastball from out of bounds to hit a moving target in stride.

So who is this mystery Lakers ball-handling wizard?

It wasn't LeBron James, who was sitting out with a minor injury. It was a 20-year-old prospect named Talen Horton-Tucker. A former 2019 second-round pick, Horton-Tucker spent most of his rookie year in the NBA G-League. He then went on to play just 48 mostly garbage-time minutes in the Lakers' six-game playoff loss to Phoenix.

This is hardly the pedigree of a future all-time playmaking great. Yet despite his lack of pro experience, he just pulled off a multi-layered passing read that only a few players ever master.

Only a few players, that is, until now. While Horton-Tucker is an intriguing prospect that may blossom by the time you read this,[103] his advanced

---

103. The Lakers, in a nod to his potential, re-signed him to a three-year, $32 million contract after the 2020–21 season.

May 11, 2021 — Knicks at Lakers
Knicks 25, Lakers 21 — 42 seconds left in first quarter

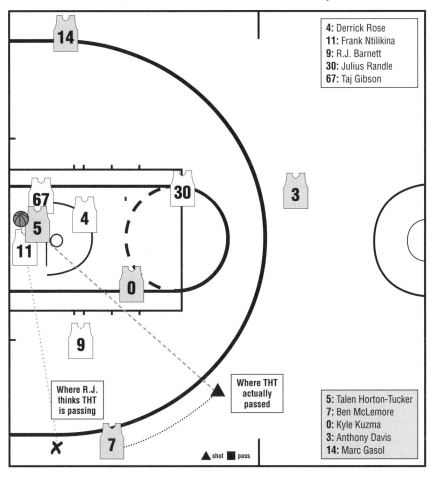

4: Derrick Rose
11: Frank Ntilikina
9: R.J. Barnett
30: Julius Randle
67: Taj Gibson

Where R.J. thinks THT is passing

Where THT actually passed

▲ shot ■ pass

5: Talen Horton-Tucker
7: Ben McLemore
0: Kyle Kuzma
3: Anthony Davis
14: Marc Gasol

playmaking sophistication at an age where he cannot legally buy alcohol reflects the massive scope of the NBA's three-point revolution. Every single current NBA player, from superstars like LeBron James to the 15th man on every roster, has been forced to showcase on-court skills they've never needed before.

So far, this book has explained how the three-point revolution transformed superstars, merged positions, and incubated a league-wide "pace and space" emphasis that combined the fast break and half-court set. It showed how the pick-and-roll became the game's primary mode of attack and defense, then dove deep into the nuts and bolts of pick-and-roll strategy from all angles while acknowledging the speed at which those schemes continue to evolve.

But each of those transformations pale in comparison to those of the players themselves. If any piece of this book has altered the way you watch an NBA game, imagine what it's done to those who play it.

In that respect, young players like Horton-Tucker have an advantage on their more experienced peers because they are closer to blank slates. They don't need to unlearn anything that the spread-out game has quickly rendered obsolete. It's easier for them to compartmentalize which skills to master and what it takes to master them. Each new draft class is more prepared than the last to pick up the ongoing rapid changes in their new profession.

In the coming chapters, we'll discuss how the Spaced Out NBA has altered shooting form, dribbling movements (or non-dribbling, as it were), and perimeter defensive techniques such as sliding one's feet and closing out on shooters.

But we will begin with passing. Why passing? The answer comes in the form of a question.

Do you remember the Talen Horton-Tucker pass I just described?

If you do, you're way more of a diehard than I thought possible. Horton-Tucker's assist isn't exactly routine, even by today's standards, but it didn't feature in ESPN's seven-minute highlight package from the game and was overshadowed by his dagger three-pointer in overtime. How did a 20-year-old second-round rookie perform a LeBron-level pass? The better question is why his remarkable feat was so easily forgotten.

This is one of the many effects of the three-point revolution that hides in plain sight. Spreading players out meant everyone needed to learn how to see the whole floor. They all needed to develop the court vision once reserved for pass-first point guards.

And that meant rediscovering something that lives inside of all of us.

THERE'S A SCENE in *The Matrix*[104] where Trinity (Carrie-Anne Moss) and Neo (Keanu Reeves) are trying to rescue their mentor Morpheus (Laurence Fishburne) from captivity within the machine-created Matrix simulation. They fend off a computerized agent who takes the form of a police officer,

---

104. The original, good one, not the ~~two~~ three sequels.

then decide to steal his vacant helicopter to get to Morpheus. One tiny problem: neither knows how to fly it.

"Not yet," Trinity clarifies.

She whips out a cellphone to dial up their ship located outside the Matrix. "I need a pilot program for a B-212 helicopter," she says to an operator named Tank (Marcus Chong). "Hurry!"

Tank pushes a few buttons to load up a picture of a helicopter. On the ship, the real Trinity's eyes flicker as the program implants onto her brain. In just a few seconds, it's done. The Matrix version of Trinity has suddenly become an expert B-212 helicopter pilot.

Mastering a new skill isn't quite that easy for a modern NBA player. But it's not *that* far off.

Thirty years ago, it was rare for an NBA player to have a private trainer on their own payroll. Nowadays, the "master trainer" is a cottage industry, with non-team-affiliated gurus competing to gain the trust of top pros, either to work with them extensively all year or just in short offseason bursts. They record their sessions—or at least the parts they want potential clients to see—post instructional videos on social media while hawking their full product, and personalize their players' sessions with proprietary film and data. Increasingly, they collaborate *with* their client's agency and team staffers on development plans that align with everyone's best interests, not just the player's.

The player development infrastructure on each NBA team is also more robust than ever. Though NBA rules permit only a head coach, three assistants, and one trainer to sit on the first row of the bench with the players, teams fill second and even third rows with specialized basketball support staff.

It takes a village to maximize team performance. The 2011–12 Charlotte Bobcats media guide references 26 basketball operations staffers. The 2020–21 Charlotte Hornets staff directory lists 43, not including the additional dozen or so assigned to their G-League affiliate Greensboro Swarm. Jobs like "player development coach," "video coordinator," and "data analyst" were occupied by a single full-time person, if that, as recently as a decade ago. Now, they are often fully formed departments of their own.

Technological advances make it laughably easy to study oneself or an opponent. In the early 1970s, Lakers coach Bill Sharman asked assistant Bill

Bertka to construct short 16-millimeter film loops of their team's games. He beamed those reels onto a projector so old that Bertka was forced to use the blunt edge of a pencil to hold the spool in place. (Then-owner Jack Kent Cooke, amazingly, told Sharman the organization *could not afford* to purchase a new one.) This was how the Lakers became the first NBA team to regularly watch game film—literally.

Nowadays, any NBA player, coach, staffer, or bozo like me can "watch film" from almost anywhere at almost any time. For those working in the NBA, it's as simple as pulling out an iPad and accessing a curated playlist from one of several league-sanctioned databases.[105] Assistant coaches spend several minutes reviewing game (or practice) clips with each player before every game. They can even go over sequences *from that specific game* while they rest on the bench. Between games, players and/or coaches can request a collection of a specific type of clip—say, every pick-and-roll in which they go left against a deep drop—and have someone send it to their device to watch on their own time.[106] Some teams have begun using virtual and/ or augmented reality to improve free-throw shooting, jumper form, and decision-making.

On top of that, many players use proprioception devices that improve subconscious muscle memory. In 2017, the NBA's official Instagram account posted a video of LeBron James catching and throwing hard passes with one hand while balancing on two plastic bubbles before an early-season Cavaliers game. Viewers were mesmerized,[107] in part because it was LeBron, but mostly because of those squishy bubble things.

What were they, and what were they doing in an NBA arena? They're called Waff Mini Elites, and they're beloved by hardcore yoga enthusiasts for improving balance, core strength, and flexibility while contorting the body in multiple directions. James was using them at the time to strengthen a balky ankle, but others use them and other similar equipment to hardwire the increasingly complex, dynamic basketball movement patterns the modern game requires.

---

105. They include Synergy Sports, Second Spectrum, and a number of others.

106. The widespread access to video is an underrated reason why NBA teams don't practice much in season anymore. Why add more wear and tear to players' bodies when a few well-targeted film sessions and walkthroughs are more than sufficient to prepare for most games?

107. The clip has nearly 3.3 million views on Instagram and tons more on other platforms.

With all these tools at their disposal, it's no wonder the average current NBA player performs athletic feats their predecessors never could. It's a lot easier to achieve peak performance with access to technology that allows players to repeatedly *visualize,* quite literally, the most microscopic in-game actions and body movements.

That word—"visualize"—illustrates the first of many reasons why the modern NBA is in the midst of an unprecedented golden age of passing. The greatest impact of the modern abundance of video is in democratizing the attributes of great passers: "feel," "court vision," and "basketball IQ."

Once upon a time, these qualities were considered inborn, if not supernatural. There's a reason the Lakers' 1979 No. 1 pick from Michigan State was nicknamed "Magic." But that was before every player, coach, analyst, and fan gained instant access to more game film than they could possibly watch in a lifetime. It's easier to anticipate an open teammate when you've overloaded your brain with visuals of similar sequences.

And it's even easier when those technological advances are occurring at the same time as an unprecedented stylistic revolution is doubling the court's practical playing surface. Indeed, the NBA's three-point revolution has simultaneously opened the floor up while forcing every player—point guard on down—to spot and deliver passes that must cut through multiple layers of help defense.

The result is that the players quite literally *see* more of the floor now than ever before. When paired with effective training techniques, modern NBA players have rapidly developed enhanced neuro-muscular processes that quickly sift through any visual clutter. The result is that *everyone* is capable of attempting and completing passes that previous generations never thought to try.

Cognitive scientists have a specific term for the skill that modern NBA players are developing by osmosis: *spatial awareness.*

In simple terms, this describes the internal process by which humans adjust their movements and behavior based on the objects or people in their line of sight. This is how we know to stop ourselves from crossing the street when we see and/or sense that a car is coming. Everyone, from the smallest infant to the oldest adult, possesses varying reservoirs of spatial awareness based on some combination of stuff they can't control (genetics, biology) and stuff they can (practice, life experience, attention). Some people are naturals depending on the context, but everyone will cross the street more effectively if they look both ways first.

The mechanism by which human beings improve their spatial awareness occurs through a process psychologists refer to as "chunking." When faced with giant blobs of information, our brain breaks down, groups, and regroups them into smaller patterns for our active working memory to recall. Human beings constantly chunk without realizing it. For example: we remember a 10-digit phone number by chunking it into three smaller groups of three, three, and four digits, respectively.[108]

Spatial awareness is, in essence, the act of chunking the overwhelming amount of information our senses take in every split second of our lives. Imagine having to cycle through every tiny element of the scene individually before deciding if it's safe to cross the street. Not only would you stay frozen in space for all eternity, but your active working memory capacity is too limited to hold the information you already analyzed as you painstakingly move from item to item. Thankfully, our brains instead chunk the scene, allowing us to quickly spot the most relevant bits to our decision to cross.

Those chunks naturally become faster and more precise with repeated exposure to the scene. When you approached the intersection for the first time, your brain built a mental map of similar intersections and life experiences to guide your decision to cross. You won't need to focus too much to identify some common intersection signals like traffic lights and crosswalks. That mental map becomes more specific each time you cross that street. What began as an abstract representation of the intersection gets closer and closer to the real thing.

The ever-increasing clarity of that mental map frees your brain to form more specific and relevant chunks each time you return to the scene. You'll notice a parked car on the side of the road the first time you cross the street, identify it as blue after the fifth time, mark its distance as halfway between the curve and the next driveway after the 10th, and encode it as a blue Honda Accord with a scratch near the left bumper on the 20th. It's always been there in reality, but you, in essence, don't "see" it—or its qualities—without repeated exposure.

---

108. In America, at least. Other countries have different chunking formats.

This is a vast oversimplification of real-life spatial awareness, since it assumes a fixed level of attention, timing, scene obstacles, and our mood at the time. But those *are* assumptions we can make more easily with *basketball* spatial awareness, even given its tactical complexity.

Like all sports, it is what psychologists call a controlled environment. The primary objective, number of players, court dimensions, and rules are always the same. Everyone is paying close attention, at least compared to life's mundane tasks. (You don't play competitive basketball while simultaneously peering at the sky, listening to headphones, and considering your lunch order.) It is an inherently visual game that requires many rapid decisions with incomplete information.

Those factors already made basketball an ideal platform for the growing scientific consensus that spatial awareness can be systematically improved with proper training, even in areas the training doesn't directly address. Now tack on the dramatically spread-out floor of the post-three-point revolution and the technological advances that ease access to highly specialized video and data. This is how every modern NBA player can receive a highly specialized spatial awareness training program that even Carrie-Anne Moss' fictional *Matrix* character would envy.

This does not fully explain the inborn qualities that separate LeBron James from Talen Horton-Tucker. Just because everyone is a better passer doesn't mean that everyone is the *same* quality of passer. Genetics and biology still play a huge role in spatial awareness and decision-making.

What if I told you the modern NBA was systematically shrinking *that* gap, too?

IN THE LATE 1980s and early 1990s, Philip Kellman was just beginning his distinguished career as a psychology professor at Swathmore College. He was also learning a new skill: how to fly an airplane.

The process was arduous. Studying for aviation tests. Logging time in flight simulators. Practicing for hundreds of hours in the air with tons of different instructors. He understood the material. He was slowly getting better at putting it into action. But he still got overwhelmed in the air.

More infuriatingly, his instructors always seemed as calm as a cucumber. They noticed stuff he missed, then offered unhelpful or non-existent explanations for *how* they saw what they saw.

"Coming in for a landing, an instructor may say to the student, 'You're too high!'" Kellman told author Benedict Carey in his 2015 book *How We Learn: The Surprising Truth About When, Where, and Why It Happens.* "The instructor is actually seeing an angle between the aircraft and the intended landing point, which is formed by the flight path and the ground. The student can't see this at all. In many perceptual situations like this one, the novice is essentially blind to patterns that the expert has come to see at a glance."

What, exactly, allows an expert to see what novices cannot? The answer is often reduced to fuzzy concepts like "intuition," "gut instinct," "reflexes," "instinct," "sixth sense," "impulse," "feeling," "knack," and several others. It's not exactly a revelation that experience improves these skills. But does that process occur naturally, or is it the result of a systemic mental tabulation?

As a cognitive psychologist whose research focused on perception, Kellman understood that his instructors were able to produce more specific chunks of spatial data than a novice like him. They both had access to the same spatial data, but the instructor could cluster more relevant signals together faster. He couldn't explain his thinking in a satisfactory way because it had become a single mental computation for him rather than the step-by-step process novices needed to master first.[109]

This is the effect of the instructor having more experience, of course. But what if there was a better way to teach novices how to make higher-level mental computations than "hope they develop it naturally through experience"?

Kellman thought so and had an idea for how to prove it. Instead of training pilots to master the technical specs of each dial or memorize each marker on a map individually, why not train them to instantly recognize what they *collectively* saw at a glance. Or, in other words: train them to develop spatial awareness of the board and map as individual units.

To do so, Kellman joined forces with Mary K. Kaiser of the NASA Ames Research Center to develop two different types of what they called Perceptual Learning Models. The experiment functioned like a computer or video game. One task was to instantly translate a combination of signals from all six dials at once into one of seven different flying maneuvers. The other was to choose one of three possible current locations on an aeronautical map of the San

---

109. This goes a long way toward explaining why great players often don't make great coaches.

Francisco region based on different fragments of a 20-second animated flight pattern. The key was that Kellman and Kaiser ran each experiment with a combination of pilots-in-training and complete novices.

The first PLM featured four pilots with between 500 and 2,500 hours of civil aviation experience and 10 undergraduate volunteers from Swarthmore and UCLA. Both groups received a five-minute orientation and two practice rounds on the device, then repeated the exercise 24 times with different alignments. After each round, they were given the correct answers and told how well they performed. They then repeated the process eight more times over the course of an hour.

The second PLM included a group of experienced pilots, who were only shown the answers and their scores after each round, and three others that were made up of novice students—one who got detailed instruction after each round, one who only received scores and answers, and the third acting a control group with no feedback whatsoever. Each group was then measured for speed and accuracy.

Each non-control group improved dramatically over the course of both programs. The non-pilots and pilots both sliced their reaction times by more than half in both scenarios while also improving their accuracy, often to significant degrees.

But the most remarkable discovery was that the novice pilots were more accurate and faster after completing the one-hour program *than the expert pilots were before they started*. One hour of Kellman and Kaiser's Perceptual Learning Model was as good at teaching students how to interpret flight dials and maps as 1,000 hours of *actually flying with an instructor*.

The study was a triumph in the emerging psychological field of perceptual learning, first codified by Eleanor Gibson in a seminal 1969 book. The idea is to use perceptual learning techniques like these to simulate the experience of making real-time decisions instead of overloading students with detailed information and hoping that experience performing the task will eventually teach them how to sift through it all. Perceptual learning has been proven to work in a variety of fields, ranging from medical students learning how to remove a gallbladder, high-school students mastering algebra, chemistry students recognizing the bonds between molecules, and much more.

There is growing evidence that perceptual learning in one task improves other adjacent skills as well. Some research has linked video games to improved visual recognition skills and hand-eye coordination. In one 2004 study, a group of 16–27-year-olds with 20/20 vision who engaged in perceptual learning to identify letters at different contrasts were also able to read a page of words faster.

Kellman and Kaiser were quick to note that their study did not measure the small matter of actually flying a plane. They weren't trying to *replace* real-life experience or more traditional classroom learning. Their point was that perceptual learning could dramatically bridge the gap between theory and practice.

Professional basketball players have a lot in common with airplane pilots. Their job requires them to translate everything they've learned in hundreds of thousands of hours of deliberate practice to a full-speed, continuous game. No matter how much they drill, how much film they study, and how many statistics they consult, each experience inside the lines is different. Those individual games are themselves composed of hundreds of smaller experiences, each of which require instant decisions without the luxury of deep thought.

Now, thanks to the three-point revolution, players must make more of those decisions faster over wider spaces. If players considered each element of the Spaced Out Era's style of play individually, the complexity would overwhelm them.

But that's not what they do. Instead, they've forced themselves to map the court as a single unit, much like the flight students in Kellman and Kaiser's study.

Whether they realize it or not, today's NBA players are using the combination of improved technology, more specific on-court reps, and robust feedback loops to form their own Court Vision Perceptual Learning Model. Their results mirror those of the pilots in Kellman and Kaiser's study. Expert passers like LeBron James keep improving, while relative novices like Talen Horton-Tucker achieve the greats' prior level in a fraction of the time. Together, they have created a playmaking golden age unlike any the NBA has ever seen.

The way the modern NBA player spots more open passes faster is by organizing the spatial data of an NBA court into more specific chunks. That, in theory, requires that they automatically form lower-level chunks first.

The best lab reproduction of that process comes from an 1897 study that asked subjects to read Morse code telegraphs over the course of a year. The results graphed as a series of asymptote curves—rapid early growth followed by a slower leveling off process over time. Some subjects only registered one curve. Others produced a second that started *at the highest level of the first,* rose dramatically, and then tapered off again. A select few reached a *third* level that began at the highest level of the second before following the same quick-rise-and-gradual-fall pattern. Each curve looked the same, but they began at exponentially higher points.

The authors of the study, a pair of Indiana University professors, asked subjects at each stage to explain their reading methods. Those who were still within the first asymptote curve said they mapped the dashes of Morse code to English letters individually before combining them into words. Those in the second said they picked up on the word structure automatically and focused on forming them into sentences. Finally, those few who produced a third curve said they could recognize full sentences automatically and took more time to ensure they combined into a coherent message.

The authors then showed the second group a message of random letters that didn't make words, then showed the third group one with random words that didn't form a coherent sentence. Each group's translation's speed dropped to its previous level.

The study's authors concluded that the three curves reflected "a hierarchy of habits." Their Morse code subjects saw letters, then words, then strings of words, etc. Mastering one stage automated their mental processing of it, freeing them to devote more attention to the next stage, then the next, ad infinitum. "Automatism is not genius," the authors wrote. "But it is the hands and feet of genius."

The passing magic we see on a nightly basis from NBA legends past and present is the result of a similar step-by-step systematic process that lurks beneath everyone's consciousness. Every player knows the game is five on five, on a 94' x 50' playing surface, with a hoop 10 feet in the air. The playmaking genius has access to the same spatial information as the novice. They've just trained themselves to *interpret* its meaning faster. A mental processing graph of a passing genius would feature some super high multiple of the 1897 study's three exponentially increasing asymptotic curves.

Imagine being plopped inside of LeBron James' body without any memory of his on-court basketball experiences. You'll need to first learn how to get past your own defender, which means working on dribbling moves, pump fakes, and the like to get shots off. You'll shock your opponent the first time you whip out a new move, exponentially less over time as you fine-tune it, then develop a counter-move and repeat the process.

This mindset requires you to see a five-on-five game on a one-on-one level. The rest of the court exists, but you may as well be blind to it. You're reading letters before you can read words.

As you master those one-on-one tools, your own defender occupies less and less of your conscious thought. You'll think more about how to draw a second defender to you and away from an open teammate. Then, you'll focus your attention on reading the third defender rotating to your open teammate. Soon, you'll automatically encode various connections between the other defenders that you can exploit to open up different teammates. You'll instantly spot the pass before the pass, the pass before the pass before the pass, etc.

If you're really good, you'll automate the entire structure of the court, allowing you to anticipate all the different ways the five defenders *might react* if you made different passes. And if you're a genius like LeBron, you'll automatically encode those *hypothetical* reactions and instead focus on how to present alternate realities to trick your opponents into opening up the pass you *really* want to make.

This is how passing magicians like LeBron James think—or, to be more accurate, *perceive*.

Most great players admit they don't think about beating their own defender because they assume it's a given. Their answers appear to reflect extreme confidence that borders on arrogance, which is seen as essential to the job of playing basketball really, really well. But it's equally accurate to conclude that their brains perceive in too advanced a way to consciously describe the game on a one-on-one level.

This is why a great pass yields a visceral joy that few other basketball experiences can. When LeBron makes one of those crosscourt no-look passes that seems to bend time and space, we think it's because he saw an open teammate others didn't. In truth, it's more like he's figured out *how to see* that open teammate in a place our primitive basketball brains never thought to look. We saw letters, maybe words. LeBron saw how they combine to form sentences.

This isn't to say that *anyone* can develop LeBron James' court vision by playing a lot of basketball. His unique combination of genetics, physiology, muscle memory, non-basketball experience, physical training, and a host of other natural factors allowed him to zip through some stages, bypass others, and advance through some of them concurrently.

But what if more could go further? What if those below LeBron's level of magic—like, say, Talen Horton-Tucker—could learn how to advance, bypass, and/or combine the stages of basketball court vision? Could you create a new hierarchy of passing habits? Could you *engineer* basketball IQ?

This is exactly what perceptual learning aims to accomplish. The pilots in Kellman and Kaier's study were using their perceptual learning model to bypass the early stages of mastering flight theory and skip ahead to the tasks that required spatial awareness. They were creating a new hierarchy of habits that began several steps ahead of more traditional learning models. They were giving the novices a head start on the experts.

And that's exactly what the Spaced Out NBA has done for passers.

LUKA DONČIĆ HAS eyes in the back of his head. Normally, this is a figure of speech, but not on March 19, 2021. On this night, a regular-season game against West rival Portland, Luka Dončić must actually have eyes in the back of his head.

With seven and a half minutes to go in the second quarter, Dončić veered right off a Dwight Powell screen, surged back to the left at a dropping Enes Kanter,[110] then stopped at the elbow to allow Powell time to complete his roll. After taking a quick glance behind him, Dončić angled his body to keep primary defender Robert Covington on his back before tip-toeing between two Blazers to the other side of the lane. He stepped slightly back and to the left, bringing his arms up to his head for the one-legged fadeaway jumper that Mavericks legend Dirk Nowitzki once made famous.

With Covington crowding him in front, guard C.J. McCollum poking around from behind, and the other Blazers gazing at him, Dončić jumped

---

110. Now legally named Enes Freedom.

March 19, 2021 — Mavericks at Trail Blazers
Trail Blazers 47, Mavericks 44 — 7:18 left in second quarter

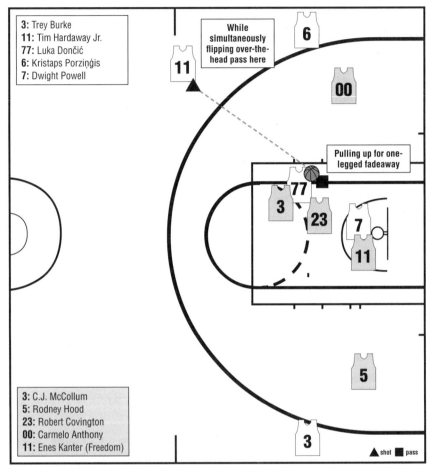

off his back foot, looked straight at the basket, and flipped the ball *directly behind him* to a wide-open Tim Hardaway Jr. on the left wing.

With every part of his body—chest, hips, knees, toes, and especially face—peering at the rim, Dončić flicked his right wrist toward the opposite perimeter. "Eyes in the back of his head!" Dallas play-by-play man Mark Followill exclaimed as Hardaway drained the three.

Eleven in-game minutes later, Dončić dribbled left off a screen and surged back to his right to attack Kanter. Covington again pursued from behind, while Dončić's screener, Maxi Kleber, held his position on the left wing instead of rolling to the hoop. Dončić picked up his dribble, took a large sideways step with his right foot to finish, and briefly lost the ball on the exchange, allowing Covington to box him underneath the right side of the hoop. Dončić regained control of the ball with a low, right-handed dribble, but now stared straight at the Blazers bench, with no passing outlets visible and his momentum stopped by the brief fumble. His only choice was to power up and finish through Kanter with Covington riding him from behind.

So Dončić arched his back, leaned forward to his left and *shoveled a right-handed pass all the way back to Kleber, spotted up for three on the left wing.*

With every part of his body—chest, hips, knees, toes, and especially face—pointed down and to the right corner, Dončić somehow extended his right arm juuuuuust far enough the other way to sneak the no-look crosscourt pass around Covington's outside shoulder into Kleber's shooting pocket. If you zoom in at the right frame, you'll see Kanter and Covington staring at Kristaps Porziņģis, the Mavericks shooter spotted up on the *right* wing. Who else could Dončić have seen? It's only after a brief pause that two Blazers swivel their heads around and notice that Dončić's actual target was on the *left* wing instead.

"How did he see that?" commentator Jeff "Skin" Wade exclaimed.

"To answer your question, 'How does he see that?'" Followill said a few seconds later, following a stoppage in play. "He's a Jedi. That's how he sees it."

"You're right," Wade responded. "He doesn't see it. He *feels* it."

How, though, did Dončić *feel* it? As far as anyone knows, he doesn't have two eyes hidden in his occipital bone, nor is he uniquely attuned to a mysterious energy field that surrounds us and binds the galaxy together.

But *something* magical must be happening, or at least something uniquely Dončić-ian. Can other NBA players drill and replicate *any* parts of that remarkable sequence? The answer, according to perceptual learning techniques, is yes—to some of it. The showmanship, precision, and/or the specific no-look pass that Dončić showcased is probably beyond the average pro.

But thanks to the combined effect of the Spaced Out Era and the loosening of illegal defense rules, every player in the league has been exposed to a never-ending court vision perceptual learning model that's repeated hundreds of thousands of similar situations. They may not know exactly where Hardaway and Kleber are standing, but they've hardwired similar spread pick-and-roll precepts through repeated film study, immersive training, and constant reinforcement via games, practices, and various on- and off-court simulations.

Put another way, every NBA player is now processing the game's bread and butter by encoding the contextual relationships between the 10 players on the floor rather than learning each's role individually. *If Help Defender A reacts this way when Ball-Handler B reaches Spot C on the court, it means Teammate D is open. If they instead react another way, it means Ball-Handler B can power to the hoop. If they react a third way, Teammate E is open.* This process reduces the vastly complicated sensations that make up the spread pick-and-roll to simpler cause-effect frameworks.

It's the same way Phillip Kellman's pilot subjects learned to translate the six dials as a unit into one of seven possibilities, just over a lifetime instead of an hour. The result is that today's NBA players are able to *see the floor,* so to speak, in ways most of their predecessors never could.

Because of that, the gap between that knowledge and actually passing the ball in high-pressure situations against equally skilled opponents is rapidly closing the more we learn about the science of spatial awareness and human decision-making. There is only one Luka Dončić, and only he can access the secret sauce that turns a great pass into a dish of "Luka Magic." But it's never been easier to provide any other player with the other core ingredients— regardless of position or role.

So let's answer the Dallas broadcasters' rhetorical question. How did Dončić see that Hardaway and Kleber were open?

In truth, we've always known that some players possess a heightened ability to sense their on-court surroundings. We've just never found a good way to describe it. The closest facsimile is "feel for the game," the long version of the term Dallas' announcers used. Passing, more so than any other skill, is an illustration of the indefinable ability to predict the future. Ergo, they *feel* the way the game *will* develop.

The other common, yet equally vague descriptor of this quality is "basketball IQ." Even without scientific research, we know intuitively that some players are encoding and processing information faster than their opponents—and often their teammates. They are *smart enough* to *anticipate* what will happen next.

And they encode information faster by, well, their heightened "feel for the game." So, now we're back where we started. When a player delivers a pass, do they feel their open teammate, or do they process that they're open?

The answer has significant ramifications. Coaches want to create an on-court environment to replicate that pass. Talent evaluators want to discover players who consistently deliver those types of passes. Players want to learn how to make that pass themselves. Fans want to know when to expect that pass again. Journalists, analysts, and bozos like me want to show you how these great players make those passes. We're all trying to figure out if great passers are feeling or calculating.

The answer, which, ironically, has been hiding in plain sight this whole time, is both.

In 1965, *The New Yorker's* Pulitzer Prize–winning journalist John McPhee wrote that then-Princeton-sensation Bill Bradley attempted "a certain number of passes that are based on nothing but theory and hope." Bradley's Princeton coaches said they called these plays "hope passes." But when McPhee told Bradley, the future New York Knicks Hall of Famer and US Senator got "sensitive," and "an edge came to his voice as he defends them."

"When I was halfway down the court, I saw a man out of the corner of my eye who had on the same color shirt I did," Bradley told McPhee while recounting an assist he generated while falling out of bounds. "A little later, when I threw the pass, I threw it to the spot where that man should have been if he had kept going and done his job. He was there. Two points."

Bradley just answered the golden question that eluded us for the next half century. What seemed like *feel for the game* to McPhee and Bradley's own coaches was in fact a calculation to Bradley himself.

He used a visual cue to spot a teammate in his peripheral vision, measured their speed at that moment, and threw the ball to the spot the teammate would reach if he continued at that same speed. There was no "hope" in Bradley's pass, other than "hope" in the laws of kinetic energy. All he did was triangulate a path between the current and likeliest future locations of his teammate. He never *saw* that player get open, just as Dončić never *saw* Hardaway and Kleber were open on the perimeter. But from their perspective, they didn't *feel* their open teammates either.

Both players *did* sense the raw materials that allowed them to make their instant calculations. Bradley saw the color of his teammates' shirt, while

Dončić mapped his teammates' spacing to similar alignments and acted based on the positioning of the most relevant help defender. Players cannot always explain how they sensed those elements because it was a subconscious process, so we say that those with elite "feel for the game" can sense them faster than others.

What, exactly, goes into those subconscious sensations? In January 2021, neuroscience graduate student and aspiring basketball analyst Evan Zaucha posted a sprawling essay on his personal website that separated "feel for the game" into three parts. Step 1: pattern recognition. Step 2: visual processing. Step 3: processing speed. The sum of these three attributes, Zaucha wrote, adds up to "feel for the game."

We can organize Bradley's explanation and Dončić's feats through these stages. First, Bradley:

> **PATTERN RECOGNITION:** "When I was halfway down the court, I saw a man out of the corner of my eye who had on the same color shirt I did."
>
> **VISUAL PROCESSING:** "The spot where the man should have been if he had kept going and done his job."
>
> **PROCESSING SPEED:** "A little later, when I threw the pass, I threw it to [that spot]. He was there. Two points."

Dončić's explanation was less detailed—"Honestly, I don't know. I just, I think, trust my teammates, depending on the spot, so it was 50 percent their job and 50 percent mine," he told reporters after the game—but I suspect his inner monologue was something of a mad lib.

> **PATTERN RECOGNITION:** *I am running pick-and-roll with* _____ [screener], *whose job is to roll hard. I see three other blue blobs out of the corner of my eye, one in the right corner, one in the left corner, and one on the* _____ [left or right] *wing.*
>
> **VISUAL PROCESSING:** *I dribble* _____ [left or right], *then cut back to my* _____ [the opposite] *to get to the middle of the floor. I can't see or feel* _____ [primary defender], *so he must be trailing behind me. I see* _____ [screener's defender] *hanging back to meet me in the lane. I swivel my head briefly to the* _____ [left or right] *and see* _____ [help defender] _____ [sinking down on me OR staying with his man] *instead of* _____ [the opposite].

PROCESSING SPEED: *I calculate that* _____ [primary defender] *won't catch up to me,* _____ [screener's defender] *will follow the roll, and* _____ [help defender] *will* _____ [try to block my shot OR stay with his man]. *I pretend to shoot, then throw to the spot* _____ [teammate spotting up] *should be if he does his job. He is there. Three points.*

In a sense, the three passes were one in the same, save a few details. Obviously, they weren't *exactly* the same, and I took some creative liberties to describe Dončić's thinking.

But the process of finding broad similarities between them is how we interpret what we see *all the time.*

There's a rectangle hanging on a set of wires in the middle of two streets with three different-colored circles stacked on top of each other. We're the ones grouping those to form the object known as a "traffic light," and *we're* the ones interpreting its meaning as "device that tells us when to cross the street." We take that processing for granted because we've been flooded with images of traffic lights since we were born. But it is there, lurking somewhere within our brains.

Cognitive psychologists have spent decades trying to decipher how and why we form those immediate, strong associations from what our eyes "see." In 1980, Anne Treisman and Garry Gelade, then professors at the University of British Columbia, proposed that we register common features such as color, movement, and shape "early, automatically, and in parallel," and only then zero in on specific individual properties.

The first stage, which they dubbed "preattentive" because it happens without us realizing it, is when our brains automatically link those elements to a mental map of similar scenes and make high-level associations that may or may not reveal a critical difference between that abstraction and what our eyes are actually seeing. If and when that superficial stage of sensory processing can't detect a relevant difference, we consciously scan for more specific clues to guide our next action. They called this the Feature Integration Theory of visual processing.

Their model argues that attention is what determines the speed and accuracy of that second stage. The more we pay attention during that conscious scan, the better we are at noticing what our brains deem most relevant in that moment. Because that attention is limited, it works best when the distinguishing feature stands out most clearly. We're more likely to notice the car darting across the intersection on a sunny day than a cloudy day, and we're more likely to spot it on a cloudy day when its headlights are on.

Though the central message of Feature Integration Theory has proven to be remarkably durable, the last four decades of research has added more specificity to its inner workings while challenging the idea that the two stages of visual processing are sequential or even separate. No study, to my knowledge, has involved current NBA players. Few measure high-level athletes of any kind.

Still, the spread-out spacing and fast-paced play of the NBA's Spaced Out Era provide a relevant environment to replicate these findings outside of the lab. Can NBA players be trained to automatically register more broad similarities within the wider on-court environment of this era? Can they then alter their attentional narrowing in the subsequent follow-up or simultaneous stage of on-court visual processing to zero in on more specific spots and throw better, more difficult passes?

In following up his 1994 pilot study, Kellman made a similar distinction when identifying the two main effects of perceptual learning. The first, "discovery," is when we learn to extract more from what we see, whether by chunking more sensory information, reorganizing it more appropriately, or better separating the relevant from the irrelevant. The second, "fluency," is when we see the same information with less cognitive effort, allowing us to act on it more quickly. You become fluent in another language when you can follow a real-time conversation, not when you first learn the words.

While discovery and fluency effects overlap, the distinction is useful, especially in a basketball context. Court vision—or feel, or basketball IQ, or whatever phrase you use—is the combination of *seeing* more and *acting* on it quicker. Dončić made those two passes against Portland by seeing broad similarities between the alignments *and* by exploiting their relevant differences sooner, more accurately, and more creatively than his peers.

That is a crucial clue to understanding how the Spaced Out Era has naturally heightened "court vision," or whatever term you use. When coaches replace slow-developing set plays with "pace and space," they nudge all of their players toward *discovering* more of the floor and processing it with adaptive *fluency* instead of rote memorization. Those lessons are reinforced by an army of player development assistant coaches through constant film study and regular on-court reinforcement.

Outside training and skill development methods increasingly target discovery and fluency effects. Most top trainers have replaced repetitive single-skill drills with ones that engage multiple sensory and/or neuromuscular tasks at the same time. One simple example is tossing players a tennis ball to catch while they dribble with one hand. More complicated examples include devices like the FITLIGHT system, composed of several discs that light up with different colors that can be arranged on a wall or even the court itself. Either tool can be altered to prioritize discovery or fluency effects while still improving both at the same time.

The sum of these methods is an NBA in which every player has a massive court vision head start on their predecessors. To the naked eye, it looks like NBA players hurl more "passes of hope." In reality, those passes result from better spatial awareness. They make quicker calculations to anticipate changes in their visual field if, as Bradley once put it, their teammates are "doing their jobs."

That two-step recognition is the essence of what is often called "basketball IQ," and the modern game engineers it on a daily basis. While few players can precisely reproduce the Luka Magic that fooled the Trail Blazers twice, they can improve their ability to discover open teammates and more fluently get them the ball.

Dončić's masterful court vision extends far enough to create alternate realities for the most relevant defenders. He is so perceptive and fluent as a passer that he can deceive opponents with a mere look or body gesture. Perhaps this is the secret sauce that defines Luka Magic.

It is on some level. But that manipulation, as it turns out, can be engineered, too.

BEFORE THERE WAS Luka Dončić or LeBron James, there was a different Los Angeles Lakers oversized point guard with a No. 2 and No. 3 on his jersey. His family called him "Earvin." We know him as "Magic."

There's never been anyone quite like Magic Johnson. Nobody, not even LeBron or that rival who played in a northeast city while hailing from a small Indiana town—single-handedly advanced the science, art, and aesthetics of passing as far as he did. You tuned into Showtime because you never knew what Magic saw or how exactly he'd get the ball there. Right hand, left hand, across his body, over the shoulder, bounce pass, chest pass, lob, wrap-around, over the head … somehow they all hit teammates in stride no matter what.

Magic's speciality was the no-look pass. He could stare directly at one teammate and instead throw to someone else he couldn't see at the precise instant he got rid of the ball. He sold the hell out of those fakes just in case a layperson missed them. My favorite is a pass he made in a 1987 game against Denver that's in every Magic highlight package. He stared left at Michael Cooper on a three-on-one fast break, mouth agape as he flashed a shocked face to the camera, while whipping a pass across his body for an A.C. Green dunk on the right. Fat Lever, the one Nuggets player back, looks like he's involuntarily playing Twister.

There's a certain aura to the no-look pass that makes it a visceral joy to see in action. You're left in awe on multiple levels: amazed that someone can pass to a teammate they can't see, delighted by the magician completing his trick.

Pulling off a no-look pass requires performing the trick before the opponent snuffs out the deception. Magic Johnson had to know Cooper and Green were running up opposite wings, as well as their relative speed and distance from the basket. He needed to make Lever think he was passing to Cooper, then pass to Green before Lever could anticipate it. All that made for an iconic highlight. A no-look pass, in other words, requires *discovery* and *fluency,* the very elements of perceptual learning.

That explains one of the modern NBA's most fascinating phenomena: it is *overflowing* with no-look passes.

Some are as showy as Magic's, with ball-handlers staring wide-eyed at a specific teammate while feeding another. Others are lookaways where ball-handlers shift their eyes in a different general direction while throwing a pass the other way. Still others are more like *never-looks* in that the ball-handler doesn't tilt their head at all while passing. Regardless, eye manipulation has become more abundant and crucial to succeeding in the Spaced Out Era. I counted 30 versions of these three no-look passing categories in a 2021 Bucks-Hawks playoff game, and that honestly felt *low.*

Stars and/or lead ball-handlers aren't the only players infected by the no-look passing bug. The more the game has spread out, the more the no-look pass has transformed from highlight to virtual necessity to beat increasingly complex pick-and-roll defensive schemes.

Help defenders are quicker, longer, and better at reading visual cues to anticipate and close off the offense's next move. But those same improvements have made them more vulnerable to no-look passes, which present fake visual cues designed to deceive. They must scramble across so much ground that even a slight look at a decoy target can freeze them in place or send them flying in the wrong direction, thereby opening up a passing lane.

That may explain *why* players may want to make more no-look passes, but how have so many mastered the art so quickly? Why did Talen Horton-Tucker's leaping, one-handed, partial-look, flying-out-of-bounds whip pass to a moving Ben McLemore seem so unremarkable? The answer begins with the spacing revolution that incubated the league's (possibly) accidental Court Vision Perceptual Learning Model.

James Worthy, the Lakers Hall of Famer and frequent recipient of Magic's dimes, once told NBA TV that his teammate "could take a snapshot of the court." He continued: "[Magic] could be in an effort to get a rebound, and when the ball hit his hands, he took a quick snapshot, and that's all he needed to take."

Worthy's use of the word "snapshot" is revealing. A snapshot, by definition, is quick and imperfect. It sacrifices specificity for width and accuracy for speed. It is meant to be a model of a scene that one generates before filling in more details. To Worthy, Magic's snapshots were simply more actionable than anyone else's.

That characterization hits on an inherent contradiction of court vision. Passing savants like Magic are said to be capable of seeing *more* of the floor, conjuring up an image of them sifting through thousands of possibilities in a split second to choose the pass none of us noticed. But Worthy's point wasn't that Johnson saw *more* with his snapshot, it's that his snapshot was *all he needed* to pick out the right pass at the right time. Magic had learned to see *less* of the floor. He only saw what he needed to see and ignored everything else.

Jeremy Wolfe, the director of the Visual Attention Lab at Harvard Medical School, developed a model that squares this contradiction. He believed that Treisman's Feature Integration Theory ignored a key element of visual processing when separating the preattentive stage from the second, more limited narrowing of attention. "It is a curious feature of these models that the parallel processes seem to have very little influence on the subsequent serial processes," he wrote in a 1989 paper in the *Journal of Experimental Psychology*.[111] He proposed that the initial preattentive phase *guides* the attentive phase, filtering out unnecessary senses and narrowing the visual sight line down to capture more specific and relevant differences. He called it, fittingly, Guided Search.

Guided Search is how Magic Johnson could determine, in a single snapshot, Green and Cooper's positions, speeds, and distances, as well as Lever's balance and how to get him to lunge at the wrong Lakers teammate. Feature Integration Theory can explain how Johnson immediately spotted a three-on-one break and then zoomed in to determine Lever's body position, but not how the former influenced the latter. In Wolfe's model, the two go hand-in-hand. The three-on-one situation guided Johnson to pay attention to Lever's positioning, which enabled him to quickly decide which teammate to feed and which to make Lever think he wanted to feed.

Wolfe has updated his model six times, most recently in a 2021 paper in the *Psychonomic Bulletin & Review*. He used the analogy of a "priority map," which is "a dynamic attentional landscape that evolves over the course of search" to show active locations that guide our next move. We see what we see because our preattentive visual system repeatedly (many, many times per second) filters a *snapshot* of reality that we can act on rather than overwhelming us with everything we *could* see in a specific scene.

That filtering system is remarkably specific and influenced by more factors than Wolfe and his colleagues initially realized.

Earlier versions of Guided Search proposed two different forms of sensory pruning: top-down and bottom-up. Top-down is controlled by the searcher's explicit and/or implicit desires. Magic Johnson wants the Lakers to score and open teammates tend to score more easily, so he is more likely to "see" open teammates than if he was a referee, scorekeeper, or neutral observer in the crowd. Bottom-up is when the properties of a specific item in the environment pop out without us actively looking for them. Johnson,

111. The paper, written while Wolfe was at Massachusetts Institute of Technology, was co-authored by Kyle R. Cave and Susan L. Franzel while they served in MIT's Department of Brain and Cognitive Sciences.

the referee, the scorekeeper, and our impartial observer in the crowd all see the difference between Lakers and Nuggets players because they're wearing different-colored uniforms.

Wolfe's 2021 update spelled out three new forms of visual filtration to make five total, but admitted that the specific number is "somewhat arbitrary" and "there are different ways to lump or split guiding forces." The more important point was that what we've already seen, even passively, has a dramatic effect on what we currently see. Vision *is learned behavior,* not inborn. The sum of Earvin Johnson's genetics, life experiences, and in-game role *taught him* how to see what others couldn't on a basketball court and pull off no-look passes like that one against Denver. It wasn't, well, magic.

If vision is learned behavior, then altering the learning environment can push more players closer to Magic's seemingly unattainable level of court vision. The Spaced Out NBA, as we've established throughout the book, has become a dramatically different learning environment over the last 15, 10, and especially five years. All of those changes have made visual search significantly easier for today's players in a variety of different ways.

The first two of Wolfe's three additions to his theory were historical priming and the possibility of reward and punishment. The first is a formal version of our earlier street-crossing analogy. We are better at spotting objects in the intersection even if we never actively look for them, which challenges Treisman's focus on direct attention. We will locate a fork faster in the kitchen than the bedroom, even though we aren't searching for a fork every time we step foot in any kitchen.

The pervasiveness of historical priming is so pronounced that it occurs even when we don't consciously view our current environment as similar to one we've experienced in the past. This is known as "contextual cueing," first coined by Yale University professors Marvin M. Chun and Yuhong Jiang in 1998.

NBA players are engaging in contextual cueing whenever they watch film. When Rudy Gobert, for example, cues up a playlist of his short rolls and repeatedly sees the corner shooter's defender sink to the middle of the lane, he's training himself to make that pass to that shooter faster, eventually reaching the point where he can do it without looking. But that film study doesn't just make Gobert better at making *that* pass in *that* alignment. It also improves his ability to deliver *any* pass to *any* open teammate on *any* spread pick-and-roll.

That is contextual cueing because he's getting better at skills he's not explicitly studying at that moment. And because the feedback loop of film study → in-game experimentation → film study → more in-game experimentation, etc. moves exponentially faster thanks to technological advances, faster pace of play, and all the other stuff discussed in this book, every player's court vision today improves by leaps and bounds through mere osmosis.

The possibility of reward or punishment also plays a role in basketball. Great passes lead to better shots, which lead to more points, which causes opportunities to get better shots and score more points on future plays.

There's evidence that the mere possibility of a reward can influence what we see even if it's not present in the scene. In basketball, those rewards include cheering fans,[112] bewildered defenders' faces, the cool thing the pass recipient might do, the prospect of the clip getting hundreds and thousands of social media impressions,[113] and myriad others beyond scoring more points.

"Selection of a category example thus appears to activate representations of prototypical category characteristics even when these are not present in the stimulus. In this way reward can guide attention to categories of stimuli even when individual examples share no visual characteristics," Clayton Hickey, Daniel Kaiser, and Marius V. Peelen, three researchers at the University of Trento in Italy, wrote in a 2015 article in the *Journal of Experimental Psychology.*

The fifth element of Wolfe's model, scene guidance, best explains why the NBA's Spaced Out Era is overflowing with no-look passes. The idea is that the type of scene your eyes see limits the possible locations of a given target.

Wolfe describes the process of searching for a sheep in a black-and-white snapshot with a grassy meadow set amid a backdrop of trees separated by a fence, with the sky looming in the distance. Your eyes automatically ignore the sky because sheep don't fly and the trees because sheep aren't known

---

112. Or booing fans for some players, i.e., Trae Young.

113. Yes, I'm theorizing that the ubiquity of social media highlights is making NBA players better at passing. No, I'm not (totally) kidding.

to hang from branches. They instead naturally gravitate to the grass even though its visual properties don't pop.

That example features two different types of scene guidance. The first is "syntactic" because it is physically impossible for sheep to fly. The second is "semantic" because sheep aren't known to be in trees, even though they *theoretically* could have climbed up there, been dropped out of a helicopter, or some other infinitesimally small possibility. Regardless, the sheep's basic properties (color, shape, size) aren't what tell the eyes to not bother searching in the sky or the trees.

There's a growing sense that "semantic" meaning plays a significant role in guiding our eyes. This seems obvious—of course what we see is influenced by how we think the world works!—but it's hard to objectively test for "meaning" in a lab setting while controlling for all other possible sensory inputs.

John M. Henderson, a psychology professor at the University of California-Davis, found a creative way around that problem. He asked several survey respondents to rate the importance of small patches of real-world pictures, plotted their responses into a "meaning map" of each image, then showed the full images to a group of students for 12 seconds each in preparation for a future test. The test was a ruse to see if the students' eye movements fixated more on his survey-created "meaning maps" or to the images' most visually salient features.

The answer was the former at every point during the 12-second interval. Even when "meaning" is subjective, the students noticed the semantic scene meanings instantly and throughout their search, even when they did not visually pop out.

Henderson's findings are significant, though his methodology has been questioned.[114] They suggest that the stuff we actually see is always influenced by what we think we should see. Our eyes already extract some form of meaning from a scene at the earliest instance of visual consciousness, and that instant processing is far more complicated than "Hey, that looks shiny!"

---

114. The main objection in the academic field is that these "meaning maps" are just a fancier way of illustrating humans' abstract physical impressions of meaning rather than truly reflecting deeper semantic meaning. Academics, right?

We see and interpret rapidly and in parallel, deriving semantic meaning and acting on it *at the same time.*

If true, it means that NBA players—especially defenders who must cover more space faster—are naturally biased to see the *perception* of how that basketball sequence *should* work at that given instant. That perception is stronger than ever thanks to the repeated exposure of film study and other training methods.

The playmaking calculation that Bill Bradley described when asked about his "passes of hope" doesn't just go one way. It's a dynamic exchange of visual signals between the passer, the defenders, and their surrounding environment. The same expertise that allows defenders' eyes to sort through eons of sensory data in an instant also makes them *more* vulnerable than ever to well-crafted illusions like … no-look passes.

No-look passes are a form of literary fiction as told by the passer. To capture their attention, the passer needs to craft a narrative that is compelling and sensible within the specific context of that game. Remember: the defender's visual processing system is already curating a narrative that makes sense to their eyes based on the situation, players involved, etc. The passer's task is to weave a tale so coherent, alluring, and believable that it fools the defender's well-informed visual narrator. No-look passes do just that.

Wolfe's Guided Search paradigm offers lots of ways they do. A no-look pass might convey a different goal than the passer intends (top down). The decoy pass' features can pop visually (bottom up)—see Magic Johnson's emotive shocked face. It can be made to look like a pass the opponent has seen before, especially recently (historical priming). It may dangle the reward of an interception or deflection (reward/punishment). But it really works when the scene itself includes more ways the fake dish might pass the semantic meaning smell test.

That is exactly what the Spaced Out Era has provided to every single NBA player. When the court is wider, more passes become possible. When more passes are possible, the illusionist can more easily use their eyes to tell coherent, compelling, and *believable* passing fiction.

It's as if the grassy meadow in Wolfe's scene with the hidden sheep covered twice as much of the picture. The semantic meaning hasn't changed. Sheep are much more likely to be in the grassy meadow than a tree, and passes are much more likely to be completed when fewer defenders are in the way.

But the viewer's eyes can't focus as narrowly to find the target. They have to consider more alternate realities, which makes them most vulnerable to illusions like no-look passes.

As if things weren't hard enough for defenders, the Spaced Out NBA's wider practical playing surface allows would-be no-look passers to see and craft no-look passes more easily. The reason is due to "crowding," a fancy term in visual search academia to describe the simple idea that it's harder to identify objects when they're close together than if they're far apart.

Crowding most profoundly affects peripheral vision. If two items within our peripheral vision are close together, their features blend into one amorphous blob. If they are spread apart, though, it's easier to discern and act on their differences. To use a simple example, I typed this sentence from the far corner of my local library while my eyes stared straight at my laptop screen. At that instant, I could tell the difference between the bookshelf to my left, the display table directly behind my laptop, and the window to my right without moving my eyes. But I couldn't determine any differences between the books on the shelf, those on the display table, or the cars in the parking lot. They appear close together in my peripheral vision, so I see them as one blob instead of several distinct objects.

The basketball court works the same way, just with more motion. Spread 10 players far out and apart from each other, and it becomes easier for each to identify the other nine's positions with just their peripheral vision. Their eyes each see more stuff within the same snapshot. To use Kellman's terminology, a less crowded visual field has improved their discovery effects.

Reducing crowding also improves their ability to act on what they see— i.e., visual fluency. Within the more constricted space of past NBA eras, players needed to pay closer attention to spot the differences between each other. Whether that manifests as converting peripheral vision to central vision or narrowing the peripheral vision itself is a subject of some debate,[115] but they needed to take more time to act either way.

Slow decision-making, of course, goes against the ethos of the Spaced Out NBA. It should come as little surprise that typical half-court NBA

---

115. There is robust evidence that perceptual learning tactics reduce the effects of crowding by reinforcing more context-specific semantic scene meaning. I'd argue this explanation describes the same phenomenon with different words.

possessions used to move much slower than they do now. The other nine players on the court were smushed closer together, which required players to take more time to survey the scene to find one pass, much less a handful of possible ones. The sport's spatial dimensions handicapped their ability to craft believable fake stories with their eyes. Only the best of the best—Bill Bradley, Magic Johnson, LeBron James, etc.—possessed enough court vision to slice through visual crowding.

Today's game has cut all that clutter out, making it a hell of a lot easier for anyone's peripheral vision to pick up distinct features. Everyone who plays today can literally see more potential no-look passes, which, in turn, makes it easier for them to craft believable fake stories with their eyes that fool defenders who themselves are forced to rely more on instant visual processing to make proper defensive rotations.

This makes the Spaced Out NBA an incredibly fertile setup for the growth of the no-look pass. It's yielding a pattern that eerily mirrors Kellman's pilot perceptual learning study. Novice NBA players like Talen Horton-Tucker gain Young LeBron–level court vision expertise in a fraction of the time, while geniuses like LeBron himself just keep improving with age.

When it comes to passing, the Spaced Out NBA is a rising tide that lifts all boats.

Chapter 10
Fake It by Taking It (A Lot)

How NBA players learn to stop worrying and let those three-pointers fly.

Utah Jazz forward Joe Ingles stood in the left corner, staring down one of the most fearsome guards in the league. Patrick Beverley, the Los Angeles Clippers' (now Minnesota Timberwolves) guard, had staked his career—his life, really—on his snarling, in-your-face defense. To say Beverley plays with emotion is like suggesting human beings live with oxygen. It is his very lifeblood.

At this moment, Beverley was doing his part to maintain the Clippers' coordinated defensive rotations, which is no easy task against this opponent. During Quin Snyder's coaching tenure from 2014 to 2022, the Jazz's offense had slowly grown into one of the modern game's platonic ideals. Their roster stacked multiple pick-and-roll operators, deadly long-range shooters, instant decision-makers, and unselfish passers around a nimble giant in Rudy Gobert with an insatiable energy for setting on-ball screens and rolling hard to the rim. That system carried the Jazz to the NBA's best record in 2021.

Now, it whirred at full power to get the Jazz one more bucket to close out the first quarter of Game 2 in their second-round playoff series against the Clippers. So far, the Clippers had matched Utah's power. They cut off Ingles' pick-and-roll with Gobert using Beverley's customary ball pressure, closed out to backup forward Georges Niang spotting up for three, contained

Niang's drive to the basket, and deterred a potential dump-off to Gobert in the lane. Niang's only option was to pass to Ingles in the corner.

Beverley knew it, too. He needed to travel a long way to reach Ingles after rotating to Gobert, but had a beeline on Niang's pass before it was even thrown. Beverley was in his trademark too-close-for-comfort spot by the time Ingles caught the ball, having rushed out like a fly attracted to light.

So what did Ingles, a 45-percent long-range marksman that every team desperately tried to stop from shooting that season, do? He did something that is hard for any modern player in that context and even more remarkable considering his own development path.

Joe Ingles shot a three-pointer. Specifically, he caught the pass with his arms extended up and out at 18 seconds and released the ball at 17.6 seconds while keeping it above his face.

At that moment, Ingles looked more like a volleyball setter than a three-point shooter. It didn't matter that Beverley's left arm extended into his face, or that Beverley's left foot planted inches from his right, or that Beverley's snarling face bore into his eyes. To Ingles, Beverley might as well have been invisible. He was going to shoot no matter what it took.

The ball hit the back rim and dropped through the hoop. Three points for Utah despite perfect defense from L.A. All because Joe Ingles, a 33-year-old undrafted free agent who only brought his slowpoke game and loopy shooting motion to Utah because the Clippers cut him in training camp seven years earlier, found enough power and accuracy to launch and make a 24-foot basket in less than half a second, without bringing the ball below his forehead.

Though the Jazz ended up losing the series in six games, this moment of triumph—which did not merit a replay—was the culmination of Ingles' years-long development from *a guy who makes threes* into a deadly NBA *shooter.*

That distinction may sound odd to you. After all, Ingles had shot 41 percent from downtown in 30 Euroleague games with Maccabi Tel Aviv in the 2013–14 season and nearly 39 percent across multiple competitions with FC Barcelona the previous season. But Ingles knew two things right away: his NBA future depended on becoming a *shooter,* and he'd never become a *shooter* if he ran out of time to get his shots off.

June 10, 2021 — Clippers at Jazz — WCSF Game 2 (UTA leads 1-0)
Jazz 27, Clippers 26 — 17.8 seconds left in first quarter

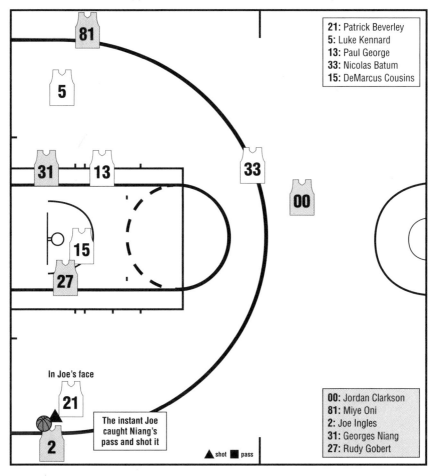

"When I first got in the NBA, I used to bring the ball down to my shins and go back up and shoot it," Ingles said during a 2021 regular-season Zoom session with Jazz media. "But I realized that a 6-foot-8 athletic guy was going to smack it into Row Zed by the time I shot."

Ingles' journey from a reticent perfectionist with the world's longest windup to an audacious gunner with a blink-and-you-miss-it release mirrors the NBA's long-range shooting evolution in the Spaced Out Era.

It's no secret that three-point shooting is the foundation of the sport today. Without long-range perimeter shooters, there is no spacing. Players take and make way more, from farther out, than ever before. If you can't hit a three-pointer, you have to be really, really, *really* good at everything else to stick in the league. Even the players who are among the best in the world at other stuff that helps a team win limit their own ceilings and create challenges for their teams if they can't (or won't) shoot. Just ask Ben Simmons or Russell Westbrook.

Everyone in the NBA, including the most old-school coaches and throwback players, holds these shooting truths to be self-evident. But what actually defines great shooting? What separates the *shooters* from the players who can make threes?

At first glance, the answer seems simple: you are a *shooter* if you make a high percentage of your threes. Polling anyone around the league, though, will reveal lots of discrepancies. Plenty of high-percentage shooters get omitted from the *shooters club*, while others who make them less often on average are granted access.

Ray Allen, the Hall of Fame guard best known for his picturesque jumper and history of daggers, said that opposing coaches used to call him "OH SHIT" because that was their reaction when he got open. Allen is a career 40-percent three-point shooter, tying him for 46th all time. Does anyone think Ray Allen is the 46th-best shooter in NBA history? You'd be mad to rank him behind Raja Bell, Otto Porter, Michael Dickerson, and Brandon Rush at least, even though they all possess higher career three-point percentages.

The current ubiquity of the long ball makes three-point percentage an even less useful proxy for long-range prowess. Once upon a time, three-point shooting was a privilege coaches (generally) bestowed to a select few who were really good at it. If you shot threes regularly, defenders assumed it was because you made them more regularly than the average pro and reacted accordingly.

Nowadays, though, everyone is allowed—nay, *encouraged*, to fire away. By everyone, we mean *everyone*. Short or tall, skinny or thick, fast or slow, shifty or direct, *everyone*. That makes it harder for defenders to delineate dangerous threats from mild ones. There are players who make a higher percentage than others, of course, but the gap between them shrinks every season. More importantly, that range no longer acts as a filter. The 33-percent shooter now behaves like the 43-percent shooter, usually at their coach's behest.

That's led to a growing incongruence between a player's three-point percentage and the way they are defended. To a fan or dispassionate analyst, it seems obvious that the 39-percent guy merits a harder closeout than the 34-percent guy. To a defender in the heat of the moment, though, they both act like shooters because each will fire when given a sliver of daylight. Even if they read the scouting report, they have fewer visual cues to zip that knowledge to the top of their already overtaxed active working memory.

This dramatic upheaval of three-point shooting norms occurred so suddenly that the NBA is still making sense of its consequences. That, of course, is the story of this book as a whole.

But one separate piece of that story is how it changed the look, feel, and craft of shooting itself. It's become more important to be a *threatening* shooter than an *accurate* one, and while the two of course overlap extensively, the latter is not a substitute for the former. Just as John Henderson's experiments revealed that our eyes draw instant meaning from sources besides visual salience, defenders rate three-point shooting threats using criteria that goes beyond their percentages. You become a *shooter* by looking and acting like a *shooter,* not simply by making more shots.

Once you do that, you gain the most precious skill of all. You gain shooting gravity. As in, the magnetic life force that pushes us to the ground so we don't float in midair.

Great NBA shooters in the Spaced Out NBA have gravity because they are magnetic forces that pull defenders toward them. Stephen Curry isn't a *shooter* because he makes lots of threes, shoots quickly, or even because he's liable to pull up from anywhere. Stephen Curry is a *shooter* because the sum of all those attributes sucks one, two, three, four, even five opponents to him to prevent him from shooting, even (and especially) when he's 35 feet from the hoop.

How do players develop shooting gravity? How can viewers measure it? Why is shooting gravity so much more meaningful now than before? The answers begin with a seismic league event that occurred four months before Ingles began his NBA career.

IF YOU'VE EVER played basketball at any level, chances are you're familiar with the phrase "triple threat." I am because legions of well-meaning youth coaches seared it into my brain. To this day, I cannot catch a basketball without hearing "*TRIPLE THREAT! TRIPLE THREAT!*" echoing in my head.

The triple threat is a specific position with a clear objective: to ready a player to shoot, pass, or dribble. When a player catches the ball, they must shift it to their hip, bend their knees, and keep their feet shoulder-width apart with their right foot slightly in front of their left. From there, they can decide if they want to rise up for a jump shot, drive to the basket, or pass to a teammate. Their defender, in theory, can't know what their opponent wants to do if they're in a triple threat. The same stance accommodates each decision, allowing the offensive player to, in theory, read the defender and *then* decide which of the three decisions makes sense in that specific moment.

The emphasis on the triple threat position came at a time when the NBA was becoming a half-court game of slow-developing set plays. Viewers increasingly saw pros holding the ball high above their heads as they waited for a teammate to get open in the next segment of the designed play. This off-balance, non-threatening position may as well have been a megaphone announcing the player's intention to pass rather than shoot or drive. It makes sense only if the goal of the sport was to follow a coach's (or point guard's) script down to the letter rather than to, you know, actually score points.

The triple threat position was an obvious remedy to that bad habit. It still allowed the player the potential to pass while also preserving the possibility of doing, well, anything else.

Abstractly, the logic behind considering the triple threat as basketball's version of the ready position in any number of other sports makes sense. *Of course* it's better for a player to be on the balls of their feet instead of upright. *Of course* it's better to offer the threat of doing three things instead of one. *Of course* it's better to leave the defense off-balance and allow yourself a chance to read their intentions before deciding your next move. For all those reasons, the triple threat is still a useful framework to help beginners learn how to play the sport.

But for all its merits, the triple threat has one gigantic flaw that makes teaching it impractical at best and counterproductive at worst, particularly in the NBA's Spaced Out Era. It is a static position, not a dynamic one.

Hesitation is built into the triple threat position's very essence. It takes time to get into it, even more time to wait to fully survey the defense out of it, and even more time to actually make a move out of it. It encourages players to stop and think before they act rather than play within the flow of movement. It was made for a game that proceeded in stages, as if the music must stop on every pass before it resumes again.

For all those reasons, the triple threat position is a decent one-on-one tactic, but an awful five-on-five approach. It misses the forest for the trees, both in theory and application. It narrows the player's focus to the man guarding them instead of promoting a wider view of the court's entire shape. It is often taught militaristically, with too many coaches emphasizing precise ball and foot placement instead of applying the general principle of a dynamic position to more practical in-game situations.

The triple threat position is especially out of step with the ethos of the modern NBA, which prioritizes spacing, fast-paced movements, mapping the entire court at once, and replacing set plays with flow. The idea of players *presenting* a triple threat is noble, but not if the cost is even a split second of hesitation.

That's why the triple threat, at least in the NBA, has been upgraded to a similar concept that is far more appropriate to today's style of play.

Like many of the modern game's principles, it spread like wildfire after Gregg Popovich and the San Antonio Spurs provided proof of concept. While its effect on the sport is felt in a number of different sectors, its most underappreciated impact is that it forced players of all shapes and sizes to learn new ways to get exponentially more long-range three-point shots off without losing their accuracy.

The summer of 2013 was brutal for Popovich and the Spurs. Game 6 of the NBA Finals against the Miami Heat. Up 3–2 in the series, up five points in this game with 28 seconds left. Champagne on ice. Fans streaming out of American Airlines Arena. All for naught thanks to a furious Heat rally punctuated by Ray Allen's legendary, game-tying three-pointer. The Spurs' loss and subsequent defeat in a close Game 7 were among the most gut-wrenching in sports history.

The pain of that defeat inspired Popovich and the Spurs to become an even better version of themselves. They were already known for their speedy ball movement, having completed their multi-year evolution from the static, post-centric style of their 1999 and 2003 titles. But Miami's blitzing pick-and-roll defensive scheme proved to be too fast even for them, if by the slimmest of margins.

So Popovich and the Spurs set out to move the ball even faster the next season. They fine-tuned a system designed to present a constant blend of activity that could keep them one step ahead of Miami's frantic defensive rotations. Popovich called it "Summertime" to evoke images of playing free and loose on a nice summer day.

"It's when you're playing. Just playing. The ball's moving, and the game's flowing," then-Spurs assistant and future Philadelphia 76ers coach Brett Brown told ESPN in 2015. "You make a decision to shoot it, pass it, drive it."

This, of course, is how every basketball team at every level wants to play. The moment when the whole becomes more than the sum of its parts is basketball nirvana. But coaches and players soon realize they can't simply speak it into existence. It's a forever-aspirational, always-elusive sort of flow state, a term psychologist Mihály Csíkszentmihályi coined to describe the feeling of being "so involved in an activity that nothing else seems to matter."

Popovich and the Spurs found a way to engineer that hoops flow state. And they did it with a single phrase, relentlessly repeated from the first days of training camp until the last seconds of their five-game annihilation of the Heat in the subsequent Finals.

Point Five!

As in Zero Point Five. As in the maximum number of seconds—or fractions of a second as it were—that each player gets to make a pass, shoot, or drive decision.

That's way less time than it takes to reposition the ball onto your hip and line your feet up to even get into a triple threat position! But the Spurs realized that modern NBA defenses, particularly Miami's, could use that time to paralyze players into indecision at best and turnovers at worst. The only way to succeed was to stay one step ahead of them, and the only way to stay one step ahead of them was to never stop to think.

"Point Five" offered a practical way to make that goal tangible for players. Stressing the need to make instant decisions works fine … until players make the wrong ones. Soon, the fear of failure takes over. Coaches and players inadvertently reinforce this when they lament their inability to take care of the ball. Without a set target for "instant decisions," players often overcorrect to make slower, more careful decisions that are less likely to result in mistakes, but kill the offense's flow. The phrase "Point Five," on the other hand, allowed Spurs players to achieve the spirit of their objectives without bogging down in procedure or worrying about absolutes.

That's especially critical because 0.5 seconds doesn't leave much, if any, time to think. The Spurs players had to (continue to) learn how to process information in a short amount of time while internalizing their new(ish) reality that an instant good decision is better than a delayed perfect one. The time limit keeps the chain moving, which ends up easing each additional players' quick decision-making accuracy as the sequence continues.

When Miami's pressure briefly resurfaced in the first two games of the Finals rematch,[116] Popovich took center Tiago Splitter out of the starting lineup, replacing him with Boris Diaw, the stocky forward whose idiosyncratic, unselfish game made him an avatar for Point Five basketball. The Spurs ran the Heat through a never-ending blender of ball and player movement in the next three games, winning the title easily while making the vaunted Miami blitzing pick-and-roll defense suddenly appear to move in slow motion.

The rest of the league watched in amazement, determined to replicate the Spurs' beauty on their teams. That next season, Steve Kerr, Stephen Curry, and the rest of the Golden State Warriors began deploying their turbocharged, spread-out version of San Antonio's "Summertime" to overwhelm the league. The triple threat was dead. The Point Five Mentality was now king.

It's important to note that Point Five is not a system, position, set play, or even style of play. It is a mindset for players to live by, measured by an actual number to reinforce the larger goal of making quick, dynamic, and collaborative decisions on the court. It is a modern application of the triple threat's purpose to prepare players to act and disguise their intentions from the defense.

Though coaches use different phrases to describe the effect a Point Five Mentality creates, the specific terminology often helps players internalize it. When Monty Williams, a Popovich disciple, took over as Phoenix Suns coach in 2019, he and general manager James Jones used the phrase

---

116. Miami won Game 2 and nearly took Game 1 as well, but the Spurs survived when severe cramping relegated LeBron James to the bench for key fourth-quarter minutes. The Spurs' air condition system broke during the game, causing sweltering temperatures inside the AT&T Center. James had a history of cramping up at the end of tight playoff games. It doesn't take much to connect the two into a coherent conspiracy theory.

constantly when describing how they wanted the Suns to play. Many writers took the message to heart, penning well-reported, detailed stories about the Suns' new "0.5 offense."

But Williams and the Suns weren't constructing a new system so much as rebranding an old one. Previous coach Igor Kokoškov also stressed a fast-moving system, except he referred to it as "The Blender" in a nod to Snyder, his former boss with the Jazz and one of his closest friends in the profession.

For whatever reason, the Suns players didn't execute "The Blender" well in Kokoškov's one season in charge, yet took to Williams' Point Five language despite it reflecting the same goal. Phoenix improved in Williams' first season, emerged as an unlikely NBA Finals team in his second, and ran away with the NBA's best regular-season record in 2021–22 before the Dallas Mavericks upset them in the second round of the playoffs. It helped that Williams had better players, of course, especially once Chris Paul arrived in Williams' second season. But the consistency and tangibility of "Point Five Mentality" played an underrated role in the Suns' re-emergence.

It's no coincidence that the rise of the Point Five Mentality coincided with the NBA's three-point revolution. It's a lot easier to make quick decisions and keep it moving when the game is playing on a larger practical playing surface. As with "pace and space," the threat of long-range shooting and the player mindset to string together multiple split-second pass/shoot/drive decisions go hand in hand. We could go around in circles debating which is the chicken and which is the egg, but they both caused each other.

Still, there is one element that has to bind the two trends together. If teams are using the Point Five Mentality to stress instant pass/shoot/drive decisions, and if those decisions are easier to make when offensive players space out on the floor, then teams must also give the defense reason to stretch out that far. The only way to do that is to shoot a lot from there, especially since each make is worth an extra point.

To stress instant decision-making as a guiding principle is to require players take and make longer shots while spending less time powering up to release them. Joe Ingles' long, loopy three-point motion isn't going to work anymore, even if that's the precise method he's used to generate the power and balance to make those shots in the past.

How does a player continue to make those shots while also getting more of them off quicker? The answer is tied directly to the rise of the Point Five Mentality. And, as it turns out, it is as much mechanical as mental.

HERE'S A QUESTION for you. What's the correct way to shoot a basketball?

Think of all the people in your basketball life who tried to help you find the answer. Think of all those instructional videos from shooting gurus. Think of all their teaching points: keep your elbow in, bend your knees, square up to the rim, spread your feet shoulder length apart, reach up with your follow through, keep your off hand on the side of the ball, let it rest somewhere between your palm and your fingertips, and all the others I'm forgetting.

What if they were all wrong?

Don't worry, they're not all "wrong" in a literal sense. All of those elements can be important to a good jump shot. Some are more important than others. But none of them get you all that close to answering the golden question posed above.

Why? Because there is no single correct way to shoot a basketball.

More to the point: there is no universal collection of elements that adds up to a perfect jumper. Chasing that elusive, universal platonic ideal will cause you to focus too narrowly on the sum of a jumper's parts instead of how each individual shooter puts them together.

This becomes especially clear in a fast-moving, spread-out game like today's NBA. To be a great NBA shooter in 2022 is to realize that function, particularly at full speed, is far more important than form.

That is the lesson Joe Ingles and so many other NBA players needed to learn to get many more three-point shots off without suffering a corresponding dip in accuracy. In fact, many players, including Ingles, have *improved* their three-point percentage with more volume. In a sense, this is another victory for perceptual learning. And it's past time for the new era of shooting gurus to realize that, too.

The NBA's three-point revolution happened so naturally that we take for granted that shots from farther away from the hoop are supposed to be harder to make. That assumption is why the line exists in the first place. The extra point is the shooter's reward for overcoming the distance difficulty.

If we're being pedantic, distance is one of many factors that make some shots harder than others. There's also the player shooting, the horizontal location on the court, the defender's positioning, the pass or dribble leading into the shot, myriad other factors, and, if we're honest, a ton of luck.[117] Still, distance is the best proxy we have. What's the alternative? Go back to every field goal counting for two points? Place sensors under the court to measure each shot distance to the decimal, so one is worth 2.1346 points and another is worth 2.9865? Have an independent judge rate the difficulty of each shot attempt?[118]

But still, longer shots are harder, right?

Well, in the 2020–21 season, the league shot 41.1 percent on five- and six-footers … and 37.8 percent on 24- and 25-footers. Players made 24-footers only slightly less often than six-footers, *notwithstanding the extra point they're worth.*

All things being equal, a six-foot shot should be much easier to make than a 24-foot shot. Who tells their six-year-old to master threes before six-footers? Yet today's NBA players have made all other things so unequal that the two shots may as well be worth a similar number of points based on this data.

The way they've done that explains why you should look back at your shooting instruction with renewed skepticism. It's not that those gurus were wrong. It's more that they were optimizing your shot for a game that did not emphasize the three-point shot like the Spaced Out NBA has. Worrying about form over function makes sense if one assumes a strong correlation between shot distance and shot difficulty. As long as the game viewed threes and two-point jumpers relatively equally, as it had throughout most of its history, it was better to be super accurate from closer in than equally accurate from all ranges. Generating *power* with your shot motion was less important than lining the elbow, feet, et al. properly.

That philosophy got flipped on its head once 24-foot shots suddenly became more important to master than six-foot shots. All those well-meaning

---

117. Or, as I prefer, "factors that are beyond humanity's current ability to understand." But I'm being a pedant in a paragraph that's already pedantic.

118. Eddie Gottlieb, the legendary Philadelphia Warriors coach and three-point skeptic, said as much in 1967, "If it is worth three points to make a standard long jump shot, well then, a twisting, driving hook, going full speed to take the pass, cutting between two big defenders—why, that must be worth six points," he told *Sports Illustrated*'s Frank Deford.

coaches now have it backwards. Great modern NBA shooters have to make lots of threes, and long ones in particular. They need to power up to reach that distance, and that power comes from the shooter's upward trajectory. To carefully line the many parts of a shot up is to detract from the power of the motion itself.

That's what today's NBA players spend the most time tinkering. They don't try to build the perfect jumper. They perfect *their* jumper by fine-tuning its energy transfer, removing any unnecessary friction to make sure it is efficient, repeatable, and fluid enough to apply to any number of in-game situations. Looseness is their platonic ideal. By worrying about function over form, players like Ingles learn how to get more shots off faster, from farther away, while moving more. They're better equipped to overcome an inaccurate pass and/or an aggressive closeout like Patrick Beverley's.

Maintaining an effective, modern NBA jump shot is not defined by aggregating key components. It's more like fine-tuning an engine, in that optimizing its overall performance is the only goal that matters. You can drive with a dent in your car. You can even survive for a while with a small puncture in your tire. But everything breaks down if there's any issue with your engine.

That makes the Point Five Mentality the modern jump shot's best friend. Its fast-moving principles align with this reimagined view of shooting mechanics. Ever notice how you perform a task better and faster once you stop overthinking it? The same principle applies double here. There's (almost) no way to overthink in half a second.

The Point Five Mentality requires players to move constantly and prioritize instant shoot/pass/drive decisions over optimal ones. Since speed is the goal, shooters have less time to line up their shot and maintain perfect form. That forces them to streamline their upward motion, removing potential sources of friction that could slow it down or throw it off balance. Not only do they develop quicker shot releases, but they also generate more power to get the ball to the rim from 24+ feet away. Each skill leads to quicker decisions. This is how long-range shooting and the Point-Five Mentality co-exist in a virtuous cycle that raises the bar on both with every passing NBA season.

Their union also helps us begin to solve one of the sport's most enduring mysteries. Just what is confidence, exactly, and why must elite NBA shooters possess an abundance of it?

IS JOE INGLES a confident basketball player? I suspect you'd say yes with a large degree of, well, confidence.

You'd have plenty of supporting evidence, even beyond the reality that all NBA players are exceedingly confident relative to the general population. Ingles has called himself the best shooter in the league, most notably before the 2018–19 season. He's a surprisingly (to some at least) loud trash talker who happily exchanges verbal barbs with everyone from star players to courtside fans. (His signature move is to blow kisses to the crowd after nailing dagger three-pointers.) He jokes openly about his, uh, unassuming look, displaying the level of self-confidence needed to poke fun at himself.

Yet as any psychologist would tell you, the line between self-belief and insecurity is razor thin. Bravado is the NBA player's trusted companion as much for its ability to mask self-doubt than remove it entirely. Many of the most outwardly brash players act that way to drown out the critical voice in their own head, placing trust in the immortal plan of faking it until they make it. Stephen Curry doesn't strut after his own made threes for kicks and giggles.

In that sense, the basketball court is an exaggerated representation of reality. Mistakes can be tolerated. Selfishness is often forgiven. But reluctance *always* stands out, both in your pickup game and in Game 7 of the NBA Finals.

Consider the Ben Simmons saga, which seemingly ended with a February 2022 trade to the Brooklyn Nets before tacking on a few new chapters to close the season. The former No. 1 pick, citing mental health difficulties, refused to play for Philadelphia despite having four years left on his maximum contract. Reluctance is what blew that saga open; specifically, Simmons' reluctance to take a wide-open layup at a crucial point in Game 7 of the 76ers' 2021 second-round upset loss to the Atlanta Hawks.

Reluctance *really* stands out now that the game is built so thoroughly around three-point shooting. The Suns of Mike D'Antoni and Steve Nash starred in a league that more viscerally feared the long-range shots' risks than its potential rewards. These days, that calculation has tipped in the complete opposite direction. To get there, players, with the help of their coaches, also needed to flip their mindset a full 180 degrees. They needed to learn to be okay—like, *really* be okay—with missing threes.

That's wayyyyy harder than it sounds for perfectionists like NBA players. It's not easy for them to nurture a mindset that they'll make any shot at any time when they inevitably miss. It's even harder to maintain that line of thought to freely attempt long, often-contested shots they make anywhere from three-to-five times out of 10 on average. Projecting supreme confidence is the only way for a player to drown out the guilt and self-doubt of falling short. Makes must be treasured. Misses must be forgotten.

Joe Ingles had that supreme confidence in 2021, but it's not natural, didn't come easily, and may go away as he recovers from a torn ACL suffered midway through the 2021–22 season. By his own admission, he tried too hard to fit in and get other players shots in his first few NBA seasons. He took a long time to consider *himself* a shooter. "I still don't, really," he told UtahJazz.com in December 2018, two months after declaring himself the game's best long-range bomber.

For years, Snyder begged him to take more threes. He even banned Ingles from slumping his shoulders, a habit Ingles possessed when he entered the NBA. "He had to be willing to miss," Snyder told ESPN in 2021. "That was the biggest thing for him to overcome. I'd rather him go 0-for-10 than 1-for-2."

Ingles repeatedly praised Snyder and his staff for nurturing the confidence he didn't naturally possess. "I've never been with a coach that can motivate you and make you feel so confident," Ingles told *GQ* before the 2021 playoffs, noting qualities that other coaches at other times might see as contradictions.

Could any other coach at any other time have coaxed Ingles to more than double his three-point attempts per game between his second and fourth NBA seasons? That we're even asking the question speaks volumes about Ingles' (lack of) natural confidence relative to his peer set. No coach, least of all Snyder, has to tell Ingles' teammate Jordan Clarkson to shoot more confidently.

But however Ingles got there, he learned to shoot three-pointers, to quote legendary broadcaster Marv Albert, with *no hesitation*. That phrase is key to understanding how the magic elixir of self-confidence blends with the new-age mindset of shooting to form an inseparable, co-dependent relationship that continues to vault Ingles and countless other modern players to higher levels of long range shooting skill.

Until this era, jump shooting followed the same underlying logic as many of life's more mundane tasks: taking our time is supposed to improve our actions. We can't take forever on everything, of course, so we weigh the trade-offs between the two with each decision. We take much less time choosing a gum flavor than picking out an engagement ring. Or we should, at least. Imagine telling your future spouse you spent just five seconds on such a monumental decision.

Jump shooting is anchored by the same perception. The main value of an open shot is the time it provides the shooter to line it up properly. Rushing is bad. Patience is good. Accuracy requires precision, and it's easier, in theory, to be more precise when you have more time.

That underlying theory is correct *when all other things are equal.* Shooters make open shots more often than contested shots and usually post better percentages on free throws than threes, two-point jumpers, or even layups. There is a right way to shoot *in theory.* Scientists use trigonometry to determine optimal launch angles, which new-age products like shooting sleeves and sensor trackers embed into their products. They add quantitative beef to methods like BEEF.[119]

But this isn't theory. And all things are never close to equal in live basketball games. Time is not a luxury any shooter has unless they're on the free-throw line. No two shots are the same. No two *shooters* are the same, and not just because their height differences change their optimal launch angles. A 24-foot practice shot in a closed gym is completely different from the same 24-foot three-pointer in a high-leverage moment of a big game with 20,000 screaming fans and millions watching on TV.

In that respect, in-game shooting is more like buying gum than picking out the right engagement ring. Perfect, as defined by taking one's time to get their form exactly right, has always been the enemy of good—i.e., getting the shot off at all. Yet until recently, shooting instruction largely operated on the opposite paradigm, emphasizing precision and accuracy before functionality.

That has started to change over the past decade. More instructors are incorporating the underlying data to fine-tune individual shooting motions instead of reconstructing them to fit a platonic ideal. That's function over

---

119. BEEF, which stands for Balance, Eyes, Elbow, and Follow-Through, is a popular acronym that shooting instructors have used for decades.

form. Perhaps the modern era is less a shooting golden age and more an escape from a decades-long dark age?

"How to make people more proficient shooters is not necessarily to get everyone to shoot the same way but to get everyone to optimize their shooting form based on their flexibility, range of motion, muscle structure," Scooter Barry, the creator of the SOLID shooting sleeve and the son of NBA legend Rick Barry, told *Sports Illustrated* in 2017.

Yet the NBA's Spaced Out Era also went one step further to shatter the speed/accuracy trade-off paradigm in the first place. In this modern style, faster shot motions don't degrade accuracy. They enhance it. That's why players of all sizes still make lots of in-game three-pointers against defenses who are trying desperately to stop those shots.

Joe Ingles offers a case study. He shot 37 percent on 2.5 threes per game in his first two seasons in Utah while largely using his old, slow shot motion. Not bad, but certainly not worthy of a *shooter*. His percentage and volume placed him squarely in the "willing to shoot but not a terribly dangerous threat" category.

He was also quite streaky. Ingles shot dreadfully over the first two months of his rookie year before picking it up as the season progressed. His sophomore season was a roller coaster: 50 percent in November, 38 percent in December, 32 percent in January, 19 percent in February, then 45 percent down the stretch. More to the point, he passed up countless three-pointers because his motion took too long. To quote ~~Wayne Gretzky~~ Michael Scott, "You miss 100 percent of the shots you don't take."

Ingles' primary motivation for speeding up his motion was to get more threes off. But his slow release was also a reflection of several biomechanical imbalances that the faster NBA made worse. He was bending his knees too much, which caused him to bring the ball too far below his waist to a crouching position. Exploding up from there required more trunk strength than he possessed at the time, so he often arched his back to compensate. The only way to regain his balance was to hold the ball in place above his head before flinging it toward the rim, which took time. His body often landed at an acute angle, causing shots to miss left and right, and the arc he generated was inconsistent.

These flaws don't show up as often when Ingles had time to gather himself and go through the long bodily process he had naturally developed, but they lept to the forefront when he was under duress. Over the course of his first two years, Ingles shot 42 percent on threes that were considered wide-open—which NBA.com defines as no defender within six feet of him—and 30 percent on all other triples. His percentage and volume increased dramatically in his third NBA season, when he shot 45 percent on 5.5 threes a game. But that open versus non-open discrepancy returned in the playoffs. Ingles shot 11-of-26 on wide open threes and 4-of-14 on all others. The "14" is as noteworthy as the "4" because it shows Ingles passed up many semi-contested threes entirely.

By then, Ingles was working to solve the root of the problem. He was bending his knees too much, following the typical emphasis of most shooting instruction. That didn't matter when he was wide open, but in all other situations, he rushed the low knee bend, which in turn exacerbated biomechanical imbalances and caused too much friction in his upward motion.

His solution to the problem was bold. He experimented with removing his jump shot's dip.

The dip describes when players naturally drop the ball down in their shooting motion before re-raising on its release. It's easy to miss in real time, but you'll begin seeing it once you know to look. Dipping is hard to avoid. When you bend your knees to jump, your arms naturally come down, too. That's why rebounders are taught to keep the ball high instead of bringing it down. If you don't actively try to keep the ball above your shoulders, it will drop down when you crouch to explode back up.

Ingles applied that same principle to minimize his low knee bend on his jump shots. He trained himself to bring the ball straight up to his head instead, releasing it before his arms had a chance to drop. The goal wasn't to remove the dip on every in-game three-point attempt, or even on most of them. It was to use that teaching point as a way to emphasize bending his knees less and thus generating a faster, smoother shooting motion.

After multiple years and millions of jump shots, Ingles felt comfortable trying a no-dip three-pointer in an NBA game. After all, you'll never know when you might need that trick. That 2021 shot against the Clippers is the most prominent example of the fruits of that labor, but there have been plenty of others.

The more important development is that Ingles can now vary his dip distance and speed to account for defensive pressure, the type of pass, and his own movement. If he only has time to dip to his chest, for example, it won't unbalance the other elements of his jumper.

Just because that method worked for Ingles' shot doesn't mean everyone else should try it, too. It'd usually be counterproductive, in fact, as it's more common to see players who don't bend their knees *enough*. Teaching them to forgo a dip would chop their motion up even more, causing them to develop even worse biomechanical habits to generate the upward energy to reach the rim from long range. But Ingles' jumper is unique, and unique jump shots require personalized solutions.

That requires instructors to reimagine how they train shooters. Proper form adapts to the individual, not the other way around. Instead, many shooting instructors draw battle lines in a frivolous "dip or no dip" debate. Some say dipping must be trained to aid the jump shot's natural upward trajectory. Others fear dipping actually slows down that motion and causes players to have too low a release point.

But adopting an ironclad position on the dip obscures its purpose to a modern jump shot. It's there to *help* streamline the body's upward energy transfer, not necessarily to *be* the body's upward energy transfer on every single type of three. To reach the three-point volume the Spaced Out NBA requires, players need to develop multiple ways to create the frictionless upward energy that gives their shots power and accuracy. That means adopting as many different dip speeds and positions as possible.

That could mean training a player to fine-tune or even elongate their dip. R.J. Barrett is a young New York Knicks' left-handed wing with a similar height and weight profile to Ingles. As a rookie in 2019–20, Barrett shot just 32 percent from three-point range. During the ensuing (long) offseason,[120] Barrett, with the help of trainer Drew Hanlen, decided to bring his elbow farther out rather than actively tuck it in, as the classic BEEF method proposes.

The move deepened Barrett's dip. Since his left arm was looser, he could use his natural momentum to bring the ball farther down before launching it back up into shooting position. Barrett and Hanlen deemed it necessary because tucking the elbow in made Barrett's shot too stiff and flat. Given his

---

120. The Knicks were not good enough to qualify for the bubble, so their 2019–20 season ended in mid-March. The 2020–21 season began for every team in late December.

body's long, lean shape, Barrett's upward energy transfer *needed* the kick start of a loose elbow and long dip to be more fluid. He improved to 40 percent from downtown on higher volume in his second season.

The common denominator between Barrett and Ingles is that they both perfected *their* jump shot rather than incorporating elements from others'. Both were aiming to shoot quicker and with less friction. They just used opposite methods to get there.

And what happens when you successfully prioritize what works *for you* instead of someone else? You build self-belief. Self-love. Trust. *Confidence.* Yes, confidence most of all.[121] And thus the modern game's virtuous shooting cycle is complete.

Shooting confidence isn't an intangible buzzword or magical property that cannot be easily defined. Sure, it can be either the cause or effect of a good jump shot. Joe Ingles is more confident because he's become a great shooter, and he also became a great shooter by growing his self-confidence. It was the chicken and the egg behind his improvement.

But the distinction is meaningless. By emphasizing the biomechanics of a jump shot's motion rather than the mechanics of its form, the Spaced Out NBA dramatically strengthened the link between the mental mindset of confidence and the tangible, detail-oriented, repetitive process of improving a jump shot. Players and coaches like to say that confidence means they trust the value of their own work over the whims of their most recent attempts. Now's the first time in NBA history that their process actually embodies that cliché. That's how guys who make threes become *shooters.*

And as Ingles and others are discovering, that reputational shift is worth far more than any three-point percentage jump.

MARCUS SMART IS a winner. His high school teams won 115 games and lost six in his three seasons. Oklahoma State won 45 percent of its games the year before Smart arrived and 64 percent when he played during his two college seasons.[122] The Boston Celtics went 25–57 the year before drafting him and have won 60 percent of their regular-season games and 10 playoff series

---

121. That's a reference to a Yoda line from Star Wars' *The Last Jedi*, which is a great movie, and I will debate anyone who says otherwise.

122. He was suspended for three games in his second year after shoving a Texas Tech fan in the closing seconds of a 65–61 loss. Oklahoma State lost all three games he missed.

since. He's received two lucrative contract extensions, fended off legions of trade rumors, and became a Boston fan favorite.

The tricky part is defining exactly *how* he's a winner. When he entered the NBA Draft in 2014, scouts lauded his "intangibles," while wondering if he had a position. That message hasn't changed much, even though the Celtics' system and core has been remarkably stable for a modern NBA franchise during his career. We just know he's a winner that makes Winning Plays™.

What does Smart actually do, then? He's known as a fierce defender with a knack for making clutch plays, which are nice qualities that help teams win. But he's also a career 32-percent three-point shooter who's only recently been deployed as a point guard and has never been an efficient primary scorer. Yet he doesn't seem to realize it. He launches nearly five threes a game on average, a rate that held steady over his first five years before increasing in the next two and dropping back slightly in 2021–22. Even Celtics fans who love his moxie not-so-silently wish he'd dial it back.

Based on three-point percentage, Marcus Smart is the complete opposite of a *shooter*. Since Smart's rookie season in 2014–15, 42 players have played at least 500 minutes in a Celtics uniform (as of 2021). Smart is seventh among them in three-point attempts per game and 26th in three-point percentage. His best shooting season (2018–19, when he made 36.4 percent from downtown) was good enough to place fifth on his own team and in a tie for 68th among shooters who qualified for the minutes leaderboard. Based on those odds, a Celtics possession that ends in a Marcus Smart three is a win for the defense. Year after year, game after game, Marcus Smart keeps handing opponents more of those wins than he should.

And yet, the Celtics usually win, further cementing Smart's reputation as a winner. It seems bad to shoot lots of three-pointers when it's proven, over a long period of time, that you're bad at making three-pointers? That must mean the Celtics are winning in spite of Smart rather than because of him, thereby invalidating his status as a winner. At the very least, he must be hurting their offense. Right?

Wrong. Dig deeper, and you find that quite the opposite is happening.

The reason has everything to do with the modern NBA's new reality. Aggression, as it turns out, has ancillary benefits that add up to something much more.

In this case, that is Boston's offense being consistently better with Smart on the court firing errant threes than with his poor shot selection on the bench. Over the course of his career, the Celtics score more points per 100 possessions with Smart on the court (110.9 on vs. 109.65 when he's on the bench and 109.2 when he doesn't suit up at all) and shoot better collectively (55.4%/55.1%/54.94% true shooting). Their three-point percentage is slightly worse (35.5%/36.3%/37%), largely due to Smart's own shooting, but they get more threes up as a team, generate a higher percentage of their shots at the rim (30.7%/30.5%/29.4%), and make more of those (62.2%/61.6%/61.5%).[123] The effect is consistent, too: Boston's offense has been better with Smart on the floor than on the bench in five of his seven NBA seasons.[124] For a guy known for defense, hustle, and long-range chucking, Smart is oddly important to the Celtics' *offensive* success.

This seemingly incongruent Smart Effect has grown in recent years, when you'd think his errant shooting reputation was sealed. During the 2020–21 season, a disappointing one for both team and player, the Celtics scored 116.1 points per 100 possessions with Smart in the game, 112.8 with him on the bench, and 114.2 in the 24 games he missed entirely. They made 38.5 percent of their threes with Smart in, launched 70.3 percent of their shots from the rim or the three-point line, and posted a true shooting percentage of 58.5—all significantly higher marks than when he wasn't in the game. Smart, meanwhile, made just 33 percent of his six three-point attempts per game, which somehow raised his career mark.

While Smart is a special case, his ability to *act* like a shooter despite not consistently doing the thing shooters are supposed to do is not unique. In 2021, Caitlin Cooper, writing for the ESPN-owned stats website FiveThirtyEight, discovered a similar effect with Eric Gordon, whose three-point percentage had tumbled from elite (44.8 percent with the New Orleans Pelicans in 2014–15) to respectable (36.4 percent over his first three years with the Houston Rockets) to ghastly (31.7 percent with a contending Rockets team in 2019–20, 32.9 percent with a dreadful Rockets team in 2020–21).

---

123. All stats are via the indispensable pbpstats.com and as of the end of the 2020–21 season.

124. It will likely be six of eight by the time you read this, but I turned this book in midway through the 2021–22 season.

But Gordon's three-point decline did not convince opponents to stop guarding him. The opposite, in fact: not only did they contest *more* of his three-point attempts in 2019–20 and 2020–21, but his mere presence on the floor in that second season dramatically improved the Rockets' ability to generate shots at the rim. The worse he shot, the *more* opponents guarded him, and thus the more space his teammates had to drive.

In theory, Gordon and Smart defy logic. In practice, they both embody an important basketball lesson that the three-point-happy Spaced Out NBA naturally thrusts in our faces: basketball moves fast. Too fast, in real time, for defenders to easily access each opponent's precise three-point percentage.

They must use superficial cues to trigger their memory of the scouting reports, sacrificing accuracy for quick decision-making. The more "real time" speeds up, the more work these superficial characteristics are forced to do, even (and especially) if the players are more informed. In plainer terms: the skill Marcus Smart and Eric Gordon possess to look like shooters causes defenders to treat them like shooters even when their three-point percentages say otherwise.

A statistician might conclude that this analysis fixates too much on two outliers. Smart and Gordon are exceptions to the larger rule that three-point percentage is an effective way to illustrate a player's shooting threat level.

That framing makes sense in a Statistics 101 textbook, but not a 2022 NBA game that hands every player a neon-green light instead of just a select few. In 2009–10, 68 players averaged at least four three-point attempts per 36 minutes—one every nine minutes they played. In 2019–20, 175 reached that threshold, a more than two-and-a-half times increase over the span of a decade.[125] The league averaged the same percentage of made threes both years (35.5 percent in 2009–10, 35.8 percent in 2019–20) but on way more attempts a decade later.

The below-average to average shooters don't leave the high-volume club anymore. In 2009–10, only 18 players who took at least four threes per 36 minutes converted below the league average from downtown. In 2019–20, by comparison, there were 75 such players, a more than fourfold increase.

---

125. Both figures only consider players who qualified for the minutes per game leaderboard that season, so they don't include minor-league call-ups and excessively injured players. Adding those folks in only widens the gap.

What is the range of acceptable—not great, *acceptable*—long-range shooting accuracy? Suppose we set one end at 33 percent (mathematically the equivalent of making half your two-pointers) and the other end at 40 percent, since anyone over that threshold is colloquially considered a "knockdown shooter." Imagine using that range to provide defenders a simple closeout guide. Anyone below 33 percent doesn't merit one at all, anyone above 40 percent merits a hard one, and use your best judgment on everyone else.

The pervasiveness of the three-point shot causes problems right off the bat. While 33 percent seems way worse than 40 percent, the difference between the two is the equivalent of less than one more make on every 10 shots. If two players take one three-pointer in each of the season's 82 games, the 40-percent shooter will make five more over the course of the season than the 33-percent shooter. That's it.

The 33-percent shooter should, in theory, attempt fewer threes, but they don't anymore. The player who just missed the 33-percent threshold in 2019–20 (Chicago guard Garrett Temple) took eight threes per 36 minutes. The guy who just eclipsed the 40-percent edge (Utah forward Georges Niang) attempted 8.8 threes per 36 minutes. They both acted like 40-percent three-point shooters even though only one actually was that season.

And the "use your best judgment" category? It's swelled beyond the point for it to be practically useful. In 2009–10, 49 players took at least one three every nine minutes and landed somewhere between 33 and 40 percent. Ten years later, 130 players did. That's more than 40 percent of the league![126] And it doesn't include Smart, Temple, or Gordon, all of whom fell beneath that 33-percent threshold that season.

The last two words of the previous two paragraphs add yet another confounding variable to this murky picture. Players' three-point percentages fluctuate year over year for reasons that are hard to attribute to anything but randomness. Many players slide from one edge of our 33–40 percent range to the other. Temple, for example, has shot as well as 39.2 percent and as poorly as the aforementioned 32.9 percent over the past six seasons. Should defenses guard him like the 39-percent version, the 33-percent version, or somewhere in between? Is there even a material difference between the three?

---

126. 41.1 percent, to be exact. Minimum 650 minutes that season.

At least Temple is somewhat consistent. Tons of players regularly move in and out of 33–40 percent entirely. Usually, these sorts of swings are caused by more than just dumb luck. Sometimes, players suffer lower-body injuries that permanently make them worse three-point shooters. Sometimes, their tireless work permanently makes them better three-point shooters. But that just adds more conflicting information for defenders to sift through in real time. Once players enter the green light three-point club, they never—okay, rarely—leave. The guy who makes a dramatic jump feels emboldened to shoot more threes, while the guy who slid will keep shooting to regain his previous touch.

Which of those two types of players merits more attention? Even a question that seems to have an obvious answer can be complicated. For example, Gordon shot more threes per game and minute during his two sub-32-percent years than in his 44-percent season in New Orleans. By contrast, New York Knicks forward Julius Randle's dramatic three-point percentage improvement from less than 28 percent in 2019–20 to more than 41 percent in 2020–21 was accompanied by an increase in volume (four attempts per 36 minutes to 5.3). Is Randle's 41-percent season more "real" than Gordon's 44-percent campaign because it happened more recently? That's difficult for defenders to answer when both players behave like the most accurate versions of themselves.

So how are defenders supposed to delineate between threats? Some argue that they can't, at least in the regular season.[127] Analysts inside and outside the league have found little consistency in teamwide three-point percentage allowed year over year, even when those franchises maintain similar personnel and/or the same coach. They'd say the best way to defend the three-point line is to not allow three-point attempts in the first place. That's an oversimplification on an individual level, but it's much less of one than "close out entirely based on their three-point percentage."

There is some value in measuring a player's percentage on more specific subcategories of three-pointers. Most players shoot better on corner threes, some (*cough* P.J. Tucker) significantly so. Some are better from one side of

---

127. The playoffs, they argue, are different because defenders face the same team multiple times, giving them more time to focus on small differences between shooters. But this effect is often mitigated by the enhanced role luck (or noise, if you're a statistician) plays in the small sample size of a short series rather than the larger 82–game sample.

the floor than the other. Some are more accurate spotting up off a teammate's pass than after one or more dribbles. Some are good stepback or sidestep shooters and others aren't. Some are like Ingles used to be: accurate when they have time and space, less accurate when they don't. Some need a perfect pass more than others. Some are dramatically affected by the three-pointer's distance and others aren't. Some shoot especially well in transition. Some are better dribbling to their left than right, and vice versa.

Many of these individual trends lean in one direction globally. Most players are better from the corner than above the break. Most players are better spot-up shooters than off-the-dribble marksmen. A good pass helps all shooters to varying degrees. Most players make shorter three-pointers more often than those from the logo. (Damian Lillard being a notable exception.) Most players shoot open threes better than contested ones. Teams incorporate those larger trends into their defensive strategies and are better at identifying dangerous three-point threats because of it.

Yet they're hardly panaceas in a modern game that forces players to cover so much ground. The threat of a drive always looms, and some shooters are better drivers than others. Some players are more vulnerable to stunts, which is when a player fakes a closeout to one shooter, but stays with their man. Everyone agrees that corner threes are better shots than above-the-break threes, but is that because they're closer to the rim or because they usually result from an effective drive-and-kick attack? Each of those complications pale in comparison to the growing reality that shooters increasingly fire just as freely in each specific moment of the game.

All of those reasons and many more explain why defenders fall for players like Marcus Smart. The judgment call of "How hard do I close out on this shooter?" is impossible for defenders to answer accurately in real time when every shooter has a green light and they have so many to worry about.

Defenders thus become even more prone to humanity's many cognitive biases. They overrate the most recent memory ("He's hot, we can't leave him open"). They fall for visual coherence ("His jumper looks pretty so he must be a shooter" or "His shot looks ugly so I don't have to guard him"). They overreact to bad shooters in the aggregate with a couple high-profile moments of brilliance in their careers. They change their approach based on the flow of that game even if the law of averages is likely to kick in

April 17, 2022 — Nets at Celtics — ECQF Game 1
Nets 114, Celtics 113 — 3 seconds left in fourth quarter

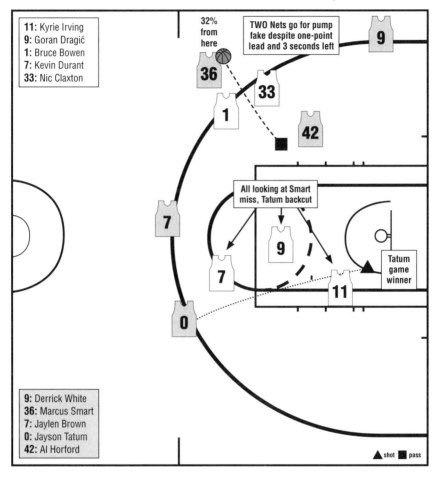

11: Kyrie Irving
9: Goran Dragić
1: Bruce Bowen
7: Kevin Durant
33: Nic Claxton

32% from here

TWO Nets go for pump fake despite one-point lead and 3 seconds left

All looking at Smart miss, Tatum backcut

Tatum game winner

9: Derrick White
36: Marcus Smart
7: Jaylen Brown
0: Jayson Tatum
42: Al Horford

▲ shot ■ pass

("He's made a couple, so I have to honor him"). And they react strongly to a confident shooter even when that confidence isn't warranted.

Marcus Smart's game was built to exploit these cognitive illusions. He is a streaky 32-percent shooter, trading impressive hot streaks for ugly cold stretches. The former repeats over highlight packages; the latter is forgotten. He has worked to make his shot motion at least look presentable. He's made several high-leverage threes in his career, giving him a (possibly unearned) reputation as a big shot maker. Above all, none of his many misses alter his supreme self-confidence, and defenders can't help but react to that.

That's how Smart possesses shooting *gravity* despite missing most of his threes. His complete disregard for acting like a 32-percent shooter overwhelms the defenders' memory of his 32-percent career three-point mark.

While Smart is a unique case, it's only because the rest of the massive pool of players who behave like deadeye long-range shooters at least come closer to making an appropriate percentage. If Smart's own stats don't deter him from launching lots of threes, how does a defender in real time make sense of a player who behaves the same way with a 38 percent career mark instead?

I'd argue the statistical picture of an NBA player's three-point accuracy has become so complex that superficial closeout judgments—the "eye test," so to speak—are in fact *more* reliable these days. Sure, it leaves defenders prone to their own cognitive biases. But those biases are noteworthy in part because they overrate *exceptions* to the rules. Usually, our snap judgments based on visual features are correct enough. If they weren't, the human race would've become extinct millenia ago instead of winning evolution's survival of the fittest. When time is of the essence, perfect becomes the enemy of good.

The problem is that even the eye test has become increasingly challenging for defenders, thanks to the Point-Five Mentality the Spurs ushered into the league after their 2014 title. Embodying it has a way of making each player's jump shot look more similar to a defender, no matter the circumstances.

Recall that Joe Ingles' incredibly fast no-dip three-pointer from the beginning of this chapter took 0.4 seconds from catch to release. If Ingles followed the Point-Five Mentality to the letter of the law, he'd have made a remarkably quick, instant decision to shoot with just one tenth of a second to spare.

But that's not how the Point-Five Mentality works. Ingles' actual shot release took 0.4 seconds, but he knew he was going to shoot much earlier. How much earlier is tough to say. Maybe he knew before Georges Niang released the pass. Maybe he knew once he spotted Beverley in the corner of his eye. Regardless, he did not catch the ball with a blank slate, survey the scene, and then rise and fire in four tenths of a second. He had to know he was going to shoot.

Put another way, the Point-Five Mentality transfers the original purpose of the triple threat to those precious split seconds *before* players get the ball. You don't catch the ball and then get into the proper position to make a shoot/pass/dribble decision. You get into the proper position to make a shoot/pass/dribble decision and then catch the ball.

While that mindset change has affected each of those potential decisions, it has most dramatically changed the look of players' in-game jump shots. The Point-Five Mentality requires players to begin their shot motion before the defense knows they're going to shoot. If they're taking a spot-up three, that means they start shooting before they even have a ball to shoot. If they're launching off the dribble, that means the move(s) they make to create separation must double as the beginning stages of their shot. Either way, defenders get even less time to gauge their closeout precisely.

The proper biomechanics of the modern players' shot preparation are subject to much debate. For years, conventional wisdom was that players should step into their shot, using their forward momentum to generate the lower-body strength to power their motion. That method is known as the "one-two" because players are planting their feet one after the other on the ground as they rise up to shoot.

But more coaches now believe the "one-two" takes too much time with players needing to take more three-pointers quickly and on the move rather than just from stationary positions. They've shifted modern conventional wisdom toward a maneuver known as "the hop," which is when a player leaps ever-so-slightly off both feet as they catch the ball, then spring up a second time to release their shot. The first hop is like a kick-start that generates the shot's lower-body power, allowing players more elasticity to control their second jump and shoot on the way up.

The hop is generally a better fit for the Point-Five Mentality because it is a single, brief two-footed leap instead of a more drawn-out one-two step. It's easier to execute it quickly before catching the ball and when attempting more contested threes.

But just like the frivolous dip-or-don't-dip debate, coaches and other shooting instructors spend too much time trying to prove the supremacy of the hop or the one-two in all cases. It's best to teach advanced players how to execute both quickly and smoothly, since certain situations will call for a hop and others will call for a one-two. The hop tends to be better on spot-up threes, but plenty of great NBA shooters use a one-two effectively. Similarly, the one-two makes sense in theory on pull-up and off-the-dribble threes, but tons of players hop into those shots instead.

Regardless, the Point-Five Mentality requires players to begin either method before the defense knows they're shooting. Most of the NBA players who dramatically improve their three-point accuracy during their careers haven't altered their form. They've instead learned how to be more prepared to shoot before they catch the ball.

One example is young star Brandon Ingram, who improved his three-point percentage and volume significantly after he was traded from the Los Angeles Lakers to the New Orleans Pelicans. Instead of widening his stance and then stepping in once he caught the ball, Ingram, with the help of Pelicans shooting coach Fred Vinson, learned to pivot his body toward the rim before receiving the pass. To use basketball jargon from a different context, Ingram learned to do more of his work early.

That kind of tip, increasingly necessitated by the widespread Point-Five Mentality, is making Ingram, Ingles, and countless others more dangerous shooters. It smooths their shooting motions, removing friction that would otherwise throw off their biomechanics. The effect is they are becoming higher-volume shooters in a league where three-point volume is increasingly essential to maintaining spacing and individual shooting gravity. They are using different dip levels and speeds to get more attempts off from different positions on the floor without sacrificing their accuracy—and often improving it to boot. Hundreds of other players are doing the same.

So how is a defender supposed to tell which shooters merit hard or soft closeouts? How do they avoid misidentifying imposters like Marcus Smart? Good luck solving those seemingly impossible tasks.

Chapter 11
Dribbling Is Footwork

How ball-handlers are developing new ways to
dribble without actually dribbling.

Giannis Antetokounmpo in the open floor. Those six words foreshadow anticipatory joy or impending doom depending on your rooting interests. The world is about to see something awesome, and everyone knows roughly what it'll look like. All that's left is for it to happen and blow our minds.

This is the scenario mean-mugging the Brooklyn Nets in the face on the night of March 13, 2016, an otherwise forgettable date in otherwise forgettable seasons for both franchises. With 10 and a half minutes left in the second quarter, Nets 10-day contract call-up Sean Kilpatrick boinks a wild floater off the side of the backboard and Antetokounmpo snatches the carom. He crosses the Nets' edge of the half-court logo, thrusting the ball in front of him with his right hand, letting it bounce well above his shoulders. He lets it dangle there, waiting to see how the Nets respond.

That's when backup Nets guard Shane Larkin turns his body slightly inward—leaving Bucks backup guard Tyler Ennis on the wing—to cut Antetokounmpo off. That's all the information Antetokounmpo needs to pounce. The dribbling served its purpose. Now it's time for his actual move,

In one motion, Antetokounmpo snatches the ball with two hands, plants his left foot onto the ground, extends both arms out as if he's throwing a chest pass to Ennis, and takes a single long stride that gets him from well

March 13, 2016 — Bucks at Nets
Bucks 31, Nets 25 — 10:32 left in second quarter

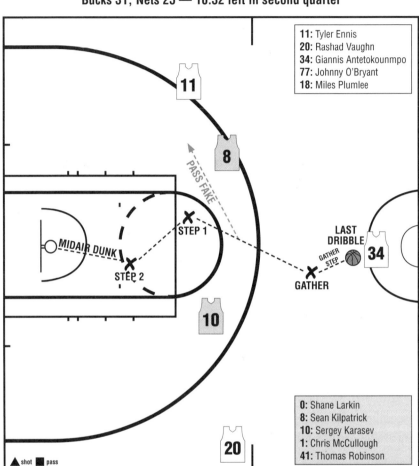

beyond the three-point line to just inside the free-throw circle. By the time Larkin swerves his head back toward Ennis, Antetokounmpo has already pulled the ball to his chest and taken a second giant stride to the edge of the dotted free-throw circle inside the paint. While Larkin raises his arms to deflect a pass that'll never arrive, Antetokounmpo lifts off his left foot, swoops through the air, and stuffs the ball through the rim with an extended right arm.

In covering 25 feet in less than two seconds, Antetokounmpo included:

- Two steps, each in a slightly different direction.
- One remarkably believable fake chest pass.

- One full horizontal extension and retraction of both arms while holding the ball.
- One extended right arm, ball palmed in hand to the rim.
- One thunderous dunk.
- Zero dribbles.
- Two points.

Zero dribbles! Yes, zero dribbles. And that was perfectly legal by the book and the view of that specific officiating crew.

The NBA is often mocked for its supposedly loose enforcement of traveling violations, but the letter of the law permits Antetokounmpo's step rhythm. Players get one step to pick up their dribble and "gather" the ball, then another two steps before they must shoot or pass. It's the same number they (and you) take in a pregame layup line. The only difference is that Antetokounmpo took his gather step 25 feet from the hoop and then covered the rest of the ground with two very long steps.

I don't blame you for struggling to find any similarity between Antetokounmpo's full-court gallop and your rec league warmup. You've seen gravity-defying NBA athletes before, but none of those guys regularly made body-shifting moves around defenders over 25 feet of the court without dribbling. These moves are breathtaking displays of athleticism, but it doesn't feel like they should be legal. How can a league allow a player to go 25 feet without dribbling? How is that *basketball?*

It is now, thanks to the ever-widening court of the Spaced Out Era colliding with a quarter-century revolution in dribbling, footwork, and the relationship between the two.

The specifics of Giannis Antetokounmpo's move against the Nets is unique to him, but the general principle is not. It's what binds Antetokounmpo to a friend like Stephen Curry, a nemesis like James Harden, and every other player of every size in the current NBA. Each has learned to optimize the gather + one-two step rhythm to stretch their moves. They, in effect, have reinvented the art of dribbling itself.

Basketball players simply do not move with the ball like they did in past eras. They leap forward, tap-dance backwards, and/or dangle the ball out alluringly to the side while still keeping their dribble alive. They hop from one spot to another like frogs on lily pads. They swing their arms through traffic and tuck the ball into their chests like running backs weaving between the tackles. They stretch it out off balance and one-handed like gymnasts during a floor exercise. They move their upper and lower bodies in opposite directions at the same time, as if they are separate puzzle pieces only loosely connected. They've even mastered the art of jumping backwards, surging directly into their defender before slamming on breaks that would make any car manufacturer jealous.

And they've learned to perform all of these neat movements in between the one thing the sport requires them to do to legally move anywhere on their own.

Dribbling, of course, is still a requirement in the NBA. The game hasn't changed *that* much. But as the game spread farther and farther out, players began using the dribble as a prop to delay, deceive, and/or absorb information about their environment. Before the Spaced Out Era, players dribbled to get from Point A to Point B. Now, they dribble at Point A to determine the move they make to get to Point B, dribble again to determine the move they make to get to Point C, and repeat as relevant until their last move to shoot or pass.

"Dribbling is footwork," former Providence College legend and ball-handling pioneer God Shammgod once told the *Washington Post*. "The hands are just an illusion."

Separating the dribbling motion from the feet has allowed the modern NBA player to navigate the court in different ways than their predecessors. Players of all sizes are using the underlying rhythm of a loose dribble to survey the scene, make a decision, and then take two maximized steps to carry out that decision via never-before-seen stepbacks, crossovers, layup finishes, Eurosteps, and many more. It doesn't matter whether the gather + two-step rhythm moves are forward, backwards, sideways, long strides, short strides, or any combination of any of the above. All are legal and all have found their place in a modern NBA that is played on a wider floor than ever before.

How did the NBA learn to reimagine the dribble, one of basketball's most fundamental elements? It learned from two slashing guards whose influence on the sport far exceeds their individual accomplishments. One is a South American legend credited with popularizing the Eurostep. The other is a counterculture American icon known simply as "The Answer."

IT TOOK FIVE games for Allen Iverson to piss off the NBA.

The fearless 76ers' rookie point guard burst onto the scene in more ways than one. He dropped 30 on Milwaukee on opening night, poured in 32 points in his team's first victory in Boston, and exchanged trash-talking barbs with the world champion Chicago Bulls while reportedly telling Michael Jordan to "get the [bleep] away from me" when No. 23 tried to calm him down.[128]

Now, he stared straight at a terse league memo, directed at him alone. Your shorts are too long. Your ankle braces cover up too much of your socks. Oh, and your signature move, the one you've used to achieve this level of instant success? It's illegal and you can't use it anymore.

The signature move in question was Iverson's crossover, in which he dangled the ball invitingly in one hand for so long *before* rapidly crossing over to the other. This, according to the league, was a palming violation.[129] Officials reviewed the tape and concluded that Iverson was cupping his hand underneath the ball before uncupping it, giving him an unfair advantage against defenders who thought he had picked up his dribble. His trademark quickness was a cheat code—literally.

Iverson was stunned. He insisted other players got away with more blatant palming violations. He claimed the league was out to get him, once saying that all this disrespect "comes with being Allen Iverson." His coach, Johnny Davis, said the referees weren't high-minded enough to understand Iverson's creativity. "What are they going to do, change the rules like they did for Wilt Chamberlain?" Davis asked rhetorically.

Oh, they tried. Iverson was whistled for palming twice in his next game, then many more times over the course of his rookie season. More league memos followed. Officials declared palming a preseason point of emphasis in 1999, 2000, 2005, and a bunch of other times behind the scenes. The NCAA did the same. Players complained. Opposing coaches complained. Well-known newspaper columnists complained. ("By god, there's slim hope

128. Dennis Rodman said: "Iverson came in here thinking he was Jumanji and was going to control the whole forest and wilderness," referencing the 1995 film adaptation of the children's book about a magical board game. The word "Jumanji" translates to "many effects" in a language native to the Zulu tribe in South Africa. The lesson of the game is that one person's decision can cause all sorts of unintended consequences—"many effects," so to speak. Rodman was presciently referring to Iverson himself as that agent of chaos.
129. A "discontinued dribble," to be technical.

for this league yet," legendary scribe Bob Ryan wrote when reporting the league memo in November 1996.)

Iverson's possibly illegal crossover became a significant talking point in every market. The 76ers' first game after the memo circulated was against the Knicks at Madison Square Garden. With one minute remaining in a tie game, Iverson missed a tough floater in the lane, but Philly retained possession on an offensive rebound. As Iverson reset the play, John Andariese, the longtime even-keeled Knicks analyst and broadcast partner of Marv Albert, jumped in. "What a horror show he is to guard," Andariese began, before adding, "He's carrying that ball with his high dribble."

When the broadcast returned from a commercial break with the 76ers leading by three with 38 seconds left, viewers saw a close-up, half-speed replay of Iverson's dribbling after that offensive rebound. "The Knicks are unhappy with Iverson's handling of the basketball and feel he's getting away with carrying the ball," Andariese said as the screen showed Iverson retreating casually to half-court to set up a pick-and-roll with teammate Derrick Coleman. "There's an example," Andariese said on Iverson's first dribble. "There's another one," he said on the second. Finally, "There's another one right there," on the third.

Albert chimed in agreement. "Big time."

"If you can do that, you can really sail by the defender," Andariese concluded. "That's something that, you know, coaching staffs are going to be talking to the league about."

This was a Knicks broadcast, on a regional TV network named after the Knicks' world-famous arena, with the Knicks' iconic broadcasters, in a game the Knicks trailed by one possession with the ball with less than 40 seconds remaining. And they in here talking about dribbling. Not the game. Not the game. They talkin' about *dribbling*.

It's impossible to overstate how much Iverson's status as a cultural threat to the league's establishment influenced the largely negative view of his signature move. At the time, the NBA's power brokers were uncomfortable, to put it mildly, with Iverson's image as an avatar for hip-hop culture. It's hard to imagine Iverson's crossover inspiring such moral outrage if he looked more like, say, John Stockton. As Thomas Beller of *The New Yorker* wrote in 2019, Iverson's crossover "managed to take the aesthetic of hip-hop and translate it into basketball."

Despite (or possibly because) of that larger noise, the debate over Iverson's crossover dribble foreshadowed a much larger sea change regarding the purpose of dribbling itself. Johnny Davis was right. Allen Iverson was targeted because he had come up with something so different from anything anyone had seen before. But even Davis and Iverson's other defenders missed the move's most revolutionary quality.

Allen Iverson didn't just introduce a new, lethal type of crossover to the basketball world. He introduced a new way to dribble, period. And while the rest of the world argued in circles about technicalities, Iverson fine-tuned his revolutionary approach to dribbling until the rest of the basketball world—including the NBA itself—understood what he pulled off and why it was the first step in a much larger off-the-dribble movement revolution.

Everything about Iverson's handle was counterintuitive to the norms of the times. It was designed to appear far looser than it actually was. He purposely committed the cardinal sin of dribbling the ball high and wayyyyy out to the side instead of tucking it into his body to shield it from defenders. He took the prevailing idea that the ball is a prized commodity to be protected at all costs and flipped it on its head. *Here's the ball. It's sitting right there, invitingly, waiting for you to swipe it. I'm letting you have it. Just reach out and take it!*

This was a well-crafted illusion that influenced defenders' behavior even if they knew they were being sandbagged. They couldn't help but relax, sit up in their stance, and/or lunge for the ball. That's exactly when Iverson made them look like fools. He lulled the defense to sleep and made his next move appear even deadlier.

The pouncing method didn't need to be a crossover. It could be a straight-line drive, pull-up jumper, a slow crossover to set up a second crossover, another fake-lazy dribble decoy, or anything else. Iverson also developed a lethal pull-back crossover move over the course of his career, switching the ball behind his back or underneath his front leg while his defender retreated. (Ask Tyronn Lue about that one.) He used an initial slow dribble to layer multiple moves on top of each other, as he did when dropping Washington's Antonio Daniels in a famous clip from the 2005–06 season.

Regardless, Iverson's initial fake-casual dribble was the most important component to his success. The next generation of pros idolized Iverson, so when they entered the league, they overwhelmingly adopted his high, slow, fake-casual dribble to enhance their own signature moves. Iverson didn't just inspire small guards, either. Taller players—starting with Tracy McGrady and continuing on to Kevin Durant—discovered that Iverson's delay tactic was an ideal fit for their long arms and stretched-out torsos, each of which allowed the high bounce to go higher while they decided between driving to the hoop and going into a seamless pull-up jumper rhythm.

Nowadays, the technique is so widespread that it has its own name: "the hang dribble." In hindsight, the hang dribble, and not the crossover, was Iverson's real signature move. The crossover just happened to be hot at the time. It was the move that Reebok highlighted in commercials for Iverson's signature shoes.

And it was on the tip of the basketball world's collective tongues thanks to another ball-handling wizard who burst onto the NBA scene a half-decade earlier.

Tim Hardaway seemed like the last guy the Golden State Warriors needed in the lead-up to the 1989 NBA Draft. Don Nelson, the Warriors coach and general manager, repeatedly said he wanted a frontcourt player. When he instead selected a six-foot guy from Texas El-Paso with the No. 14 pick, the locals were confused. "Nelson Thinks Tall, Drafts Small," read one *San Francisco Examiner* headline. "I was expecting someone a little taller than a sportswriter who can barely touch the top of his refrigerator," wrote *The Press Democrat* columnist Bob Padecky.[130] Nelson, of course, got the last laugh when Hardaway immediately became a sensation, teaming with Chris Mullin and Mitch Richmond to form the iconic Run TMC trio.

In college, Hardaway developed a signature move that became known as the "UTEP Two Step." He would perform a normal-speed crossover one way, then rapidly cross back the other before exploding to the rim. (He adopted the move from Pearl Washington, a former New York City high-school legend and Syracuse standout who couldn't stick in the NBA.) It got a new name once he unleashed it in the pros: the "killer crossover."[131]

The killer crossover was a rapid-fire move that staggered opponents before they realized it was coming. Hardaway galloped into the move, delivered two

---

130. The Warriors planned to trade their two first-round picks at No. 14 and No. 16 to the Indiana Pacers for the No. 7 selection before Indiana backed out at the last minute. Had the deal gone through, Nelson said the Warriors would have taken power forward Randy White, who went No. 8 to Dallas. White was out of the league within five years.

131. Magic Johnson is reputed to be the first person to use that term.

punches when most players barely had time to get in one, then exploded out of it. The cadence of the move was fast (setup) then super-duper fast (the crossover itself), then fast again (the finish). Or as Magic Johnson said in 1991: "It's bang bang and you're dead."

To make that happen, Hardaway kept his body "in the box," to use his words. He was crouched in an explosive position, keeping his dribble as low to the ground and as much within his shoulders as possible. This, in turn, limited the distance it traveled while crossing from one hand to the other. By staying low to the ground the whole time, Hardaway didn't give off any signals that his defender could use to anticipate the move. Then, it happened so fast that viewers often blinked and missed it.

Hardaway was just beginning his second act with the Miami Heat when Iverson's version sparked such intrigue in the fall of 1996. Their deadly crossovers forever linked the two in NBA history, but the similarities ended there. Their relationship was icy during their playing days and is still tense long after both have retired.

Iverson's crossover didn't just threaten Hardaway's as the game's signature small man move. It did so while running on a theory that was 180 degrees removed from its supposed model.

Whereas Hardaway used his killer crossover like a boxer connecting on a rapid one-two punch sequence, Iverson deployed his like a baseball pitcher changing speeds or arm angles. Forget keeping the ball "in the box," as Hardaway insisted. Iverson used his hang dribble to instead widen the strike zone considerably. He played on the defender's tendency to watch the ball, dangling it out to his side while letting it levitate up as far as his chin. The higher and farther it bounced, the deadlier the effect when Iverson snatched it out of midair to cross over low to the ground. The cadence of his move was slow (the setup), super slow (the stationary high and wide dribbles), and then fast times two (the crossover itself and the finish). It was more like bang … baaaaaang … baaaaaang … until you got bored, *then* bang-bang and you're dead.

This added another layer to the core basketball concept of moving at different speeds when handling the ball. Many before Iverson perfected head, eye, and body fakes in which they stood up in their stance before crouching back to explode. Others, like Hardaway, used the crossover itself as their change of pace while keeping their body in the same position.

But Iverson changed speeds by varying the height and width of his actual dribbles. The act of pounding the rock wasn't just a means to legally go from one spot to another. It could also be a tool to deceive, a way to sneak more steps in than otherwise permitted, and/or a way to hypnotize defenders while his feet moved separately. It turned his hands into an illusion.

The hang dribble also gave Iverson time to read his defender. Instead of worrying about protecting the ball low to the ground, Iverson could devote more mental energy toward analyzing his defender's foot position, torso, eyes, knee bend, or any other cue that might reveal their next move. He could wait for the defender to seal his own fate, whereas Hardaway made his killer crossover decision right away.

Plus, Iverson's approach provided room to position his own body to best sell the lie. He could thrust his shoulders, hips, and/or torso forward while the ball was still hovering in mid-air, then snatch it to cross them all over in the other direction. Unlike Hardaway, whose body gave off no signals, Iverson's flooded defenders' senses with a bunch of false ones to disguise the truth. In essence, Iverson used the time between dribbles to deploy the same fakes, jabs, or other body gyrations that were previously only available to players before they put the ball on the floor.

Iverson got all the benefits of dribbling without any of the drawbacks. And therein lies the controversy that engulfed his crossover.

If you're purposely hanging the ball in midair as long as possible, are you really maintaining your dribble, or are you—in spirit if not in letter—*discontinuing* it? How could anyone do that without placing their hand underneath the ball? Why even require dribbling if you can moonwalk willy nilly during the time it takes for gravity to push the ball down to the ground?

Hardaway, to this day, insists the answer to all those questions is "no." Here's a sample of his comments on Iverson's move:

December 1996, before their first matchup: "He carries the ball. The NBA sent a memo and said he carries the ball and travels with it."

March 2000, in a segment that aired during a Celtics-76ers NBC game: "My crossover's just coming down, you go one way, and whoosh, come back another way. Like Isiah [Thomas] used to do it, like Magic [Johnson] used to do it. It's just easy and it's fundamental. Kobe [Bryant] and Iverson's dribble is a carry, and that's why they're calling it."

2017, in an interview with NBA.com's Scott Howard-Cooper: "I'm going to tell you this—and I tell everyone this—Allen Iverson carried the basketball." (That one prompted a classic Iverson response: "I carried my crossover all the way into the Hall of Fame," he told Bleacher Report's Jonathan Abrams.)

2018, in an interview with FOX Sports' Chris Broussard: "Carry and a travel. It is what it is. I'm not being critical of anybody. I'm just telling the truth. … I came down. I didn't carry. I didn't set my man up. I just did it. It was in the flow of the game."

2020, on ESPN's *Now Or Never* ESPN+ show: "Well I think he carried. I just think he carried and they let him carry, because that was his move. Everybody said he carried."

November 2021, before a Warriors-Hornets game: "To me, Iverson is a bad analogy for what I used to do because he used to carry. Point blank. He carried it all the way to the Hall of Fame, as he said, which is true. I have no gripes with that. But at the park, he wouldn't have gotten away with that. It is what it is."

Why is this such a hot-button issue for Hardaway? There are a lot of messy layers to peel back: ego, sour grapes, style, legacy, and, of course, the dramatic Iverson-inspired cultural revolution that swept the sport in the late 1990s and early 2000s.

But one (two-part) basketball question is at the heart of the debate. Where on the ball, and for how long, can a player put their hand without being considered to have picked up their dribble?

The current NBA rulebook clearly states that the hand cannot go directly under the ball. "A player who is dribbling may not put any part of his hand under the ball and (1) carry it from one point to another or (2) bring it to a pause and then continue to dribble again." That means a violation occurs if the hand is under the ball *and* the player is either moving from one point to another OR stopping long enough to register a pause.

The problem is there's a lot of gray area between "directly on top of the ball" and "directly underneath the ball."

Picture the ball like a round clock. Dribbling with the hand at 12 o'clock is clearly legal, while doing so with the hand at six o'clock isn't. But does that mean everything in between 12 and six, or six and 12, is kosher? What if a player executes a crossover at four o'clock, but their fingers briefly brush somewhere between five and six o'clock while getting in position? Is three o'clock governed any differently than nine o'clock? How long must the hand linger on something resembling six o'clock to be considered a "pause?" Does it matter where the ball is positioned within the hand—i.e., fingertips, palm, etc.—assuming the ball-handler has avoided six o'clock?

Iverson's hang dribble pushed these gray areas to their limits. All crossovers, to some degree, require shifting the hand below 12 o'clock to the side. How else does one, you know, cross the ball over? Many before Hardaway tested that limit in the 1960s and early-to-mid 1970s, including, but not limited to, Earl Monroe and a slick point guard named Archie Clark. Once the league rubber-stamped their moves, they could not stick to a strict "12 o'clock only" interpretation of carrying. Hardaway would've been whistled for palming if he tried his killer crossover in the 1960s.

But Hardaway's crossover, like the signature ones before it, was so low to the ground that it was pointless and physically impossible for his hand to approach six o'clock. Even if he wanted to carry the ball, it would have thrown off the whole cadence of the move. This is why Hardaway made it a point to say that he "didn't set his man up" and his killer crossover "was in the flow of a game." Translation: I didn't have the luxury of stopping, dancing around in place, and messing with my hand placement while my teammates snoozed on the opposite side.

Iverson, of course, had carte blanche to dribble a lot. His one-on-one style rubbed many the wrong way and may have contributed to his absence of deep playoff runs outside of his 2000–01 MVP season. That claim has and will be endlessly debated.

But Iverson certainly wasn't messing around with those slow, long hang dribbles. Like a pitcher using the entire strike zone and more, Iverson pushed his hand to different parts of the ball while performing his hang dribbles. Technically, he operated within the rules as long as he avoided placing his hand directly underneath the ball—at six o'clock exactly. Five o'clock with the hand inches from the six? Iverson tested that limit, and the NBA, after many attempts to rein him in, had little choice but to agree. Was Iverson operating within the spirit of the law? It depends on who you asked.

Regardless, Iverson was the first player to actively push these boundaries. While other players naturally shifted their hand position while executing their moves, Iverson's entire game was built on exploiting the space between

12 and six o'clock. He could make it seem like he was picking up his dribble, continuing one way, or anything in between. That unpredictability made him appear quicker, much like a pitcher's slow change-up makes their fastball seem faster by comparison. It seemed unfair to defenders at the time because nobody else thought to use the period *between* dribbles as a means to deceive. In hindsight, Iverson hacked dribbling itself.

As the league cracked down on his most blatant violations, Iverson more clearly toed the line with his hand placement. He trained himself to let the ball roll off his fingers somewhere between 12 and 6 o'clock instead of tempting himself to place his hand underneath the ball. Palming violations dropped, shattered ankles skyrocketed, and his counter moves to that deadly crossover proved to be just as vicious.

It was one small way Iverson became a cultural icon and model to the next generation. Many current players point to him as their favorite growing up, which Iverson consistently repays by effusively praising the ways they've continued to advance the game. "Those guys are next level," he said of Stephen Curry and Kyrie Irving in a 2015 *Showtime* documentary. "I didn't have the handle they do." When Memphis' Ja Morant dropped 52 points in a late-February game in the 2021–22 season, including a thunderous dunk over Spurs big man Jakob Poeltl, Iverson tweeted a picture of a Grizzlies No. 12 jersey draped over his 2001 MVP trophy. "Pass the torch OG," Morant responded, with a photoshopped picture of the two players standing together in uniform. The mutual appreciation between Iverson and today's stars is, to me at least, endearing and refreshing.

Inspired by Iverson, today's players are iterating on his hang dribble concept. They found different ways to lengthen and exploit the beats *between* dribbles, when their defenders are most blind to their intentions. And though Iverson's signature finishing move required him to dribble again, others realized they could use the hang dribble's same delay mechanism to set up a different kind of move.

One where they didn't have to dribble at all.

MANU GINÓBILI ANNOYED the hell out of the Denver Nuggets. Mostly because they couldn't stop him, though they weren't willing to concede that point easily at the time. But the specific way in which they couldn't stop him drove them mad.

"I'm just going to put it on tape, give it to my son, and tell him this is how to play basketball," coach George Karl said. "Just put your head down and run into people. I guess that's the new brand of basketball."

Karl said that minutes after Ginóbili came off the bench to score 32 points in an 86–78 San Antonio Spurs win in Game 3 of their 2005 first-round series. Many of those points came from kamikaze drives that ended in buckets, glancing blows, and/or free throws.

Finally, with the game out of reach in the closing seconds, the Nuggets had enough. When Ginóbili surged down the lane one final time, Greg Buckner wound up and struck him on the left elbow, Kenyon Martin jabbed him in the ribs, and Carmelo Anthony unleashed a two-handed smackdown on both of Ginóbili's shoulders. Anthony got tossed, but it could have been any one of them.

Karl later said he loved Ginóbili and was engaging in a form of gamesmanship.[132] Nevertheless, his comments inspired others to voice long-hidden gripes with the Argentinian import's fearless style. "His hair goes wild, and it looks like someone just murdered him," then-SuperSonics star Ray Allen said during the Spurs' six-game second-round series win. Phoenix's Shawn Marion joked during the Western Conference Finals that the Suns needed to take acting lessons to guard Ginóbili. Detroit's Ben Wallace flung his headband in disgust after getting whistled for a blocking foul on Ginóbili in Game 1 of the NBA Finals, which sparked a game-clinching 19–4 San Antonio run.

This was how Manu Ginóbili's image as a flopper metastasized. "I had that year in 2005 where my reputation started to go up because George Karl started to say it and he said it to a million newspapers; you know because I had the long hair and all of that," Ginóbili said in 2016. "But I don't think I was."

These complaints concealed the real issue: the league didn't understand Ginóbili's idiosyncratic style of play. Karl wasn't *that* far off when he called it "put your head down and run into people." (Okay, the "put your head down" part was wrong.) Ginóbili surged straight at defenders and trusted

---

132. "Manu and George are from the same basketball gene pool," former Charlotte Hornets coach and Karl teammate Allan Bristow told the *San Antonio Express-News* after Game 3. "I guarantee you, if George Karl was picking sides, he'd take Manu first."

his feet to figure out a path around and through them. It was aggressive and downright reckless to outsiders. Sean Elliott, the former Spurs player and current broadcaster, put it perfectly when he said Ginóbili "looks like a squirrel running through traffic trying to dodge cars."[133]

"Running" was the most apt word for it. That's because Ginóbili's mad dashes to the rim conspicuously did not include the tool that is supposedly required for players to advance the ball themselves: a dribble.

That, more than anything, confused the hell out of his NBA opponents. Falling down while bouncing the ball to get somewhere felt in tune with the spirit of the game. Falling down while clutching the ball to squeeze through tiny creases seemed unnatural, as if Ginóbili was trying to get hit first and score second. Hence, the flopping accusation.

But while Ginóbili's opponents complained about his wild drives to the hoop, they began taking notes on his methods. They found that his footwork consisted of two legal, long and diagonal steps, each of which followed a hard thrust forward to build up momentum. The first step doubled as a probe for more information and a trick to draw a reaction, much like Allen Iverson's hang dribble was designed to read and hypnotize the defender. The next step cut hard the other way, leaving the defender swatting at air or uncontrollably jutting their unbalanced body into Ginóbili's.

The "fake one way to go hard the other" cadence of Ginóbili's move worked the same way as Iverson's deadly crossover, with two main differences. The first is that Ginóbili's steps were faster and more direct. He changed speeds and directions, but his paths to the hoop were straighter than Iverson's.

The second, of course, is that Ginóbili couldn't dribble after executing his signature move. He instead improvised different ways to finish the play, all of which flummoxed shot blockers who were not used to his driving rhythm. Fundamentally, though, both stars lengthened and exploited the times and spaces between the ball's bounces. Their dribbling was footwork and every other part of their body was an illusion.

By 2007, those within league circles had settled on a name for Ginóbili's move that blended his non-American nationality status with his foreign

---

133. This line was relayed by Steve Kerr, the current Warriors coach whose final NBA season was with the Spurs in 2002–03, Ginóbili's rookie year.

footwork. The Spurs again split the first two games of their first-round playoff series against a red-hot Denver Nuggets team, dropping Game 1 at home before striking back in Game 2. Though Ginóbili had not starred in either game, his unique rim-attacking game again put the Nuggets on tilt.

Well, one player in particular: a 21-year-old guard named J.R. Smith. The talented former preps-to-pros draftee had become an effective, though often erratic, bench scorer in his first year with Denver, but was having a nightmare of a time dealing with Ginóbili. During the three-day break between Games 2 and 3, Smith decided to vent some frustration with his bench counterpart.

"He's got that Eurostep that's unbelievable," Smith said. "Yeah. He takes an extra step every time he gets to the paint. It always works for him. They never call it a walk. I might try it."

Eurostep. The term folks in the league used was out in the open, henceforth forever associated with an Argentinian.[134] Soon, the "Eurostep" was everywhere. American stars like Dwyane Wade adopted it. Coaches like Kentucky's John Calipari began teaching it to their future NBA stars. A decade later, the Eurostep is as fundamental a phrase as "crossover" or "behind the back." We have J.R. Smith of all people to thank.

It is ahistorical to say Ginóbili "invented" the Eurostep. The move, insofar as one might define it as one or more long, non-direct post-dribble strides to avoid defenders, dates back to the 1960s, if not further in the past. Elgin Baylor, the former Los Angeles Lakers great who was the prototype to today's athletic wing stars, used a similar side step in his heyday. So did Julius Erving, Magic Johnson, and lesser-known American players like former Rockets guard Lewis Lloyd. A 2018 ESPN feature story traced the move's origins to a Serbian overseas pro named Vladimir Cvetković.

Most agree that the first tipping point in the move's popularity occurred when several top European-born players filtered into the league in the late 1980s and early 1990s. Croatian-born stars Toni Kukoč and Dražen Petrović had been taught to use their two allowed steps to avoid defenders,

---

134. The ways the press wrapped their heads around Smith's terminology in print is amusing in hindsight. The Associated Press report notes that Ginóbili "has been driving past Smith with what Smith terms his 'Eurostep'" [sic]. The *Rocky Mountain News* felt the need to clarify that Ginóbili was "a native of Argentina who once played in Italy." *Colorado Gazette* columnist David Ramsey assumed Smith misspoke. "Eurostep?" he wrote. "Remember, Ginóbili hails from South America."

even and especially if they went in opposite directions. Lithuanian-born star Šarūnas Marčiulionis incorporated those methods into a downhill attacking style that Ginóbili later perfected. While their methods were (begrudgingly) accepted and sometimes celebrated, they were not widely imitated until Ginóbili emerged in the early 2000s.

Ginóbili never claimed to invent the Eurostep, and in fact has repeatedly said he wasn't reinventing the wheel. So why do so many players, coaches, and fans associate Ginóbili with the Eurostep instead of those other early adopters?

The answer is a combination of the versatility of Ginóbili's steps and the wider changes occurring throughout the league that laid the groundwork for today's Spaced Out Era. Ginóbili was the right player who came along at the right time.

In truth, the term "Eurostep" doesn't do Ginóbili's move justice. It's not a single step at all. It's more like a flexible, intentional three-step process to slice through defenses *after* picking up the dribble.

That differentiates it from Baylor, Erving, and the other American stars who perfected one- and even two-step methods to elude defenders. Even Marčiulionis, a fellow lefty who picked up his dribble early and stepped diagonally to slice through defenders, was too bulky to cover nearly as much ground on his drives. Ginóbili, on the other hand, applied finesse, speed, and explosiveness to a move that was previously used as a power attack.

There were two ways Ginóbili did that. The first was by stretching out the move's start and end points so it could work equally effectively in tight and wide spaces. Like Iverson, Ginóbili created ambiguity by waiting until the last possible moment to gather the ball into his hand. Sometimes, he threw the ball out ahead of him before snatching it on the run. Sometimes, he crouched low to perform one final power dribble before exploding up to begin his two-step finish. Sometimes, he jabbed hard in one direction, then gathered the ball, then took two more steps the other way. Regardless, he was dribbling to assess the situation and give off false signals. His actual move to get by the defender could wait until he gained more information.

By customizing the precise instant he officially terminated the dribble, Ginóbili discovered how to take an extra step on his drives without officially taking an extra step.

The best way to understand this supposed contradiction is to try it out yourself. If you're able, put this book down, grab a basketball, and find your nearest indoor or outdoor hoop. Start warming up as if you're in a pregame layup line. Go casually, but not *too* casually.

As you do so, make special note of the thud of your steps, the last time the ball bounces on the ground, and the exact moment you snatch it to go into your shot. If you're shooting a normal righty layup off the inside foot, you'll perform some sort of left-right-left step routine before releasing the ball. The last bounce will occur sometime before that first beat, you'll gather it sometime just before the second one, and then your feet will tap the floor in a one-two count while you bring the ball up to lay it in.

Guess what: you just took three steps! One was to gather the ball, and the other two were to set up your layup. Would you say you traveled? Of course not! It should've felt like something you do all the time at full speed. There's a reason that movement is allowed, but raising your pivot foot even slightly from a standstill position isn't. If we weren't allowed a gather step and a one-two count, nobody would ever drive and this sport would look more like water polo.

There's no rule stating that those three steps *have* to be forward, equally long, or even in the same direction at all. It may feel natural to gather the ball and then take two strides forward, and that may be the spirit of the initial rule. But as long as a player takes one gather step followed by a one-two into a shot or pass, any direction, length, or speed is theoretically possible. With enough intent, leg strength, creativity, and muscle memory, three steps can go a long way.

Manu Ginóbili was one of the first NBA players to show just how long. He intentionally performed the gather + one-two step count at many different speeds and directions to elude off-balance defenders, customizing every inch of space and beat of time during all three parts of the process. He gathered the ball at many different points: up above his shoulders, down near his knees, square at his chest, with either hand, and even sometimes while wrapping it around his back. From there, he could reposition it throughout those additional two steps, deploying pass fakes before shooting, shot fakes before passing, and anything else that might throw off defenders.

As Ginóbili spun the ball around his body like a windmill, he was plotting the best one-two step path to get the easiest shot. He stepped sideways,

May 24, 2005 — Spurs at Suns — WCF Game 2 (SA leads 1-0)
Spurs 103, Suns 102 — 1:55 left in fourth quarter

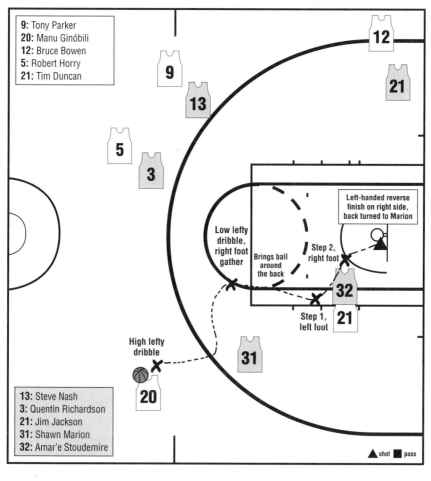

9: Tony Parker
20: Manu Ginóbili
12: Bruce Bowen
5: Robert Horry
21: Tim Duncan

Left-handed reverse finish on right side, back turned to Marion

Low lefty dribble, right foot gather

Brings ball around the back

Step 2, right foot

Step 1, left foot

High lefty dribble

13: Steve Nash
3: Quentin Richardson
21: Jim Jackson
31: Shawn Marion
32: Amar'e Stoudemire

▲ shot ■ pass

forward, backward, diagonally, in sharp zig-zags, and anything in between to weave through defenders who were usually bigger and slower than him. He possessed remarkable leg strength and ankle flexibility, which allowed him to juke defenders like a football scatback. He also swung his arms while stepping, giving him an extra kick of momentum to surge forward.

Finally, he made sure to cover as much ground as possible with his last legal step. He understood that a traveling violation is triggered by the *third* post-gather step, which meant he, in effect, was allowed 2.999999999999 steps after his gather, not two flat. He could plant that last foot into the ground, float horizontally over long distances in the air, twist his upper body to find the right finishing angle, and still avoid a travel as long as his other foot stayed off the floor until he released the ball. That took a level of athleticism that fans didn't fully appreciate at the time. Though Ginóbili mostly played below the rim, he generated as much hang time as some of the game's highest flyers.

All this took a level of creativity that previous players hadn't displayed. Though it often appeared otherwise, Ginóbili was not, in fact, charging forward and then falling down at the slightest sign of contact. He was instead using the slight pause of his own gather step to rapidly pick up defensive cues so he could then slice through them using an ever-growing menu of finishing steps. He hit them at acute angles, forcing blocking fouls.

The zig-zag move that became known as the Eurostep was one such example. Before Ginóbili, few players thought to use their one-two post-dribble count as a move/countermove combination and even fewer possessed the core strength and full-body elasticity to actually pull it off in real time.

Ginóbili, on the other hand, possessed both qualities. He used his first stride to draw a reaction from the defender, then finished them off with the second stride. If the defender bit on the first step, the second went in the opposite direction. We now call that a Eurostep. But he could also continue to stride forward if the defender didn't bite, or he could use his second step to slice through them diagonally. He never predetermined his move, even though he seemed, to use Karl's words, to be "putting his head down and running into people."

Tying Ginóbili's legacy to the Eurostep itself sells him short. It's true that his version of that specific move inspired Dwyane Wade, James Harden, Giannis Antetokounmpo, and millions of players worldwide to add it to their bags.

But just as the narrow focus on Iverson's crossover downplays his role in transforming the very technique of dribbling, harping on Ginóbili's "Eurostep" takes for granted that he showed players they could drive without dribbling. He took the gather + two-step rhythm once used to *finish* full-speed driving moves and turned it into the move itself. Or, more accurately, the moves, plural.

That innovation spread like wildfire across the NBA. Empowered by 2004's crackdown on hand-checking, a new generation of perimeter stars suddenly found they could dance more freely with the ball than ever before.

Brute strength was on the way out. Agility was on the way in. What better way to showcase your agility than to surge forward like Manu Ginóbili and then use your allotted gather + two-step rhythm to slip around and through defenders who no longer could use their hands to stop you? In an instant, strong, yet jet-quick penetrators like Wade, LeBron James, Kobe Bryant, and others added their own flavor to Ginóbili's post-dribble style. If he wasn't traveling, neither were they. Right?

Well, sort of. It turned out the league had one more loophole they needed to close before they caught up.

THE 2008–09 SEASON was one Washington Wizards fans would prefer to forget—and that's saying something given the franchise's woeful history.[135]

Their offseason decision to octuple down on a core with zero playoff series victories to its name was going horribly wrong.[136] Gilbert Arenas, in the first year of a six-year, $111 million contract, was set to miss most of a second straight season with a left knee injury. Running mates Caron Butler and Antawn Jamison were underperforming and rolling their eyes at a group of young teammates that seemed to lack basic professionalism. A 1–10 start cost longtime coach Eddie Jordan his job, and interim Ed Tapscott wasn't faring much better.

One moment, at around 3:30 PM ET on the first Sunday after New Year's, made Wizards fans forget about all that misery. For a brief instant, those few remaining broken-down Wizards fans sitting inside Verizon Center or by their televisions erupted in a roar. What could've possibly caused such a hopeless fanbase to react as if their team won the championship?

LeBron James *finally* got called for traveling.

The Wizards clung to a two-point lead with 10.5 seconds left as the Cavaliers inbounded at half court. James crossed the ball between his legs, hopped backwards to draw Butler out of his stance, and surged past him to his left, swinging the ball over his head to avoid a second defender. He took a massive leap off his right foot to split two Wizards at the free-throw

---

135. The franchise has not won 50 games since 1978 and has been through its fair share of scandals, promising eras cut short, and almost everything in between. (And that list of fans includes me.)

136. They beat the Chicago Bulls in the first round in 2005 with Larry Hughes as the third star instead of Caron Butler.

line, then finished the move with a left-right one-two step sequence into a powerful layup while being fouled.

But as James surged to the hoop to finish, outside official Bill Spooner greeted him with a series of whistles. The call was for traveling. No game-tying basket, no accompanying foul to give Cleveland a chance to take the lead. Finally, a small source of karmic retribution for Wizards faithful who remembered the uncalled James traveling violation that cost them a crucial Game 3 victory in their first-round playoff series three years earlier.

"He traveled!" Wizards announcer Steve Buckhantz shouted in shock. "A traveling has been called on LeBron James!"

James was baffled. "Bad call," he said bluntly after the game. "We all make mistakes." Then, he uttered a phrase that would become immortal in basketball lore:

"I took a crab dribble."

A what?

"A hesitation dribble, and then two steps."

Come again?

"It's a play that you don't see in this league much but myself," he elaborated. "It's one of those plays where you have your trademark play, and that's one of my plays. It kind of looks like a travel because it's slow, and it's kind of like high steps. But it's a one-two, just as fluent as any other one-two in this league. I got the wrong end of it, but I think they need to look at it again and need to understand that's not a travel.

"What happens is when you take a crab dribble and you hesitate, that is not one step, because you still basically have a live ball," he said after another follow-up question. "And then when you go into your one-two that's when the steps get counted. So if you look at the play, I take a crab dribble and find a crease and then I take my one-two. So it's a perfectly legal play, something I've always done and always been successful with."

Within hours, "crab dribble" became one of the most popular (proto) memes in modern NBA history. Most fans and media had never heard this term before, and many players even admitted their ignorance. Images and videos of James' face superimposed on crab legs flooded the Internet. (One argued, facetiously, that LeBron didn't travel because 18 itty bitty crab steps was the same as one human step.) An increasingly loud cacophony of James critics began using "crab dribble" as a catch-all term for the special treatment The King supposedly received from the league.

"A crab dribble is when you, uh, travel," Caron Butler said, echoing their thoughts.

The silly ensuing conversation overlooked two critical points. First: the "crab dribble" is a real basketball move. It's when a player uses their back to shield their defender, crouches down, and dribbles while hopping their feet to the side like a crab. It's usually performed when posting up, but it can also carve out space underneath the hoop, ward off a pressuring defender in the backcourt, or, as James showed, feign a step backward as part of a perimeter hesitation move.

Secondly, and more importantly, James traveled anyway. The crab dribble was irrelevant. The actual confusion centered on when, exactly, James gathered the ball to terminate his dribble. Did he do that and *then* take a one-two step, as he claimed, or did he take three steps?

The answer is three steps. The call was correct. LeBron was wrong. But the margin was a lot narrower than the naked eye suggested.

James *almost* nailed the footwork using hacks similar to Iverson's and Ginóbili's signature moves. Had LeBron taken that first giant leap forward *before* gathering the ball, that step wouldn't have counted as one of his two permitted ones. Instead, LeBron, perhaps fearful of a second Wizard reaching in for a steal, snatched the ball over his head just *before* his toes could lift off the ground for that giant stride. That meant it counted as one of his post-gather steps, which meant the extra two he took added up to three, which is illegal. That very slight mistiming made all the difference.

In practice, at least. The actual language of the 2008–09 NBA rulebook was far less clear.

"A player who receives the ball while he is progressing or upon completion of a dribble, may use a two-count rhythm in coming to a stop, passing or shooting the ball," it read. "The first count occurs: (1) As he receives the ball, if either foot is touching the floor at the time he receives it. (2) As the foot touches the floor, or as both feet touch the floor simultaneously after he receives the ball, if both feet are off the floor when he receives it. The second occurs: (1) After the count of one when either foot touches the floor, or both feet touch the floor simultaneously."

The one word conspicuously absent from that paragraph? "Step."

Instead, the rule referenced a "two-count rhythm" that is *related* to when the players' feet touch the floor, but is obfuscated with legalese that muddies their precise relationship. It's sort of like counting to two once the player picks up his dribble, except that count starts at slightly different points. If you can say "one-two" naturally without an abnormally long break between the two words, the move was legal. If you couldn't, it wasn't.

Talk about a subjective measure! No two people count the same way, so of course nobody could agree on traveling violations.

By relying on a "count" rather than the feet actually hitting the ground, the rule unofficially considered post-dribble steps legal if they seemed like natural extensions of the move itself. It rested on the theory that players made dribble moves consciously and then finished the play in a continuous motion. "Two-count rhythm" was enough to cover the natural transition between the two.

The sudden rise of the Eurostep and the dribbling creativity of Iverson and his disciples shattered that framework. How could the Eurostep be considered a "dribbling move" when players had to terminate their dribble before executing it? How did the "one-two count" apply to the tempo changes and gather ambiguity of Iverson's hang dribble? Referees found themselves at a loss trying to assess those moves with the letter of the traveling law at the time. Neither required extra steps, but they didn't necessarily shift from gather to finish in a continuous motion, either.

James' one-of-a-kind athletic profile presented another complication. As a high school phenom and early NBA sensation, James developed a jump stop-esque move to leap through creases and finish around the basket. While the jump stop had been a common driving tactic for years, James' footwork was different. Whereas prior jump stoppers needed to leap off both feet to generate enough power to pull the move off, James was so explosive that he could leap off one foot and cover as much ground, if not more, than most people's two-footed hops.

That revealed an additional gray area in the traveling rule's language. A two-footed jump stop was considered a non-continuous move because the leap itself requires a slight pause to execute properly. Those players were thus required to maintain a pivot foot upon landing, so they could only use a jump stop if they landed on both feet, then went back up off both feet.

(Iverson, ironically, was adept at doing just that to elude bigger defenders for short jumpers and floaters.)

LeBron, however, interpreted his signature move differently. Because his initial leap was a one-footed move, he wasn't "jump stopping." Instead, he was performing something now known as a "pro hop"—a slow, yet continuous move in which his launch step operated as the first part of his "two-count rhythm." It didn't matter that the first step *looked* like a jump stop and traveled as far as a jump stop. It couldn't be one because it was off one foot rather than two.

By that logic, he should be allowed to take *another* legal step before incurring a traveling violation. If people thought it looked like a travel, that was because they weren't looking at his feet. Why should he be blamed for possessing supreme athletic gifts that allowed him to fly off one foot when most players could only dream of levitating off two?

The league initially disagreed, telling James that referees were instructed to view his move as a jump stop and thus a traveling violation. But they found it impossible to enforce consistently, only following through in a few isolated incidents. Despite James' repeated claims that the league took away his signature move, referees mostly let him get away with it.

The confusing status of James' one-footed jump stop/pro hop move was not the specific reason he got called for a travel on that pivotal January 2009 afternoon in D.C. As Spooner reiterated to a pool reporter, James took three steps after his gather regardless. But that history, combined with the rise of the Eurostep and the influx of players who mimicked Iverson's dribbling techniques, helps explain why the crab dribble controversy was the league's last straw. Nobody knew what traveling was, and players had exploited that vagueness to make a mockery of the rulebook definition. Something needed to be done to fix that.

That something trickled out a couple months later. In a story published in March of 2009, vice president of referee operations Joe Borgia told ESPN's Henry Abbott that officials had long been told to permit two post-gather steps, even if the rule's language did not explicitly state that. "We really don't reference the rulebook," he said.

To rectify this problem, Borgia drafted a new version of the traveling rule that the league approved that summer. "A player who receives the ball while he is progressing or upon completion of a dribble, may take two steps in coming to a stop, passing or shooting the ball," it read. No more "counts." No more confusion. The unwritten rule had become a written one. Players got two steps before they were whistled for traveling.

Though NBA officials pushed back on the idea that they had "changed" the definition of traveling,[137] the significance of that language alteration (or clarification, if you prefer) would soon become clear. The players' creativity had outstripped the written rules of the game. The league was forced to play catch up.

This was not the last time they fell behind.

JAMES HARDEN AND Giannis Antetokounmpo aren't best friends. It's probably a stretch to say they are mortal enemies, especially now that Antetokounmpo has a title and Harden has moved to Philadelphia by way of the Brooklyn Nets. But they undeniably sniped at each other for the better part of a calendar year.

The subject of their beef was simultaneously silly and enlightening. First, Harden dismissed Antetokounmpo's 2019 MVP Award as a narrative choice rather than one based on merit. Then, Antetokounmpo declined to pick Harden in the first-ever NBA All-Star draft, joking that he "wanted somebody that's gonna pass the ball." When ESPN's Rachel Nichols referenced Antetokounmpo's comments in a sitdown interview with Harden, the then-Rockets star took a dramatic left turn.

"I wish I could just be seven feet and run and just dunk," Harden said, citing his gaudy assist numbers to refute Antetokounmpo's dig. "Like, that takes no skill at all. I've got to actually learn how to play basketball and have skill, you know? I'll take that any day."

Harden was being somewhat facetious, even if the lingering frustration about his image was real. But the intensity of his comment was also revealing, especially since Harden prefaced his criticisms by claiming he hadn't heard Antetokounmpo's TNT comments. (Suuuurrre you didn't.) The two men were rivals, and not especially respectful ones at the time. It was only a matter of time before the subtle jabs became less subtle.

---

137. During a preseason conference call, then-executive vice president of basketball operations Stu Jackson insisted, "We have not changed the traveling rule, nor how we enforce the rule." Instead, Jackson said the league had merely changed "some antiquated language in our existing rule as it related to steps."

Rivalries tend to be defined by contrasting traits that each side is quick to wield as a cudgel against the other. Harden saw himself as an artist and Antetokounmpo as a brute. He painted masterpieces while Antetokounmpo got undue credit for coloring within the lines. He developed his bag of tricks, whereas Antetokounmpo won the genetic lottery.

Meanwhile, Antetokounmpo saw himself as a complete player, relentless worker, and leader, not a guy who monopolized the ball to score a lot of points. He played within the natural flow of the action. He didn't make excuses or blame outside forces when he came up short. He didn't try to trick referees or game the rulebook. He succeeded with *honor,* unlike Harden's public image as a trickster.

But the best rivalries occur when their bluster belies the reality that the two sides have much more in common than not. They fight over their small differences *because* their objectives and desires are so similar. Neither side wants to admit their enemy is the opposite side of the same coin, so they fixate on surface-level differences to avoid facing deeper truths. As legendary psychologist Carl Jung first proposed, the negative personality traits we amplify in our rivals are often the ones we repress in ourselves.

Harden left no doubt about the negative (basketball) personality trait he chose to amplify in his rival. He attacked Antetokounmpo's individual skill level with the subtlety of a car crash, matching the absurdity of his complaint with the (likely) lie that preceded it. Either Harden was prepared to address Antetokounmpo's TNT joke, or he wasn't and somehow barfed out the unskilled comment as a defensive mechanism.

Either way, his response offered a brief and indirect glimpse into the on-court revolution that both players were (and are) leading in opposite directions. No two players in the Spaced Out Era have done more to expand the creativity of modern footwork. Together, Harden and Antetokounmpo have built on the legacies of Ginóbili, Wade, Iverson, James, and others to reimagine the way players use their steps and dribbles. Their efforts have redefined the way players move with the ball.

Whether either player wants to admit it, their forms of on-ball creativity are two sides of the same coin. The foundation of their styles and, yes, skill, is in stretching the limits of "dribbling." They just do it in completely opposite ways—literally.

The most important element to both of their signature moves goes by two names. The more technical term is "gather step." You've probably heard that one before, or at least understand that a player must gather the ball between terminating their dribble and going up into a shot or pass. (At least I hope so, since this is the 29th time I've used the word "gather" in this chapter.)

It also goes by a different name that you may not know unless you're an advanced player, trainer, or coach. That phrase is "zero step." As in, "Giannis Antetokounmpo and James Harden's moves are deadly because of the way they use the 'zero step.'"

So what the heck is a "zero step"? Taken literally, it's a contradiction. "Zero," as in nothing, and "step" as in how your feet move. It's a step … that does not count as a step? Forgive the uninitiated person who is having trouble understanding how players are allowed to take a step that doesn't count as a step. (Maybe use "gather step" instead when convincing your friend that NBA players aren't constantly getting away with traveling).

In practice, though, the "zero step" isn't a contradiction at all. Remember the mental exercise you did earlier as you casually shot a layup? You might not have realized it then, but you took a step after your last dribble, but before you put two hands on the ball to begin your layup motion. It wasn't within your dribble, but it wasn't exactly in your shooting motion, either. Instead, it exists on the border of the two, like the neutral zone in football or a safe zone in Capture the Flag.

Do steps in this gray zone count as dribbles, post-dribbles, or neither? Historically, this question has been answered differently at different levels of basketball. Lower-level leagues did (and still do) adopt a stricter interpretation of this intermediary stage, placing it in the post-dribble category. Professional leagues like the NBA and FIBA, on the other hand, tended (and still tend) to take a more liberal approach. Cynics claim they do so for business reasons—i.e., engineering more highlights. The boring truth is that top pros are the only people with enough athletic coordination to make the distinction matter.

How have players used the stage between dribbling and shooting (or passing)? Before the rise of Iverson, Ginóbili, and their early disciples, the answer was "not much." The league thought it had corralled their innovations when it explicitly permitted two steps after gathering the ball. But while that alteration more clearly defined the dribble and post-dribble stages of a move, it did not address the zone between them.

How much could players really extract from such an abbreviated transition stage? A lot, as it turns out. Especially once Giannis Antetokounmpo and James Harden showed them.

Antetokounmpo's lessons began in earnest early in the 2014–15 season, his second in the league. His intriguing flashes of novelty as a rookie faded as the Bucks sank to the bottom of the standings, and grew homesick. Armed with renewed confidence, familiarity, an offseason of hard work, a rival to push him (No. 2 overall draft pick Jabari Parker), and a new coach in Jason Kidd that demanded he showcase his versatility, Antetokounmpo began to display his revolutionary potential.

His fast breaks caught the most attention. Every week yielded a new clip of him going from well beyond the three-point line to the rim without dribbling. His strides looked more like a giant animal's or high-tech robot's than a human being's. He didn't run, he *galloped*. And he did it while stretching his arms in impossible ways, as if he was performing real-life imitations of Michael Jordan at the end of *Space Jam*.

The intense focus on Antetokounmpo's stride length was understandable, but the more remarkable fact was that he didn't cover all that ground in a straight line. It'd be one thing if Antetokounmpo performed a more extreme in-game version of the dunk contest that players take to jam from the free-throw line.

Antetokounmpo, though, was terminating his dribble way beyond the three-point line and taking indirect paths around defenders to get to the hoop. Against Detroit, he executed a left-to-right Eurostep that took him from beyond the three-point line on the left wing to a lefty finger roll in the middle of the paint. Against Miami, he gathered the ball a step beyond the arc at the top of the key, leapt violently to his left to get around a defender, then hopped off one foot to his right to finish with a finger roll with plenty of room to spare. Imagine how much ground he could have legally covered without those pesky opponents in the way?

Antetokounmpo advanced the Eurostep popularized by Ginóbili to a whole new level. Like Ginóbili, Antetokounmpo used the first of his two allotted post-dribble steps to set up the defender before punishing them with the second. But while Ginóbili used his two to surge directly into his defenders at sharp forward angles, Antetokounmpo often sidestepped his prey. He was (almost) always taller and longer than those defenders, so it made more sense to hop around them while stretching his arms to the rim.

The length of Antetokounmpo's strides created a paradox. His transition mad dashes were incredibly fast in sum, yet each individual step of those full-court sprints was remarkably slow. As a general rule, short steps build up speed, while long steps slow it down. (Short steps hold force in reserve, while long steps thud all that energy in place upon landing.)

Antetokounmpo, however, showed how to get the best of both worlds. It took time for each of his feet to stride forward, yet they covered so much ground as a whole that he could take fewer of them to get from Point A to Point B. The balance and power he maintained on each individual step created the effect of stopping to change direction when he was still moving. He (sort of) invented a jump stop with a one-foot landing.

Antetokounmpo wasn't the first player to tailor his Eurostep to move horizontally. Others, most notably Dwyane Wade, perfected a variation of Ginóbili's move that combined a short first step with a long second one that sharply changed directions, a contrast he enhanced by swinging the ball over and around his body.

But Antetokounmpo showed a way for players to create the same effect with a long first step as well. He could cover as much ground as possible to the side after a long first step. Eventually, he could step in a left-right, left-center, right-center, center-right, right-right, left-left, or right-left combination. He possessed the leg strength and body flexibility to cover as much court space as possible with both strides.

In 2015, Antetokounmpo was still rail thin and raw. He often predetermined his moves, allowing defenders to anticipate them and take charges. He was too easily bumped off his path and committed a healthy barrel of turnovers. He still couldn't shoot from the perimeter—and, in fact, was told not to by his head coach. Those factors initially limited his movement revolution to transition play.

But Antetokounmpo and the Bucks were slowly transferring his superpowers to half-court situations. They artificially engineered fast-break-like conditions against set defenses, encouraging Antetokounmpo to use the space teams gave him to shoot as a runway to attack the basket. The faster he moved, the longer his strides in any direction. The Bucks began hanging

Antetokounmpo farther back from the three-point line so he could build up the same forward momentum he used on the break.

These tactics, while primitive for today's game and possibly even for the times, laid the groundwork for more extreme ones like Kidd's Point Giannis experiment and Mike Budenholzer's five-out offensive system. The former weaponized Antetokounmpo to push tempo, while the latter cleared out obstacles that previously got in the way of his extreme tap-dancing. Both approaches provided Antetokounmpo's long strides space to land. Luckily for him and the Bucks, the sport was rapidly spreading out.

While most observers were captivated by Antetokounmpo's stride length, there was also an undercurrent of confusion. Everyone understood that Antetokounmpo's freakish athleticism allowed him to cover more ground with his steps than his peers. But this much more ground? That seemed unnatural. Players should not be able to move through a third of the court without bouncing the ball. How had he found a way to do that legally?

The answer was the zero step. When it came to classic on-ball skills, Antetokounmpo was indeed raw at the time. But in terms of the timing, technique, and cadence of his zero step, Antetokounmpo's skill level was light years ahead of a typical player's with his NBA experience, even those who were also supremely gifted athletes. That was how he wove around defenders like they were traffic cones.

As an impoverished child in Greece, Antetokounmpo could not afford many amenities that most of the developed world takes for granted. He was exposed to the NBA largely through YouTube highlight videos he watched at Internet cafes, at which he spent one hard-earned dollar for about 30 minutes of access. Several players intrigued him, including Kevin Durant, Magic Johnson, Scottie Pippen, and Kobe Bryant. But the one that most captured his heart was Allen Iverson.

"I played basketball because of him," Antetokounmpo told TNT during 2022's All-Star Weekend. "I wanted to be like Allen Iverson growing up."

Antetokounmpo loved The Answer's aggressive style. His toughness. His cornrows, which Antetokounmpo briefly adopted. And, crucially, his crossover, which Antetokounmpo also adopted despite growing to become nearly a foot taller than its creator. "When [big brother Thanasis] played two-on-two, I was coming down, doing the crossovers, acting like I was

Iverson." Antetokounmpo said in 2019's *Finding Giannis* documentary, mimicking Iverson's high dribble and low switch of hands.

Antetokounmpo never mastered his idol's signature move, but he did even better to incorporate Iverson's more valuable hang dribble into his full-speed attacks. He saw how Iverson used the slow, high bounce of the ball to bait defenders into revealing their intentions and give off false signals of his own. Antetokounmpo also observed Iverson waiting until the last possible instant to place his hand back on the ball to attack, heightening the contrast between the hang dribble and his next move.

As Antetokounmpo grew to seven feet and continued his own basketball journey, he applied the same qualities of Iverson's hang dribble to gather the ball as late as possible when terminating his dribble. With his obscene height and stride length, Antetokounmpo's dribbles took more time to go from hand to floor than any perimeter player in NBA history. He used these long gaps to step all over the place, read his defenders, and gyrate his body to send them false cues.

Like Iverson, Antetokounmpo mastered the ability to take one last high dribble, jab an exaggerated step in one direction, wait for that foot to hit the floor, and *then* gather the ball as it still hovered in midair to preserve the two additional steps the rules allowed. He turned two already long strides into three even longer ones, with the first not counting for traveling purposes. A zero step, if you will.

That zero step was also the nexus point of Harden's signature stepback move. Harden, like Antetokounmpo, mastered the art of stretching out his gather so that it could act as an unofficial third legal step. The only difference was that Harden's move went backwards instead of really far forward. It was a mirror image of Antetokounmpo's.

In Harden's early days in Oklahoma City, he looked more like Manu Ginóbili 2.0 than the innovative player he eventually became. The comparison was a bit superficial, since both were lefties with a knack for slipping to the rim like a knife cutting through butter. Still, that version of Harden more closely aped the Spurs legend's direct downhill attacking style instead of the wholly unique approach he later displayed in Houston. Because of that, his post-gather steps got more attention than his zero step.

That changed once Harden became the on-court avatar of the Rockets' analytics revolution. His game, already tailor-made to fit Daryl Morey's holy threes-or-layups ethos, became even more in tune with them when he started using his gather step as a foul-drawing magnet. He learned to snatch the ball out of midair at different points, then swing it through his defenders' arms as he took his two post-dribble steps to power through their chests and hips. He drew all the same blocking fouls that Ginóbili once induced with his low center of gravity, plus all those extra reach-ins that barely deterred his path to the basket. He even learned to clandestinely use one arm to clamp his defenders' hands onto his other one, an underhanded tactic that succeeded for years before referees learned to snuff it out.

Cheap or not, Harden's foul-drawing skill was powered by his zero step mastery. He used it to dangle the ball invitingly to defenders in much the same way Iverson enticed his prey. But while Iverson hung the ball loosely by his side, Harden kept his dribble close to his body so he could snatch it and swing his arms through his defenders' body in a single motion. He was able to speed up his gather to catch the defender before they pulled their hands back, but he could also slow it down to bait them to reach into the cookie jar.

The unpredictability of Harden's varied gather points made it nearly impossible for defenders to maintain a balanced defensive stance. When they weren't getting left in the dust, off-balance defenders often reached in and/or committed blocking fouls. Harden's wide hips and tree-trunk legs made his two post-gather steps strong enough to withstand a wide variety of glancing blows, while his manipulation of the zero step provided ideal driving angles to activate that core strength. Like Iverson and Antetokounmpo, Harden used the previously overlooked stage *after* the dribble to create an advantage, *then* the two finishing steps to exploit it.

That serves as the backdrop for Harden's novel, deadly effective, controversial, and (eventually) widely adopted stepback three-pointer. The time spent mastering the zero + one-two footwork cadence to go forward in tight spaces early in his career informed his task to then perfect it backwards. That, as it turns out, didn't end up taking long.

Harden's stepback three-pointer was a triumph of imagination as much as a technical marvel. The value of the zero + one-two step footwork is in allowing players to cover much more space to reach valuable on-court landmarks without dribbling. The basket itself is the most obvious one. The

Eurostep took over the league because it offered a creative, deadly way for players to get there.

But the Spaced Out Era taught teams that there are other spots on the floor that are worth reaching in as few dribbles as possible. The most notable one is the three-point line, since jumpers from behind that barrier count for an additional point. Harden, and the Rockets, internalized that truth better than their peers. So he used the zero + one-two step motion to reach that landmark as well, particularly when dribbling with his weaker right hand.

The Beard began his signature move the same way players executed stepback jumpers in the past. He used his last dribble to jab hard to the basket before hopping backwards off that inside foot to create separation. But instead of putting two hands on the ball right away, Harden waited until his back leg hit the floor to do so. This, according to the now-revised language in the NBA rulebook, permitted him to take two *more* steps backward to create extra separation. The move looked more like a double stepback, but the longer first leap served as the zero step.

It takes a ton of coordination to perform Harden's "double" stepback move legally. (*Philadelphia Inquirer* reporter Keith Pompey posted a fun clip of Harden and assistant coach Sam Cassell loudly critiquing Joel Embiid as he attempted to replicate the move during Harden's first 76ers practice in February of 2022.) Harden is correct that he wasn't blessed with Antetokounmpo's body. But he did possess one athletic superpower that made his stepback jumpers and drives equally deadly.

In 2016, Harden took one of his many trips to the headquarters of the Peak Performance Project (P3 for short) in Santa Barbara, California. Founded by Dr. Marcus Elliott, a Harvard-trained physician, the P3 lab has become a hotbed to test for athletic indicators that are most conducive to the athletes' specific sport. Harden posted ordinary marks compared to his high-level basketball peers, with one notable exception. In anything related to *deceleration*, Harden was miles ahead of his fellow hoopers and way ahead of the thousands of athletes P3 tested in any sport. "He has the best all-around NBA braking system we've ever measured," Elliott told ESPN in 2016.

Harden uses his remarkable ability to stop on a dime when executing his trademark stepback three. He is able to surge forward, instantly leap back, and still go against his body's natural momentum into a balanced, straight up-and-down three-point shot with enough power to reach the rim

April 15, 2018 — Timberwolves at Rockets — WCQF Game 1
Rockets 47, Timberwovles 40 — 2:30 left in second quarter

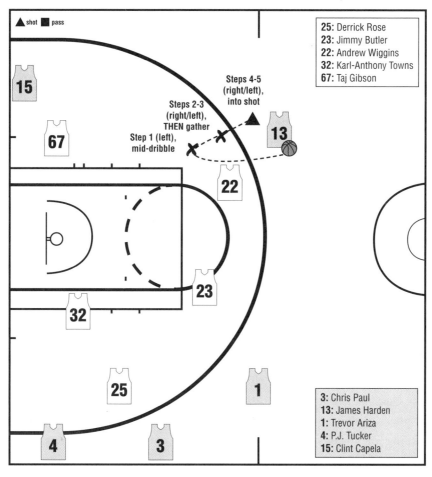

accurately. At his best, Harden was more proficient on his stepback threes than most players on spot-up triples. On top of that, defenders couldn't break fast enough to avoid slamming into him for three-shot fouls and four-point plays. Without his superpower for stopping, Harden's signature move would have lost its bite.

Yet Harden wouldn't have been able to showcase his brakes without mastering that elongated zero step to go backwards as well as forward. Players typically use the stepback as a counter to the threat of a drive, but Harden's zero step skill expanded his range of possible finishing moves. He could pick up the ball mid-leap and shoot a normal stepback off two feet, snatch it after landing to preserve his two additional steps backwards or sideways, or even plant his back foot down and surge forward without technically double-dribbling. A fake drive to set up a stepback to then set up a drive after all? Sure, why not? He hadn't gathered yet.

That wide range of options made Harden's rapid speed changes each seem quicker. Defending Harden one-on-one, especially at the peak of his powers, is mentally draining, especially if you've studied him closely. The more you know about him, the more your mind swirls with possibilities. He enhances your paralysis by keeping his dribble alive as long as possible, endlessly bouncing the ball and layering zero steps on top of zero steps until your concentration inevitably wanes. That's when he switches to quickly gather the ball and execute his finishing move. Your brain is exhausted just thinking about it. The Rockets' isolation-heavy style made you go through that over and over and over again.

The stepback three is the most demoralizing of Harden's finishing moves. "Death by 25-foot stepback jumper" is a fate no defender endured before Harden came along. Defenders either shifted weight from heel-to-toe too slowly to contest his shot, or they rushed the technique and flew wildly into him. Neither was a good outcome.

This completely bewildered opponents. Warriors coach Steve Kerr replied to a tweet of a Harden highlight by calling its legality an "embarrassment." (He later claimed he intended to send a direct message.) Three weeks later, Stephen Curry exaggeratedly mimicked Harden's double stepback in a game, earning an obvious traveling violation. Some coaches and analysts, most notably ESPN's Jeff Van Gundy, advocated for defenders to give Harden an open stepback three instead of risking a three-shot foul or four-point play trying to contest it. In 2019, Milwaukee Bucks guard Eric Bledsoe played *behind* Harden during a midseason game, deliberately letting him drive so he couldn't take a stepback three.[138] The Utah Jazz used a similar tactic in their first-round playoff series against Houston later that season, albeit less successfully. Harden's footwork was so counterintuitive that it was upending some of the sport's most basic norms.

---

138. The Bucks wanted Harden's primary defender to chase him from behind while giant center Brook Lopez protected the basket, but Bledsoe admitted he modified (or misinterpreted) the strategy to purposely let Harden drive in front of him.

The same was true of Antetokounmpo's. He had unlocked the secret to striding really, really far forward, while Harden used the same knowledge and technique to step farther backwards. For each, the act of bouncing the ball on the floor was a prelude, with the post-dribble stage making up the meat of their move. They hacked dribbling.

The rest of the league has quickly followed suit. Players stride farther forward, delay their gather even longer, and hop farther backwards. Some purposely stride *shorter* to throw off defenders used to those long Eurosteps. Others convert some of their post-dribble steps into tiny hops that hover just above the ground like a stone skipping across water. The creativity of the modern ball-handler knows no bounds. This is a golden age of ball-handling innovation, powered by what happens *after* the dribble ends.

The NBA's rulebook is finally starting to catch up. In 2017, FIBA, international basketball's governing body, became the first to put the gather step in writing, adding specific language that wasn't in the NBA's bylaws at the time. Two years later, the NBA created a new section in their rulebook to define the gather:

> For a player who receives a pass or gains possession of a loose ball, the gather is defined as the point where the player gains enough control of the ball to hold it, change hands, pass, shoot, or cradle it against his body.
>
> For a player who is in control of the ball while dribbling, the gather is defined as the point where a player does any one of the following:
>
> Puts two hands on the ball, or otherwise permits the ball to come to rest, while he is in control of it;
>
> Puts a hand under the ball and brings it to a pause; or
>
> Otherwise gains enough control of the ball to hold it, change hands, pass, shoot, or cradle it against his body.

The league again branded this move as a clarification of existing guidelines rather than a "rule change." But adding *an entire separate section* to define the gather was a significant alteration, however they wanted to define it. It institutionalized three separate stages of ball-handling: the dribble, the gather, and the post-gather. All three could be manipulated, which meant each needed to be regulated.

Most important of all, only one of the three actually included dribbling. The other two showcased a different set of skills that were only loosely connected to bouncing the ball.

With the league fully on board with a three-pronged view of ball-handling, we must consider two related overarching questions. First: What does it mean to be a ball-handling wizard now? And second: What even is functional NBA athleticism today?

AARON HOLIDAY IN THE OPEN FLOOR. Those six words foreshadow, well, nothing, unless you're an NBA scout, assistant coach, pro personnel executive, or one of the other two NBA-playing Holiday brothers. Such is the case with 25-year-old backup combo guards who become forgettable throw-ins in larger trades.[139]

This is the scenario blankly staring the Charlotte Hornets in the face against Holiday's Washington Wizards on the night of November 22, 2021. With two and a half minutes to go in the first quarter, budding Charlotte star LaMelo Ball tosses a lazy crosscourt pass that Holiday easily intercepts. The Wizards' backup, who checked into the game 30 seconds earlier to spell star Bradley Beal, races back the other way.

Holiday crosses the half-court line at an angle, juts his shoulders by Hornets wing Kelly Oubre, and throws the ball several feet ahead with his left hand, letting it bounce up to his right shoulder five feet in front of the three-point line on the right wing. He brings his right hand to the outside of the ball, letting it dangle as he veers his head toward Hornets forward Miles Bridges. At the same time, Holiday slips his left hand ever-so-closely toward the ball without touching it. He's waiting to see how Bridges, the lone Hornet back, will react.

That's when the young Hornets forward turns toward Holiday while balancing ever-so-slightly on his left leg so he can quickly hop back toward Deni Avdija, the second-year Wizards forward sprinting up the wing. Bridges is trying to convince Holiday that he's chosen to stop the ball, but Holiday isn't fooled. He has all the information he needs to see Bridges' intention to play the pass.

---

139. After being part of the complex, five-team, sign-and-trade deal that sent Russell Westbrook to the Lakers, Holiday was then sent to Phoenix at the 2022 trade deadline for … cash.

The dribble has served its purpose. Now it's time for Holiday's actual move.

In one rapid sequence, Holiday lets his right foot hit the floor, extends his right hand while swiveling his head as if he's throwing a chest pass to Avdija, and takes a single long stride that brings his left foot to just inside the free-throw line. By the time Bridges turns his back thinking he's won the battle of wits, Holiday has already pulled the ball back to his right and taken another long stride to the edge of the dotted free-throw circle. As Bridges squares up for an Avdija finish that never comes, Holiday lifts off his right foot and glides for a point-blank righty layup.

It's been less than five years since Giannis Antetokounmpo wowed a half-empty Barclays Center crowd with a similar open-floor ball-fake move. That play, in which Antetokounmpo took a single dribble from half court and soared from 25 feet to the basket in two long strides, was impossible to even imagine before he came along. Now, *less than five years later,* a 6'3" backup combo guard who was traded for cash two-and-a-half months later duplicated his feat while adding an even more convincing ball fake and an extended one-handed, outside-footed layup.

And it was all perfectly legal, both by the book and the view of that officiating crew.

Holiday manipulated all three stages of his move to fit those guidelines. He followed Iverson's example to let his final dribble hang up by his shoulder while he gave off false signals. He followed Ginóbili's lesson to use the time between his last dribble and his first post-dribble step to survey the scene. He adopted Harden's trick of gathering the ball *just* after taking a long "zero" step, thereby preserving his two remaining ones. He mimicked Antetokounmpo's two long post-gather diagonal strides. For good measure, he also duplicated Steve Nash's signature one-handed, outside-footed finish. Like most members of the NBA's rank and file, Holiday had mastered the game's newest art: moving with the ball without dribbling it.

His lovely, but long-forgotten move against Charlotte was a small sign that the NBA's post-dribble revolution is now complete. Over the last few years, players of all sizes have become well-schooled in the ball-handling ideals of Iverson, Ginóbili, Antetokounmpo, Harden, and others. They know that when the dribble ends, the real move is just beginning.

The widespread, rapid adoption of those innovators' tactics did not occur by accident. By widening the playing surface and speeding up the game's tempo, the Spaced Out Era elevated the importance of movement efficiency to best cover that extra ground.

(It's also no accident that this ball-handling revolution occurred at the same time the fitness community at large realized the importance of core exercise and stability training. Players today aren't just leaner than their predecessors. They're also better at balancing on one leg, changing direction quickly, and maintaining their speed over longer distances. This book has and will continue to reference ways the Spaced Out NBA is both a cause and an effect of these training methods, but a full dissection of those specific fitness training changes is beyond the scope of this book.)

The open floor gives offensive players more space to delay and deceive with their steps and dribbles, mostly because it gives them more room to step, period. That's more room to fit deadly individual moves, such as a crossover, Eurostep, or spin, into longer stories that develop with each step and body fake.

The impact of that extra space on the floor cannot be overstated. Basketball, at its core, has always been a game built on deception. Great ball-handlers have always been vivid on-court storytellers, particularly gifted at weaving captivating mysteries that turn their decisive moves into twists defenders never see coming. It always pays to make defenders think you can do anything before you commit.

Nowadays, they craft those narratives in a significantly larger, more open space instead of within the tighter confines of previous eras. Much of the ball-handling exposition in the past occurred while players were standing still. In the Spaced Out Era, it happens on the move, since both the ball-handler and defender have more room to travel before they each reach their preferred destinations. Often, the time *between* steps and dribbles has become the ideal spot to lay out trails of clues, red herrings, and the other plot devices that make up a good mystery.

It wasn't the moves themselves—the crossover, Eurostep, pro hop, stepback three, etc.—that made Iverson, Ginóbili, James, Antetokounmpo, and Harden pioneers. It was the ways they used previously unexplored sections of their handle, like the gap between dribbles, the gather stage, and the two post-gather steps, as storytelling devices. They showed modern ball-handlers how to break down and optimize each to deceive their opponents.

This is the final and arguably most profound downstream effect of the NBA's three-point revolution. The more the game's surface area widened, the more it necessitated completely new ways to actually move with the ball. The elongated gather step, the "hang" part of the hang dribble, and the long, slow post-dribble strides became pages of great modern ball-handling stories. Since none of them directly involve dribbling, the modern NBA player, quite literally, must move in a far different way than his predecessor.

The necessity of that harsh reality has been the mother of several new training techniques to improve players' functional "Spaced Out basketball" athleticism.

One you'll spot right away is known as the "toe drag." Taking long strides without losing balance and/or blowing out a knee ligament is exceedingly difficult, especially when opponents—and their body parts—get in the way. To gain more power and balance, players learned to slide the back toe along the ground when lurching their front foot forward, thereby redistributing force the lead leg would otherwise have to absorb on its own. That, in turn, preserves more power for the front foot to take a stronger, more on-balance second step, whether it's farther forward, sideways, or even to stop forward momentum and explode up while the defender flies out of the play. The "toe drag" has thus become an essential element in today's longest, slowest, most diagonal, and most powerful Eurosteps.

The toe drag is one of several biomechanical tricks players now deploy to maximize the impact of their strides. Ever notice players swinging their arms to and fro on their drives? The cynical reason is to clear out obstacles and/or draw cheap fouls, which is somewhat true.[140] But the more important reason they do is that the swinging motion propels their body farther forward, giving it the extra push needed to power through perimeter defenders and dislodge rim protectors. Plus, it's also a good way to perform pass fakes. The same motion Aaron Holiday used to fool Miles Bridges also helped him to cover more ground on his next two steps.

Armed with those tactics, leaner bodies, stronger core muscles, a more open floor, and the proof of concept of past innovators, modern players

140. James Harden has entered the chat.

April 26, 2022 — Timberwolves at Grizzlies — WCQF Game 5 (Tied 2-2)
Timberwolves 85, Grizzlies 72 — 8.1 seconds left in third quarter

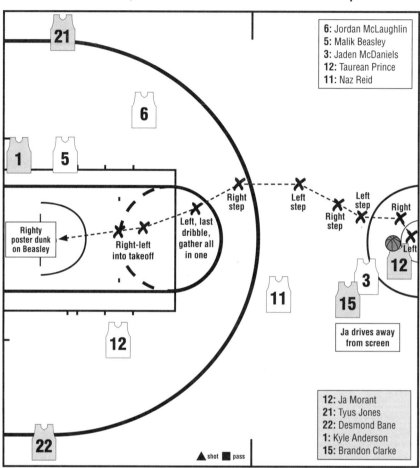

are taking the precepts of the post-dribble movement to new places. A few examples:

- Kyrie Irving created space for his go-ahead stepback shot in Game 7 the 2016 NBA Finals with a Harden-esque reverse gather + one-two step footwork toward his strong hand rather than his weak one.

- Harden has tried out more elaborate gather methods, such as a behind-the-back motion into a stepback without dribbling. He also experimented with a one-legged stepback three in a preseason game, a la Dirk Nowitzki's one-legged fadeaway.

- Kyle Anderson, a tall, skinny point forward affectionately known as "Slo Mo," built his entire game out of performing longer, slower post-dribble strides than his opponents. Consider him the NBA's Tim Wakefield.

- Some gifted guards, including Memphis sensation Ja Morant and Utah's Donovan Mitchell, will leap *backwards* with their second step, hang in midair until their opponents go down, and shoot a de-facto fadeaway layup or floater before their foot hits the ground.

- Bigger players such as Dallas' Luka Dončić and the Clippers' Paul George use that second step more like a one-footed jump stop, driving their foot deep into a backpedaling defender to force them on their heels before rising straight up to finish before committing a charge.

- Players of all sizes now take two itty-bitty post-gather steps to set up outside-foot finishes that sneak the ball up to the hoop before defenders can leap to block it.

- Morant, whose jaw-dropping athleticism is unlike any point guard's in NBA history, deploys similarly quick one-two post-gather footwork to explode to the rim like he's shot out of a cannon. He uses the equivalent of a football four-point stance to marry the power of a two-footed jump with the forward momentum of a one-foot gather step leap. That's legal as long as a) his two rapid post-gather steps aren't perfectly simultaneous, and b) the foot not used as the gather step's takeoff point hits the ground first. This footwork allows Morant to dunk on poor fools like San Antonio's Jakob Poeltl in an early March 2022 game, but also allows him to stop on a dime for his deadly floater. Minnesota second-year wing Anthony Edwards is developing the same footwork on his strong drives as well.

- Some players take long, low steps that skim the ground as if there's an invisible jump rope in the lane. Charlotte's LaMelo Ball uses this tactic to sneak his lovely passes through windows that otherwise wouldn't exist. Mitchell sometimes pairs a long, high stride with a second low "skim step" before releasing a layup or one of his signature crosscourt whip passes.

The power of the zero step concept can be extended to spot-up situations. Players now are able to avoid pesky traveling calls by leaping ever so slightly while receiving the pass. If they time it just right, they possess the ball *before* landing and thus have not established a pivot foot.

The same trick can be used to catch the ball on the move, which enables them to attack a gap in the defense before they even have the ball. This maneuver, known as a "go-and-catch," originated overseas before becoming popular in a spread-out NBA with more gaps that defenses rush to shut quickly. As long as players timed their sprinting strides to catch the pass just *after* one foot hit the ground, they still had two more to use if they wanted to shoot or pass without dribbling.[141] These, in essence, are "zero steps."

In the Spaced Out NBA, proper step timing, *not* dribbling, is the way players move with the ball. God Shammgod's axiom that dribbling is footwork and the hands are an illusion has never been more apt. Basketball athleticism nomenclature must adapt to the times as well.

What does it mean to be explosive? Quick? Crafty? *Athletic?* Now that every player customizes their stepping cadence to move fast, slow, and every speed in between over an ever-widening court, these terms must be deployed far more precisely. Craftiness and athleticism are one in the same these days, if they weren't already. It does everyone a disservice to treat them as opposites.

The failure to specify and modify NBA-specific athletic qualities has cost teams dearly. The most notable example was when supposed "athleticism" concerns contributed to Dončić getting selected *after* "NBA athletes" Deandre Ayton and Marvin Bagley despite starring at a young age in the far superior Spanish ACB and Euroleague, each composed of the best grown men not in the NBA. Ayton became a quality player in Phoenix, though he never reached Dončić's level. Bagley, meanwhile, flopped with the Kings before they dumped his salary in a 2022 deadline deal with Detroit.[142]

These devastating mistakes were based on a view of NBA athleticism that was becoming dated. In truth, Dončić, despite his famous conditioning troubles, *is a far superior athlete for the modern NBA.* His ability to maintain balance on one foot while covering large distances allowed him to play at his own pace and fool defenders with his vision and creativity. Bagley could

---

141. But only one more if they ended up needing to dribble.

142. Much of the next paragraph applies to No. 5 pick Trae Young as well, albeit in a slightly different way since Young's size scared teams rather than his quickness and/or first step.

leap over anyone, but that wasn't much good without the leg strength and balance to do so within the flow of a modern NBA game.

Yet Bagley was universally considered the more athletic prospect due to his chiseled body, whereas Dončić had to make up for his lack of athleticism with craftiness that many feared wouldn't scale as easily against NBA defenders.

Why did so many NBA folks make this error? The answer lies with the post-dribble movement revolution that has accelerated in the Spaced Out Era. In particular, it showed the folly of the term "first step."

If we're being literal, every move requires multiple steps, and a "first step" is one small part of that process. In practice, it had become a catch-all term imprecisely used to describe many different types of basketball athleticism, if not basketball athleticism itself. To be athletic *was* to have a quick "first step."

Using "first step" interchangeably with other distinct athletic qualities was less damaging in previous eras because the game was more constrained. One quick first step to get past a defender was more likely to be decisive enough to reach the basket or pivot into a makeable shot. The game was more start-and-stop, heightening the value of a quick first move.

But once the three-point revolution spread the game farther out, the importance of going from 0 to 60 dwarfed in comparison to the capability of executing rapid shifts *between* 0 and 60. Previously, the first step got players far. In the Spaced Out Era, they still have a long way and many steps to go. The value of the "first step" shifted to a means to set up the next steps, much like the dribble now serves to set up the post-dribble stage of a move.

Elongated gathers, slow post-dribble strides, and the zero step further chip away at the importance of making a quick first move. Semantically, is the zero step the first step, or something else? More to the point, these tactics double as ways to restart moves midway through their completion, as if each step becomes a new "first step."

While many harped on Dončić's average "first step," they missed how he more than made up for it with the rest of his steps. He traversed the court like a distance runner, slowly accumulating small advantages with his steps before delivering finishing blows with his final one. His acceleration was average, but his *deceleration* rivaled and possibly exceeded even Harden's. Had those talent evaluators who missed on Luka adopted a more well-rounded view of basketball athleticism. they might have declared Dončić's "last step" to be among the most vicious in the history of the draft.

That might not have counted for as much if Dončić entered the NBA 15 years ago, but in a "post-dribble" world, the "last step" is as important an athletic skill as any in the sport. The Eurostep is a last step move. So is the "double" stepback three. So, even to an extent, is Iverson's hang dribble. They aren't so deadly by accident. They each packed a serious punch because their practitioner engineered his steps to cover lots of ground with as few dribbles as possible.

A few years ago, only innovators like Antetokounmpo or Harden possessed that ingenuity. Now, it's become a form of basketball athleticism a non-playoff team's 11th man deploys in-game without most of us batting an eye. That's how quickly the Spaced Out Era transformed the ideals of a two-decade dribbling revolution into basketball dogma. This is how players move with the ball in their hands now.

It was time for defenders to adapt.

Chapter 12
Beyond Man-to-Man

Defensive technique and footwork get long-overdue updates.

In the vast majority of his 320 regular-season games and 39 playoff contests in Houston's Toyota Center, James Harden was an unstoppable offensive force. His 360th visit was a different story.

On December 8, 2021, Harden brought his road-weary Nets into Houston on the second night of a back-to-back. In the previous season, Harden dazzled in his first return trip to the city in which he cemented his professional reputation, albeit in front of a reduced crowd due to COVID-19 restrictions. With Kevin Durant resting and Kyrie Irving still away from the team after refusing the coronavirus vaccine, the Nets needed Harden to repeat that feat against a young Rockets team on a six-game winning streak following a 1–20 start to the season.

Instead, Harden experienced the full scope of a league that was catching on to his many tricks.

Rookie guard Josh Christopher stripped Harden twice in the open floor, the second after picking up Harden full court *and* getting spun on a lightning-quick Harden crossover. Second-year combo forward Jae'Sean Tate lunged out under control on Harden's signature stepback, which Harden tried and failed to circumvent with an exaggerated leg kick that failed to draw a foul. Former teammate Eric Gordon forced a turnover by thrusting his hip out to cut off Harden's driving angle without reaching in with his hands. Talented big man Christian Wood ran step-for-step with raised arms as Harden surged downhill, held his chest back so Harden couldn't jump into him to draw contact, then leapt ever so slightly off his back foot to swat Harden's meek layup attempt.

That was just in the second quarter!

In the end, Harden shot 4–16 from the field, committed eight turnovers, and looked like a shell of the star he had been in Houston. The Rockets won by 10, gaining a small measure of revenge after Harden's ugly trade demand the season prior.

This was one of several out-of-character Harden performances to start the 2021–22 season. The same player who revitalized one-on-one basketball, popularized the stepback three-pointer, sliced to the basket at will, and paraded endlessly to the free-throw line was finding it harder to pull off each of those feats.

Most commentators knew exactly why.

"Those are the calls that James Harden's not getting anymore," Rockets broadcaster and former 10-year NBA veteran Ryan Hollins said after one of Christopher's two strips. "You know, when he creates all the contact. Now he's not being rewarded."

Hollins' point, echoed by many others, didn't apply to the rest of this game since Harden managed to generate 16 free throws. But he was correct that Harden *was* getting fewer calls on his drives to the basket, at least at the time.[143] And while it will never be its official stance, this trend was indeed by the league's design.

In the summer of 2021, the NBA confirmed its long-reported intention to crack down on "non-basketball moves," i.e., overt foul-drawing tactics that had long annoyed players and viewers. Those included shooters jumping into defenders, ball-handlers "abruptly veering off their path … into a defender," unnatural leg kicks on jump shots, and off-arm hooks into defenders while gathering the ball—all Harden specialties.

Harden was not the only player that used them, which the league drove home by omitting him from their initial wave of examples that would be

---

143. Harden's free-throw rate was already bouncing back after dropping precipitously during the first month of the season and kept rising during and after he engineered another trade, this time to the Philadelphia 76ers.

violations under the new mandate. But his all-around mastery of foul-hunting tricks had turned him into the personification of the "non-basketball moves" the league aimed to eliminate. "We're getting away from the gimmicks," NBA president of league operations Byron Spruell told ESPN.

These changes were widely applauded as several stars' free-throw rates plummeted in the first few weeks of the season. Drives that once ended with whistles turned into contested finishes at the hoop, turnovers, more difficult floaters, or short-range jumpers. Defenders felt emboldened to play more physically, making it even harder to attack the basket. Referees (initially) erred on the side of swallowing their whistles.

Harden bore the brunt of these changes, but he was hardly alone. Damian Lillard, Devin Booker, Luka Dončić, Bradley Beal, and others saw their free-throw rates and scoring efficiency plummet in the early part of the season. It took time for each to adjust their games to keep pace. (Interestingly, Atlanta's Trae Young, considered to be the other main target of these new points of emphasis along with Harden, did not experience much of a drop.)

As their production declined, teams suddenly found it harder to score. The league's average offensive efficiency, which had risen from 105.9 points per 100 possessions in 2014–15 to 112.9 in 2020–21, was on pace for a steep decline after the first month of the season. Spaced Out NBA skeptics rejoiced, and even its most enthusiastic proponents were happy to see some balance restored.

"I love what I'm seeing. I think the game has a more authentic feel," Warriors coach Steve Kerr said during an off-day media availability.

"Can I also say how satisfying it's been to watch the game of basketball without all those bullshit calls," Draymond Green said unprompted after an early-season win.

"Best thing the league has done in recent history," tweeted Wizards forward Kyle Kuzma.

Few considered the many other reasons for the (temporary) league-wide offensive decline. Several of the aforementioned stars, most notably Harden and Lillard, were nursing and/or recovering from core muscle injuries. Historically, offense improves as the season progresses, when travel fatigue sets in, injuries pile up, and the teams who fall out of contention lose the zeal for defending. (The 2021–22 season proved to be no exception, though it didn't quite reach the highs of the previous season.)

Most notably, the league's three-point shooting percentage was way down from the previous season. The league as a whole made 36.7 percent of its three-pointers in the 2020–21 season, the highest mark in NBA history, and eclipsed 39 percent on those logged as "open," which has only happened one other time since the league began using tracking data.

The reasons for that early-season trend were numerous, but few, if any, directly related to officiating. Not only was regression statistically inevitable to some degree, but key in-game conditions had changed. Fans were no longer absent from arenas due to COVID-19 restrictions, a quirk that most players and coaches believe aided shooters because empty gyms feature fewer background obstacles that affect depth perception. The NBA also switched their official ball manufacturer from longtime partner Spalding to Wilson over the summer, and several players admitted, publicly and privately, that they were still adjusting to its different feel. "Not to make an excuse or anything, but it's just a different basketball," Clippers star Paul George told reporters early in the season. "It doesn't have the same touch or softness as the Spalding ball had."

Yet each of those factors were overlooked as the public rushed to praise the new officiating points of emphasis. After decades of seemingly tipping the scales in the offense's favor, a fix to aid defenses seemed refreshing. Finally, mercifully, the natural balance of the game was being restored. It would no longer be impossible to play defense in the NBA.

But while the so-called "2021 rule changes" certainly *helped* defenses, they weren't solely responsible for its (mini) revival. Instead, they helped showcase the gradual transformation in defensive technique and theory already in progress. With them now in place and the kind shooting environments of fanless post-pandemic arenas (hopefully) in the rearview, the effects of that defensive evolution—which had been hiding in plain sight—are now easier to spot.

It's often said that sport strategies proceed in cycles. If so, are we at the beginning of a new one?

This book is about an NBA revolution that metastasized slowly over multiple decades, accelerated dramatically over just a few years, and has forced us to reconsider the previously sacred norms governing the sport's fundamentals. It is a story about three words that begin with the letter "S":

"shooting" plus "speed," which add up to the increased "space" that offenses use and defenses must cover.

It is also a story, above all, about *faith*. Showing faith in players' on-court creativity and instincts. The leaps of faith they must take to make a move or deliver a pass before a teammate knows to look for it. Maintaining faith in shooting rhythm and confidence even when the shots aren't going in. Modern basketball rewards decisive action, which only occurs when one has more faith in a positive outcome than fear of a negative one. These concepts, to some degree, were out of step with traditionalists' views of basketball.

They're *especially* antithetical to a traditional view of defense. Good defense is seen as a matter of willpower, persistence, intensity, and grit. It is militaristic, defined by following a set of rules to the letter. It is *drilled* into players by snarling coaches who never seem content, lest any seeds of satisfaction sprout into oak trees of complacency. Bad defense indicates a lack of effort, which stems from a breakdown in commitment. How often do you hear a coach say they "can't teach effort" after a bad *offensive* performance?

Everyone working for an NBA team knows that effort is nothing without proper technique and strategy. Yet that, in many ways, can bias them and other avid fans *more* to this oversimplified image of defense. The culture of defense is discipline, and discipline requires repetition. But that can become problematic when the techniques themselves are taught as ironclad laws to be followed precisely rather than broader concepts to apply to increasingly unique in-game situations. Plus, the more thoroughly a coach drills their techniques, strategies, and schemes, the easier it is to see each subsequent failure to stop an opponent from scoring as a breakdown in player execution rather than the coach's own overarching design. "We gotta drill this more" becomes the default solution.

This made defense especially susceptible to the elimination of hand-checking, relaxation of zone defense rules, and the practical doubling of the playing surface on account of the ensuing three-point revolution. In theory, they should have inspired the same level of defensive innovation as we saw on the other end. Instead, the "effort bias," so to speak, kept too many stuck in their ways while endlessly complaining that the league made it impossible to play defense anymore. We've all heard variations of these gripes. "Back in my day, you could get in guys' faces. Now you can't even touch them. ... If Michael Jordan played now, he'd average 200 points a game. ... It's so much easier for today's players. But this is what the NBA wants." Yada yada yada. The flip side is a small offseason tweak to curtail a minor offensive advantage (unnatural foul-drawing tactics) is overstated as the salvation for defense itself.

What if those same people asked themselves if defenses had it too *easy* all those years? What if the Spaced Out Era was *correcting* a decades-long structural imbalance in defense's favor rather than tipping the scale unduly toward offense? What if the ongoing revolution was exposing defensive inefficiencies that had always lingered beneath the surface?

The first step for defense's, uh, defenders to adapt was to consider those questions. Not to form an opinion on them, to be clear, for those are subjective opinions that are a matter of one's taste. Instead, the purpose of reframing these questions is to realize that if offense now requires versatility, then perhaps good defense shouldn't be defined as effortfully following a bunch of rules to the letter of the law.

It was time for defense to evolve. It was time for it to match the offense's fluidity. It was time to build more flexible defensive schemes, techniques, and fundamentals.

"BEND YOUR KNEES! Get low! Slide your feet!"

"Stay between your man and the basket!"

"Never cross your feet, unless you want to fall on your ass!"

"Chop your feet when closing out on a shooter!"

These are but a few of the defensive rules that your coaches seared into your head from a young age.

They're also wrong.

Okay, not *entirely* wrong. Most were correct once upon a time, likely when you learned them. But each, to varying degrees, relies on an assumption that no longer applies as the game spreads out. To teach them as ironclad fundamentals is to be out of step with the reality of the Spaced Out NBA.

That does not mean they are useless. Getting low is generally important for playing good defense—*generally* being the operative word. "Never bend your knees" would be stupid advice. It is still important to stay in front of your man. On-balance closeouts are good. Falling on your ass is bad.

But they are useful as *principles* or *guidelines*, not *rules*. Rules are *followed*. Principles are *applied* to a wide variety of in-game situations. For years, these theories of defense have been taught like rules, not principles. That's a good way to ace a test, but an awful way to adapt to the dynamic, fast-paced, wide tapestry of the current NBA style of play.

Defensive slides, for example, have long been seen as the proper way to move your feet in every defensive situation. That attitude presumes the defender starts from the exact same position at the exact same time as the offensive player, with no help and no room to recover if beat. Assuming *all that*, yes, sliding gives the defender the best chance to keep the offensive player in front of them. One quick slide out and in covers more ground while staying on balance than any other movement from a stationary position.

How often is an NBA defender in that position in a 2022 game? What happens if (when) they still get beat? Now what?

Defenders are often, if not constantly, in "now what" situations these days. While modern players go one on one, they start from farther away from the hoop, after more fluid ball movement, with more finishing moves, fewer teammates, and/or more off-ball opponents near their driving lanes. Otherwise, the game is played entirely on the move, all the way out to well beyond the three-point line. Defenders almost always will get beat to some spot before, during, and/or after their opponent's move. They rarely have the luxury of a *mano a mano* battle where they have time to size up their opponent, get down in their stance, and square them up before they act. They are constantly helping, closing out on shooters, slipping around or through on-ball screens, and switching assignments.

Is sliding the best way to make up for those inherent time and/or space deficits? Of course not! Would you, in any context other than basketball, reach someone ahead or behind you by turning to the side and sliding your feet without crossing one over the other? Of course not. You turn and run. Specifically, you use shortcuts and fewer steps to catch up to the person you're pursuing. You can't worry about not letting them out of your sight again without getting them back in your sight first.

Basketball, especially modern basketball, requires a series of micro movements from even-strength, leading, and trailing positions. A good defender must know when to slide, when to turn and run, and how to shift between the two to beat offensive players to their desired end point. They must toggle between those movement patterns while using some obstacles in their environments (help defenders, the sideline) and avoiding others (screens). They mix some step-and-slide maneuvers with sideways hops off either foot, long steps over their other foot—a maneuver known as a "cross step" or "crossover step"—short steps to decelerate, coming up in their stance to avoid hard picks (sometimes called "getting skinny"), and running directly alongside the opponent.

There is no one way to move when keeping up with shifty offensive players over wider spaces. Why teach players otherwise?

One reason for the misconception is that sliding was long assumed to be the only way defenders could maintain balance while moving laterally, changing direction, and absorbing body contact. An off-balance defender is a useless defender, especially when sitting flat on their behind. Sticking to slides, particularly low step-slides with no crossing of the feet, was seen as the safest way, the *only* way, to avoid that embarrassing fate.

That was and still is true in close quarters, when offensive players are using power moves that cause early body contact. In those situations, getting low gives defenders much-needed leverage,[144] while the step-slide approach is more than sufficient to address any lateral direction change within such tight confines. Before 2004, most scoring situations were in these closer quarters.

But the same qualities that make a low step-slide effective in the trenches dramatically limits its range of motion. The extra time it takes to pick up the front foot, plant it back down, and then drag the back foot along the ground in a typical slide dramatically limits a defender's lateral mobility. Spreading the game out magnified that weakness, especially because the offensive player also had more space to get a head start to build up speed. The more room offensive players get to turn defenders, execute multiple slides, and shift through multiple speed gears, the less balanced a step-sliding defender becomes over time. That movement is built to handle first-step moves, not multi-step ones.

That lesson did not sink in immediately. Instead, the 2004 decision to police all forms of hand-checking further reinforced the step-slide myth. Defenders didn't just use a hand-check to impede their opponent's progress. They also did it to maintain *their own balance* as they slid their feet, much like we grip railings for stability when walking on steep or shaky surfaces.

---

144. This is why the best low-post defenders aren't necessarily tall, but all have low centers of gravity.

Losing the guard-rail of the hand-check further magnified the importance of balanced feet.

But because the step-slide was itself seen as a balanced movement in all situations, many interpreted the loss of hand-checking as a reason to *reinforce* the step-slide method even more. That interpretation failed to realize that the sport's self-imposed spatial constraints intrinsically linked step-sliding and hand-checking together. Taking one away (hand-checking) exposed the other (the step-slide).

That became especially clear once the game spread out. One-on-one defenders got roasted repeatedly, especially as perimeter offensive stars introduced post-dribble moves like the Eurostep. Hand-checking became the boogeyman that allowed the step-slide method to skate free. At least for a while.

To some, defenders seemed (and still seem) to be facing an impossible task. *There's too much space to stay in front of these guys without my precious hand-check! Care to give me a fighting chance?* They certainly faced a harder task at a minimum, in that a group of five players will always have more trouble covering a surface area of 35(ish) by 46 feet than 20(ish) by 46 feet. But impossible? Hardly.

It just required accepting the simple, grave truth that the way they used to cover the court may not work when it doubles in size. They needed to learn new ways to keep up. They needed to think more like pursuers than stationary guards. They needed to cross step, turn and run, get skinny, stay upright on the move, backpedal if necessary, absorb body blows in the chest without bringing the arms down, use their hips for leverage and stability instead of their hands, shade ball-handlers one way or another instead of squaring them up, and mirror opponents' footwork to anticipate their next move and arrive there first. Above all, they had to train their bodies to stay on balance no matter how they moved their feet.

Sounds tough, right? Well, yeah, it's not *easy*. But there is one group of athletes that must learn, from an early age, how to backpedal, turn and run, cross their feet, and still change direction in open spaces instantly while staying on their feet if they want to succeed at the highest levels. If they can learn those tricks, so could NBA defenders.

They are NFL defensive backs.

This, in fairness, isn't an apples-to-apples comparison. Defensive backs can, of course, use their hands to jam receivers within the first five yards and get repeated stoppages to catch their breath. But any advantage they possess over NBA defenders pales in comparison to *all* the extra space they must cover.

A football field is nearly four times as long and more than three times as wide as an NBA court. If we suppose a very (very) rough estimate of a 20-yard pass route on one side of the field, a defensive back is primarily responsible for 1,600 square feet. Even if a basketball defender today is stuck on an island with an offensive player 30 feet from the hoop—an extreme scenario—they're only covering *less than half the space of our hypothetical NFL defensive back*. Plus, their man must also dribble a basketball while they run.

The point is not to assert that NFL defensive backs are better athletes than NBA players. It's to illustrate how the modern NBA puts primary defenders in spatial positions that are much closer to football than they were in the past. The multi-step, multi-direction, and multi-speed compound moves highlighted in Chapter 11 more closely resemble the route-running patterns of wide receivers, just with less top-end speed and more acute tempo and directional shifts. How can we update defensive techniques for the current NBA? "Make them more like those of NFL defensive backs" is a good place to start.

How do defensive backs move?

Certainly not by mimicking the traditional step-slide-only method indoctrinated in past basketball players, because if they did they'd be lucky to stay in their receivers' zip code. Instead, they sometimes backpedal, sometimes cross step sideways, sometimes surge toward the ball, sometimes turn and sprint with them, and always know to switch instantly between each depending on the receiver's route and the coverage/situation. They stay on balance no matter their footwork by drilling to remove wasted steps or movements that might throw off their bodies' speed or control.

One key area of focus is the transition between backpedaling and breaking on the ball. Some football coaches teach a "T step," which is when a defensive back swings their back leg out to the side while keeping their front foot facing forward to make the shape of a T. Other coaches swear by the "bicycle step," which involves defensive backs leaning up on the balls of their back foot and pushing off it. "T step" advocates believe their approach adds more leg stability and power, while "bicycle step" proponents feel their method is the more natural of the two. In truth, NFL players must be proficient at both to address different in-game situations. (In that respect, the "T step vs. bicycle step" debate is similar to the "dip or no dip" jump shot argument from Chapter 10.)

Regardless, the success of either method hinges on two key factors that NBA pros are beginning to adopt as well.

The first is hip flexibility, i.e., the ability to swivel them smoothly in any direction at any point. That requires excellent core strength, but also a loose torso that enables a wide range of motion. The hips, and not the feet, are the most important body part for an NFL defensive back.

Talent evaluators study how well defensive backs can "flip their hips," i.e., swing them from one side of the body to another. Bulk the hips up too much, and it'll take too long to flip their weight from one side to another. Leaving the hips unattended, though, forces other body parts to overcompensate to make any sharp cut. Only by striking the ideal balance between the two can defensive backs change speed and direction on balance with a single rapid hip turn. With optimized hips, it shouldn't matter if a defensive back's feet are spread far apart, close together, or crossed one in front of the other.

The best modern NBA defenders are also elite hip flippers. It's no accident that so many of them have wide torsos and bulging calf muscles. Players like Draymond Green, P.J. Tucker, Marcus Smart, Kawhi Leonard, Jrue Holiday, Ben Simmons, and Jimmy Butler don't have prototypical spindly basketball bodies. Many were considered subpar NBA athletes or stuck between positions. How do they all possess an uncanny ability to stay with (supposedly) much quicker offensive players? The hips don't lie.

Specifically, their hip strength and flexibility negate the need to step-slide to maintain balance. They of course *can* when appropriate, particularly in close quarters. But their loose hips allow them to also cross their feet, turn and run, backpedal, hop, plant off either leg, and seamlessly shift between each form of movement to cover more ground in fewer steps. Not only are they able to *stay in front* of more players, but they can also recover more quickly when beat. Their hip flexibility keeps them from opening up too much or jutting too far in the offensive player's path—however their feet move. Players that stick to sliding, by contrast, are toast once they fall behind their driver.

Their ability to access such varied footwork patterns is what makes them so difficult to beat in so many different on-court situations, on and off the ball. That pairs nicely with the other key NFL defensive back attribute that NBA players are only now adopting: a technique known as "dissociation."

Dissociation refers to an athlete's ability to move one part of their body without that momentum moving any others. In football, dissociation is how defensive backs are able to flip their hips without turning their shoulders or chests, allowing them to keep their eyes on the receiver, quarterback, and (if necessary) the ball. Basketball in the post-hand-check era, on the other hand, requires a slightly different form of the skill that trainers refer to as "upper/lower-body dissociation." In other words: moving the body parts below the hips without also moving those above the waist in the same direction.

While football is a far more violent sport overall, basketball players touch each other more frequently than receivers and defensive backs because the playing surface is much smaller. In order to "beat your man to the spot," every single basketball drive features at least one battleground moment when the defender stands their ground as the offensive player tries to surge through a gap. If the offensive player gets through with no contact whatsoever, they win. If the defender gets to the spot early enough to draw a charge or force the offensive player to double back, they win.

But the vast majority of driving situations fall between those two extremes. Whenever an offensive player changes their speed or direction on a drive, they are marking the end of one micro-move and the beginning of another. Each of those moments are likely to result in some sort of body contact with the defender trying to beat their man to the spot.

These crucial mini-collisions, which decide the success and failure of each drive, have become far more frequent in the Spaced Out Era. This seems counterintuitive, but spreading the game out has given offensive players more room to attack, stitch multiple micro-moves together, and perfect the post-dribble tactics described in the last chapter.

Offensive players won the vast majority of those battles for most of the post-hand-check era. That makes sense: it's easier to strengthen and balance one's lower body moving forward than backwards or sideways. Defenders of all shapes and sizes were in desperate need of a way to turn those skirmishes into fairer fights without using their hands. Upper/lower-body dissociation became the key to cracking that seemingly impossible code.

Though the rules delineating legal and illegal contact are byzantine and highly situational, they do entitle defenders a certain amount of space. If they keep their body parts—most notably their arms, but really anything that can protrude—within that ever-shifting imaginary line separating them from their opponent, they're considered to be in a "legal guarding position" and thus are not responsible for any resulting contact. If not, they get whistled for the foul. That's an oversimplification, but it's a useful one to see why modern defenders so badly needed to learn how to dissociate their upper and lower bodies while on the move.

Eradicating hand-checking outside the low-post in 2004 exposed just how much perimeter defenders used the tactic as a crutch to conceal poor movement habits. Once offenses began to spread out, shoot threes, and use all that extra space to drive unimpeded to the hoop, defenders learned the hard way they had not built their bodies to move their feet *and* keep their arms from chopping down on the offensive player on those inevitable mini-collisions. Stiff hips and weak core muscles didn't matter as much when defenders could use their hands and forearms to slow the driver's momentum. Now, they did.

Exploiting this asymmetry is the nuts and bolts of the much-maligned skill of foul-drawing. The way the best drivers "create contact" is they surge underneath and through the defenders' hips, chest, and/or torso at acute angles. They jump into defenders' bodies to disarm their upper-body strength so thoroughly that they can't help but drop their arms lower. The contact down below, initiated by the offensive player, is legal and thus deemed a no-call, assuming it's not a straight-on collision. They're hoping the aftershock of the legal contact they create will either yield the angle needed to complete the drive/finish, or create natural momentum that brings the defenders' arms down for a foul. Ideally, they get both.

Without hand-checking and with far more distance to cover, modern perimeter defenders *and* rim protectors found it incredibly difficult to avoid those negative outcomes. That is, until they started to master upper/lower-body dissociation. Only then could they absorb the legal body contact down below and keep their arms from coming down and fouling drivers.

Ironically, they have James Harden (and other foul hunters, to a lesser extent) to thank for motivating them.

Each of Harden's foul-drawing tricks is designed to exploit defenders' slightest movement asymmetries. The stepback leg kick, the armbar, the unnaturally high gather in traffic, the swinging arms before finishing, and the horizontal jump into rim protectors' chest all target defenders' arms once Harden initiates lower body contact. Harden was exposing sneaky hand-checking, much like a flop (usually) exaggerates illegal contact that already exists rather than conjuring it out of thin air. Yet Harden became so good at recognizing these situations that it was more like he willed future hand-checks into existence.

In response, coaches told their players to tuck their arms as far into their bodies as possible to avoid providing Harden any form of bait to exploit. Some players made a show of clasping both hands behind their back, well aware of the symbolism of such actions. In essence, this meant maintaining the same verticality on the perimeter that big men had to perfect at the rim.

That task may seem impossible to some. How could anyone move with offensive maestros like Harden *and* hold their hands back? But it only seems impossible because basketball players never had to do it before. Football defensive backs do it beyond five yards. So do soccer players to avoid committing handball violations. So do athletes in many other sports contested over large playing surfaces. Why couldn't NBA players learn to do it, too?

The defense you see now is a product of that ongoing transition. It started when the Warriors showcased the value of versatile, switching defenders. It accelerated as a response to Harden's foul-drawing heyday in the late 2010s. Now, it hides in plain sight on every defensive possession among players of all shapes and sizes. Even big men shaped like Anthony Davis, Giannis Antetokounmpo, Rudy Gobert, and Nikola Jokić built their training regiments around agility and core flexibility to become expert upper/lower-body dissociators.

This leveling-up process was *already occurring* before the 2021 crackdown on "non-basketball moves." The key word there is "process."

To achieve the defensive versatility prized in a switch-heavy game, players needed core strength to hold their ground, hip flexibility to rotate laterally, and light feet that could slide, cross over, and backpedal equally well. Many of the best defenders of the late 2010s share certain characteristics: wide hips, thick thighs, long arms, lean chests, and "positionless" designations. They formed and inspired the "Draymond Generation."[145]

For a time, sturdy and stocky alone took some players, and even teams, a long way. In February 2020, the Houston Rockets dealt lone big man Clint Capela in a three-team trade to bring in wing stopper Robert Covington, forming a front line anchored by the 6'5" Tucker and 6'7" Covington. This drastic move was deemed necessary to open up space for Harden and Russell Westbrook on offense, but despite their incredibly short front line, the Rockets held their own defensively after the trade and were downright stifling in the minutes Covington and Tucker shared the floor.[146] Neither was a traditional rim protector or long-armed perimeter stopper, but each's unique combination of hip flexibility and core strength enabled the Rockets to contain dribble penetration at its source.

Houston's micro-ball experiment fell short of the promised land, in part because defensive rebounding proved to be an Achilles heel during the regular season and in a five-game second-round playoff loss to the eventual champion Lakers. (That, plus LeBron James and Anthony Davis being amazing.) But the Rockets had conducted a fascinating experiment that simultaneously revealed the power of building a defense around upper/lower-body dissociation experts and the limits of assuming that only smaller players can achieve that level of mastery.

The more teams used on-ball screens to force slower and/or shorter defenders to switch onto stars, the more everyone—small and big guys alike—realized they needed an upper/lower-body dissociation crash course. They needed to prepare for the moment they'd be forced to dance with Trae Young, chase Stephen Curry through a maze of screens, close out on Harden's stepback threes, cut off Kawhi Leonard's battering ram drives, contest the seemingly uncontestable jump shot of Kevin Durant, or root out Jokić in the mid-post.

---

145. Seerat Sohi, then at Yahoo! and now at The Ringer, coined that term in a January 2021 feature story in a nod to the Warriors' do-everything defensive savant.

146. The Rockets allowed just 105.1 points per 100 possessions in the regular season when Covington and Tucker were both on the court, according to the advanced stats subscription site Cleaning the Glass. That ranked them in the 91st percentile among two-man combinations who shared the floor for at least 100 possessions.

These slow, subtle improvements—initially hidden as long-range shooting and unnatural foul-drawing tactics rose to unsustainable levels in fan-less pandemic play settings—are now revealing themselves. In fact, I'd argue the scourge of foul-hunting became more obvious *because* defenders were already beginning to improve their upper/lower-body dissociation. The aftershocks of the body contact the offensive players created were now less severe, so defensive fouls that would've been obvious in the past were closer to the border. Players like Harden and Young had to resort to more underhanded tactics to get the whistles they received in the past.

That makes the league's crackdown on "non-basketball moves" the straw that fully broke the camel's back. Not only did they eliminate many of those increasingly common borderline calls, but they also incentivized a new, legal type of physical on-ball defense that, to some degree, brought back the aggressive ball pressure often associated with hand-checking.

Though these officiating points of emphasis predictably leveled off as the 2021–22 season continued, players like Harden are learning that they need to work harder to keep winning those many micro-collisions that occur on every drive. It's harder for drivers to finish around the basket and get to the free-throw line when they're forced to take bumpier paths to get in position to do either in the first place.

So while the new points of emphasis certainly helped defenders, it's more accurate to say they helped the viewing public better appreciate the ways they were already adapting their technique and biomechanics to cover the extra space the Spaced Out NBA suddenly required them to cover.

Those adjustments were happening on the team level, too.

THE CONVENTIONAL WISDOM of the Spaced Out Era was that limiting three-point *attempts* indicated a smart defensive process. Opponent three-point *percentage* tends to fluctuate wildly between games and seasons even among teams with the same personnel and scheme. So the fewer threes you surrender, the less vulnerable you are in the long run to those random hot streaks.

That makes the 2019–20 season a key pivot point in recent history. On one side: the 10 teams that gave up the highest proportion of three-point attempts. On the other: the top 10 in fewest points allowed per 100 possessions.[147] I've bolded the teams in both categories.

MOST THREES ALLOWED (BY PERCENTAGE OF TOTAL OPPONENT SHOTS)	BEST DEFENSES (POINTS ALLOWED/100 POSSESSION)
Toronto Raptors	**Milwaukee Bucks**
Miami Heat	**Toronto Raptors**
Milwaukee Bucks	Los Angeles Lakers
Sacramento Kings	**Boston Celtics**
Charlotte Hornets	**Los Angeles Clippers**
New York Knicks	Indiana Pacers
Los Angeles Clippers	Philadelphia 76ers
Boston Celtics	Oklahoma City Thunder
Golden State Warriors	**Miami Heat**
Denver Nuggets	T: Orlando Magic / Utah Jazz

That's not a typo. Four of the five best defensive teams in the league—and five of the top 10—allowed opponents to take tons of threes.[148] (The Lakers, the other top-five defense, ranked in the middle of the pack in threes allowed by this measure.) For one season at least, the measure that once indicated a good defensive process emphatically suggested the exact opposite.[149]

This didn't mean teams should've suddenly stop guarding the three-point line. The correlation between three-pointers allowed and defensive aptitude was much stronger in the 2020–21 season.

Still, this counterintuitive 2019–20 season trend represented more than a mere statistical blip. It was an indication that defensive schemes were starting to address the fundamental problem that dogged them throughout the Spaced Out Era. Just how does a defense cover the two most valuable pieces of real estate on the floor—the basket *and* the three-point line—when they're 25 feet apart?

---

147. Data via the advanced stat subscription site Cleaning the Glass, which filters out garbage time.

148. Orlando nearly made it six of 10, but finished 11th-worst (or 19th-best) in three-point attempts surrendered.

149. The trend was more pronounced before March's COVID-19 shutdown, so the bubble environment is not the cause.

As discussed in Chapters 6 and 7, the initial answer was to keep a big man back at the rim, play the pick-and-roll two-on-two with drop coverage, stay close to shooters, and induce pull-up, mid-range jumpers. Soon, though, those two-point jumpers had become threes. Not only was this vaporizing drop coverage's math edge, but offenses were using too much space on the floor to rely on a strategy built to avoid defensive rotations.

The 2019–20 season was the moment several teams made a key decision. Giving up a ton of threes isn't great. But giving up layups is far worse. If barricading the basket resulted in a few more threes going up, so be it.

The math had tilted in favor of this view. Now that every team replaced most of their long two-point jumpers with threes, a semi-open long-range bomb from an average shooter (say, 35 percent or so from downtown) wasn't as valuable proportionally as it was when teams took more long two-point jumpers.

So let's make another chart. On one side: the 10 teams that allowed the lowest proportion of restricted area shot attempts in 2019–20. On the other: our same top-10 defensive efficiency list. We'll again bold teams on both sides.

FEWEST SHOTS AT THE RIM (BY PERCENTAGE OF TOTAL OPPONENT SHOTS)	BEST DEFENSES (POINTS ALLOWED/100 POSSESSION)
Milwaukee Bucks[150]	**Milwaukee Bucks**
Brooklyn Nets	**Toronto Raptors**
Orlando Magic	Los Angeles Lakers
Miami Heat	**Boston Celtics**
Utah Jazz	**Los Angeles Clippers**
Toronto Raptors	Indiana Pacers
Los Angeles Clippers	Philadelphia 76ers
Boston Celtics	**Oklahoma City Thunder**
Golden State Warriors	**Miami Heat**
Oklahoma City Thunder	T: **Orlando Magic** + **Utah Jazz**

150. The Bucks lapped the field in rim protection, both in terms of attempts (29.1 percent of opponent shots, compared to 31.2 percent for second place Toronto) and percentage (55.1 percent, compared to Toronto's 59.7 percent). No team had finished first in both categories in the same season since the 2006–07 Houston Rockets.

Those numbers make a lot more sense. The teams that turned the restricted area into a no-fly zone prospered, even and especially if they gave up more threes.

Yet even as most of those good defenses aligned strategically in their quest to protect the basket, their tactics wildly diverged.

The Bucks, as discussed in Chapter 7, doubled down on drop coverage, choosing to live with the shots it naturally surrendered even if they were threes instead of twos. Utah adopted a similar approach around multi-time Defensive Player of the Year Rudy Gobert, while Orlando tilted that way to a lesser extreme to protect their less mobile center, Nikola Vučević.

The Raptors and Heat, on the other hand, took the opposite approach. Instead of playing more conservatively, they protected the basket with constant perimeter pressure that often included what seemed like double teams on the ball before scrambling with frantic defensive rotations.

Toronto's scheme in particular was bonkers. Raptors players swarmed to the ball like bees to honey, then flew out to perimeter shooters as if they'd been shot out of a cannon. At their best, they appeared to have eight defenders on the court. At their worst, they looked like they had only three. The margin between the two was razor thin.

Yet each teams' high-risk tactics worked. The Raptors finished as the league's No. 2 defense behind the Bucks, while the ninth-ranked Heat surged to another level in their surprising NBA Finals run in the post-COVID-19 bubble.

Despite appearing like organized chaos, there was a method to both teams' madness. Neither team had a towering giant like Gobert or Brook Lopez to wall off the paint, so they did it collectively. All five players sank down into a shell in advance of every pick-and-roll, then sprayed back out once the ball got kicked to three-point shooters. Ideally, the five-man unit's shape expanded and contracted ad infinitum while the offense probed in vain for a path through. Their five-man defensive alignment looked like someone blowing heavily into a brown paper bag.

Their emphasis on preemptively forming a collective shell differentiated them from teams who blitzed the pick-and-roll with two players and relied on speedy rotations to make up the four-on-three deficit. The pressure the Heat and Raptors put on ball-handlers was less aggressive, but more proactive. The

September 17, 2020 — Heat vs Celtics — ECF Game 2 (MIA leads 1-0)
Celtics 94, Heat 91 — 3:49 left in fourth quarter

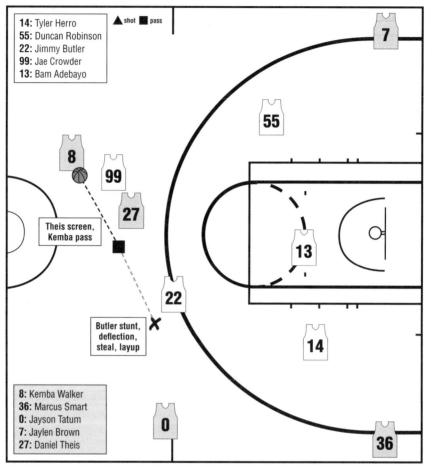

third, fourth, and fifth players didn't rotate after the fact. They *pre-rotated* to high-leverage spots on the floor in unison with the on-ball defenders.

One area in particular became the nexus of their coverages. Whereas traditional drop coverage barricades the restricted area, the Heat and Raptors prioritized the free-throw line extended to stop drives at their source. They took up permanent residence at the nail (see Chapters 6–8) and its surrounding suburbs. They prioritized stopping ball-handlers from clearing that first line of defense and were willing to allow as much sideways ball movement along the three-point line as offenses wanted in return. Picture Gandalf telling the Balrog, "You shall not pass," in *The Lord of the Rings*.

There were subtle differences between the two teams. Toronto was more willing to gamble in passing lanes to force turnovers, while Miami preferred to stunt down and back out to paralyze offensive players rather than explicitly go for steals. (The latter approach stopped Giannis Antetokounmpo in his tracks in the Heat's 2020 second-round playoff upset.) Both teams were heavy zone defense practitioners, but Miami's added wrinkle was to place its longest perimeter defenders up top and its shortest in the corners.

Yet each showed the rest of the league a model for a third type of defensive pick-and-roll scheme that maintained the spirit of a deep drop's paint protection while using the timely off-ball switches and collective sink-and-recover tactics of more flexible strategies. Eventually, their principles added new elements to conservative and aggressive styles alike. This was a new way forward for defenses who were getting their asses kicked by two decades of offensive innovation.

The hyperactive, yet coordinated defensive philosophies of Miami and Toronto dovetailed with the work players were doing on their own to optimize their bodies and technique to cover so much extra space. Their new physiques were natural fits for defensive systems that flooded multiple bodies to dangerous driving lanes before spraying out to shooters. Even if they had to execute an excessively long closeout to remotely bother a dangerous long-range marksman, they could at least fly out all full speed knowing teammates were drilled to help out and keep the basket area under control. There was no point in hesitating.

The success of the Heat, Raptors, and other teams who prioritized the rim over the three-point line in 2019–20 was also the final domino in a long-overdue reconstruction of proper closeout technique.

The spread-out game exposed the faulty logic that governed closeout teaching points. For decades, coaches instructed defenders to chop their feet with a series of stutter steps as they raced toward potential shooters. (Some pro coaches still teach this method, even though it's outdated.) This method assumed that chopping one's feet was the best and only way to stay on balance to get a hand in the shooter's face and not get beat by a drive.

But this assumption, much like the step-slide, is wrong for coordinated high-level athletes like professional basketball players. It prioritizes the wrong outcome (a potential drive where help can arrive) over an actual open three.

Worse, it badly underestimates the capacity of the human body—especially those of elite NBA pros. Anyone running at full speed indeed must take a bunch of little, choppy steps to slow down on balance. But it takes time and space for human beings to get to full speed. Far more time and space, as it turns out, than the basketball court allows.

Ato Boldon, the excellent NBC track and field analyst and two-time 100-meter Olympic medalist, once told ESPN that sprinters need anywhere from 30 to 50 meters to reach their top speed. That means 30 to 50 percent of a 100-meter race is in an acceleration stage where sprinters are not yet going as fast as they possibly can. That distance translates to anywhere from 100 to 160 feet. The entire basketball court—the whole damn thing—is 94 by 50 feet!

More to the point, the space one covers when closing out on a shooter is a tiny fraction of that space. For the sake of argument, let's say a player must cover 20 feet on a closeout. That's a damn long closeout! And it corresponds to … six meters. The first 100-meter sprinter to reach their top speed in six meters will make Usain Bolt look like a tortoise.

The point is that basketball players are so, so, soooooooooooo far away from reaching a top speed where they'd need to take many small steps to slow down. Telling them to chop their feet when contesting a three-point shot slows their closeout down out of of a Grand Canyon sized excessive abundance of caution. NBA players' height and weight profiles may strain the muscles required to stop and pull in the opposite direction more than sprinters or other athletes, but not *that* much more. Any technique that prioritizes staying on balance on a proportionally constrained NBA floor over reaching the shooter in the first place is putting the cart a zillion meters before the horse.

The better closeout strategy for high-level players is to take normal steps toward shooters, then lunge out horizontally at them while raising their arms to bug the shot on the way. If you're trying to make up ground as quickly as possible, you'd never take a bunch of itty-bitty steps. Putting your hands up while you chop your feet doesn't do much to distract shooters either. They're too far into their motion and too focused on the rim to even notice an outstretched arm, especially now that they catch and release the ball so quickly.

The best way to spook the shooter into mistiming their motion or passing up the shot entirely is to cramp their lower-body space. The fewer steps it takes to cover the distance between you and their base, the better. In fact, leaving your feet to leap *out* toward their waists rather than up to their eyes is an excellent tactic. Modern jump shooters ignore outstretched arms, but find it harder to focus on their motion when they feel someone charging into their landing zone. That's the best way to make them uncomfortable.

Better yet, using fewer steps lends itself *better* to staying in the play if the shooter pump fakes and drives. Assuming one's horizontal lunge stays low to the ground, there's less strain on the knee when the front foot lands and quickly plants to change direction. Leaping high into the air, on the other hand, forces one knee to absorb the entire force of the ensuing landing. (This is why one of the most important skills for any high-flyer to train is how to land properly.) The more players stopped chopping their feet, the more they stopped underestimating their own bodies.

The final teaching point was to emphasize closing out to the shooter's side rather than directly into their path. This covered a contingency the many-small-choppy-step method ignored, since the whole point was to ensure defenders stayed between the shooter and the basket. That made more sense when long-range bombers took an eternity to get their shots off, but it wasn't realistic against the lightning-quick releases of the Spaced Out Era. Many defenders who got the long-steps-to-horizontal-lunge footwork down still made the mistake of closing out square to the shooters, causing a surge in three-shot fouls and four-point plays.

The fix is to fly out with their bodies positioned to the side of the shooter and arms raised diagonally into their line of sight. Some coaches insist on closing out to their opponent's strong hand. Others prefer their players rush past the other side to avoid accidentally brushing the shooter's arm and committing a foul. But the specific side is less important than picking a side in the first place. The ultimate goal is to encroach on the shooter's space down below without drifting into their "landing zone," not to block their shot.

This updated closeout method has also (somewhat) neutered the growing "one-dribble three" trend.[151] A pump fake, one-dribble three, whether of the sidestep, stepback, or step-in variety, remains a deadly weapon for long-

---

151. I first saw the term in a 2020 Ringer feature by Michael Pina, who now writes for *Sports Illustrated*.

range shooters against unbalanced closeouts. But now defenders possessed better technique to lunge out to alter the first shot, land on the balls of their feet, and instantly jump back the other way to bother the shooter from behind or the side.

That's forced shooters to develop more sophisticated methods to get their shot off or drive to make an additional play for a teammate. Possessions that once required one pass to create an open three-point look now needed two, three, four, or more to get any shot at all. It wasn't enough to be a spot-up *shooter* anymore. Those role players also needed to be able to drive gaps, relocate along the three-point line, cut to the basket, and make high-level passing reads to find the next open teammate.

As these closeout techniques evolved, so too did teams' strategies to meet the challenge of quick ball movement over wider playing surfaces. For all the justified praise the Warriors receive for their on-ball switching innovation, their ability to shapeshift and scramble efficiently *off the ball* made an even greater impact on the sport's future. They were the first team to regularly perform the scram switches, peel switches, X-outs, veer backs, and other collective forms of swapping assignments that we covered in Chapters 7 and 8. It wasn't long before the rest of the league drilled these principles, too.

The X-out in particular has transformed three-point defense. Instead of making each player recover to their original assignment, the X-out calls for the man closest to the first shooter to close out to them while the initial help defender beelines to cover the next most logical pass. (It's called "X-out" because the two defenders are criss-crossing to form an X.) This was a paradigm-shifting tactic that added layers of complexity to spot-up play.[152] All of a sudden, defenses could move one step ahead of ball movement rather than always having to react to it. Long closeouts grow shorter when the burden of accounting for that extra space can be shared.

The combination of evolved team-wide scramble tactics, much-needed new techniques, and a renewed emphasis on collective paint protection has yielded a resurgence in aggressive pick-and-roll defensive schemes. More teams are employing 2019–20 Raptors and Heat-like strategies that flood multiple players to the ball, basket, and strong side.[153] Even more conservative

---

152. Or, to use this book's nomenclature, "advantage exploitation play."

153. "Strong side" means the side of the floor in which the ball is currently located.

April 20, 2022 — 76ers at Raptors — ECQF Game 3 (PHI leads 2-0)
76ers 97, Raptors 97 — 3:41 left in overtime

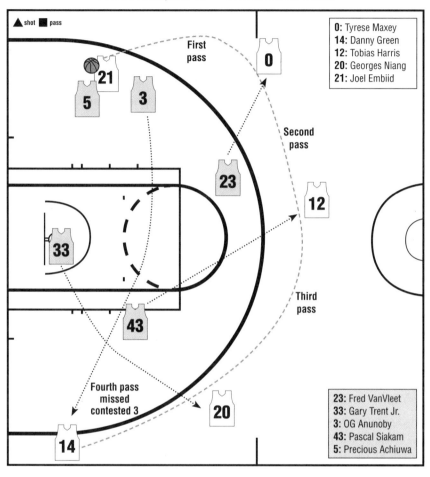

▲ shot ■ pass

First pass

Second pass

Third pass

Fourth pass missed contested 3

0: Tyrese Maxey
14: Danny Green
12: Tobias Harris
20: Georges Niang
21: Joel Embiid

23: Fred VanVleet
33: Gary Trent Jr.
3: OG Anunoby
43: Pascal Siakam
5: Precious Achiuwa

drop pick-and-roll schemes are not dropping as far back and tasking a third player—known as the "low man"—to sink to the middle of the lane to offer extra support for a drive or roll.

Why? Since defenders have never been better at closing out on shooters, the risk of deploying a scheme that requires long closeouts and rotations is less severe than it was even a few years ago. That's on top of the players themselves getting leaner, more teams deploying "small" lineups of like-sized players, and players of all sizes internalizing a collective mindset needed to execute on- and off-ball switches seamlessly.

These developments have allowed coaches to install more malleable defensive schemes. They can create more specific defensive game plans on the fly to address their opponents' personnel and tendencies instead of worrying that too much change might confuse their players. In-game adjustments have become far easier to make.

There's been a well-chronicled resurgence in zone defenses across the league, particularly those sprinkled in at various points through a game to throw the offense a curveball. This trend, though, is not as revolutionary as it often seems. Players are already covering "zones" of the floor when they X-out, make low man rotations, and perform other preemptive help principles as part of their teams' base man-to-man defense. An actual zone isn't really that different anymore.

The next big defensive scheme in the NBA isn't, in fact, a single groundbreaking scheme. Instead, it's developing the capability to seamlessly shift between multiple ones. This should have been obvious in hindsight. The Spaced Out Era made offense significantly more flexible. The only way to stop it is to reimagine defense in the same way.

NBA teams and players are still wrapping their collective heads around this concept. No mindset change can fully alleviate the challenge that comes from having to defend twice as large a practical playing surface with the same number of players.

But this evolution didn't just begin the day the NBA confirmed it was cracking down on "non-basketball moves." It was already happening behind the scenes. Even if the effect of these under-the-hood defensive developments on the 2021–22 season specifically leveled off, any sign of offensive decline is significant given the exponential offensive growth that preceded it in the last decade.

If defense is starting to catch up, how long will it take? Are we already seeing the offense's counter?

Epilogue
Means to the Same End

The NBA's tactics of the future will be inspired by ones from its past.

DeMar DeRozan is a self-proclaimed stubborn person. Tell him that his game, his plan, his strategy won't work, and he will leave no stone unturned to will it into existence somehow. Stubbornness *defines* DeRozan, usually for the better, occasionally for the worse.

In 2010, DeRozan, after a nondescript rookie season that kept him off either All-Rookie team, tweeted, "Don't worry, I got us" when star Chris Bosh departed Toronto for the Miami Heat in free agency. Nobody asked him to bear the burden of rebuilding the Raptors' franchise back to respectability. It certainly didn't happen overnight. It included many postseason failures. But DeRozan completed the deed eight years later, even as the Raptors traded him to San Antonio to acquire Kawhi Leonard, the final piece of their championship puzzle.

DeRozan's famous stick-to-itiveness shows up in other places, too. Displeased with his ball-handling during the 2013–14 season, DeRozan spent all summer doing everything with his left hand—including writing. ("My [one-year-old] daughter probably could understand [my handwriting] It looks like hers," he told the *National Post* in 2014.) Seven and a half years later, DeRozan, frustrated by a 5–9 second-half performance from the charity stripe in a Chicago Bulls home win over the lowly Orlando Magic, practiced free throws on the United Center floor while maintenance workers prepared for the NHL's Chicago Blackhawks game the following night. As the wood panels dwindled around him, DeRozan, to date an 85-percent shooter from the line, took free throw after free throw, refusing to count any until he made 10 in a row. Eventually, according to ESPN, he stopped at 250—or 25 sequences of 10 in a row.

Stubbornness is what explains DeRozan's long-standing refusal to join the NBA's three-point revolution, even as it utterly transformed the sport around him. He has instead famously chosen to master the mid-range shot the Spaced Out NBA was supposedly erasing. With the exception of the 2017–18 season, DeRozan has never attempted more than three three-pointers per game.

Even that outlier season, in typical DeRozan fashion, was a result of his stubbornness. He recalled a coach telling him the summer before that he needed to shoot threes to last in the league. In response, he refused to take them in the 2016–17 season. "It was just me being an asshole, I'm gonna be honest," DeRozan said in a 2020 appearance on J.J. Redick's *Old Man and the Three* podcast. When he continued to draw criticism for his long-range reluctance even after averaging 27 points per game that season, DeRozan gave in for just one year to prove that he could. (He attempted 3.6 a game that season, his last with Toronto, making 31 percent.)

"My whole mindset switched to say, 'Man, I don't give a damn what nobody says. I can shoot threes. Stop saying I *can't* shoot them just because I *don't* shoot them. There's a difference between can't and don't,'" he told Redick. "So that was my mindset. That year, I just had a moment. The next year came, and I just was myself."

Following a three-year stint in the shadows with increasingly nondescript San Antonio teams, DeRozan signed a much-maligned free-agent deal with the Chicago Bulls. Many panned Chicago's decision to give DeRozan an $85 million deal at age 31, especially with fellow ball-dominant perimeter scorer Zach LaVine already on the team.[154] Would they maximize each other's games? Should the Bulls have instead signed better defenders and three-point shooters with that money?

---

154. The cost was actually higher than that, because Chicago also surrendered veteran forward Thaddeus Young and multiple draft picks in a sign-and-trade to allow DeRozan to receive his three-year, $85 million deal.

Instead, DeRozan grew into something else entirely: an MVP candidate, at age 32, for one of the best teams in the Eastern Conference.

"The 32-year-old version of DeRozan has morphed into ... the 32-year-old version of [Dirk] Nowitzki," John Hollinger, the onetime Memphis Grizzlies executive and current writer at The Athletic, wrote in March of 2022, referencing the season Nowitzki won his only NBA title.

Let's be clear: the success of DeRozan and his throwback game does not portend a reversion to the pre–Spaced Out Era style. Offenses, down dramatically in the early part of the season, were normalizing by December and continued to trend up after the worst of the Omicron COVID-19 wave. Stars who initially struggled with the new officiating points of emphasis adjusted. Officials again called more incidental contact in the offense's favor. James Harden started climbing back to his customary spot near the top of the free-throw attempt leaderboard.

By the start of the new calendar year, the league's average offensive efficiency had risen back above that of each season prior to 2018–19. That was also the last full season before a global pandemic forced fan-less game environments that, on balance, favored offenses.

This was bound to happen. While sports proceed in cycles, seismic stylistic shifts are rare and take far longer than a year to fully metastasize. They aren't supposed to thoroughly transform a sport in less than a decade. The existence of this book is proof that we are coming out of an exceptional moment in basketball history.

Still, DeRozan's perseverance in the face of overwhelming change around him may foreshadow a resurgence in some older tactics bathed in fresh coats of paint. While the days of the 1990s and early-2000s slugfests are gone for good, there are elements of those days that will be remembered, reshaped, and repurposed for modern times. We're already starting to see this happen.

Take the mid-range and post-up games, old-school elements that DeRozan prizes to the point of symbolizing the cliché complaint of the Spaced Out Era. To hear some former players, coaches, and commentators tell it, these supposed pillars of "back in my day" ball were demonized and then shoved aside by eggheads who scoffed at their inefficiency while ignoring their artistry and selective utility.

That point has always been overstated. Post-ups remain effective vehicles to force double teams, initiate off-ball movement, and punish switches in moderation. Meanwhile, the decline in the mid-range game was mostly driven by role players exchanging long two-point jumpers for threes. The self-created superstar pull-ups glorified by DeRozan and other proponents of the *lost art of the mid-range* have largely remained. It's more accurate to say the Spaced Out Era viewed the mid-range shot like past eras treated the long-range bomb: as a privilege bestowed to a select group of players who have earned it.[155]

Nevertheless, it's fair to say that the Spaced Out NBA has turned the post-up and mid-range jumper into effective counters instead of core objectives. That represents a significant shift, even if critics code it in strawman arguments that get taken literally.

Yet that same reality also presents an opportunity for each to be revived given the current state of the game. The more defenses focus attention on stopping Plans A and B, the more vulnerable they become to Plan C. And Plan C is right in DeRozan's wheelhouse.

"A lot of teams will live with [mid-range shots]," he told NBC Sports Chicago in December 2021. "I look at it like, if a team will live with that, why not try to figure out how to master that and be dominant with that?"

During his three years in San Antonio, DeRozan kept playing his way, leaving no stone unturned in his quest to do it better. He improved his playmaking and recycled more moves from past eras into his bag.[156] He swapped true "long twos" from just inside the three-point line for shorter two-point jumpers from around the free-throw arc. He became more of a point guard that took pride in generating threes for his teammates instead of for himself. His scoring efficiency, supposedly capped by his analytic-unfriendly shot profile, soared even before his Chicago breakout.

Now, his persistence—*stubbornness*—is paying off in multiple ways. Recent innovations in individual defensive technique and strategy, combined with the crackdown on offensive foul-hunting tactics, have chipped away

---

155. I'd argue the mid-range shot receives disproportionate attention because many pundits are former stars who would have been granted the privilege to take mid-range shots had they played today.

156. My favorite DeRozan move is the reverse rip-through Eurostep into a lefty floater from a standstill position in the mid-post. It combined James Harden's gather, Kevin Durant's arm swing through the defender, and the off-hand, off-foot finish occasionally deployed by Larry Bird and Kobe Bryant. Few players are put in a position to even attempt the move in a modern game, but that didn't stop DeRozan from perfecting it.

at the symbiotic relationship between threes and layups. It still exists, of course. The threat of the three opens space to drive for layups, and vice versa. But defenses are better at getting out to shooters *and* stopping teams from getting to the hoop off the dribble than they were even three years ago.

DeRozan's mid-range-oriented skill set has thus become more comparatively valuable. He's so damn good at making those shots that he can score efficiently on that sub-optimal diet when others can't. Fewer defenders regularly guard mid-range artists like him, so they are more vulnerable to his bag of tricks. Because he's not trying (as hard) to generate threes or layups, he's less affected by new defensive techniques or increased physical play on the ball. Plus, his Kobe Bryant-esque signature pump fake was less impacted by the crackdown on "non-basketball moves" because he was close enough to his defender to jump naturally into a mid-range shot and still create contact.

Not everyone can be DeMar DeRozan. For one, good luck matching his maniacal work ethic, intense film study, and steadfast belief in his own style of play. For another, DeRozan was benefiting from the rest of the Bulls, particularly LaVine and All-Star center Nikola Vučević, taking a step back to spread the floor for him. The future DeMar DeRozans of the world can't play their game if their teammates all ditch the three-ball and fancy themselves as mid-range artists.

Plus, given the renewed emphasis on collective basket protection, any rise in mid-range shots will likely come at the expense of layups instead of threes. If defenses continue to make it harder to get all the way to the hoop on a drive, that'll lead to more jumpers overall, whether they count for three or two.

Still, the longer DeRozan ages gracefully, the more he will inspire his peers to follow his lead. Being a "three-level scorer" who can drive, shoot the three, and operate in the mid-range area is already a necessity for the superstar class. As we advance into the 2020s, the same may become true for all types of players, too.

There are other budding trends that bear watching as the game advances into the future. For example, the very concept of attacking the basket is morphing into the broader concept of "rim pressure." Taken literally, the phrase refers to, well, *putting pressure on the rim* in some capacity. It does not specify how to apply said pressure, even if we associate the term with off-the-bounce drives.

In truth, there are many ways to generate "rim pressure." The simplest is to have one guy attack off the dribble while shooters spread out on the floor, theoretically forcing defenses to pick their poison. The Rockets pushed this basic concept to extreme levels around James Harden, which inspired others to preach the gospel of five-out spacing while centralizing their offense around elite perimeter drivers. But once defenses improved their techniques for covering those drivers in space, those teams struggled to generate "rim pressure" when those drivers couldn't get to the hoop.

The 2020 playoffs went a long way toward bursting the bubble (pun intended) of five-out spacing as the *one ring to rule them all* offense. The teams who succeeded—namely the Lakers, Heat, and Nuggets—relied on a mix of constant off-ball movement, timely cutting, hard rolls when appropriate, drives, and even the dreaded post-ups to pressure the rim. Each scored signature playoff victories against opponents (Houston, Milwaukee, L.A. Clippers, and Boston) who leaned heavily on exceptional on-ball attackers to collapse defenses.[157]

Because driving to the hoop in a traditional sense promising to be more challenging in the near future than it was at the height of the Spaced Out Era, offenses must diversify their rim pressure methods to create the *effect* of a drive to the cup. There are several ways teams already do this.

In Utah, Rudy Gobert's rim-rolls paired with Donovan Mitchell's on-ball shiftiness to power the best offense in the NBA (at least in the regular season). Teams like Phoenix, Miami, and Golden State use well-timed off-ball cuts to collapse defensive shells and open up their shooters. The 2019–20 title-winning Lakers team specialized in turning every live-ball rebound into a 94-foot half-court possession, with big men like Anthony Davis leaking out to the rim, guards sprinting to the corner to provide spacing, and LeBron James' pinpoint passing doing the rest. The Clippers, Nets, and Warriors have unleashed shaky-shooting, bowling-ball sized "guards" like Bruce Brown, Terance Mann, and Gary Payton II as inverted pick-and-roll screeners who catch the ball at the high post and attack the ensuing four-on-three situations. Other teams have and will co-opt and improve these tactics.

---

157. As noted in Chapter 8, the Bucks' postseason failure inspired their decision to emphasize the dunker spot, which proved critical in their march to the 2021 championship.

April 27, 2022 — Nuggets at Warriors — WCQF Game 5 (GSW leads 3-1)
Warriors 90, Nuggets 90 — 2:15 left in fourth quarter

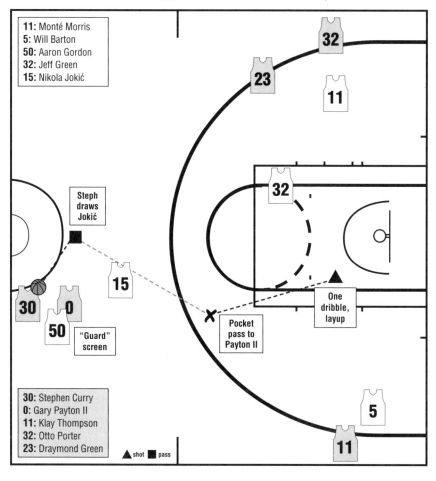

11: Monté Morris
5: Will Barton
50: Aaron Gordon
32: Jeff Green
15: Nikola Jokić

Steph draws Jokić

One dribble, layup

"Guard" screen

Pocket pass to Payton II

30: Stephen Curry
0: Gary Payton II
11: Klay Thompson
32: Otto Porter
23: Draymond Green

▲ shot ■ pass

On top of those, effective post-ups are increasingly becoming a deadly and aesthetically pleasing form of rim pressure. Not the slow-developing, endless backdown post-ups of the 1990s, which got erased for good with the 2001 relaxation of zone defense. The *modern* post-up is a quick timing maneuver in which the post player seals his man deeper in the paint in sync with the ball-handler's vision. It is a read that results from a pick-and-roll action, scramble situation, and/or transition sequence, not a set play. It can involve letting the defender front, clearing the opposite side out, and throwing a lob over the top.

These instantaneous post moves are increasingly effective ways to punch through smaller gaps in a defense's shell. That's especially true when the players doing the deed are punishing switching smaller defenders while the taller men pull the larger ones away from the hoop with their new three-point proficiency. The old-fashioned post up was big on big with the small throwing the entry pass. The new-school post up is big on small, or small on smaller, with anyone throwing the entry pass.

Ultimately, the harder defenses work to stop teams from reaching the hoop via the dribble, the more they must get there with passing or movement. Posting up, cutting, and rim-rolling each relies on pinpoint passing, which, as noted in Chapter 10, is in the midst of a golden age that could become even golder. As longtime skills trainer and analyst David Thorpe wrote in a December 2021 TrueHoop newsletter, "the pass" is the key NBA skill of 2022.

What about on defense?

One trend worth watching is the deployment of dominant "rim protectors" farther out on the floor. Modern big-man play already requires many of them to come up higher on pick-and-rolls to stop elite pull-up shooters like Stephen Curry and Damian Lillard. But with perimeter defenders more adept at challenging from behind and schemes more in tune with sink-and-recover tactics that protect the rim collectively, does it still make sense to confine players like Gobert and Joel Embiid to the paint when their mammoth size, improved agility, and long arms can effectively shut down other high-leverage areas on the court?

We've already seen teams emulate a key Warriors adjustment from 2015 and stick their biggest defender on the opponent's least threatening perimeter shooter.[158] The Celtics, owners of the league's best defense in 2021–22, use rising center Robert Williams in this role within their base defense. Why couldn't a team extend that idea to place their tallest player at the top of a zone, as Minnesota did with Kevin Garnett two decades ago? What about having *them* guard powerful perimeter drivers like Kawhi Leonard, LeBron James, or Luka Dončić? What's so scary about them switching out on a

---

158. After falling behind 2–1 in their second-round series with the Memphis Grizzlies, the Warriors elected to have center Andrew Bogut "guard" Memphis' Tony Allen, a notorious non-range shooter. That way, Bogut could roam off him in a one-man zone to help everyone else. Teams quickly copied the tactic, even against far more willing three-point shooters than Allen.

quick guard when they are more able to pursue from behind and can count on their teammates to help quicker?

Perhaps the Cleveland Cavaliers' surprising early-season success will inspire those types of adjustments. With a roster overloaded with big men and devoid of wing players, coach J.B. Bickerstaff started a jumbo front line of three near-seven footers in Jarrett Allen, Lauri Markkanen, and rookie Evan Mobley. Most figured Cleveland lacked the lateral mobility to cover the perimeter properly. Instead, the Cavaliers regularly switched Allen and Mobley onto opposing guards, trusting that the other could anchor the paint behind them. They functioned like a modern-day Twin Towers, propelling Cleveland near the top of the defensive rankings after finishing in the bottom six in each of the previous four seasons.

As Cleveland's giant front line thrived, there was talk of the Cavaliers "bucking the NBA's small-ball trend." That's part of the ESPN headline on Brian Windhorst's December 28 feature story in which Cavaliers general manager Koby Altman admits their "tall ball" strategy was intentional and inspired by recent teams: "The Bucks had Giannis [Antetokounmpo] and [Brook] Lopez. The Lakers had LeBron, [Anthony] Davis, and [Dwight] Howard," Altman told Windhorst. "They played big and they won."

Altman is correct that size *was* a key element to the 2021 Bucks and 2020 Lakers. But they did not buck the NBA's small-ball trend, and neither are the Cavaliers.

That's because the small-ball trend didn't exist in the recent past, doesn't exist today, and will not exist in the future. Neither, in fact, has or will its counterpart. Size does not explain the Warriors revolutionizing the sport, the Rockets emerging as their top foil, the Lakers and Bucks winning the league's two most recent titles, or Cleveland's surprising re-emergence to start the 2021–22 season.

Those teams succeeded for one reason above all else: they optimized the game's expanded space to their benefit. If you take one thing away from this book, let it be that sentence.

The revolution that upended the NBA, which centered around an on-court landmark created in 1979 and dramatically accelerated 35 years later once several different forces that originated anywhere from one year to three decades before fused into a chain reaction, was not about David defeating Goliath. It was about *space*. Specifically, *using* more of it instead of playing the game within a self-constrained sandbox.

It's true that the initial wave of the Spaced Out NBA gave little guys more of a fighting chance. But over time, the victors of this seminal moment in NBA history have proven to be the players, teams, coaches, and executives who have found the most creative ways to use the game's additional space to their benefit—no matter their size.

Reducing the Spaced Out Era to a triumph of small over large misses its most revolutionary quality. It ushered in new opportunities and shattered long-held truths about the game. It made size immaterial in either direction. It prioritized skill, democratized it, then redefined it to account for regularly stretching each possession over an exponentially larger playing surface.

That is why the key figures of this NBA moment come in so many different shapes and sizes.

- The 7' Nigerian-born Greek point guard who overcame homelessness, poverty, racial discrimination, and (less significantly, of course) never playing above Greece's second division as a youth to become an icon and NBA champion.
- The stocky Arizona State penetrating guard with devious curiosity and gigantic thighs.
- The 7' silky-smooth scorer who couldn't bench press 135 pounds as a rookie.
- The supremely gifted Chosen One who somehow turned out better than expected.
- The 300-pound Serbian behemoth with deft vision and touch.
- The 7'2" Cameroonian volleyball star who didn't touch a basketball until the age of 15 and sat out his first two full seasons due to injury.
- The slithery 6'3" point guard from Murray State who credits his father for being his "first hater."
- The 6', exacting, sometimes evil basketball genius whose on-court intellect inspires and annoys in equal measure.
- The grinning, pudgy 6'7" Slovenian who kicks your ass while working his way into shape every season.
- The four-star, San Diego State product with hands so gigantic that he was nicknamed "The Klaw."

- The 6'6" bowling ball from Saginaw who looked more like a football player.
- The razor-thin 6'3" sharp-shooter from Davidson who heads a royal family of long-range marksmen.

What do all have in common? An ability to use that extra space to enhance their skill and physiological advantages. They differ only in the means by which they accomplish that goal.

It's fitting, then, that this seminal era in basketball history came full circle in 2022, with the Warriors reclaiming their place as the NBA's Gold(en) standard.

Many of the ingredients that elevated the 2021–22 Warriors to the franchise's fourth championship in eight years were familiar to even the most casual NBA fan. Stephen Curry (and, eventually, Klay Thompson) whipped defenses into a frenzy with his long-range shooting, magical playmaking, and relentless off-ball movement. Draymond Green anchored the defense while gluing the many components of the Warriors' chaos engine together with his one-of-a-kind blend of muscle and precognition. A deep roster of overlooked talents packaged essential complementary skill sets in unconventional arrangements. Steve Kerr affably kept the structure sturdy enough to become an organizational credo, yet fluid enough for players to color outside the lines.

But these Warriors had also evolved to address the league-wide revolution they inspired. Curry bulked up to absorb more punishment inside the arc, whether it came on his own drives or those of larger opponents who targeted him for switches on the other end. They tinkered their defensive approach: more collective paint protection off the ball, (slightly) less switching. They channeled Andrew Wiggins into his best self, unleashed Jordan Poole as a chaos multiplier, uncovered Gary Payton II as a new-age positionally-fluid utility player, rehabilitated veterans like Otto Porter and Nemanja Bjelica, and sharpened Kevon Looney's often-overlooked contributions.

These small edges, combined with their own institutional knowledge, overcame a league that seemingly caught up to them. This was most evident in the championship series against the Boston Celtics, a physically imposing opponent powered by a shape-shifting defense that dominated the league like no other in the Spaced Out Era.

Through three games, that defense ground the Warriors to a halt. Boston deployed a form of drop coverage on Curry's pick-and-rolls, the very strategy that Curry and his ilk once rendered untenable. But these Celtics were making it work, in large part because their players had learned to stay with the Currys of the world in space. Curry got his, but the Celtics cut off the Warriors' trademark offensive flow and wore Curry down over the course of the game.

The Warriors' star responded with a virtuoso performance, torching Boston's coverages for 43 points as Golden State squeaked out a late win to tie the series at 2. Afterwards, the Celtics repeatedly insisted they would not deviate from their plan to defend Curry's pick-and-rolls two-on-two. As great as Curry was individually, the Celtics did not want to unleash his greatest superpower: when the *threat* of his individual greatness occupies so much defensive attention that the rest of the Warriors get to play with a constant man advantage over acres of space.

"We can mix it up there, being more physical, make some unders on him when he's that high. We have been good as far as that," coach Ime Udoka said. "But the fact that he's such a willing and good playmaker I think makes it tougher to go after him, as opposed to other guys who don't want to get off the ball."

But in the end, even the most disciplined defense of the Spaced Out Era couldn't help themselves. In Game 5, the Celtics held Curry to a nearly unprecedented off shooting night, but lost by double digits anyway as the rest of the Warriors took advantage of the extra attention Curry drew to wake up from their series-long offensive slumber. Three nights later, the Warriors broke the Celtics' defense for good, using Curry as a decoy to open space for everyone else before going back to him to finish the weary Celtics off down the stretch.

The structure of the Warriors' 2022 triumph—three games stuck in the mud, followed by a pivotal Game 4 adjustment whose downstream effects flip the schematic terms of engagement for good—mirrored their first taste of ultimate success against Cleveland in 2015. There were, of course, key differences between the two titles. The opponents, for one: no balanced supporting cast to worry about in 2015, no LeBron James to fear in 2022. The hole-poking method in 2022 was their superstar, rather than 2015's lineup change before Game 4. But both were defined by the Warriors forcing their opponent to cover the extra space on the court that maximized their skill and physical advantages.

Same franchise. Same formula. Same end. The only difference was the means they used to get there.

The message to start this book was that the sport you watch today only vaguely resembles the one you watched 30, 20, 10, or even five years ago. That is still true. All you need to do is pause the screen at the start of any half-court possession and draw a box around the first and last offensive players. You're bound to find one end delineated by a ball-handler 40 feet from the hoop and the other marked by two shooters deep in both corners. Repeat that exercise with any classic game—they're all there on YouTube, *trust me*—and you'll see the difference.

But as we ponder the future of NBA gameplay, we'd be smart to consider the lesson of DeMar DeRozan's stubbornness. Ultimately, the sport is still basketball. The object of the game is still to launch a ball through a cylinder 10 feet above the ground. There are still five players on each team working together to accomplish that goal. The game still lasts 48 minutes. The team with the most total points at the end of that time still wins.

Any strategy, tactic, concept, philosophy, movement, and fundamental we hold dear to our hearts is a means to those ends. And means can *always* change.

Acknowledgments

June 5, 2020, is a day I will never forget. It was the day I took a buyout from the only job I ever had, ending a 10-year run with SB Nation. It was also the day I opened a cold email from Triumph acquisitions editor Clarissa Young. Subject line: "Triumph Books - Xs and Os Basketball Book." The timing could not have been more serendipitous if you scripted it in a movie. Thank you, Clarissa, for believing in this project, and thank you to the higher power that brought us together precisely when my career was at its lowest point.

There are so many people who were essential to getting this book over the finish line. It's not a stretch to say they've changed my life. While there are too many to name in such a short section, a few deserve special mention.

Thank you to my editor, Jesse Jordan, for your patience as I dawdled on the manuscript, your reassurance during our many phone calls, and your insight in sharpening my ideas. Thank you for believing in me when I didn't believe in myself. Thank you to Bill Ames and the rest of the team at Triumph for taking a chance on me despite my lack of book-writing experience. Special thanks to Patricia Frey for bringing the graphics to life—and for dealing with my many failed attempts to explain the idea behind them.

Thank you to my many co-workers at The Athletic and SB Nation for your guidance, your company, and your sometimes-inadvertent work fine-tuning these concepts. In particular: Tom Ziller for setting an incredible example; Brian Floyd and Ryan Nanni for keeping me sane; Jenn Holmes for pushing me to think bigger; Whitney Medworth for widening my perspective on fandom; and Ben Epstein for bickering with me so much that our banter became a podcast.

Thank you to colleagues, subjects, and anyone else involved in the basketball and sports media worlds. Whether you provided direct feedback on the text, shared insight into the NBA's evolution, or simply inspired me with your work, this book would not have happened without you. Special thanks to Seth Partnow, Jake Fischer, and Joseph Perry for counseling me on the stuff nobody tells you about before signing a book deal.

Thank you to the Plainview and Syosset libraries for providing access to key research databases and a quiet place to write. I'd thank everyone that uploads complete classic games on YouTube, but I don't want to out you.

Thank you to my family and friends for their love, support, and gentle ridicule whenever I needed to be knocked down a peg. To my brother, Josh, and my stepfather, Larry, for cheering me on. To my grandmother, Tama, and my aunt Pam for checking in on me. To my uncle Brad for personifying my target audience with your self-proclaimed *old school* basketball sensibilities. To the family I married into—Randie, Marty, Eddie, Nadine, Scott, Molly, Penny, and Sophie—for their endless reservoirs of positive energy. To my friends for keeping me humble with their constant roasts. To Ron Meyers, the most reliable pal through thick and thin. RIP.

To my mom, Jana, for showing me how much good can be accomplished when you don't care who gets the credit. You taught me what it means to be kind, attentive, and, most of all, *understanding* of others, no matter their background or expertise. I've yet to meet a more thorough line editor.

To my dad, Vince, for, among other things, sparking my love of basketball with all those father-son trips to watch the mid-1990s Washington Bullets. Everything I do, I do for you. RIP.

Finally, to Hillary, Vivienne, and Myles: Thank you for being you. Thank you for your happy days, your sad days, and for sharing every part of them with me. Thank you for hugging me when I needed a hug, metaphorically kicking me in the pants when I needed motivation, and for roping me back to reality when I got too deep in my own head. I love you all more than any words could convey.

—Mike Prada
June 2022

References

Abbott, Henry. 2007. "George Karl: Just Kidding, Manu Is Great." *TrueHoop*, ESPN, April 18, 2007. https://www.espn.com/blog/truehoop/post/_/id/3266/george-karl-just-kidding-manu-is-great.

———. 2008. "Traveling to Europe." *TrueHoop*, ESPN, October 7, 2008. https://www.espn.com/blog/truehoop/post/_/id/5443/traveling-to-europe.

———. 2009. "Jamal Crawford's Street-Legal Shake-N-Bake." *TrueHoop*, ESPN, December 22, 2009. https://www.espn.com/blog/truehoop/post/_/id/11664/jamal-crawfords-street-legal-shake-n-bake.

———. 2009. "NBA Traveling: Always Been a Tough Rule to Call." *TrueHoop*, ESPN, March 4, 2009. https://www.espn.com/blog/truehoop/post/_/id/6037/nba-traveling-always-been-a-tough-rule-tocall.

———. 2009. "NBA Traveling: A Rule That's Unclear to Players." *TrueHoop*, ESPN, March 4, 2009. https://www.espn.com/blog/truehoop/post/_/id/6036/nba-traveling-a-rule-that-s-unclear-toplayers.

———. 2009. "NBA Traveling: 'We Really Don't Reference the Rulebook.'" *TrueHoop*, ESPN, March 4, 2009. https://www.espn.com/blog/truehoop/post/_/id/6035/nba-traveling-we-really-don-t-reference-therulebook.

———. 2009. "Traveling Violation: NBA on Rule Change." *TrueHoop*, ESPN, October 23, 2009. https://www.espn.com/blog/truehoop/post/_/id/9963/traveling-violation-nba-on-rule-change.

———. 2009. "The Two Step." *TrueHoop*, ESPN, October 16, 2009. https://www.espn.com/blog/truehoop/post/_/id/7097/the-two-step.

———. 2010. "Still Bickering about LeBron James' 'Travel.'" *TrueHoop*, ESPN, May 6, 2010. https://www.espn.com/blog/truehoop/post/_/id/15740/still-bickering-about-lebron-james-travel.

Abrams, Jonathan. 2010. "NBA Imports Euro Step and Other Moves of a Global Game." *New York Times*, November 18, 2010. https://www.nytimes.com/2010/11/18/sports/basketball/18moves.html.

———. 2017. "Allen Iverson Answers Everything: 2017 MVP, Rest as BS…and Breaking Ankles." *Bleacher Report*, April 25, 2017. https://bleacherreport.com/articles/2705401–allen-iverson-answerseverything-2017–mvp-rest-as-bsand-breaking-ankles.

———. 2018. "It's a Good Time to Be P.J. Tucker." *Bleacher Report*, Turner Sports, October 17, 2018. https://bleacherreport.com/articles/2801074–its-a-good-time-to-be-pj-tucker.

Abramson, Mitch, and Stefan Bondy. 2014. "Jason Kidd Spins Story about Brooklyn Nets Breakup, Which Landed Him with Milwaukee Bucks." *New York Daily News*, October 19, 2014. https://www.nydailynews.com/sports/basketball/nets/kidd-ing-jason-spins-story-brooklyn-nets-breakuparticle-1.1979962.

Ahissar, Merav, and Jeremy M. Wolfe. 2021. "Guided Search 6.0: An Updated Model of Visual Search." *Psychonomic Bulletin & Review* 28: 1060–92, Springer. https://link.springer.com/epdf/10.3758/s13423–020–01859–9.

Alamar, Ben. 2016. "Data Helping NBA Players Redefine Meaning of Athleticism." *ESPN*, September 25, 2016. https://www.espn.com/nba/story/_/id/17636581/data-helping-nba-players-redefine-meaningathleticism.

Aldridge, David. "Here's the Real Jackson Five." *ESPN*, October 13, 1999. http://www.espn.com/premium/nba/columns/aldridge_david/102706.html.

———. 2020. "'We Tried to Rehearse the Randomness': Ray Allen's Epic Finals 3-Pointer Was No Accident, and the Greatest 3 Ever." The Athletic, January 9, 2020. https://theathletic.com/1513411/2020/01/09/we-tried-to-rehearse-the-randomness-ray-allens-epic-finals-3-pointerwas-no-accident-and-the-greatest-3–ever/.

———. 2021. "'Scoring Is What's Pretty': Why Elite NBA Defenders Still Struggle to Get Paid." The Athletic, February 4, 2021. https://theathletic.com/2364266/2021/02/04/nba-free-agency-whyelite-defenders-struggle-to-get-paid/.

———. "The Warriors, like all champions, refuse to leave the stage." The Athletic, 17 June 2022, https://theathletic.com/3368175/2022/06/17/aldridge-the-warriors-like-all-champions-refuse-to-leave-the-stage/.

Alter, Tommy, performer. 2020. "Episode 20: DeMar DeRozan." The Old Man and the Three, created by J.J.Redick, season 2020, episode 20, ThreeFourTwo Production, October 8, 2020, Apple Podcasts.

———, performer. 2020. "Episode 30: Chris Paul." The Old Man and the Three, created by J.J. Redick, season 2020, episode 30, ThreeFourTwo Production, December 9, 2020, Apple Podcasts.

Amick, Sam. 2020. "Jimmy Butler Unplugged: On Miami, Giannis, Minnesota, Philly and Everything In Between." The Athletic, September 2, 2020. https://theathletic.com/2038637/2020/09/02/jimmybutler-unplugged-on-miami-giannis-minnesota-philly-and-everything-in-between/.

Amick, Sam, and Eric Nehm. 2021. "From Burst Bubble to Champions: Inside the Incredible NBA Title Run by Giannis Antetokounmpo and the Bucks." The Athletic, July 21, 2021. https://theathletic.com/2719538/2021/07/21/from-burst-bubble-to-champions-inside-the-incredible-nba-title-runby-giannis-antetokounmpo-and-the-bucks/.

Anderson, Ben. 2021. "Jazz Biggest Adjustment for Game Two: Shoot Better." KSL Sports, June 10, 2021. https://kslsports.com/461221/jazz-biggest-adjustment-for-game-two-shoot-better/.

Anderson, Sam. 2013. "Why Basketball Won't Leave Phil Jackson Alone." New York Times, May 19, 2013. https://www.nytimes.com/2013/05/19/magazine/why-basketball-wont-leave-phil-jackson-alone.html.

Andrews, Malika. 2018. "How the '4–Point Line' and Other Court Markings Are Changing the NBA." ESPN, Disney, December 18, 2018. https://www.espn.com/nba/story/_/id/25559428/the-4–point-linejust-beginning-nba-latest-trend.

Antetokounmpo, Giannis, and Marques Johnson, performers. 2016. "Giannis Antetokounmpo Breaks Down the 'Euro-Step.'" FOX Sports Wisconsin, season 2016, April 1, 2016 YouTube video. https://www.youtube.com/watch?v=LHV1Yt4pcTo.

Apricot, Eric. 2016. "Explain One Play: Illegal Screen Calls Wipe Out Two Curry 3s." Golden State of Mind, Vox Media, January 17, 2016. https://www.goldenstateofmind.com/2016/1/17/10781712/warriorsvs-pistons-video-analysis-highlights-stephen-curry-threes-illegal-screens.

Arnovitz, Kevin. 2011. "The Miami Heat on a String." Miami Heat Index, ESPN, April 19, 2011. https://www.espn.com/blog/truehoop/miamiheat/post/_/id/6313/the-miami-heat-on-a-string.

———. 2011. "Sixers at Heat, Game 1: 5 Things I Saw." Miami Heat Index, ESPN, April 16, 2011. https://www.espn.com/blog/truehoop/miamiheat/post/_/id/6191/sixers-at-heat-game-1–5–thingsi-saw.

———. 2013. "Spurs-Heat Game 2 Takeaways." TrueHoop, ESPN, June 10, 2013. https://www.espn.com/blog/truehoop/post/_/id/59526/spurs-heat-game-2–takeaways.

———. 2014. "NBA's New Replay Center Will Help Game." TrueHoop, ESPN, October 24, 2014. https://www.espn.com/blog/truehoop/post/_/id/70972/nbas-new-replay-center-will-help-game.

———. 2016. "While the Grizzlies' Grit 'N' Grind Is Perfect Branding, It Might Also Be the Team's Most Fatal Flaw." ESPN, Disney, April 19, 2016. https://www.espn.com/nba/story/_/id/15234297/how-grit-n-grind-defines-grizzlies-better-worse.

———. 2017. "Playing the Longer Game." ESPN The Magazine, ESPN, October 20, 2017. https://www.espn.com/espn/feature/story/_/page/enterpriseBucks/how-giannis-antetokounmpobucks-plan-take-warriors.

———. 2022. "'A Basketball Savant': How DeMar DeRozan Is Driving the Bulls to Title Contention." ESPN, March 3, 2022. https://www.espn.com/nba/insider/insider/story/_/id/33406334/abasketball-savant-how-demar-derozan-driving-chicago-bulls-title-contention.

Arnovitz, Kevin, and Kevin Pelton. 2021. "Why the Pick-and-Roll Is the Single Most Important Play in the NBA." ESPN, July 1, 2021. https://www.espn.com/nba/insider/story/_/id/31728952/nba-playoffs-2021–why-pick-roll-single-most-important-play-nba.

Aschburner, Steve. 2010. "LeBron a Point Forward? Well, He Wouldn't Be the First." NBA, December 15, 2010. http://www.nba.com/2010/news/features/steve_aschburner/12/15/point-forward/index.html.

———. 2016. "Q&A: Milwaukee Bucks Forward Giannis Antetokounmpo." *NBA*, November 16, 2016. https://www.nba.com/news/q-and-a-milwaukee-bucks-giannis-antetokounmpo.

———. 2018. "'Randomness' from New Coach Budenholzer Gives Bucks Fresh Direction." *NBA.com*, Turner Sports, November 1, 2018. https://www.nba.com/news/bucks-budenholzer-changing-teamsways.

Associated Press. 1947. "Arena Cage League Bans Zone Defense." *The Troy Record*, January 17, 1947, Newspapers.com.

———. 1978. "NBA urged to accept 3-point shot." *New York Daily News*, July 16, 1978, 1, Newspapers.com.

———. 1998. "Bulls Have Neutralized Jazz Pick-and-Roll Play." *Deseret News*, June 7, 1998. https://www.deseret.com/1998/6/7/19384179/bulls-have-neutralized-jazz-pick-and-roll-play.

———. 2007. "Karl Not Concerned by Lack of Scoring from Nuggets Bench." *The Daily Sentinel* [Grand Junction, Colo.], April 27, 2007, Newspapers.com.

———. 2009. "Cleveland Cavaliers LeBron James Not Convinced He Walked." *ESPN*, January 6, 2009. https://www.espn.com/nba/news/story?id=3814635.

———. 2009. "Washington Wizards Call LeBron James' 'Crab Dribble' Traveling." *ESPN*, January 5, 2009. https://www.espn.com/nba/news/story?id=3812091.

The Association for Professional Basketball Research. 1947. *Basketball Association of America League Minutes 1946–49*. APBR. http://www.apbr.org/baaminutes.html.

The Athletic. *Heart of Gold: The Golden State Warriors' Remarkable Run to the 2022 NBA Title*. Triumph Books, 2022.

"Atlanta Hawks Coach Mike Budenholzer on His Offense." 2015. *BBALLBREAKDOWN*, created by Nick Hauselman, season 2015, January 5, 2015, YouTube video. https://www.youtube.com/watch?v=5Igt0KLIbc.

Awh, Edward, et al. 2012. "Top-down versus Bottom-up Attentional Control: A Failed Theoretical Dichotomy." *Trends in Cognitive Sciences* 16 (8): 437–43. https://doi.org10.1016/j.tics.2012.06.010.

Ayers, Coleman, director. 2016. "Allen Iverson." *Attention to Detail*, By Any Means Basketball, September 18, 2016, YouTube video. https://www.youtube.com/watch?v=G4qIscXHY5s&list=PLPQGFn96QoEiSEBBx22W23ejWdq5d-xJv&index=32.

———. 2016. "How to Become a Lockdown Defender: On-Ball Defense." *By Any Means Basketball*, August 10, 2016, YouTube video. https://www.youtube.com/watch?v=5vPIPB0_iP0.

———. 2017. "Why Basketball Players Are the Best Athletes in the World." *By Any Means Basketball*, September 27, 2017, YouTube video. https://www.youtube.com/watch?v=YwHYkpVcGMo.

———. 2018. "How to Dominate Without Even Dribbling!" *By Any Means Basketball*, September 16, 2018, YouTube video. https://www.youtube.com/watch?v=fG2GkU_Ws4g.

———. 2019. "Allen Iverson's Handles Broken Down to a Science." *By Any Means Basketball*, YouTube fideo. https://www.youtube.com/watch?v=00eLhSDw62Y.

———. 2019. "Basketball vs. Football Players: Which Is the Better Athlete?" *Attention to Detail*, By Any Means Basketball, October 6, 2019, YouTube video. https://www.youtube.com/watch?v=1A1d5nBMwiE.

———. 2019. "Giannis Antetokounmpo." *Attention to Detail*, By Any Means Basketball, April 28, 2019, YouTube video. https://www.youtube.com/watch?v=DB3wJU6Pcr0.

———. 2019. "How to 'Stretch the Rules' by Keeping Your Dribble Alive." *By Any Means Basketball*, May 19, 2019, YouTube video. https://www.youtube.com/watch?v=2cF2kb7hyJQ.

———. 2020. "The Forgotten Key to Lockdown Defense: Recovering." *By Any Means Basketball*, September 8, 2020, YouTube video. https://www.youtube.com/watch?v=bXB5NsJlQ4s.

———. 2020. "Jrue Holiday." *Attention to Detail*, By Any Means Basketball, November 21, 2020, YouTube video. https://www.youtube.com/watch?v=qg_T7KChXnU.

———. 2021. "How Jrue Holiday Locks Up Everything." *By Any Means Basketball*, July 18, 2021, YouTube video. https://www.youtube.com/watch?v=HpI2lJOxCv0.

———. 2021. "How the BEST Athletes Shift Their Weight." *By Any Means Basketball*, March 28, 2021, YouTube video. https://www.youtube.com/watch?v=bE1ZNmc5xZY.

———. 2021. "Should We Really Always Be Getting Low on Defense?" *By Any Means Basketball*, April 13, 2021, YouTube video. https://www.youtube.com/watch?v=7cu2BlZdK3I.

———. 2021. "What Makes Davion Mitchell a Lockdown Defender." *By Any Means Basketball*, October 22, 2021, YouTube video. https://www.youtube.com/watch?v=i1PUZp1Y2Dw.

Balas, Benjamin, et al. 2009. "A Summary-Statistic Representation in Peripheral Vision Explains Visual Crowding." *Journal of Vision* 9 (12). https://jov.arvojournals.org/article.aspx?articleid=2122150.

Baldinger, Brian. 2020. "Stephon Gilmore Breaks Down His Technique & How to Be an Elite DB." *NFL Media*, June 9, 2020, YouTube video. https://www.youtube.com/watch?v=RwJYVKqRIH4&.

Baldinger, Brian, and Ron Jaworski. 2019. "Xavier Rhodes Breaks Down How to Guess Routes, His Technique, and Today's Top WRs." *NFL Media*, July 10, 2019, YouTube video. https://www.youtube.com/watch?v=F6kYFFoVOp4&.

Ballard, Chris. 2012. "21 Shades of Grey." *Sports Illustrated*, May 21, 2012. https://vault.si.com/vault/2012/05/21/tim-duncan-21-shades-of-gray-spurs-nba.

———. 2013. "Three for All." *Sports Illustrated*, June 10, 2013. https://vault.si.com/vault/2013/06/10/three-for-all.

———. 2013. "Warriors' Stephen Curry Perfecting the Imperfect Art of Shooting." *Sports Illustrated*, April 2, 2013. https://www.si.com/nba/2013/04/02/stephen-curry-golden-state-warriors-three-pointshooting.

———. 2015. "Sources: Jerry West Threatened to Resign over Thompson-Love Deal." *Sports Illustrated*, June 11, 2015. https://www.si.com/nba/2015/06/11/jerry-west-klay-thompson-kevin-love-deal.

———. 2015. "Warriors: From One-Dimensional and One-and-Done to NBA Title Favorites." *Sports Illustrated*, February 19, 2015. https://www.si.com/nba/2015/02/19/golden-state-warriors-stevekerr-stephen-curry-klay-thompson-joe-lacob.

———. 2019. "Get Your Freak On." *Sports Illustrated*, April 8, 2019. https://vault.si.com/vault/2019/04/08/get-your-freak.

Barnard, Bill. 1990. "In the NBA of the '90s, Tough Defense Has Kept Scores in the 70s." *Los Angeles Times*, March 4, 1990, ProQuest.

Basketball Reference. n.d. "2004–05 NBA Preseason Odds." *Basketball-Reference*. https://www.basketballreference.com/leagues/NBA_2005_preseason_odds.html.

Beck, Howard. 2009. "N.B.A. Launches a Multimedia Rule Book Online." *New York Times*, October 15, 2009, ProQuest.

Beckham, Jeff. 2012. "Analytics Reveal 13 New Basketball Positions." *Wired*, April 30, 2012. https://www.wired.com/2012/04/analytics-basketball/.

Begley, Ian. 2013. "Woody: Stop switching on pick-and-rolls." *ESPN*, 26 December 2013, https://www.espn.com/blog/new-york/knicks/post/_/id/51799/woody-stop-switching-on-pick-and-rolls.

———. 2020. "Mike Woodson Q&A: Knicks Coaching Candidate on Why He's Right for the Job." *SNY*, June 24, 2020. https://sny.tv/articles/mike-woodson-qa-knicks-coaching-candidate-on-why-hesright-for-the-job.

Bejjanki, Vikranth R., et al. 2014. "Action Video Game Play Facilitates the Development of Better Perceptual Templates." *Proceedings of the National Academy of Sciences* 111 (47): 16961 6. https://www.pnas.org/content/111/47/16961.

Beller, Thomas. 2019. "James Harden's Transcendent Step-Back." *New Yorker*, January 25, 2019. https://www.newyorker.com/culture/culture-desk/an-overanalysis-of-james-hardens-step-back.

Bernreuter, Hugh. 2011. "Draymond Green Gives Football a Shot, but Will Stick with Michigan State Basketball." *MLive*, June 23, 2011. https://www.mlive.com/sports/saginaw/2011/06/draymond_green_gives_football.html.

Bickley, Dan. 2010. *Return of the Gold: The Journey of Jerry Colangelo and the Redeem Team*. Morgan James Publishing.

Birdsong, Devon. 2019. "Tim Duncan: The Very Spursiest." *Pounding the Rock*, Vox Media, February 21, 2019. https://www.poundingtherock.com/2019/2/21/18231480/tim-duncan-the-very-spursiest.

Black, James. "What Do NFL Scouts Look for in Cornerback Prospects?" *Big Blue View*, Vox Media, January 21, 2020. https://www.bigblueview.com/2020/1/21/21075082/what-do-nfl-scouts-look-forin-cornerback-prospects-nfl-draft.

Blair, Jeff. 2009. "LeBron's No Traveller." *Globe and Mail*, October 26, 2009. https://www.theglobeandmail.com/sports/lebrons-no-traveller/article792217/.

Bois, Jon, performer. "We Decided to Erase the Three-Pointer." *Chart Party*, season 2016, SB Nation, July 6, 2016, YouTube video. https://youtu.be/hhB1vPM8ItA.

Boisvert, Zak. 2017. "Golden State's Switching Concepts." *PickandPop*, May 30, 2017. https://pickandpop.net/2017/05/golden-states-switching-defense-concepts/.

———. "Boston Celtics Scram Switch (Brad Stevens)." May 24, 2018, YouTube video. https://www.youtube.com/watch?v=C-U5Lxj8o6Y.

Bondy, Stefan. 2021. "Immanuel Quickley Has Added Outer Space to His Shot Chart." *New York Daily News*, May 2, 2021. https://www.nydailynews.com/sports/basketball/ny-knicks-immanuelquickley-20210502–xfeykuamoreh7fuqwiuj2zxuqm-story.html.

Bonett, Bobby. 2012. "LeBron James' Late Travel Against the Clippers." *Newsday*, January 12, 2012. https://www.newsday.com/sports/basketball/lebron-james-late-travel-against-the-clippers-1.3448436.

Bontemps, Tim. 2013. "Refs Won't Keep Garnett from Going 'Full Throttle.'" *New York Post*, October 14, 2013. https://nypost.com/2013/10/14/refs-wont-keep-garnett-from-going-full-throttle/.

———. 2017. "The 15-Year Chain Reaction that Led to the NBA's Current Offensive Explosion." *Washington Post*, February 21, 2017. https://www.washingtonpost.com/news/sports/wp/2017/02/21/the-15-year-chain-reaction-that-led-to-the-nbas-current-offensive-explosion/.

———. 2021. "NBA Pleased with Progress in Officiating Non-Basketball Moves, Sees No Evidence of Increased Physicality." *ESPN*, November 2, 2021. https://www.espn.com/nba/story/_/id/32536415/nba-pleased-progress-officiating-non-basketball-moves-sees-no-evidence-increased-physicality.

Bontemps, Tim, and Kevin Pelton. "NBA Playoffs: Why Teams Are Combating the Offensive Revolution by Going to Zone Defense." *ESPN*, September 25, 2020. https://www.espn.com/nba/story/_/id/29963960/nba-playoffs-why-teams-combating-offensive-revolution-going-zone-defense.

Boot, Walter R., et al. 2006. "Detecting Transient Changes in Dynamic Displays: The More You Look, the Less You See." *Human Factors* 48 (4): 759–73. https://pubmed.ncbi.nlm.nih.gov/17240723/.

———. 2009. "Stable Individual Differences in Search Strategy?: The Effect of Task Demands and Motivational Factors on Scanning Strategy in Visual Search." *Journal of Vision* 9 (3): 7. https://doi.org 10.1167/9.3.7.

Boswell, Thomas. 2021. "Elgin Baylor Was the Prototype for Every NBA Icon that Followed." *Washington Post*, March 22, 2021. https://www.washingtonpost.com/sports/2021/03/22/elgin-baylor-nbahistory/.

Bracker, Milton. 1942. "10,000 Fans Are Mad About It." *New York Times*, January 25, 1942, ProQuest.

Branch, John. 2006. "Arrow Points to the Jump Ball's Demise." *New York Times*, March 31, 2006. https://www.nytimes.com/2006/03/31/sports/ncaabasketball/arrow-points-to-the-jump-balls-demise.html.

Brandt, Gil. 2016. "The Perfect CB: Marcus Peters' Hips, Darrelle Revis' Technique…" *NFL*, June 16, 2016. https://www.nfl.com/news/the-perfect-cb-marcus-peters-hips-darrelle-revis-technique-0ap3000000670010.

———, performer. 2020. "Explaining James Harden's 'Put on the Brakes,' Rapid Deceleration Ability." *3CB Performance,* YouTube video. https://www.youtube.com/watch?v=fAPXMhbm3cI.

Brar, Rajpal. 2020. "The Science behind Single-Leg 'Power Jump' LeBron Uses." *Silver Screen and Roll*, Vox Media, June 19, 2020. https://www.silverscreenandroll.com/2020/6/19/21296182/lebron-jamessingle-leg-power-jump-breakdown-youtube-video-3cb-performance-lakers-highlights-nba.

Brenkus, John, creator. 2017. "The Science Behind the Greek Freak's Skills." *ESPN*, YouTube video. https://www.youtube.com/watch?v=hWIq6ymuh7g.

Brenner, Jordan. 2018. "The Most Lethal Two-Step in the NBA." *ESPN*, November 8, 2018. https://www.espn.com/nba/story/_/id/25206602/most-dangerous-two-step-game.

Brier, Noah. 2018. "Pareto Principle (AKA 80/20 Rule) [Framework of the Day]." *Noah Brier*, October 1, 2018. https://www.noahbrier.com/archives/2018/10/pareto-principle-aka-80–20–rule/.

Brockmole, James R., and John M. Henderson. 2006. "Recognition and Attention Guidance during contextual Cueing in Real-World Scenes: Evidence from Eye Movements." *Quarterly Journal of Experimental Psychology* 59 (7): 1177–87.

"Brook Lopez." 2018. *The Lowe Post*, created by Zach Lowe, season 2018, ESPN, December 18, 2018, Apple Podcasts.

Brown, Jerry. 2005. "Brownie Points - Spurs' Ginóbili Must Have Idolized Laimbeer, Ainge." *East Valley Tribune*, May 22, 2005. https://www.eastvalleytribune.com/sports/brownie-points---spurs-Ginóbilimust-have-idolized-laimbeer-ainge/article_107a5e6c-1b3d-5fe4–9bff-0704176259cb.html.

Bryan, William L., and Noble Harter. 1899. "Studies on the Telegraphic Language. The Acquisition of a Hierarchy of Habits." *The Psychological Review* 6 (4).

Bryant, Kobe, creator. 2017. "Kobe Bryant Details How Future NBA Stars Can Learn from the Greats." *Granity Studios*, ESPN, YouTube video. https://www.youtube.com/watch?v=hI0DqGSNo04.

Bunkley, Nick. 2008. "Joseph Juran, 103, Pioneer in Quality Control, Dies." *New York Times*, March 3, 2008. https://www.nytimes.com/2008/03/03/business/03juran.html.

Calver, Charlie. 2021. "Joe Ingles on the NBA Playoffs and His Reputation as a 'Trash Talker.'" *GQ Australia*, May 23, 2021. https://www.gq.com.au/fitness/sport/joe-ingles-on-the-nba-playoffs-and-hisreputation-as-a-trash-talker/news-story/bf9a6ddc90f063a0cbebd843d0c870e4.

Canzano, John. 2014. "Punching out Joey Crawford, and the Issues on NBA Officiating." *Oregonian*, May 16, 2014. https://www.oregonlive.com/sports/oregonian/john_canzano/2014/05/canzano_part_five.html.

Caparell, Adam. 2021. "Quit Complaining: The NBA Is So Much Better After the Rules Changes." *Complex*, November 12, 2021. https://www.complex.com/sports/nba-so-much-better-after-rules-changes/.

Caplan, Callie. 2021. "Mavs Fail to Capitalize on Luka Dončić's Nifty Passes and Near Triple-Double in Key Loss to Trail Blazers." *Dallas Morning News*, March 19, 2021. https://www.dallasnews.com/sports/mavericks/2021/03/20/luka-Dončić's-crafty-passing-mavs-offensive-firepower-prove-too-little-toolate-vs-portland/.

Caple, Jim. 2016. "Perfect 100: How to Run Olympics' Fastest Event the Right Way." *ESPN*, August 12, 2016. https://www.espn.com/espn/feature/story/_/id/17277615/perfect-100–meters-how-run-olympicsfastest-event-right-way.

Carey, Benedict. 2014. *How We Learn: The Surprising Truth About When, Where, and Why it Happens*. Random House.

Carney, Patrick, and Dan Krikorian. 2021. "Off-Ball 'Next Defense,' Steve Donahue, and Brazil's 'TriplePost Action.'" *Slappin' Glass*, Substack, March 7, 2021. https://slappinglass.substack.com/p/off-ballnext-defense-steve-donahue.

———. 2021. "The 'Peel Switch': A Primer." *Slappin' Glass*, Substack, January 24, 2021. https://slappinglass.substack.com/p/the-peel-switch-a-primer.

Carpenter, Les, and Thomson News Service. 1996. "Allen-town? Rookie Allen Iverson is Taking Philadelphia by Storm." *Daily News* [Lebanon, Pa.], November 14, 1996, 13.

Carr, Kyle. 2019. "One Year Later: Recovering from the Broken Pieces of Kidd's Reign." *Brew Hoop*, Vox Media, January 22, 2019. https://www.brewhoop.com/2019/1/22/18191833/a-year-recoveringbroken-pieces-and-an-epidemic-milwaukee-bucks-jason-kidd.

Castelhano, Monica S., and Chelsea Heaven. 2011. "Scene Context Influences without Scene Gist: Eye Movements Guided by Spatial Associations in Visual Search." *Psychonomic Bulletin & Review* 18: 890–6. https://doi.org/10.3758/s13423–011–0107–8.

Castelhano, Monica S., and Richelle L. Witherspoon. 2016. "How You Use It Matters: Object Function Guides Attention During Visual Search in Scenes." *Psychological Science* 27.

Castellaw, Collin. 2019. "3 Reasons Why You Get Beat on Defense | Basketball Defense Techniques." *Shot Mechanics*, August 12, 2019, YouTube video. https://www.youtube.com/watch?v=AZl-Abt3A9s.

Cato, Tim. 2016. "Mark Cuban Still Thinks the 2006 Finals Were 'Worst Officiated Finals' in History." *Mavs Moneyball*, Vox Media, February 3, 2016. https://www.mavsmoneyball.com/2016/2/3/10910840/

———. 2017. "FIBA's Rule Change Has American Players Super Excited for Hoops Overseas." *SB Nation*, Vox Media, August 17, 2017. https://www.sbnation.com/nba/2017/8/17/16164332/fiba-travelingamerican-players-rule-change-gather-step.

———. 2018. "The Impossible, Demoralizing Task of Guarding James Harden, Explained by Players and Coaches." *SB Nation*, Vox Media, April 13, 2018. https://www.sbnation.com/2018/4/13/17233598/james-harden-highlights-defense-houston-rockets-nba-playoffs.mark-cuban-2006–nba-finals-worst-officiated-history-mavericks-heat.

———. 2020. "One-on-One with Luka Dončić's Trainer: Inside his Slovenian Quarantine Workouts." The Athletic, June 12, 2020. https://theathletic.com/1869297/2020/06/12/1–on-1–with-luka-Dončić'strainer-inside-his-slovenian-quarantine-workouts/.

Cawthon, Raad. 1996. "NBA Puts the Squeeze on Iverson." *Philadelphia Inquirer*, November 12, 1996, 47.

Center for Disease Control and Prevention. 2020. "COVID-19 and Your Health." https://www.cdc.gov/coronavirus/2019–ncov/need-extra-precautions/older-adults.html. Accessed 11 February 2020.

Charania, Shams. 2021. "NBA to Implement Rules to Limit Fouls on Non-Basketball Moves." The Athletic, June 22, 2021. https://theathletic.com/news/nba-to-implement-rules-to-limit-fouls-on-non-basketballmoves-sources/4AW9CaoPoehb/.

Chau, Danny. 2021. "Trust the Processing: Why Cade Cunningham's Vision Could Make Him a Star." *The Ringer*, July 26, 2021. https://www.theringer.com/nba/2021/7/26/22593326/cade-cunninghamnba-draft-luka-Dončić.

Chavez, Luciana. 2007. "U.S. Beefs up for FIBA: Players Bigger, Tougher in '07." *McClatchy-Tribune Business News* [Washington, D.C.], August 27, 2007, ProQuest.

Chiang, Anthony. 2021. "Butler Must Make Adjustment to Being Guarded by Antetokounmpo." *Miami Herald*, May 24, 2021, A18.

Christensen, Sebastian Martinez. 2011. "Manu Ginóbili on Heat and Euro-Step - Miami Heat Index." *TrueHoop*, ESPN, March 14, 2011. https://www.espn.com/blog/truehoop/miamiheat/post/_/id/5262/manu-Ginóbilion-heat-and-euro-step.

Chun, Marvin M., and Yuhong Jiang. 1998. "Contextual Cueing: Implicit Learning and Memory of Visual Context Guides Spatial Attention." *Cognitive Psychology* 36: 28–71.

Chung, Susana T.L., et al. 2001. "Spatial-frequency and Contrast Properties of Crowding." *Vision Research* 41 (14): 1833–50, Science Direct. https://www.sciencedirect.com/science/article/pii/S0042698901000712?via%3Dihub.

———. 2005. "Learning Letter Identification in Peripheral Vision." *Vision Research* 45: 1399–1412, Science Direct. https://www.sciencedirect.com/science/article/pii/S004269890500009X.

Cianfrone, Matt. 2018. "Modern Moves: Giannis Antetokounmpo's Eurostep." *FanSided*, January 24, 2018. https://fansided.com/2018/01/24/modern-moves-giannis-antetokounmpo-eurostep-bucks/.

Clarke, Alasdair D. F., et al. 2018. "Stable Individual Differences in Strategies Within, but Not Between, Visual Search Tasks." *PsyAirXiv*. https://doi.org10.31234/osf.io/bqa5v.

———. 2019. "Seeing Beyond Salience and Guidance: The Role of Bias and Decision in Visual Search." *Vision* 3.3 (46), Crossref. https://doi.org 10.3390/vision3030046.

Claxton, Gary, and Bradley Sawyer. 2019. "How Do Health Expenditures Vary Across the Population?" *Peterson Center on Healthcare and KFF*. https://www.healthsystemtracker.org/chart-collection/health-expenditures-vary-across-population/#itemstart.

"Closeout Defense - Dan Burke - Basketball Fundamentals." 2018. *FIBA*, December 13, 2018, YouTube video. https://www.youtube.com/watch?v=4RuYhzwnzDE.

Cohen, Ben. 2016. "The Golden State Warriors Have Revolutionized Basketball." *Wall Street Journal*, April 6, 2016. https://www.wsj.com/articles/the-golden-state-warriors-have-revolutionized-basketball-1459956975?mod=article_inline.

———. 2017. "James Harden's Secret Talent Is Slowing Down." *Wall Street Journal*, February 11, 2017. https://www.wsj.com/articles/james-hardens-secret-talent-is-slowing-down-1486667420.

———. 2017. "The Rockets Shoot from Outer Space." *Wall Street Journal*, May 1, 2017. https://www.wsj.com/articles/the-houston-rockets-shoot-long-3-pointers-from-outer-space-1493563578?mod=article_inline.

———. 2018. "The First Shots of the NBA's 3-Point Revolution." *Wall Street Journal*, April 12, 2018. https://www.wsj.com/articles/the-first-shots-of-the-nbas-3-point-revolution-1523542076?mod=article_relatedinline&mod=article_relatedinline.

———. 2018. "The NBA Team With a 4–Point Line." *Wall Street Journal*, April 16, 2018. https://www.wsj.com/articles/philadelphia-76ers-4–point-line-1523818220.

———. 2018. "One Eurostep for Manu. One Giant Leap for Mankind." *Wall Street Journal*, August 9, 2018. https://www.wsj.com/articles/eurostep-nba-youth-basketball-1533823846.

———. 2020. "The World's Best Athletes Are Now Better at Shooting." *Wall Street Journal*, August 4, 2020. https://www.wsj.com/articles/nba-bubble-shooting-soccer-empty-stadiums-11596539693.

———. 2021. "Has the NBA's Scoring Bubble Burst?" *Wall Street Journal*, November 4, 2021. https://www.wsj.com/articles/nba-offense-scoring-fouls-new-ball-11636002666.

Collier, Jamal. 2022. "DeMar DeRozan and His Late-Career Renaissance with the Chicago Bulls." *ESPN*, January 12, 2022. https://www.espn.com/nba/story/_/id/33041567/demar-derozan-late-careerrenaissance-chicago-bulls.

Conway, Tyler. 2019. "Stephen Curry: I'd Have Gotten Away with Stepback If I Was 'Somebody Different.'" *Bleacher Report*, Turner Sports, January 6, 2019. https://bleacherreport.com/articles/2814222–stephen-curry-id-have-gotten-away-with-stepback-if-i-was-somebody-different.

———. 2020. "Tim Hardaway Sr. Talks Michael Jordan, Space Jam, Allen Iverson, More in B/R AMA." *Bleacher Report*, Turner Sports, August 20, 2020. https://bleacherreport.com/articles/2905555–tim-hardaway-sr-talks-michael-jordan-space-jam-allen-iverson-more-in-br-ama.

Cooper, Caitlin. 2021. "Is the Mere Threat of a Three Enough to Affect a Defense?" *FiveThirtyEight*, Disney, September 24, 2021. https://fivethirtyeight.com/features/is-the-mere-threat-of-a-threeenough-to-affect-a-defense/.

Cooper, Luke, director. 2021. "Behind the Process: Trae Young." Performance by Alex Bazzell. *Through the Lens*, season 1, episode 1, March 4, 2021, YouTube video. https://youtu.be/TjCaFbJE3jY.

Coston, Tyler. 2020. "How to Play Modern Defense | Step 1 | Sprint Stop Closeout." *PGC Basketball*, August 21, 2020, YouTube video. https://www.youtube.com/watch?v=ovS7JZcdIno.

———. 2020. "Lockdown Defense: Lock Left Like Kobe Bryant." *PGC Basketball*, 23 September 2020, YouTube video. https://www.youtube.com/watch?v=RWhHU-OGwkY.

Covino, Steve, and Rich Davis, performers. 2020. "Tim Hardaway Critiques Allen Iverson, Manu Ginóbili, James Harden's Signature Moves." *Now or Never*, ESPN, July 28, 2020, YouTube video. https://www.youtube.com/watch?v=lbZL0wwwe5g.

Craft, Kevin. 2019. "A Step Too Far." *Slate*, April 4, 2019. https://slate.com/culture/2019/04/nba-eurosteptravel-allen-iverson-crossover.html.

Creech, Jenny Dial. 2018. "Steve Kerr Explains His Tweet Critical of James Harden." *Houston Chronicle*, February 5, 2018. https://www.chron.com/sports/rockets/article/Steve-Kerr-explains-tweet-critical-James-Harden-12547247.php.

Crowe, Jerry. 2008. "How Basketball Became Three-Dimensional." *Los Angeles Times*, May 6, 2008. https://www.latimes.com/archives/la-xpm-2008–may-06–sp-crowe6–story.html.

Csikszentmihalyi, Mihaly. 1990. *Flow: The Psychology of Optimal Experience*. Harper & Row.

CSN Philadelphia. 2020. "Sixers Home School: The Night Allen Iverson Crossed Over Michael Jordan." *NBC Sports*, April 2, 2020. https://www.nbcsports.com/philadelphia/76ers/sixers-home-school-nightallen-iverson-michael-jordan-crossover.

Dakhil, Mo. 2020. "Why Is One of the NBA's Most Effective Plays a Dying Art?" *Bleacher Report*, Turner Sports, September 1, 2020. https://bleacherreport.com/articles/2906132–why-is-one-of-the-nbasmost-effective-plays-a-dying-art.

Daley, Arthur J. 1939. "Zone Defense Hit as Stalling Tactic." *New York Times*, January 31, 1939, ProQuest.

———. 1952. "A Real 'Goon' Game." *New York Times*, December 21, 1952, ProQuest.

Davis, Seth. 2005. "The Rise of Saint Paul." *Sports Illustrated*, February 28, 2005. https://vault.si.com/vault/2005/02/28/-the-rise-of-saint-paul.

Deb, Sopan. 2021. "What Is a Foul in the NBA? It's Always Evolving." *New York Times*, December 23, 2021. https://www.nytimes.com/2021/12/23/sports/basketball/nba-fouls.html.

Deford, Frank. 1966. "A Tiger Who Can Beat Anything." *Sports Illustrated*, October 24, 1966. https://vault.si.com/vault/1966/10/24/a-tiger-who-can-beat-anything.

———. 1967. "Shooting for Three." *Sports Illustrated*, November 27, 1967. https://vault.si.com/vault/1967/11/27/shooting-for-three.

Dell'Apa, Frank. 1991. "A Long Way from Dr. J." *Boston Globe*, December 13, 1991, ProQuest.

Dempsey, Christopher. 2007. "Nuggets Coach Benching J.R. Smith." *Denver Post*, May 1, 2007.

———. 2008. "Ginóbili's Style Stings." *Denver Post*, May 1, 2005. https://www.denverpost.com/2005/05/01/Ginóbilis-style-stings/.

———. 2013. "Basketball Fundamentals Becoming Fancy." *Denver Post*, July 6, 2013. https://www.denverpost.com/2013/07/06/basketball-fundamentals-becomingfancy/#ixzz2Yflw1KZF.

Denison, Rachel N., et al. 2018. "Humans Incorporate Attention-Dependent Uncertainty into Perceptual Decisions and Confidence." *National Academy of Sciences* 115(43): 11090–5. https://www.pnas.org/content/115/43/11090/tab-article-info.

DePaula, Nick. 2018. "How James Harden's Sneakers Have Fueled His MVP Season." *ESPN*, May 10, 2018. https://www.espn.com/nba/story/_/id/23465402/how-james-harden-sneakers-fueled-mvp-season.

Deveney, Sean. 2005. "Spurs' Ginóbili, Legend of the Fall." *Washington Post*, June 12, 2005. https://www.washingtonpost.com/archive/sports/2005/06/12/spurs-Ginóbili-legend-of-the-fall/dfa6002d-ed94–4931–967d-5ac55c062ee9/.

Devine, Dan. 2021. "RIP, Elgin Baylor, the Overlooked Prometheus of the Modern NBA." *The Ringer*, Spotify, March 23, 2021. https://www.theringer.com/nba/2021/3/23/22347219/elgin-baylor-losangeles-lakers.

Dopirak, Dustin. 2021. "'What Is That?': Mike Woodson Not Sure What a Pack-Line Defense Is, Wants His D to be 'Hard-Ass.'" *Daily Hoosier*, May 26, 2021. https://www.thedailyhoosier.com/what-is-thatmike-woodson-not-sure-what-a-pack-line-defense-is-wants-his-d-to-be-hard-ass/.

Dosher, Barbara Anne, and Zhong-Lin Lu. 1998. "Perceptual Learning Reflects External Noise Filtering and Internal Noise Reduction Through Channel Reweighting." *Proceedings of the National Academy of Sciences* 95 (23): 13988–93.

Dowsett, Ben. 2017. "The Genesis of Mike D'Antoni's Gravity-Based Offense." *Basketball Insiders*, October 12, 2017. https://www.basketballinsiders.com/the-genesis-of-mike-dantonis-gravity-basedoffense/.

———. 2021. "The Fouls You Won't See On 3-Point Shots This Season (And Some You Still Will)." *FiveThirtyEight*, ESPN, October 19, 2021. https://fivethirtyeight.com/features/the-fouls-you-wontsee-on-3-point-shots-this-season-and-some-you-still-will/.

———. 2021. "NBA Offenses Are in a Funk. Will It Last?" *FiveThirtyEight*, ESPN, November 4, 2021. https://fivethirtyeight.com/features/4–reasons-why-nba-offenses-have-struggled-so-far-and-whythey-could-turn-it-around/.

Drew, Trafton, et al. 2016. "Searching While Loaded: Visual Working Memory Does Not Interfere with hybrid Search efficiency but Hybrid Search Uses Working Memory Capacity." *Psychonomic Bulletin and Review* 23: 201–12.

Dubay, Curtis. 2009. "The Rich Pay More Taxes: Top 20 Percent Pay Record Share of Income Taxes." *The Heritage Foundation*. https://www.heritage.org/poverty-and-inequality/report/the-rich-paymore-taxes-top-20–percent-pay-record-share-income-taxes.

Duncan, Nekias. 2020. "How Miami Slowed Down Giannis Antetokounmpo in Game 1." *Basketball News*, September 1, 2020. https://www.basketballnews.com/stories/how-miami-heat-slowed-down-giannisantetokounmpo-milwaukee-bucks-game-1–nba-playoffs.

———. 2021. "Why Isn't James Harden Getting to the Free-Throw Line?" *Basketball News*, October 26, 2021. https://www.basketballnews.com/stories/why-isnt-james-harden-getting-to-the-free-throwline.

Duncan, Tim, performer. 2008. "Inside the Mind of Tim Duncan." *NBA*, season 2008, January 30, 2008, YouTube video. https://www.youtube.com/watch?v=gyqsTKkqdtY.

Duprez, Mike. 2012. "Those Pesky Lithuanians." *The Lexington Dispatch*, August 8, 2012, ProQuest.

Eberhardt, Doug. 2017. "A Complete Guide to How NBA Teams Defend the Pick-and-Roll." *SB Nation*, VoxMedia, April 18, 2014. https://www.sbnation.com/2014/4/18/5601402/nba-pick-and-roll-defenseplayoffs-2014.

———. 2014. "The Heat's Aggressive, Incredible Defense Makes a Difference vs. Pacers." *SB Nation*, Vox Media, May 24, 2014, https://www.sbnation.com/nba/2014/5/24/5747396/miami-heatdefense-indiana-pacers-nba-playoffs-2014.

———. 2014. "Setting Screens Is Not a Lost Art." *SB Nation*, Vox Media, May 22, 2014. https://www.sbnation.com/nba/2014/5/22/5731522/nba-screens-tim-duncan-marcin-gortat.

Eisenberg, John. 2003. "Players Carried Away with the Art of Dribbling." *Baltimore Sun*, February 24, 2003. https://www.baltimoresun.com/news/bs-xpm-2003–02–24–0302240218–story.html.

Ellentuck, Matt. 2019. "Joe Ingles Is Somehow the NBA's Best Trash Talker." *SB Nation*, Vox Media, January 15, 2019. https://www.sbnation.com/nba/2019/1/15/18183791/joe-ingles-nba-trash-talk-blake-griffin.

"Episode 25: Stephen Curry's Trainer Brandon Payne." 2018. *The Habershow*, created by Tom Haberstroh, episode 25, NBC Sports, Apple Podcasts. https://podcasts.apple.com/us/podcast/episode-25-stephen-currys-trainer-brandon-payne/id1443174829?i=1000456275581.

Ericsson, K. Anders, et al. 2009. "Toward a Science of Exceptional Achievement." *The New York Academy of Sciences* 1172 (1): 199–217.

Esnaashari, Farbod. 2021. "Paul George Believes New NBA Wilson Basketball Is Why Players Are Struggling Shooting." *Sports Illustrated*, November 2, 2021. https://www.si.com/nba/clippers/news/paulgeorge-new-wilson-ball-is-why-players-are-struggling-shooting.

ESPN. 2018. "How Manu Ginóbili's Eurostep Changed the Game." *ESPN*. https://www.espn.com/video/clip/_/id/26379646.

ESPN.com News Services. 2009. "Despite Rewriting Rule, NBA Says Traveling Same." *ESPN*, October 23, 2009. https://www.espn.com.au/nba/news/story?id=4589994.

ESPN.com News Services, and Henry Abbott. 2009. "NBA on Traveling: Two Steps Are Better than One." *ESPN*, October 15, 2009. https://www.espn.com/nba/news/story?id=4563546.

Evans, Rich. 1999. "Rule Changes Put Premium on Athleticism." *Deseret News*, December 5, 1999. https://www.deseret.com/1999/12/5/19478966/rule-changes-put-premium-on-athleticism.

Fabritz, Paul J. 2021. "You've Been Taught to Close Out the Wrong Way!" *PJF Performance*, January 26, 2021, YouTube video. https://www.youtube.com/watch?v=zr9nGPTYVEE.

Fader, Mirin. 2022. *Giannis: The Improbable Rise of an NBA Champion*. Hachette Books.

Fader, Mirin. 2022. "The Many Dimensions of DeMar DeRozan." *The Ringer*, February 18, 2022. https://www.theringer.com/nba/2022/2/18/22939702/demar-derozan-chicago-bulls-all-star.

Falk, Aaron. 2018. "Q&A: Joe Ingles Keeps Climbing the Jazz's 3-Point Leaderboard, but He Doesn't Consider Himself a Shooter." *Utah Jazz*, December 6, 2018. https://www.nba.com/jazz/news/qa-joe-ingleskeeps-climbing-jazzs-3-point-leaderboard-even-if-he-doesnt-really-consider.

Falk, Ben. 2017. "Do the Bucks Stop Here?" *Cleaning the Glass*, 5 April 2017, https://cleaningtheglass.com/do-the-bucks-stop-here/.

———. 2019. "Bucking the Trend." *Cleaning the Glass*, February 21, 2019. https://cleaningtheglass.com/bucking-the-trend/.

Favale, Dan. 2014. "What Tyson Chandler Knows That Mike Woodson Doesn't." *Bleacher Report*, Turner Sports, January 23, 2014. https://bleacherreport.com/articles/1933165–what-tyson-chandlerknows-that-mike-woodson-doesnt.

Fehd, Hilda M., and Adriane E. Seiffert. 2008. "Eye Movements During Multiple Object Tracking: Where do Participants look?" *Cognition* 108 (1): 201–9.

Feigen, Jonathan. 2014. "Rockets' Harden a Eurostep above the Rest." *Houston Chronicle*, December 16, 2014. https://www.houstonchronicle.com/sports/rockets/article/James-Harden-A-Eurostep-above-therest-5961323.php.

———. 2018. "Why James Harden Isn't Traveling on His Step-Back 3-Pointers." *Houston Chronicle*, April 17, 2018. https://www.houstonchronicle.com/texas-sports-nation/rockets/article/Why-James-Harden-isn-t-traveling-on-his-step-back-12841154.php.

Feinstein, Andrew. 2019. "A History of the Denver Nuggets and San Antonio Spurs in the NBA Playoffs." *Denver Stiffs*, Vox Media, April 12, 2019. https://www.denverstiffs.com/2019/4/12/18307802/ahistory-of-the-denver-nuggets-and-san-antonio-spurs-in-the-nba-playoffs.

FIBA. 2005. "FIBA Referee Education (Volume I)." YouTube video. https://www.youtube.com/watch?v=3tDw8GJ50HQ.

Fierberg, Emma. 2021. "NBA Referee on James Harden's Step-Back Jumper Not Being a Travel." *Business Insider*, January 13, 2021. https://www.businessinsider.com/nba-referee-james-harden-step-backjumper-travel-basketball-zach-zarba-2018–4.

Filios, Chris. n.d. "The "Next" Defensive Trends in Basketball by Chris Filios." *Men's Basketball Hoop Scoop*. https://www.mensbasketballhoopscoop.com/the-next-defensive-trend-in-basketball-by-chrisfilios/#google_vignette.

Finger, Mike. 2007. "Iverson Keeps Nuggets Confident." *San Antonio Express-News*, April 26, 2007, 06D.

———. 2020. "For Spurs and Bryant, Rivalry Was Forged in Respect." *San Antonio Express-News*, January 27, 2020. https://www.expressnews.com/sports/columnists/mike_finger/article/Mike-Finger-Kobe-15006500.php.

Finnan, Bob. 2009. "James Claims 'Crab Dribble' Within the Rules." *Morning Journal*, January 7, 2009. https://www.morningjournal.com/2009/01/07/james-claims-crab-dribble-within-the-rules/.

Fischer, Jake. 2017. "Can Lonzo Ball's Jumper Make It in the NBA?" *Sports Illustrated*, October 19, 2017. https://www.si.com/nba/2017/10/19/lonzo-ball-jumpshot-form-lakers-ucla-lavar-ball.

Fisher, Harry A. n.d. "Spalding's Official Collegiate Basket Ball Guide." *Wikimedia Commons*, New York, The American Sports Publishing Company. https://commons.wikimedia.org/wiki/File:Spalding%27s_official_collegiate_basket_ball_guide_(IA_spaldingsofficia02fish).pdf.

Flannery, Paul. 2016. "Draymond Green Surprised Himself and Became a Star." *SB Nation*, Vox Media, February 16, 2016. https://www.sbnation.com/2016/2/16/10987022/draymond-green-warriors-nbaunexpected-star.

FOX Sports. "Tim Hardaway: My Crossover Was Better Than Iverson's." *In The Zone Podcast*, created by Chris Broussard, season 2018, episode 58, FOX Sports, May 24, 2018, Apple Podcasts. https://podcasts.apple.com/us/podcast/ep-58-tim-hardaway-my-crossover-was-better-thaniversons/id1193331363?i=1000412166822.

Franko, Iztok. 2021. "Meet Anze Macek, Luka Dončić's Slovenian Trainer." *Dallas Magazine*, October 1,2021. https://www.dmagazine.com/sports/2021/10/meet-anze-macek-luka-Dončićs-sloveniantrainer/?ref=mpw.

Frauenheim, Norm. 2004. "Bronze Weighing Heavy on U.S. Men: NBA Stars Find Little Consolation in Finishing 3rd." *Arizona Republic*, August 29, 2004, C.20, ProQuest.

Friedell, Nick. 2019. "Steve Kerr—Warriors Limited James Harden by Innovating Defense." *ESPN*, December 25, 2019. https://www.espn.com/nba/story/_/id/28369823/steve-kerr-warriors-limitedjames-harden-innovating-defense.

———. 2021. "Golden State Warriors' Draymond Green Enjoying Games More Without 'Terrible Calls.'" *ESPN*, October 31, 2021. https://www.espn.com/nba/story/_/id/32515758/golden-state-warriorsdraymond-green-enjoying-games-more-terrible-calls.

Friedman, Jason. 2007. "Rocket Science: Daryl Morey Brings Hard-Core Statistical Analysis to the NBA." *Houston Press*, October 31, 2007. https://www.houstonpress.com/news/rocket-science-daryl-moreybrings-hard-core-statistical-analysis-to-the-nba-6540549.

Frikki, Coach, director. 2021. "How Elite Shooters Turn Their Feet (Improve Your Jumper)." Season 2021, Coach Frikki, March 4, 2021, YouTube video. https://www.youtube.com/watch?v=-W7eAnNwOSo.

Gaine, Chris. 2017. "Remembering One of the NBA's Biggest Failed Experiments: The "New Ball."" *Complex*, April 12, 2017. https://www.complex.com/sports/2017/04/new-ball-nba-spalding.

Ganguli, Tania. 2018. "Brook Lopez Is the Next Frustrated, Highly Paid Lakers Veteran." *Los Angeles Times*, February 1, 2018. https://www.latimes.com/sports/lakers/la-sp-lakers-newsletter-20180201–story.html.

Garcia, Jeff. 2019. "Steve Kerr Recalls Rookie Manu Ginóbili's 'Eye-Popping' Talent." *News 4 San Antonio*, March 28, 2019. https://news4sanantonio.com/sports/spurs-zone/steve-kerr-recalls-rookie-manuGinóbilis-eye-popping-talent.

———. 2020. "WATCH: Spurs Great Manu Ginóbili Reveals the Origin of his 'Eurostep.'" *News 4 San Antonio*, April 24, 2020. https://news4sanantonio.com/sports/spurs-zone/watch-spurs-great-manuGinóbili-reveals-the-origin-of-his-eurostep.

Garrison, Drew. 2013. "Chris Bosh Is the Key to the Heat's Pick-and-Roll Defense." *SB Nation*, Vox Media, October 16, 2013. https://www.sbnation.com/nba/2013/10/16/4831376/chris-bosh-videobreakdown-blitz-miami-heat.

Gill, Julian. 2017. "Reliving Manu Ginóbili's Best Post-Season." *Pounding The Rock*, Vox Media, July 19, 2017. https://www.poundingtherock.com/2017/7/19/15991210/manu-Ginóbili-san-antonio-spurspistons-nuggets-supersonics-suns-best-playoffs-2005.

Gilmartin, Joe. 1997. "Jazz Denies Reliance on Pick-and-Roll." *Arizona Republic*, June 4, 1997, Newspapers.com.

Given, Karen. 2017. "NBA's Forgotten Co-Founder and the Shot Clock's True Origin Story." *WBUR*, April 7,2017. https://www.wbur.org/onlyagame/2017/04/07/leo-ferris-shot-clock-nba-founder-hall-offame.

Gold, Jason M., et al. 2004. "Characterizing Perceptual Learning with External Noise." *Cognitive Science* 28 (2): 167–207. https://doi.org10.1016/j.cogsci.2003.10.005.

Goldaper, Sam. 1979. "N.B.A. Preview: New Faces and Some Gimmicks." *New York Times*, October 7, 1979. https://www.nytimes.com/1979/10/07/archives/nba-preview-new-faces-and-some-gimmicks.html.

———. 1986. "Pro Basketball; Nelson Credits Celtic Style for Success." *New York Times*, March 20, 1986. https://www.nytimes.com/1986/03/20/sports/pro-basketballnelson-credits-celtic-style-for-success.html.

Goldberg, Rob. 2019. "James Harden Rips Criticism of Step-Back: 'I'm Tired of Hearing That's a Travel.'" *Bleacher Report*, Turner Sports, September 29, 2019. https://bleacherreport.com/articles/2855857–james-harden-rips-criticism-of-step-back-im-tired-of-hearing-thats-a-travel.

Golliver, Ben. 2021. "Giannis Antetokounmpo, Bucks Came Back Better, Smarter, Steadier." *Washington Post*, May 31, 2021. https://www.washingtonpost.com/sports/2021/05/31/giannis-antetokounmpomilwaukee-bucks-sweep-miami/.

———. 2021. "NBA Set to Crackdown on 'Non-Basketball Moves' Used to Draw Fouls." *Washington Post*, September 27, 2021. https://www.washingtonpost.com/sports/2021/09/27/nba-fouls-nonbasketball-moves/.

Gomez, Jesus. 2016. "The Warriors' Screens Aren't Any More Illegal than Everyone Else's." *SB Nation*, Vox Media, May 18, 2016. https://www.sbnation.com/2016/5/18/11680940/golden-state-warriorsillegal-screens-analysis.

Gonzales, Maximo. 2019. "NBA Replay Center Explains that Giannis Antetokounmpo's Eurostep Was Legal." *Clutch Points*, May 20, 2019. https://clutchpoints.com/bucks-video-nba-replay-center-explainsgiannis-antetokounmpo-eurostep-was-legal/.

Goss, Nick. 2020. "IT Calls Out Giannis for Comments on Defending Butler in Game 1." *NBC Sports Boston*, September 1, 2020. https://www.nbcsports.com/boston/celtics/isaiah-thomas-calls-out-giannisantetokounmpo-comments-defending-jimmy-butler.

Gottlieb, Will. 2019. "The History of James Harden's Deadliest Move." *The Ringer*, March 5, 2019. https://www.theringer.com/nba/2019/3/5/18249912/james-harden-side-step-houston-rockets.

———. 2020. "'Harder Than Man': Why the NBA Fell in Love with Zone Defense This Year." *Bleacher Report*, Turner Sports, August 17, 2020. https://bleacherreport.com/articles/2895082–harder-thanman-why-the-nba-fell-in-love-with-zone-defense-this-year.

Grange, Michael. 2021. "Inside the Off-Season Makeover that Transformed R.J. Barrett's Shot." *SportsNet*, April 11, 2021. https://www.sportsnet.ca/nba/article/inside-rj-barretts-transformation-one-nbasdeadliest-shooters/.

Greece, Michelle R., and Aude Oliva. 2009. "The Briefest of Glances: The Time Course of Natural Scene Understanding." *Psychological Science* 20 (4): 464–72. https://www.ncbi.nlm.nih.gov/pmc/articles/PMC2742770/.

Greene, Nick. 2019. "The 3-Point Line Is Passe. All Hail Shooting from the Logo." *Slate*, October 29, 2019. https://slate.com/culture/2019/10/shooting-from-the-logo-trae-young-damian-lillard.html.

Grieben, Raul, et al. 2020. "Scene Memory and Spatial Inhibition in Visual Search." *Attention, Perception, & Psychophysics* 82: 775–98, Springer. https://link.springer.com/article/10.3758/s13414–019–01898–y.

Haberstroh, Tom. 2011. "Spoelstra Brings Ducks' Spread to NBA." *TrueHoop*, ESPN, December 22, 2011. https://www.espn.com/nba/truehoop/miamiheat/story/_/id/7378111/nba-oregon-ducks-football-muse-erikspoelstra-miami-heat.

———. 2012. "The Eurostep Bowl: Wade vs. Ginóbili." *TrueHoop*, ESPN, November 28, 2012. https://www.espn.com/blog/truehoop/miamiheat/post/_/id/16069/the-eurostep-bowl-wade-vs-Ginóbili.

———. 2014. "Should the NBA Add a 4–Pointer?" *ESPN*, February 25, 2014. https://insider.espn.com/nba/insider/story/_/id/10515372/jamal-crawford-the-nba-top-4-point-shooters-nba.

———. 2015. "How the NBA Learned to Stop Worrying and Love the Bomb." *ESPN*, June 3, 2015. https://www.espn.com/nba/playoffs/2015/story/_/id/12993098/nba-35-year-war-3-pointer.

———. 2016. "How Do Kawhi Leonard—and Steph Curry—Train Their Brains? Strobe Lights (Yes, Really)." *ESPN*, November 9, 2016. https://www.espn.com/nba/story/_/id/18002545/kawhileonard-strobe-light-training-nba.

———. 2017. "LeBron's Secret Workout Yoga 'Bubbles' Could Start a Pregame Revolution." *Bleacher Report*, Turner Sports, November 3, 2017. https://bleacherreport.com/articles/2742306–lebrons-secret-workout-yoga-bubbles-could-start-a-pre-game-revolution.

———. 2017. "The Washington Wizards and Virtual Reality." *ESPN*, February 7, 2017. https://jov.arvojournals.org/article.aspx?articleid=2765520.

———. 2019. "Secret Guard-en: The Story of Luka Dončić's Undercover Steph Curry Workout." *NBC Sports*, January 24, 2019. https://www.nbcsports.com/philadelphia/nba-insider-tomhaberstroh/secret-guard-en-story-luka-Dončićs-undercover-steph-curry-workout.

Hack, Damon. 2004. "U.S. Men Get to See How the Game Is Played." *New York Times*, August 19, 2004, D3, ProQuest.

Haefner, Joe. 2010. "Drill & Video - Improving Defensive Quickness & Debunking the 'Don't Cross Your Feet' Myth." *Breakthrough Basketball*, April 8, 2010. https://www.breakthroughbasketball.com/defense/debunking-cross-feet.html.

Haimoff, Elliott, director. 2014. "33STR8: Bill Sharman and the Greatest Winning Streak in Pro Sports History." Written by Joe Ide. *Global Science Productions*, September 9, 2014, YouTube video.

Hardee, Daniel. 2018. "How Andre Iguodala, Warriors Trolled James Harden's Offensive Game." *Golden State of Mind*, Vox Media, December 18, 2018. https://www.goldenstateofmind.com/2018/12/18/18146855/nba-2018–news-golden-state-warriors-houston-rockets-andreiguodala-james-harden-stephen-curry.

Harris, Anthony M., and Roger W. Remington. 2020. "Late Guidance Resolves the Search Slope Paradox in Contextual Cueing." *Psychonomic Bulletin & Review* 27: 1300–8. https://doi.org10.3758/s13423–020–01788–7.

Harris, Conor. 2021. "How Basketball Players Can Massively Improve Their Mobility." *Conor Harris*, October 4, 2021. https://www.conorharris.com/blog/how-basketball-players-can-massively-improvetheir-mobility.

Harvey, Buck. 2005. "Ginóbili vs. His Opposite: Manu a Mano." *San Antonio Express-News*, May 11, 2005, 1C.

———. 2005. "More Manu? What Spurs Need, Minute by Minute." *San Antonio Express-News*, May 17, 2005, 1D.

———. 2005. "A Name Game: Hoop Language of Spurs Leader." *San Antonio Express-News*, May 18, 2005, 1C.

———. 2005. "Old Spur vs. New Spur: Karl as Manu." *San Antonio Express-News*, May 2, 2005, 01D.

———. 2007. "Manu Goes Back, and That's a Sign." *San Antonio Express-News*, April 26, 2007, 1D.

Hauseman, Nick, director. 2018. "Is James Harden's Stepback Legal???" Performance by Ronnie Nunn. *BBALLBREAKDOWN*, season 2018, February 3, 2018, YouTube video. https://www.youtube.com/watch?v=ToAIL4J3jIA.

———. 2019. "Explaining the Gather Step to Basketball Fans." Performances by Devin Williams, et al. BBALLBREAKDOWN, October 7, 2019, YouTube video. https://www.youtube.com/watch?v=J5xGKioMsIo.

———. 2021. "Giannis and Bucks Have New Trae Young Strategy, Shoot Down Hawks." *BBALLBREAKDOWN*, June 26, 2021, YouTube video. https://www.youtube.com/watch?v=7DvInrNawpQ.

———. 2019. "How James Harden Is Exploiting the NBA Part 1." Performance by Ronnie Nunn. *BBALLBREAKDOWN*, January 10, 2019, YouTube video. https://www.youtube.com/watch?v=gYLrITIVG08.

Hayes, Taylor R., and John M. Henderson. 2019. "Scene Semantics Involuntarily Guide Attention during Visual Search." *Psychonomic Bulletin & Review* 26 (5): 1683. https://pubmed.ncbi.nlm.nih.gov/31342407/.

Haynes, Chris. 2018. "Steve Kerr on Iverson, Nash, Durant and the Most Influential Players." *ESPN*, March 27, 2018. https://www.espn.com/nba/story/_/id/22925181/steve-kerr-iverson-nash-durantmost-influential-players.

———. 2020. "Anthony Davis Wanted to Guard Jimmy Butler." *Yahoo! Sports*, October 7, 2020. https://sports.yahoo.com/anthony-davis-wanted-the-task-of-guarding-jimmy-butler-and-it-paid-off-ingame-4-155631906.html.

Heisler, Mark. 1996. "Unpolished Gem: 76ers' Brash Rookie Allen Iverson Does It His Way as He Takes the NBA by Storm." *Los Angeles Times*, December 29, 1996. https://www.latimes.com/archives/la-xpm-1996-12-29-sp-13703-story.html.

———. 2005. "All Even and Not Close." *Los Angeles Times*, June 17, 2005. https://www.latimes.com/archives/la-xpm-2005-jun-17-sp-nba17-story.html.

Helin, Kurt. 2012. "Don Nelson Says He Got Small Ball Idea from Red Auerbach." *Pro Basketball Talk*, NBC Sports, 30 August 2012, https://nba.nbcsports.com/2012/08/30/don-nelson-says-he-got-smallball-idea-from-red-auerbach/.

———. 2012. "League Admits LeBron Did Travel in Final Seconds Wednesday." *Pro Basketball Talk*, NBC Sports, January 12, 2012. https://nba.nbcsports.com/2012/01/12/league-admits-lebron-did-travelin-final-seconds-wednesday/.

———. 2019. "NBA to Better Define Traveling Rule, Increase Enforcement, Explain Rule to Players, Fans." *Pro Basketball Talk*, NBC Sports, September 20, 2019. https://nba.nbcsports.com/2019/09/20/nbato-better-define-traveling-rule-increase-enforcement-explain-rule-to-players-fans/.

Henderson, John M., et al. 2019. "Meaning and Attentional Guidance in Scenes: A Review of the Meaning Map Approach." *Vision* 3 (19): 189.

Henderson, John M., and Taylor R. Hayes. 2017. "Meaning-Based Guidance of Attention in Scenes as Revealed by Meaning Maps." *Nature Human Behavior* 1: 743–47. https://www.nature.com/articles/s41562-017-0208-0.

———. 2019. "Scene Semantics Involuntarily Guide Attention during Visual Search." *Psychonomic Bulletin & Review* 26 (5): 1683–9. https://doi.org10.3758/s13423-019-01642-5.

Henson, Mike. 2019. "Giannis Antetokounmpo: NBA Star's Rise from 'Hustling' on Athens Streets to MVP Award." *BBC*, July 1, 2019. https://www.bbc.com/sport/basketball/48832050.

Herbert, James. 2014. "Raptors' DeMar DeRozan Trying to Become Ambidextrous." *CBS Sports*, October 1, 2014. https://www.cbssports.com/nba/news/raptors-demar-derozan-trying-to-becomeambidextrous/.

———. 2016. "How NBA Leading Scorer DeMar DeRozan Has Taken His Game to Another Level." *CBS Sports*, November 17, 2016. https://www.cbssports.com/nba/news/how-nba-leading-scorer-demarderozan-has-taken-his-game-to-another-level/.

———. 2017. "How the Raptors Got Sick of Playoff Letdowns and Broke All Their Bad Habits." *CBS Sports*, December 14, 2017. https://www.cbssports.com/nba/news/every-nba-teams-mostunderrated-move-in-2021-offseason-including-free-agency-trades-and-draft/.

———. 2017. "Tim Hardaway Stakes Claim to Crossover: 'Allen Iverson Carried the Basketball.'" *CBS Sports*, March 14, 2017. https://www.cbssports.com/nba/news/tim-hardaway-stakes-claim-tocrossover-allen-iverson-carried-the-basketball/.

———. 2018. "Bucks' Khris Middleton Feels a New Vibe in Milwaukee, Sees 'a Whole New Giannis This Year.'" *CBS Sports*, October 8, 2018. https://www.cbssports.com/nba/news/bucks-khris-middletonfeels-a-new-vibe-in-milwaukee-sees-a-whole-new-giannis-this-year/.

Hermsmeyer, Josh. 2018. "For a Passing League, the NFL Still Doesn't Pass Enough." *Five ThirtyEight*, ESPN, September 6, 2018. https://fivethirtyeight.com/features/for-a-passing-league-the-nfl-stilldoesnt-pass-enough/.

Herring, Chris. 2013. "Mike Woodson's Coaching Evolution." *Wall Street Journal*, April 2, 2013. https://www.wsj.com/articles/SB10001424127887323646604578400683248448650.

———. 2022. *Blood in the Garden: The Flagrant History of the 1990s New York Knicks*. Atria Books.

Hickey, Clayton, et al. 2015. "Reward Guides Attention to Object Categories in Real-World Scenes." *Journal of Experimental Psychology* 144: 264–73.

Hicks, Dave. 1978. "3-Point Ploy: More Wow, Less Pow in NBA." *Arizona Republic*, June 30, 1978, 1, Newspapers.com.

Hicks, Jamison, et al. 2019. "Signal Detection in American Football Play Calling: A Comprehensive Literature Review." *Cogent Psychology* 6 (1). https://doi.org10.1080/23311908.2019.1703471.

Highkin, Sean. 2017. "NBA Explains Why James Harden's Ridiculous Eurostep Wasn't a Travel." *Rockets Wire*, USA Today, November 15, 2017. https://rocketswire.usatoday.com/2017/11/15/nba-explains-whyjames-hardens-ridiculous-eurostep-wasnt-a-travel/.

Hillyer, John. 1989. "Nelson Thinks Tall, Drafts Small." *San Francisco Examiner*, June 28, 1989, 55.

Hockrow, Ross, and Turner Sports, directors. 2019. "Finding Giannis." Performance by Giannis Antetokounmpo. Triple Threat Television, February 16, 2019.

Hofmann, Rich. 2018. "Gray Lines and Red Corners: Why Brett Brown's New Favorite Word is 'Gamify.'" The Athletic, September 27, 2018. https://theathletic.com/553549/2018/09/27/gray-lines-and-redcorners-why-brett-browns-new-favorite-word-is-gamify/?redirected=1.

Hollinger, John. 2022. "Midrange Messiah DeMar DeRozan Morphs into Mid-Career Dirk in Rarest of NBA Seasons." The Athletic, March 3, 2022. https://theathletic.com/3143728/2022/03/03/hollingerdemar-dirk-derozan-is-turning-midrange-analytics-on-its-head/.

Holmes, Baxter. 2014. "Marcus Smart Has Intangibles." *Boston Globe*, June 20, 2014. https://www.bostonglobe.com/sports/2014/06/19/intangibles-set-marcus-smart-apart/0EtUrGrds1Opoogla6OhWI/story.html.

Howard-Cooper, Scott. 2017. Twitter, March 14, 2017. https://twitter.com/SHowardCooper/status/841701162432651264.

"How Kevin Durant and DeMar DeRozan Are Winning with the Midrange." 2021. *Thinking Basketball*, created by Ben Taylor, season 2021, December 17, 2021, YouTube video. https://www.youtube.com/watch?v=59epmjId_z0.

"How NFL Players Train to Become ELITE: Meet the Footwork King." 2020. *NFL Media*, December 31, 2020, YouTube video. https://www.youtube.com/watch?v=t4l4kSdb_dY&.

"How to Train Like a Defensive Back: Improve Backpedaling, Explosiveness, Jamming & More." 2019. *NFL Media*, August 7, 2019, YouTube video. https://www.youtube.com/watch?v=umEc8T9vC1U.

Hulleman, Johan, and Christian N.L. Olivers. 2015. "The Impending Demise of the Item in Visual Search." *Behavioral and Brain Sciences* 1 (1): 1–76.

Hyun, Joo-seok, et al. 2009. "The Role of Attention in the Binding of Surface Features to Locations." *Visual Cognition* 17: 1–2. https://www.ncbi.nlm.nih.gov/pmc/articles/PMC3824248/.

Iko, Kelly. "Hit Traps and Peel Switches: The Two Chess Moves that Ended a Rockets Era." The Athletic, October 1, 2020. https://theathletic.com/2103866/2020/10/01/hit-traps-and-peel-switches-the-twochess-moves-that-ended-a-rockets-era/.

Income, Net. 2014. "The Latest in Jason Kidd Controversy." *Nets Daily*, Vox Media, June 29, 2014. https://www.netsdaily.com/2014/6/29/5854286/the-latest-in-jason-kidd-controversy.

Isola, Frank. 2014. "Mike Woodson Confronts Knicks Center Tyson Chandler about Critical Comments: Source." *New York Daily News*, January 22, 2014. https://www.nydailynews.com/sports/basketball/knicks/woodson-confronts-chatty-knicks-center-chandler-source-article-1.1587197.

"Is The GIANNIS Euro Step Legal?" 2018. *BBALLBREAKDOWN*, created by Nick Hauseman, February 12, 2018, YouTube video. https://www.youtube.com/watch?v=D1b_wZF81X0.

"James Harden's Step-Back 3-Pointer Is the Most Important Move in the NBA." 2019. *Signature Shots*, created by Kirk Goldsberry, ESPN, October 21, 2019, YouTube video. https://www.youtube.com/watch?v=w6p-UJJntgE&list=RDQMFa2lYQ6cLZ0&start_radio=1.

Jares, Joe. 1972. "Busy as a Bee in the Business of Basketball." *Sports Illustrated*, November 27, 1972. https://vault.si.com/vault/1972/11/27/busy-as-a-bee-in-the-business-of-basketball.

Jasner, Phil. 1996. "Iverson Dribbles into Trouble." *Philadelphia Daily News*, November 11, 1996, 59.

———. 1996. "Keeping His Guard Up: Iverson Grows Weary, Wary of Criticism." *Philadelphia Daily News*, November 12, 1996, 53.

Jenkins, Lee. 2015. "Doing Their Fair Share." *Sports Illustrated*, March 9, 2015. https://www.si.com/nba/2015/03/10/atlanta-hawks-jeff-teague-kyle-korver-mike-budenholzer.

———. 2015. "In His Own Sweet Time." *Sports Illustrated*, February 23, 2015. https://vault.si.com/vault/2015/02/23/in-his-own-sweet-time.

———. 2019. "The Giant Killer: Draymond Green Dares You to Define Him." *Sports Illustrated*, November 7, 2019. https://www.si.com/nba/2016/05/17/draymond-green-warriors-michigan-statestephen-curry-steve-kerr-nba-playoffs.

Jerez, Ernesto, creator. 2019. *Manu Eterno*. ESPN Latin America, *ESPN*. https://www.espn.com/watch/player/roadblock/_/id/28fec957-0875-4852-9786-5574d7767aa0.

Johnson, Ernie, et al., performers. 2009. *Inside the NBA*. Turner Broadcasting Company, YouTube video. https://www.youtube.com/watch?v=Y0MN6JM-7Xo.

Jonez, Dragonfly. 2018. "Why Filayyyy Is the Preacher of the Basketball Internet." *Bleacher Report*, Turner Sports, July 23, 2018. https://bleacherreport.com/articles/2787099–filayyyy-nba-voiceoverpower-50.

Juma, Calestous. 2016. *Innovation and its Enemies: Why People Resist New Technologies*. Oxford University Press.

Juran, Joseph M. 1974. "The Non-Pareto Principle; Mea Culpa." *The Juran Institute*. https://www.juran.com/wp-content/uploads/2021/03/The-Non-Pareto-Principle-1974.pdf.

Kahneman, Daniel, and Tversky Amos. 1979. "Prospect Theory: An Analysis of Decision under Risk." *Econometrica*.

Kalman, Samuel, and Bosch Jonathan. 2020. "NBA Lineup Analysis on Clustered Player Tendencies: A New Approach to the Positions of Basketball & Modeling Lineup Efficiency of Soft Lineup Aggregates." *MIT Sloan Sports Analytics Conference*.

Kantor, Jodi. 2012. "The Competitor in Chief." *New York Times*, September 2, 2012. https://www.nytimes.com/2012/09/03/us/politics/obama-plays-to-win-in-politics-and-everything-else.html.

Karl, George, et al. 2014. *In-Game Innovations: Genius or Gimmick?* Hosted by Kevin Arnovitz, February 28, 2014, MIT Sloan Sports Analytics Conference, Boston, MA, United States. Panel Discussion.

Katz, Dan, and Eric Sollenberger, directors. 2020. "The Last Dance Finale, Karl Malone, and Mt Rushmore of Grit Week Moments." Performance by Karl Malone. *Pardon My Take*, season 2020, Barstool Sports, May 20, 2020, Apple Podcasts.

Katz, Milton S., et al. 2007. *Breaking Through: John B. McLendon, Basketball Legend and Civil Rights Pioneer*. University of Arkansas Press.

Kawakami, Tim. 2014. "Former Suns GM Steve Kerr on the Stoudemire for Curry Almost-Trade in 2009: 'We Were Very Far Down the Road.'" *San Francisco Chronicle*, February 11, 2014. http://blogs.mercurynews.com/kawakami/2014/02/11/former-suns-gm-steve-kerrs-view-on-the-stoudemirefor-curry-almost-trade-on-draft-night-2009–we-were-very-far-down-the-road/.

Kawashima, Daniel. 2020. "How the Rockets Undersized Defense Has Shut Down OKC." August 21, 2020, YouTube video. https://www.youtube.com/watch?v=29BHvn-p-1c.

———. 2020. "How the Zone Defense Is Taking Over the NBA Playoffs: Heat vs. Celtics." September 22, 2020, YouTube video. https://www.youtube.com/watch?v=7T7hfqJr-08.

———. 2020. "The Truth About the Rockets Extremely Undersized Defense." March 4, 2020, YouTube video. https://www.youtube.com/watch?v=nopjLG5_Yjo.

Keh, Andrew. 2015. "Jason Kidd's Past Meets, and Beats, His Present (and Future)." *New York Times*, March 20, 2015. https://www.nytimes.com/2015/03/21/sports/basketball/jason-kidds-past-meets-andbeats-his-present-and-future.html.

Kellman, Philip J. 2002. "Perceptual Learning." *Stevens' Handbook of Experimental Psychology*, edited by R. Gallistel, vol. 3, 259–299. John Wiley & Sons.

Kellman, Philip J., et al. 2008. "Perceptual Learning and the Technology of Expertise: Studies in Fraction Learning and Algebra." *Pragmatics & Cognition* 16 (2): 356–405.

Kellman, Philip J., and Patrick Garrigan. 2009. "Perceptual Learning and Human Expertise." *Physics of Life Reviews* 6 (2): 53–84. https://doi.org10.1016/j.plrev.2008.12.001.

Kellman, Philip J., and Mary K. Kaiser. 1994. "Perceptual Learning Modules in Flight Training." *Proceedings of the Human Factors and Ergonomics Society Annual Meeting* 38 (18): 1183–1187, SagePub. https://journals.sagepub.com/doi/10.1177/154193129403801808

Kellman, Philip, and Christine Massey. 2013. "Perceptual Learning, Cognition, and Expertise." *Psychology of Learning and Motivation* 58: 117–65.

Kelly, Danny. 2013. "An Illustrated Guide to Playing Cornerback with Richard Sherman." *SB Nation*, Vox Media, September 20, 2013. https://www.sbnation.com/nfl/2013/9/20/4747480/richard-shermannfl-darelle-revis-seahawks-cornerback.

Kendrick, Kirsten. 2021. "From Seattle U to the Lakers: How Elgin Baylor Changed Basketball." *KNKX*, March 23, 2021. https://www.knkx.org/sports/2021–03–23/from-seattle-u-to-the-lakers-how-elginbaylor-changed-basketball.

Kepner, Tyler. 2004. "U.S. Manages to Hold Off Lithuania's 3-Point Barrage." *New York Times*, April 29, 2004.

Kharpertian, Devin. 2015. "Brook Lopez Was Contacted by Jason Kidd for Bucks, but Never Considered Leaving." *The Brooklyn Game*, July 9, 2015. https://thebrooklyngame.com/brook-lopez-contactedjason-kidd-bucks-never-considered-leaving/.

Klores, Dan, director. *Black Magic*. ESPN, 2008.

Klostermann, Andre, et al. 2020. "Perception and Action in Sports. On the Functionality of Foveal and Peripheral Vision." *Frontiers in Sports and Active Living* 1 (66). https://www.frontiersin.org/articles/10.3389/fspor.2019.00066/full#B22.

Koch, Robert. 1999. *The 80/20 Principle: The Secret to Achieving More with Less*. Reprint ed., Currency.

Koreen, Eric. 2014. "Raptors Like Last Year's Hand." *National Post*, July 11, 2014, 22.

———. 2016. "DeMar DeRozan Was the Raptors Star Hiding in Plain Sight." *SB Nation*, February 10, 2016. https://www.sbnation.com/2016/2/10/10906722/demar-derozan-toronto-raptors-all-star.

Kram, Zach. 2020. "The Biggest Playoff Upsets in Recent NBA History." *The Ringer*, September 9, 2020. https://www.theringer.com/nba/2020/8/19/21374534/biggest-playoff-upsets-nba-history.

———. 2021. "If You Thought Playing NBA Defense Was Hard, Try Quantifying It." *The Ringer*, May 11, 2021. https://www.theringer.com/nba/2021/5/11/22423517/nba-defense-analytics-nikolajokic.

Krentzman, Jackie. 1989. "Nelson Takes Hardaway in 1st Round." *Press Democrat* [Santa Rosa, Calif.], June 28, 1989, 25.

Kuchar, Mike. 2016. "Reading the Wide Receiver's Hips to Teach Man Coverage." *USA Football Blogs*, April 14, 2016. https://blogs.usafootball.com/blog/1047/reading-the-wide-receiver-s-hips-to-teach-mancoverage.

Kuhn, Gustav, and Benjamin W. Tatler. 2005. "Magic and Fixation: Now You Don't See it, Now You Do." *Perception* 34 (9): 1155–61. https://doi.org10.1068/p3409bn1.

———. 2010. "Misdirected by the Gap: The Relationship Between Inattentional Blindness and Attentional Misdirection." *Consciousness and Cognition* 20 (2): 432–36.

Kussoy, Howie. 2021. "Years after Jason Kidd's Failed Coup, Nets and Bucks Thriving Without Him." *New York Post*, June 5, 2021. https://nypost.com/2021/06/05/years-after-jason-kidds-failed-coup-nets-andbucks-thriving-without-him/.

Laczkowski, Matt. 2016. "When It Comes to Hoops, Traveling Is a Two-Step Program." *Baltimore Sun*, February 23, 2016. https://www.baltimoresun.com/maryland/carroll/opinion/ph-cc-sp-laczkowskicolumn-0222–20160223–column.html.

Larsen, Andy. 2017. "John Stockton on Karl Malone, Michael Jordan, the Pick-and-Roll, Watching His Kids Play and More." *KSL*, March 24, 2017. https://www.ksl.com/article/43613394/john-stocktonon-karl-malone-michael-jordan-the-pick-and-roll-watching-his-kids-play-and-more.

Lee, Michael. 2021. "Elgin Baylor Is the Reason the Word 'Superstar' Exists." *Washington Post*, March 23, 2021. https://www.washingtonpost.com/sports/2021/03/23/elgin-baylor-original-superstar/.

Leitch, Will. 2012. "Rocket Man." *GQ Magazine*, October 16, 2012. https://www.gq.com/story/jeremy-lin-gq-november-2012–cover-story.

Lev, Maria, et al. 2014. "Training Improves Visual Processing Speed and Generalizes to Untrained Functions." *Scientific Reports* 4. https://doi.org/10.1038/srep07251.

Levi, Dennis M., et al. "Sequential Perceptual Learning of Letter Identification and 'Uncrowding' in Normal Peripheral Vision: Effects of Task, Training Order, and Cholinergic Enhancement." *Journal of Vision* 4 (20). https://jov.arvojournals.org/article.aspx?articleid=2765520.

Lewis, Michael. 2009. "The No-Stats All-Star." *New York Times*, February 13, 2009. https://www.nytimes.com/2009/02/15/magazine/15Battier-t.html.

Libanoff, Mitch. 2020. "Viewing Skills in Tandem." *The Stepien*, November, 3 2020. https://www.thestepien.com/2020/03/11/viewing-skills-tandem/.

Lippert, Jack K. 1924. "Extensive Changes Noted in 1924–1925 Basket Ball Rule Book." *Pittsburgh Press*, October 26, 1924, Newspapers.com.

Lleras, Alejandro, et al. 2020. "A Target Contrast Signal Theory of Parallel Processing in Goal-Directed Search." *Attention, Perception, & Psychophysics* 82: 394–425, Springer. https://link.springer.com/article/10.3758/s13414–019–01928–9.

Loomis, Phil. n.d. "Essential Movement Qualities: Hip Internal Rotation." *Athletes' Acceleration*, https://athletesacceleration.com/hip-internal-rotation/.

Lorenzo, Tom. 2015. "Brook Lopez Was Contacted by Jason Kidd but Never Seriously Considered Leaving." *Nets Daily*, Vox Media, July 9, 2015. https://www.netsdaily.com/2015/7/9/8922531/brook-lopezrumors-nba-jason-kidd-free-agency.

Los Angeles Lakers. 2018. "Bill Sharman Q&A." *LA Lakers*, NBA, November 10, 2018. https://www.nba.com/lakers/history/bill_sharman_q_a_111018.html.

Lowe, Zach. 2013. "Are George Karl's Denver Nuggets for Real?" *Grantland*, ESPN, February 12, 2013. http://grantland.com/features/are-george-karl-denver-nuggets-really-title-contenders/.

———. 2013. "Blow the Whistle: The NBA's Precarious Officiating Issues." *Grantland*, ESPN, October 23, 2013. https://grantland.com/the-triangle/blow-the-whistle-the-nbas-precariousofficiating-issues/.

———. 2013. "Flameout?" *Grantland*, ESPN, June 18, 2013. https://grantland.com/features/couldgame-6–end-lebron-james-miami-heat-magical-season/.

———. 2013. "Lockdown: How the Heat Defense Redefined the Eastern Conference Finals." *Grantland*, ESPN, May 31, 2013. https://grantland.com/the-triangle/lockdown-how-the-heat-defenseredefined-the-eastern-conference-finals/.

———. 2013. "A Third-Rate Babylon: The Knicks' Potential Problems This Year and Beyond." *Grantland*, ESPN, October 14, 2013. https://grantland.com/the-triangle/a-third-rate-babylon-theknicks-potential-problems-this-year-and-beyond/.

———. 2013. "Three-Heat?" *Grantland*, ESPN, October 29, 2013. https://grantland.com/features/canlebron-james-miami-heat-win-third-nba-title/.

———. 2014. "Farewell, Woody: The Knicks Clean House." *Grantland*, ESPN, April 21, 2014. https://grantland.com/the-triangle/farewell-woody-the-knicks-clean-house/.

———. 2014. "Milwaukee's Makeover: How the Bucks Decided to Buckle Down and Play for the Future." *Grantland*, ESPN, December 9, 2014. https://grantland.com/the-triangle/milwaukeesmakeover-how-the-bucks-decided-to-buckle-down-and-play-for-the-future/.

———. 2018. "Manu Ginóbili Has Built a Legacy of Love for Team in His Storied Career." *ESPN*, August 27, 2018. https://www.espn.com/nba/story/_/id/17262551/manu-Ginóbili-built-legacy-love-teamstoried-career.

———. 2018. "These Plays and Matchups Will Decide Rockets-Jazz, Celtics-76ers." *ESPN*, May 2, 2018. https://www.espn.com/nba/story/_/id/23378599/zach-lowe-rockets-jazz-celtics-76ers-nba-playoffs.

Lu, Zhong-Lin, et al. 2011. "Visual Perceptual Learning." *Neurobiology of Learning and Memory* 95 (2): 145–51.

Lu, Zhong-Lin, and Barbara Anne Dosher. 1998. "External Noise Distinguishes Attention Mechanisms." *Vision Research* 38 (9): 1183–98.

Ludden, Johnny. 2002. "Little Big Manu - Spurs Guard a Success Story by Any Measure." *San Antonio Express-News*, September 2, 2002, 1C.

———. 2005. "Is Manu a Flopper?" *San Antonio Express-News*, June 5, 2005, 1C.

———. 2005. "Marked Manu." *San Antonio Express-News*, October 29, 2005, 1C.

———. 2006. "Blazing a Euro Trail." *San Antonio Express-News*, October 1, 2006, 5N.

Luhm, Steve. 1997. "Jazz Put Rockets Near Extinction." *Salt Lake Tribune*, May 28, 1997, C1, ProQuest.

MacMahon, Tim. 2020. "The Houston Rockets Are Daring Teams to Outmuscle Their Micro-Ball Defense." ESPN, March 5, 2020. https://www.espn.com/nba/story/_/id/28837914/the-houston-rockets-daringteamsoutmuscle-their-micro-ball-defense.

———. 2020. "The Evolution of the James Harden-Giannis Antetokounmpo Feud." *ESPN*, August 2, 2020. https://www.espn.com/nba/story/_/page/nbareturn29560382/the-evolution-jamesharden-giannis-antetokounmpo-feud.

———. 2021. "Utah Jazz Wing Joe Ingles Has No Business Leading the NBA in This One Stat." *ESPN*, May 5, 2021. https://www.espn.com/nba/story/_/id/31389506/utah-jazz-wing-joe-ingles-nobusiness-leading-nba-one-stat.

MacMullan, Jackie. 2010. "2010 NBA playoffs: Kobe Bryant Perfected His Game by Watching Film." *ESPN*, June 4, 2010. https://www.espn.com/nba/playoffs/2010/columns/story?columnist=macmullan_jackie&page=kobefilmstudy-100604.

MacMullen, Jackie, et al. 2019. *Basketball: A Love Story*. Penguin Random House.

Macquet, Anne-Claire, and Koffi Kragba. 2015. "What makes Basketball Players Continue with the Planned Play or Change It? A Case Study of the Relationships Between Sense-Making and Decision-Making." *Cognition, Technology & Work* 17: 345–353.

Madden, Mark. 1995. "Drastic Steps." *Pittsburgh Post-Gazette*, March 5, 1995, F-3.

Mahoney, Rob. 2013. "James Harden Walks the Traveling Line." *Sports Illustrated*, January 16, 2013. https://www.si.com/nba/2013/01/16/james-harden-traveling.

———. 2017. "Chris Paul's Most Dangerous Weapon? His Eyes." *Sports Illustrated*, April 11, 2017. https://www.si.com/nba/2017/04/11/chris-paul-court-vision-passing-clippers-nba-playoffs.

———. 2021. "Milwaukee Sacrificed a Winning Formula to Find Its Best Self." *The Ringer*, April 22, 2021. https://www.theringer.com/nba/2021/4/22/22397331/milwaukee-bucks-giannisantetokounmpo.

Maisonet, Eddie. 2017. "The Miseducation of the 2004 U.S. Men's Olympic Basketball Team." *Bleacher Report*, Turner Sports, September 5, 2017. https://bleacherreport.com/articles/2731575-themiseducation-of-the-2004-us-mens-olympic-basketball-team.

Makovski, Tal. "What Is the Context of Contextual Cueing?" *Psychonomic Bulletin & Review* 23: 1982–8. https://doi.org10.3758/s13423-016-1058-x.

Malone, Karl, et al., performers. 2012. "Karl Malone Shows the Art of the 'Pick-and-Roll.'" *NBATV*, season 2012, National Basketball Association, October 17, 2012, YouTube video. https://www.youtube.com/watch?v=US-h15qVBCc.

Mann, J. Kyle, performer. 2020. "Tim Hardaway and the Origins of the Crossover in the NBA." *Ball the Right Moves*, The Ringer, April 23, 2020, YouTube video. https://www.youtube.com/watch?v=GLOEhp4G2qg.

Mannix, Chris. 2014. "Jason Kidd, Bucks Defeat Nets in His Anticipated Return to Brooklyn." *Sports Illustrated*, November 19, 2014. https://www.si.com/nba/2014/11/20/jason-kidd-bucks-defeat-nets-in-returnto-brooklyn.

Mansfield, Aaron. 2020. "James Harden and Giannis Antetokounmpo: A Timeline of Their Feud." *Complex*, February 28, 2020. https://www.complex.com/sports/james-harden-giannis-antetokounmpo-feudtimeline.

Maurer, Mitchell. 2017. "One Step Forward, One Step Back: Will the Bucks Defense Ever Change?" *Brew Hoop*, Vox Media, December 5, 2017. https://www.brewhoop.com/2017/12/5/16739012/one-stepforward-one-step-back-will-the-milwaukee-bucks-defense ever change-jason-kidd-giannis.

Mayberry, Darnell. 2021. "DeMar DeRozan Takes over Another Fourth Quarter in Bulls' Win over Knicks." *The Athletic*, December 3, 2021. https://theathletic.com/2995235/2021/12/03/demar-derozan-takesover-another-fourth-quarter-in-bulls-win-over-knicks/.

McCallum, Jack. 1986. "The Incredible Shrinking Court." *Sports Illustrated*, November 3,1986. https://vault.si.com/vault/1986/11/03/the-incredible-shrinking-court-in-an-era-whenthe-big-man-is-ever-more-dominant-when-seven-foot-forwards-and-six-seven-guards-are-notuncommon-some-astute-students-of-nba-basketball-believe-that-the-players-have-outgro.

———. 1991. "The Breaks of The Game." *Sports Illustrated*, November 11, 1991, 90–95.

———. 2003. "How to…Own Your Own Country." *Sports Illustrated*, October 27, 2003. https://vault.si.com/vault/2003/10/27/how-toown-your-own-country-after-his-star-turn-with-the-spursmanu-Ginóbili-is-all-the-rage-in-argentina.

———. 2004. "Third World." *Sports Illustrated*, September 6, 2004. https://vault.si.com/vault/2004/09/06/third-world.

———. 2007. *Seven Seconds or Less: My Season on the Bench with the Runnin' and Gunnin' Phoenix Suns*. Touchstone.

———. 2005. "Off to the Races." *Sports Illustrated*, June 13, 2005. https://vault.si.com/vault/2005/06/13/off-to-the-races.

———. 2013. "Pop Art." *Sports Illustrated*, April 29, 2013. https://vault.si.com/vault/2013/04/29/pop-art.

McCormick, Brian. 2015. *Fake Fundamentals*. Kindle ed., 180Shooter.com.

McCormick, Brian T., et al. 2014. "A Comparison of the Drop Step and Hip Turn Techniques for Basketball Defense." *International Journal of Sports Science & Coaching* 9 (4): 605–13.

McCrary, Cody. 2018. "Steve Kerr: 'I Could See Manu Playing When He Is Like 58.'" *San Antonio Express-News*, March 19, 2018. https://www.mysanantonio.com/sports/spurs/article/Steve-Kerr-I-could-see-Manu-playing-when-he-is-12765690.php.

McGeachy, Ashley. 2011. "For Brown and 76ers, Being in the Zone an Untenable Spot." *Philadelphia Inquirer*, October 7, 2011, Newspapers.com.

McKern, James. 2018. "Joe Ingles' Shooting Confidence: 'I Feel Like I Should Make Every One of Them.'" *Sporting News*, October 5, 2018. https://www.sportingnews.com/au/nba/news/nba-utah-jazz-joeingles-confidence-three-point-shooting/1u1w2s5jqeot319dvo0srdofrv.

McLendon, John B. 1965. *Fast Break Basketball: Fundamentals and Fine Points*. Hardcover ed., ParkerPublishing.

McPhee, John. 1965. "A Sense of Where You Are." *New Yorker*, January 23, 1965. https://www.newyorker.com/magazine/1965/01/23/a-sense-of-where-you-are.

Medina, Mark. 2018. "Exclusive: A Sitdown with Warriors Guru Andre Iguodala." *San Jose Mercury-News*, September 28, 2018. https://www.mercurynews.com/2018/09/28/warriors-andre-iguodala-on-hishealth-last-seasons-playoffs-and-life-after-basketball/.

Mettler, Everett, and Philip J. Kellman. 2014. "Adaptive Response-Time-Based Category Sequencing in Perceptual Learning." *Vision Research* 99: 111–23. https://doi.org10.1016/j.visres.2013.12.009.

Millard, Lourens, et al. 2020. "Factors Affecting Vision and Visio-Spatial Intelligence (VSI) in Sport: A Review of the Literature." *Asian Journal of Sports Medicine* 11 (3).

Miller, Brian T., and Wesley C. Clapp. 2011. "From Vision to Decision: The Role of Visual Attention in Elite Sports Performance." *Eye & Contact Lens: Science & Clinical Practice* 37 (3): 131–9.

Miller, Matt. 2013. "How Do Scouts Break Down NFL Cornerback Prospects?" *Bleacher Report*, June 29, 2013. https://bleacherreport.com/articles/1686545–how-do-scouts-break-down-nfl-cornerbackprospects.

Miller, Ryan. 2021. "The Story Behind Joe Ingles' Historic 3-Point Run." *KSL*, March 23, 2021. https://next.ksl.com/article/50131654/the-story-behind-joe-ingles-historic-3-point-run.

Miller, Stuart. 2011. "A Basketball League Where Steinbrenner and 3-pointers Started." *New York Times*, December 24, 2011. https://www.nytimes.com/2011/12/25/sports/basketball/a-basketball-leaguewhere-steinbrenner-and-3-pointers-started.html?_r=0.

Mitchell, Sam, et al., performers. 2017. "The 3-Point Revolution." Season 2017, episode Part I: The History of the 3-Point Shot, NBA TV, November 20, 2017, YouTube video.

Moehringer, J.R. 2019. "Kevin Durant's New Headspace." *Wall Street Journal*, September 10, 2019. https://www.wsj.com/articles/kevin-durants-new-headspace-11568119028.

Monroe, Mike. 2004. "Nuggets Begin Courtship of Manu." *San Antonio Express-News*, July 3, 2004, 1D.

———. 2006. "Ginóbili Again Imposes His Will." *San Antonio Express-News*, May 18, 2006, 4D.

———. 2005. "Ginóbili Proves Big off Bench Again." *San Antonio Express-News*, May 3, 2005, 5D.

———. 2007. "Notebook: Citing 'That Shot,' Karl Benches Smith for Remainder of Series." *San Antonio Express-News*, May 2, 2007, 9D.

———. 2007. "Smith's Turnover Crushes Nuggets." *San Antonio Express-News*, April 29, 2007, 14C.

———. 2007. "Smith Works at Staying Focused." *San Antonio Express-News*, April 25, 2007, 6C.

———. 2007. "Spurs Answer Nuggets." *San Antonio Express-News*, January 11, 2007, 1D.

———. 2007. "Spurs Take Down Nuggets." *San Antonio Express-News*, January 11, 2007, 1D.

Montville, Leigh. 1996. "Flash Point." *Sports Illustrated*, December 9, 1996. https://vault.si.com/vault/1996/12/09/flash-point-flummoxing-foes-with-his-crossover-dribble-and-lightningquickness-allen-iverson-the-sixers-rookie-point-guard-has-the-nba-buzzing.

Moorhead, Couper. 2021. "Heat-Bucks Game 1: Enter the Cage Fight." *Miami Heat*, NBA, May 23, 2021. https://www.nba.com/heat/news/heat-bucks-game-1–enter-cage-fight.

Moran, Aidan, and Nuala Brady. 2010. "Mind the Gap: Misdirection, Inattentional Blindness and the Relationship Between Overt and Covert Attention." *Consciousness and Cognition* 19 (4): 1105–6.

Moran, Malcolm. 1998. "Jazz Make Some Points—but Too Few." *Chicago Tribune*, June 11, 1998. https://www.chicagotribune.com/news/ct-xpm-1998–06–11–9806110382–story.html.

Moreau, David, et al. 2011. "Spatial Ability and Motor Performance: Assessing Mental Rotation Processes in Élite and Novice Athletes." *International Journal of Sport Psychology* 42: 525–547.

———. 2012. "Enhancing Spatial Ability Through Sport Practice." *Journal of Individual Differences* 33: 83–88.

Moreau, David, and Andrew R.A. Conway. 2013. "Cognitive Enhancement: A Comparative Review of Computerized and Athletic Training Programs." *International Review of Sport and Exercise Psychology*,6 (1): 155–183. https://doi.org10.1080/1750984X.2012.758763.

Most, Steven B. 2010. "What's 'Inattentional' about Inattentional Blindness?" *Consciousness and Cognition* 19 (4): 1102–14.

Muench, Jesse, creator. 2020. "Are You Calling Travels Wrong? Basketball Rules Explained." *Get Handles Basketball*, YouTube video. https://www.youtube.com/watch?v=Xwi3W4_XXlg.

Muench, Jesse, performer. 2018. "Is the James Harden Step Back Really a Travel?" *Get HandlesBasketball*, September 23, 2018, YouTube video. https://www.youtube.com/watch?v=G-MQRcwtWts.

Murphy, Dylan. 2018. "Changing the Angle." *The Basketball Dictionary*, Medium, January 30, 2018. https://medium.com/the-basketball-dictionary/change-the-angle-8fb89e26aca9.

———. 2018. "Under-Two." *The Basketball Dictionary*, Medium, January 15, 2018. https://medium.com/the-basketball-dictionary/under-two-2acb712a4c8f.

Murray, James. 1961. "Los Angeles Lakers: Behind-the-Scenes with Elgin Baylor and His Teammates." *Sports Illustrated*, January 30, 1961. https://vault.si.com/vault/1961/01/30/a-trip-for-ten-tall-men.

Myers, Bob, et al. "Basketball Analytics: Hunting for Unicorns." Hosted by Zach Lowe and Howard Beck. *MIT Sloan Sports Analytics Conference*, March 1, 2019, YouTube video. https://www.youtube.com/watch?v=OQ76ddgZmt0&. Panel Discussion.

National Basketball Association. n.d. "Bob Cousy - Celtics Legend." *Boston Celtics*. https://www.nba.com/celtics/history/legends/bob-cousy.

———. 2019. "NBA Board of Governors Approves Clarification of rule governing Traveling Violations." *NBA*, September 20, 2019. https://www.nba.com/news/board-governorsclarification-traveling-official-release.

———. 2019. "New Language in NBA Rule Book Regarding Traveling Violations." *NBA Official*, October 1, 2019. https://official.nba.com/new-language-in-nba-rule-book-regardingtraveling-violations/.

National Football League. n.d. "The Evolution of the NFL Rules." *NFL*. https://operations.nfl.com/the-rules/evolution-of-the-nfl-rules/.

Naughton, John. 2013. "Why Power Has Two Meanings on the Internet." *The Guardian*, January 6, 2013. https://www.theguardian.com/technology/2013/jan/06/power-laws-internet-john-naughton.

NBA, director. 2010. "Manu Ginóbili and His 1,2 Step." *Turner Sports*, December 6, 2010, YouTube video. https://www.youtube.com/watch?v=VSpF6OFvXl8.

NBA. n.d. *NBA Rules History*. National Basketball Association, https://cdn.nba.net/nba-drupal-prod/nbarules-changes-history.pdf.

———. 2019. "New Language in NBA Rule Book Regarding Traveling Violations." *NBA Official*, October 1, 2019. https://official.nba.com/new-language-in-nba-rule-book-regarding-traveling-violations/.

NBA Communications. 2013. "NBA Board of Governors Approves Rules Changes." *NBA*, July 18, 2013. https://pr.nba.com/nba-board-of-governors-approves-rules-changes-2013–14–season/.

Nehm, Eric. 2018. "Milwauk-3: Bucks Plan to Let It Fly from Beyond the Arc." The Athletic, October 17, 2018. https://theathletic.com/594561/2018/10/17/milwauk-3–bucks-plan-to-let-it-fly-from-beyond-thearc/.

———. 2018. "New Bucks Coach Mike Budenholzer Is Implementing His Type of Offensive Pace." The Athletic, October 9, 2018. https://theathletic.com/578741/2018/10/09/new-bucks-coach-mikebudenholzer-is-implementing-his-type-of-offensive-pace/.

———. 2019. "Giannis Antetokounmpo Unplugged: Bucks Star Sounds off about His Playoff Performance and Team's Tough Finish." The Athletic, May 30, 2019. https://theathletic.com/1001604/2019/05/30/giannis-antetokounmpo-unplugged-bucks-star-sounds-off-about-hisplayoff-performance-and-teams-tough-finish/.

———. 2019. "This Bud's for You! Bucks Coach Mike Budenholzer Is Passionate about Details (and Video)." The Athletic, April 25, 2019. https://theathletic.com/935847/2019/04/25/this-buds-foryou-bucks-coach-mike-budenholzer-is-passionate-about-details-and-video/.

———. 2020. "Bucks Guarding Jimmy Butler—Why Not Use Giannis Antetokounmpo?" The Athletic, September 1, 2020. https://theathletic.com/2036880/2020/09/01/bucks-guarding-jimmy-butlerwhy-not-use-giannis-antetokounmpo/.

———. 2020. "Cleansing, Clearing and 2.9-ing: How the Bucks' Brook Lopez Protects the Paint." The Athletic, August 14, 2020. https://theathletic.com/1976623/2020/08/14/cleansing-clearingand-2–9–ing-how-the-bucks-brook-lopez-protects-the-paint/.

———. 2020. "Game 1 Thud: Giannis Stumbles for Bucks as Jimmy Butler Delivers for Heat." The Athletic, September 1, 2020. https://theathletic.com/2035987/2020/09/01/game-1–by-the-starsgiannis-stumbles-for-bucks-jimmy-butler-delivers-for-heat/.

———. 2020. "How a Promising Bucks Season Was Derailed and What's Next?" The Athletic, October 2, 2020. https://theathletic.com/2046373/2020/10/02/how-a-promising-bucks-season-was-derailedand-whats-next/.

———. 2020. "Where It All Went Wrong (Again): Takeaways from the Bucks' Playoff Exit." The Athletic, September 9, 2020. https://theathletic.com/2048182/2020/09/09/where-it-all-went-wrong-again-4–takeaways-from-the-bucks-playoff-exit/.

———. 2021. "Bucks' Adjustments and Switching Defense Show Their Willingness to Evolve." The Athletic, March 12, 2021. https://theathletic.com/2444562/2021/03/12/bucksadjustments-and-switching-defense-show-their-willingness-to-evolve/.

———. 2021. "Bucks Begin to Experiment with New Defensive Tendencies." The Athletic, February 16, 2021. https://theathletic.com/2385475/2021/02/16/bucks-starting-to-switch-it-up-on-defense-ilike-that-were-open-minded-now/.

———. 2021. "Bucks-Heat Game 2 Preview: Giannis' Defensive Role & 2 Other Adjustments to Watch For." The Athletic, May 24, 2021. https://theathletic.com/2608433/2021/05/24/bucks-heat-game-2–preview-giannis-defensive-role-2–other-adjustments-to-watch-for/.

———. 2021. "Bucks' New Offense Is Excelling with Addition of 'The Dunker' Area." The Athletic, January 11, 2021.

———. 2021. "Bucks Struggle Against Jazz's Pick-and-Roll Strategy." The Athletic, January 9, 2021. https://theathletic.com/2311953/2021/01/09/quin-snyders-pick-and-roll-strategy-againstbucks-highlights-need-for-change/.

———. 2021. "The Evolution of the Milwaukee Bucks' 'Dunker' Spot and How It Could Help Them Break Through the Playoff Wall." The Athletic, May 19, 2021. https://theathletic.com/2559992/2021/05/19/the-evolution-of-the-milwaukee-bucks-dunker-spot-and-how-it-couldhelp-them-break-through-the-playoff-wall/.

———. 2021. "Giannis Antetokounmpo and His Continuing Basketball Evolution: What He Tells Us About His Growth as a Player." The Athletic, November 29, 2021. https://theathletic.com/2980356/2021/11/29/giannis-antetokounmpo-and-his-continuing-basketball-evolutionwhat-he-tells-us-about-his-growth-as-a-player/.

———. 2021. "Giannis Antetokounmpo Slams Clippers as Bucks Switch with Success." The Athletic, February 28, 2021. https://theathletic.com/2417881/2021/02/28/giannis-antetokounmpo-milwaukeebucks-dunk-win/.

———. 2021. "I Asked Giannis about Guarding Kevin Durant. 'Let's Have a Conversation.' So We Did." The Athletic, June 16, 2021. https://theathletic.com/2654741/2021/06/16/bucks-giannisantetokounmpo-kevin-durant-defense-game-5/.

———. 2021. "The Odd Couple: How 'Frasier' Explains Why Lopez and Budenholzer's Eclectic Partnership Drives the Bucks' Defense." The Athletic, June 2, 2021. https://theathletic.com/2473273/2021/06/02/the-odd-couple-how-frasier-explains-why-lopez-and-budenholzerseclectic-partnership-drives-the-bucks-defense/.

———. 2021. "One on One with Giannis Antetokounmpo on the Bucks' NBA Championship: 'It's Crazy. It's F—ing Crazy.'" The Athletic, July 23, 2021. https://theathletic.com/2723411/2021/07/23/oneon-one-with-giannis-antetokounmpo-on-the-bucks-nba-championship-its-crazy-its-f-crazy/.

———. 2022. "NBA 75: At No. 24, Giannis Antetokounmpo Has Become One of the Game's Most Decorated Players in Less Than a Decade." The Athletic, January 18, 2022. https://theathletic.com/3073534/2022/01/18/nba-75–at-no-24–giannis-antetokounmpo-has-become-one-of-thegames-most-decorated-players-in-less-than-a-decade/.

Nelson, Glenn. 1996. "Iverson Puts League on Its Heels." Seattle Times, December 9, 1996. https://archive.seattletimes.com/archive/?date=19961209&slug=2364087.

Nelson, Jameer, and Ben Stinar, performers. 2020. "Drew Hanlen." Court Vision Podcast, season 1, episode 16, September 4, 2020, Apple Podcasts. https://podcasts.apple.com/us/podcast/court-vision-podcast/id1517089005.

Newberry, Paul. 2005. "Hawks get Marvin Williams, load up." The Sumter Item, Associated Press ed., June 29, 2005, ProQuest.

Newman, Bruce. 1979. "The N.Y. Rens Traveled a Long Hard Road to Basketball's Hall of Fame." *Sports Illustrated*, October 22, 1979. https://vault.si.com/vault/1979/10/22/yesterday-the-ny-rens-traveled-a-long-hard-road-to-basketballs-hall-of-fame.

———. 1980. "Now It's Bombs Away in the NBA." *Sports Illustrated*, January 7, 1980. https://vault.si.com/vault/1980/01/07/now-its-bombs-away-in-the-nba-traditionalists-may-blanch-but-probasketball-is-going-downtown-with-the-three-point-shot-the-celtics-especially-have-fired-shotsheard-round-the-nba-world-but-most-teams-have-yet-to-explo.

———. 1991. "To the Point." *Sports Illustrated*, February 11, 1991. https://vault.si.com/vault/1991/02/11/to-the-point.

New York Times.1924. "Basketball Body Rearanges Rule: Seeks to Establish Uniform Interpretation of Code for Next Season." *New York Times*, April 12, 1924, 11, ProQuest.

———. 1926. "Guide Lists Changes in Basketball Code." *New York Times*, October 31, 1926, S7, ProQuest.

———. 1927. "Basketball Inventor Hits Dribble Ruling." *New York Times*, April 11, 1927, ProQuest.

Nichols, Rachel, performer. 2020. "James Harden Talks Rockets' Small-Ball Lineup, Giannis' Assist Joke & MVP Standings." *The Jump*, ESPN, February 28, 2020.

Nicholas, Rachel, writer. 2019. "NBA league exec explains how traveling will be called in 2019–20." Performances by Amin Elhassan, et al. *The Jump*, season 2019, ESPN, October 9, 2019.

Nike Basketball, director. 2008. "Manu Ginóbili." *Nike Signature Moves*, season 2008, YouTube video. https://www.youtube.com/watch?v=u0FAar0QNeg.

Noh, Stephen. 2021. "DeMar DeRozan Keeps Moving Forward by Looking Backwards." *Noh's Notebook*, Substack, September 26, 2021. https://stephnoh.substack.com/p/demar-derozan-keeps-movingforward.

North, Jamie S., et al. 2009. "Perceiving Patterns in Dynamic Action Sequences: Investigating the Processes Underpinning Stimulus Recognition and Anticipation Skill." *Applied Cognitive Psychology* 23 (6): 878–894.

———. 2017. "Identifying the Micro-relations Underpinning Familiarity Detection in Dynamic Displays Containing Multiple Objects." *Frontiers in Psychology* 8 (963).

O'Connor, Kevin. 2016. "Lessons from the Pick-and-Roll Masters." *The Ringer*, December 19, 2016. https://www.theringer.com/nba/2016/12/19/16077164/nba-pick-and-roll-lou-williams-kemba-walkerdraymond-green-f9a1ec934a2a.

———. 2019. "Steph Curry's Game Is More Than Just His Shot." *The Ringer*, February 12, 2019. https://www.theringer.com/nba/2019/2/12/18221183/steph-curry-warriors-2019–all-star-gamecharlotte.

O'Donnell, Ricky. 2020. "This James Harden 'Travel' Is Actually Totally Legal. Here's Why." *SB Nation*, Vox Media, February 23, 2020. https://www.sbnation.com/nba/2020/2/23/21149538/james-hardentravel-eurostep-rockets-vs-jazz.

Orsborn, Tom. 2005. "Pistons Lament Call, Game That Got Away." *San Antonio Express-News*, June 12, 2005, pp.3S.

Ortiz, Jorge L. 2001. "Foul Calls / NBA Players, Coaches Being Fined at Record Rate for Outbursts Aimed at Officials." *SFGATE*, January 10, 2001. https://www.sfgate.com/sports/article/Foul-Calls-NBAplayers-coaches-being-fined-at-2966385.php.

O'Shaughnessy, Haley. 2020. "James Harden vs. Giannis Antetokounmpo Is the NBA's Latest Beef." *The Ringer*, February 28, 2020. https://www.theringer.com/nba/2020/2/28/21158131/james-hardengiannis-antetokounmpo-nba-beef.

O'Shaughnessy, Haley, director. 2021. "Deep Dive: Legalizing Defense." Performance by Jordan Ligons. *Spinsters*, season 1, episode 4, Blue Wire, April 20, 2021, Apple Podcasts.

Ostler, Scott. 2005. "Ginóbili Has Become the Spurs' Mane Man." *SFGATE*, June 11, 2005. https://www.sfgate.com/sports/ostler/article/2005–NBA-FINALS-Ginobili-has-become-the-Spurs-2513561.php.

Pack, Weston, et al. 2013. "Involuntary Attention Enhances Identification Accuracy for Unmasked Low Contrast Letters Using Non-Predictive Peripheral Cues." *Vision Research* 89: 79–98. https://www.sciencedirect.com/science/article/pii/S0042698913001650X.

Padecky, Bob. 1979. "Angry Mieuli Quits Post." *Sacramento Bee*, June 26, 1979, Newspapers.com.

———.1989. "Nellie's Tune: 'Don't Worry, Be Happy.'" *Press Democrat* [Santa Rosa, Calif.], June 28,1989, 25.

Paris, Adam. 2017. "Milwaukee vs. Boston: Bucks Drop Behind Early, Can't Catch Up to Celtics." *Brew Hoop*, Vox Media, December 5, 2017. https://www.brewhoop.com/2017/12/5/16736224/milwaukee-vs-boston-bucks-celtics-game-review-december-4.

Partnow, Seth. 2019. "The Lost Art of the Inartful Midrange." The Athletic, September 13, 2019. https://theathletic.com/1205425/2019/09/13/seth-partnow-analysis-the-lost-art-of-the-inartfulmidrange/.

———. 2019. "The New NBA Heliocentrism: How Teams Revolve More Around Today's Stars Than They Ever Have Before." The Athletic, December 6, 2019. https://theathletic.com/1427059/2019/12/06/the-new-nba-heliocentrism-how-teams-revolve-more-around-todays-stars-than-they-ever-havebefore/.

———. 2021. "Disappointing Knicks, Surging Cavs and Stagnant Mavericks: Evaluating What We've Learned so Far This NBA Season." The Athletic, December 15, 2021. https://theathletic.com/3003170/2021/12/15/disappointing-knicks-surging-cavs-and-stagnant-mavericks-evaluatingwhat-weve-learned-so-far-this-nba-season/.

———. 2021. The Midrange Theory. Triumph Books.

———. 2021. "NBA Offense Is Way Down. What Are the Reasons—No, It's Not the Ball—and How Many Are Here to Stay?" The Athletic, November 3, 2021. https://theathletic.com/2930213/2021/11/03/nba-offense-is-way-down-what-are-the-reasons-no-its-not-the-ball-andhow-many-are-here-to-stay/.

Pasquarelli, Len. 2004. "Expect More Illegal Contact Penalties in 2004." ESPN, March 27, 2004. https://www.espn.com/nfl/columns/story?columnist=pasquarelli_len&id=1771047.

Patrick, Dan. 2001. "Outtakes: Tim Hardaway (Uncut)." ESPN, December 6, 2001. https://www.espn.com/talent/danpatrick/s/2000/1129/910739.html.

Payne, Brandon, performer. 2019. "Every Exercise Steph Curry's Trainer Makes Him Do." The Assist, season 1, episode 3, GQ, September 19, 2019. https://www.gq.com/video/watch/every-exercise-steph-currys-trainer-makes-him-do.

Peacock, Candace E., et al. 2019. "The Role of Meaning in Attentional Guidance During Free Viewing ofReal-World Scenes." Acta Psychologica 198: 10288. https://pubmed.ncbi.nlm.nih.gov/31302302/.

———. 2021. "Meaning and Expected Surfaces Combine to Guide Attention During Visual Search in Scenes." Journal of Vision 21 (1). https://doi.org10.1167/jov.21.11.1.

Pedziwiatr, Marek A., et al. 2021. "Meaning Maps and Saliency Models Based on Deep Convolutional Neural Networks Are Insensitive to Image Meaning When Predicting Human Fixations." Cognition 206.

Pelton, Kevin, and Kevin Arnovitz. 2018. "How the NBA Got Its Groove Back." ESPN, May 24, 2018. https://www.espn.com/nba/story/_/id/23529256/how-nba-got-groove-back.

Penn, Nate. 2012. "Dunk'd: An Oral History of the 2004 Dream Team." GQ Magazine, July 27, 2012. https://www.gq.com/story/2004-olympic-basketball-dream-team.

Pereira, Effie J., and Monica S. Castelhano. 2019. "Attentional Capture Is Contingent on Scene Region: Using Surface Guidance Framework to Explore Attentional Mechanisms During Search." Psychonomic Bulletin & Review 26: 1273–81, Springer. https://doi.org10.3758/s13423–019–01610–z.

Perez, Rob. 2021. "A Tribute to Manu Ginóbili, the NBA's Most Memorable Improv Act." Action Network, September 23, 2021. https://www.actionnetwork.com/nba/manu-Ginóbili-retirement-spurs-tribute.

Perry, Mark J. 2008. "Top 20% of NBA Players Scored 80% of Total Points." American Enterprise Institute. https://www.aei.org/carpe-diem/top-20-of-nba-players-scored-80-of-total-points/.

Petrov, Alexander A., et al. 2005. "The Dynamics of Perceptual Learning: An Incremental Reweighting Model." Psychological Review 112 (4): 715–43.

Pina, Michael. 2019. "God Shammgod Created a Legendary Move. His NBA Coaching Crossover Could Be Even Bigger." Washington Post, March 5, 2019. https://www.washingtonpost.com/sports/2019/03/05/god-shammgod-created-legendary-move-his-nba-coaching-crossover-could-be-even-bigger/.

———. 2020. "The Rise of the One-Dribble 3-pointer." The Ringer, August 5, 2020, Spotify. https://www.theringer.com/nba/2020/8/5/21353968/nba-three-point-shooting-one-dribble.

———. 2021. "Bucks' Defense Was Built for This Moment." Sports Illustrated, July 14, 2021. https://www.si.com/nba/2021/07/14/nba-finals-bucks-defense.

———. 2021. "Is Nets' James Harden's Decline Real or Temporary?" Sports Illustrated, December 2, 2021. https://www.si.com/nba/2021/12/02/james-harden-brooklyn-nets-decline-temporary.

Pluto, Terry. 1990. Loose Balls: The Short, Wild Life of the American Basketball Association. Simon & Schuster.

Povtak, Tim. 2005. "Ginóbili's Unusual Style Makes Sense to Spurs." Baltimore Sun, June 12, 2005.

Powell, Shaun. 2017. "Doubt, Disdain Marked Most NBA Teams' First Forays into 3-Point Land." NBA, February 21, 2017. https://www.nba.com/news/history-3-pointer-evolution-nba-game-larry-birdstephen-curry-james-harden.

Prada, Mike. 2013. "How the Denver Nuggets Hide Their Cutters in Half-Court Situations." SB Nation, Vox Media, March 20, 2013. https://www.sbnation.com/nba/2013/3/20/4128104/denver-nuggetsbreakdown-oklahoma-city-thunder.

————. 2014. "Giannis Antetokounmpo Is Making Traveling Impossible to Call." *SB Nation*, Vox Media, December 5, 2014. https://www.sbnation.com/nba/2014/12/5/7343451/giannis-antetokounmpotraveling-milwaukee-bucks.

————. 2015. "Atlanta Hawks Playoff Preview: Nobody Gives the East's Best Team Any Respect." *SB Nation*, Vox Media, April 16, 2015. https://www.sbnation.com/nba/2015/4/16/8269373/atlantahawks-preview-nba-playoffs-2015.

————. 2015. "Giannis Antetokounmpo Is Reinventing the Game." *SB Nation*, Vox Media, February 11, 2015, https://www.sbnation.com/nba/2015/2/11/7980435/giannisantetokounmpo-nba-slam-dunk-contest-2015.

————. 2015. "There's a New Dribble Move Taking the NBA By Storm." *SB Nation*, Vox Media, February 15, 2015. https://www.sbnation.com/nba/2015/2/15/8037121/nba-yo-yo-dribble-chris-pauljohn-wall.

————. 2016. "The Hornets Built a Beautiful Offense Without Really Changing All That Much." *SB Nation*, Vox Media, March 29, 2016. https://www.sbnation.com/2016/3/29/11320144/charlotte-hornetsbreakdown-analysis-offense-three-pointers-steve-clifford.

————. 2017. "Draymond Green Is the NBA's Ultimate Defensive Mastermind. Here's Why." *SBNation*, June 2, 2017, YouTube video. https://www.youtube.com/watch?v=Gyt1EFkB7gs.

————. 2017. "Marcus Smart Is a Terrible Shooter Who's Somehow Essential to the Celtics' Offense." *SB Nation*, Vox Media, December 6, 2017. https://www.sbnation.com/2017/12/6/16739088/marcussmart-shooting-stats-terrible-celtics-offense-works.

————. 2017. "Why the NBA's Premier Defender Is at His Best When Guarding Nobody?" *SB Nation*, Vox Media, April 25, 2017. https://www.sbnation.com/2017/4/25/15420756/draymond-green-defensebreakdown-nba-warriors-blazers.

————. 2019. "The Bucks' One Trick to Forming an Elite Defense." *SB Nation*, Vox Media, December 24, 2019. https://www.sbnation.com/nba/2019/12/24/21035620/milwaukee-bucks-defense-rimprotection-three-pointers-stats-giannis-lopez-brothers.

————. 2020. "How the Raptors' Defense Is Making Other Teams See Ghosts." *SB Nation*, Vox Media, February 12, 2020. https://www.sbnation.com/nba/2020/2/12/21129554/toronto-raptors-defensenick-nurse-zone-box-and-one-trap-switch-analysis.

————. 2020. "The New Standard Brow-er." *Prada's Pictures*, Substack, October 21, 2020. https://mikeprada.substack.com/p/the-new-standard-brow-er.

————. 2020. "Putting Their Best Foot Backwards." *Prada's Pictures*, Substack, October 8, 2020. https://mikeprada.substack.com/p/putting-their-best-foot-backwards.

————. 2020. "Robert Covington and P.J. Tucker Are Redefining Rim Protection." *SB Nation*, Vox Media, March 4, 2020. https://www.sbnation.com/nba/2020/3/4/21163408/houston-rockets-robertcovington-p-j-tucker-defense-rim-protection.

————. 2020. "Stunt Doubles." *Prada's Pictures*, Substack, September 4, 2020. https://mikeprada.substack.com/p/stunt-doubles.

Prasad, Aryanna. 2021. "Kyle Kuzma Is Loving the NBA's New Restrictive Rules on Foul Drawing." *The StepBack*, FanSided, October 29, 2021. https://fansided.com/2021/10/29/kyle-kuzma-nba-fouldrawing-rules/.

Price, S.L. 1989. "Warriors Take Guard, Then Think Big." *Sacramento Bee*, June 28, 1989, 23.

Pryor, Gibson. 2020. "Miami Heat 2–3 Zone Defense." *NBA Film Room*, January 4, 2020, YouTube video. https://www.youtube.com/watch?v=MA8–5Rn5_64&.

————. 2020. "Miami Heat's Defensive Gameplan vs Giannis - Bucks vs Heat Preview" *NBA Playoffs Film Room*, Half Court Hoops, August 29, 2020, YouTube video. https://www.youtube.com/watch?v=XwVkriJPZ3Y.

Pyzdek, Thomas, and Joseph A. DeFeo. 2019. "Pareto Principle (80/20 Rule) & Pareto Analysis Guide." *Juran*, March 12, 2019. https://www.juran.com/blog/a-guide-to-the-pareto-principle-80–20–rulepareto-analysis/.

Quinn, Sam. 2021. "Giannis Antetokounmpo Wants to Guard Kevin Durant in Game 6, but That's Not a Cure-All for Bucks' Defense." *CBS Sports*, June 16, 2021. https://www.cbssports.com/nba/news/giannis-antetokounmpo-wants-to-guard-kevin-durant-in-game-6–but-thats-not-a-cure-all-forbucks-defense/.

Radcliffe, JR. 2019. "Seven Takeaways from TNT Documentary 'Finding Giannis.'" *Milwaukee Journal Sentinel*, February 16, 2019. https://www.jsonline.com/story/sports/nba/bucks/2019/02/16/seventakeaways-tnt-documentary-finding-giannis/2894438002/.

Rafferty, Scott. 2021. "Giannis Antetokounmpo Taking on the Kevin Durant Assignment Is More Complicated Than It Might Seem." *Sporting News*, June 17, 2021. https://www.sportingnews.com/ca/nba/news/nba-playoffs-2021–giannis-antetokounmpo-taking-on-the-kevin-durant-assignment-is-morecomplicated-than-it-might-seem/b5k51j6jbx4z1x9cbf1493j4p.

Rafferty, Scott. 2020. "Have the Los Angeles Lakers Found Their Jimmy Butler Stopper?" *Sporting News*, October 8, 2020. https://www.sportingnews.com/ca/nba/news/stat-just-happened-have-the-losangeles-lakers-found-their-jimmy-butler-stopper/lui2uxk2036k1plx8t1mwrk7m.

Rains, Rob, and Helen Carpenter. 2011. *James Naismith: The Man Who Invented Basketball.* Temple University Press.

Ramsay, Jack. 2001. "Good Riddance to Illegal Defenses." *ESPN*, April 12, 2001. http://static.espn.go.com/nba/s/2001/0412/1171902.html.

Ramsey, David. 2001. "Nuggets' Chances Rest with Bench." *Colorado Gazette*, April 27, 2001.

Raskin, Alex. 2016. "Nobody Knows Head Coaches Like Brook Lopez." *Wall Street Journal*, October 5, 2016. https://www.wsj.com/articles/nobody-knows-head-coaches-like-brook-lopez-1475711728.

Reid, Jordan. 2019. "What to Look for When Scouting: Cornerbacks." *The Draft Network*, July 26, 2019. https://thedraftnetwork.com/articles/what-to-look-for-when-scouting--cornerbacks.

Reilly, Rick. 1998. "Counter Point." *Sports Illustrated*, March 9, 1998. https://vault.si.com/vault/1998/03/09/counter-point-philadelphias-allen-iverson-may-be-the-quickest-man-in-the-nba-but-hes-in-nohurry-to-conform-to-the-image-the-league-prefersor-to-his-coachs-idea-of-how-the-game-shouldbe-played.

Riege, Anine, et al. 2021. "Covert Eye-Tracking: An Innovative Method to Investigate Compliance with Instructions." *Psychological Research* 85: 3084–93, Springer. https://doi.org10.1007/s00426–020–01451–9.

Rieken, Kristie. "Harden Scores 38 as Rockets Even Series with Warriors." *Associated Press*, May 7, 2019. https://apnews.com/article/616ea36daae84605b3437bb5f99cfc03.

Rocca, Andre, et al. 2018. "Creative Decision Making and Visual Search Behavior in Skilled Soccer Players." *PLoS One* 13 (7). https://doi.org10.1371/journal.pone.0199381.

Rodriguez, Carter. 2016. "The Night Linsanity Died at the Hands of the Miami Heat." *Hot Hot Hoops*, Vox Media, February 26, 2016. https://www.hothothoops.com/2016/2/23/11100332/night-linsanitydied-hands-miami-heat-jeremy-lin-wade-lebron-knicks.

Rooney, Paula. 2002. "Microsoft's CEO: 80–20 Rule Applies to Bugs, Not Just Features." *CNN*, October 3, 2002. https://www.crn.com/news/security/18821726/microsofts-ceo-80–20–rule-appliesto-bugs-not-just-features.htm.

Rose, Jalen, performer. 2009. "LeBron James Crab Dribble - Jalen Rose Explains." *First Take*, season 2009, ESPN, January 5, 2009, YouTube video. https://www.youtube.com/watch?v=DpQBD672HkQ.

———. 2013. "The Rise of the Euro Step." *ESPN NBA Countdown*, season 2013, YouTube video. https://www.youtube.com/watch?v=3Y0ZxlEHsas.

Roth, David. "The NBA Ball that Everyone Hated." *VICE Sports*, February 23, 2017. https://www.vice.com/en/article/wnmz79/the-nba-ball-that-everyone-hated-throwback-thursday.

Ruiz, Steven. 2016. "Are the Warriors Getting Away with an Insane Number of Illegal Screens?" *For The Win*, USA Today, March 22, 2016. https://ftw.usatoday.com/2016/03/are-the-golden-state-warriorsgetting-away-with-an-insane-number-of-illegal-screens.

Ruyuan, Zhang, and Duje Tadin. 2019. "Disentangling Locus of Perceptual Learning in the Visual Hierarchy of Motion Processing." *Scientific Reports* 9: 1557. https://www.nature.com/articles/s41598–018–37892–x.

Ryu, Donghyun, et al. 2014. "The Contributions of Central and Peripheral Vision to Expertise in Basketball: How Blur Helps to Provide a Clearer Picture." *Journal of Experimental Psychology, Human Perception, and Performance* 41 (1).

Saarela, Toni, and Michael H. Herzog. 2010. "The Effect of Spacing Regularity on Visual Crowding." *Journal of Vision* 10 (10): 1–7. https://jov.arvojournals.org/article.aspx?articleid=2121115.

Sachare, Alex. 1979. "NBA Three-Pointers Cause a Furor." *Associated Press*, October 27, 1979, 1, Newspapers.com.

Saget, Bedel, and Xaquin G.V. 2011. "The Crossover on Display." *New York Times*, May 25, 2011. https://www.nytimes.com/video/sports/basketball/100000000831937/the-crossover-on-display.html.

Salzberg, Charles. 1987. *From Set Shot to Slam Dunk: The Glory Days of Basketball in the Words of Those Who Played It.* E.P. Dutton.

Sampaio, Jaime, et al. 2016. "Defensive Pressure Affects Basketball Technical Actions but Not the Time-Motion Variables." *Journal of Sport and Health Sciences* 5: 375–80, Science Direct. https://www.sciencedirect.com/science/article/pii/S2095254615000587.

San Antonio Spurs. 2018. "Gracias Manu." *Spurs.* https://www.nba.com/spurs/graciasmanu.

Sandomir, Richard. 2020. "Peter Brancazio, Who Explored the Physics of Sports, Dies at 81." *New York Times*, May 16, 2020. https://www.nytimes.com/2020/05/16/obituaries/peter-brancazio-deadcoronavirus.html.

Saunders, Laura. 2018. "Top 20% of Americans Will Pay 87% of Income Tax." *Wall Street Journal*, April 6, 2018. https://www.wsj.com/articles/top-20–of-americans-will-pay-87–of-income-tax-1523007001.

Scaletta, Kelly. 2014. "The NBA's Key Plays Still Begin with an Evolving Art: The Screen." *Bleacher Report*, Turner Sports, March 13, 2014. https://bleacherreport.com/articles/1992086–the-nbas-key-playsstill-begin-with-an-evolving-art-the-screen.

Schaefer, Rob. 2021. "DeRozan's Midrange Mastery Fueling Bulls in Crunch Time." *NBC Sports*, December 21, 2021. https://www.nbcsports.com/chicago/bulls/demar-derozans-midrange-mastery-transformingbulls-crunch-time.

Schill, Hayden M., et al. 2020. "Axis of Rotation as a Basic Feature in Visual Search." *Attention, Perception, &Psychophysics* 82: 31–43.

Schilling, Dave. 2018. "Traveling in the NBA: The Price of Making Art." *Bleacher Report*, Turner Sports, April 28, 2018. https://bleacherreport.com/articles/2771640–traveling-in-the-nba-the-price-ofmaking-art.

Schmerfeld, David. 2020. *Optimum Pass/Run Ratio in NFL.* https://davidschmerfeld.github.io/nfl-optimum-pass-run-ratio/.

Schoenfeld, Bruce. 2016. "What Happened When Venture Capitalists Took Over the Golden State Warriors." *New York Times*, April 3, 2016. https://www.nytimes.com/2016/04/03/magazine/what-happened-when-venture-capitalists-took-over-the-golden-state-warriors.html.

Schuhmann, John. 2020. "Film Study: A Look at the Rockets' Switch-Happy Defense." *NBA*, Turner Sports, July 2, 2020. https://www.nba.com/news/film-study-rockets-switching-happy-defense.

Schultz, Rob. 2009. "Penney for His Thoughts." *Wisconsin State Journal*, June 30, 2009, B.1.

Schwartz, Jason. 2014. "The Amazing Pace." *Grantland*, ESPN, April 26, 2014. https://grantland.com/features/nba-dleague-rgv-vipers-houston-rockets-future-of-basketball/.

Seifert, Kevin. 2004."Rating NFL Cornerbacks." *Minneapolis Star-Tribune*, September 8, 2004, ProQuest.

Seitz, Aaron, and Takeo Watanabe. 2005. "A Unified Model for Perceptual Learning." *Trends in Cognitive Sciences* 9 (7): 329–34.

———. 2009. "The Phenomenon of Task-Irrelevant Perceptual Learning." *Vision Research* 49 (21): 2604–10.

Sepkowitz, Leo. 2019. "How the NBA Got Its Handles." *Bleacher Report*, February 12, 2019. https://bleacherreport.com/articles/2820399–how-the-nba-got-its-handles.

Sheridan, Chris. 1997. "Rockets Cry 'Foul' about Utah's Tactics." *Associated Press*, May 23, 1997, ProQuest.

Sherman, Randy. 2021. "Early Offense Ideas: Transition Drag Screens." *FastModel Sports*, June 18, 2021. https://team.fastmodelsports.com/2021/06/18/transition-drag-screens/.

Sherwin, Bob. 2005. "Ginóbili Refines Act and Helps Spurs Close Curtain on a Series." *New York Times*, May 21, 2005. https://www.nytimes.com/2005/05/21/sports/basketball/Ginóbili-refines-act-andhelps-spurs-close-curtain-on-a.html.

———. 2005. "Spurs' Ginóbili No Flop When 'Acting.'" *Chicago Tribune*, May 21, 2005. https://www.chicagotribune.com/news/ct-xpm-2005–05–21–0505210155–story.html.

Shioiri, Satoshi, et al. 2018. "Spatial Representations of the Viewer's Surroundings." *Scientific Reports* 8: 7171. https://doi.org10.1038/s41598–018–25433–5.

Shirk, George. 1983. "Guess Again—Forget Offense; Defense Is Key for Sixers and Lakers." *Philadelphia Inquirer*, May 24, 1983, ProQuest.

Shoals, Bethlehem. 2006. "Sweet Fields of Unfastened Terrain." *McSweeneys*, October 12, 2006. https://www.mcsweeneys.net/articles/sweet-fields-of-unfastened-terrain.

Shomstein, Sarah, et al. 2019. "Intrusive Effects of Task-Irrelevant Information on Visual Selective Attention: Semantics and Size." *Current Opinion in Psychology* 29: 153–9. https://doi.org10.1016/j.copsyc.2019.02.008.

Shultz, Alex. 2019. "James Harden Says the Rockets Might Be 'the Best-Dressed Team in the History of Sports.'" *GQ*, September 12, 2019. https://www.gq.com/story/james-harden-vol-4–sneakerinterview.

Simmons, Bill, and Jalen Rose, directors. 2015. "Kobe Bryant on Russell Westbrook and the Thunder, His Plans for the Future, and More." *Grantland Basketball Hour*, season 1, ESPN, February 23, 2015.

Simmons, Rusty. 2013. "Rockets Rout Warriors by 31." *San Francisco Gate*, February 5, 2013. https://www. sfgate.com/warriors/article/Rockets-rout-Warriors-by-31–4254231.php.

———. 2013. "Training Camp Day 1: Head Coach Mark Jackson Sets Serious Tone." *San Francisco Chronicle*, September 28, 2013. https://blog.sfgate.com/warriors/2013/09/28/training-camp-day-1–mark-jackson-sets-a-serious-tone/.

Slappin' Glass. 2020. "European Pick n' Roll Defense—"Next" Coverage." May 17, 2020, YouTube video. https://www.youtube.com/watch?v=lbD7WS0QGxc.

Smith, Sam. 2001. "If Zone Defenses Come In, Stars May Go Out." *Chicago Tribune*, April 1, 2001. https:// www.chicagotribune.com/news/ct-xpm-2001–04–01–0104010375–story.html. Accessed 28 August2018.

———. 2005. "Spurs Put Foreign Flair to Good Use." *Chicago Tribune*, June 11, 2005.

Smith, Sekou. 2009. "It's Official: Two Steps OK: NBA: Rule Enforcement Will Not Change. League Changes 'Antiquated Language,' Not Traveling Rule." *Atlanta Journal-Constitution*, October 25, 2009, C.1.

———. 2009. "NBA's New Rule Paves Way for Two Steps." *Atlanta Journal-Constitution*, October 23, 2009. https://www.ajc.com/sports/basketball/nba-new-rule-paves-way-for-two-steps/AblrxEvGuoexvIrPKp4bjJ/.

Sneed, Brandon. 2017. "Steph Curry's Secrets to Success: Brain Training, Float Tanks, and Strobe Goggles." *Bleacher Report*, Turner Sports, February 22, 2017. https://bleacherreport.com/articles/2693694–steph-currys-secrets-to-success-brain-training-float-tanks-and-strobe-goggles.

Sohi, Seerat. 2017. "How the NBA Was Saved on the Back of a Napkin." *Sports Illustrated*, November 5, 2019. https://www.si.com/nba/2017/08/28/nba-shot-clock-history-invention-leo-ferris-george-mikan.

———. 2018. "Manu Ginóbili Will Forever Live in Basketball's Soul." *SB Nation*, Vox Media, August 28, 2018. https://www.sbnation.com/2018/8/28/17789068/manu-Ginóbili-retires-san-antonio-spurslegacy-soul.

———. 2021. "Draymond Green's Influence on the Modern NBA." *Yahoo! Sports*, January 15, 2021. https://www.yahoo.com/now/the-draymond-generation-why-undersized-bruisers-are-ideal-intodays-nba-140009989.html.

———. 2021. "Meet the Coaches Who Scrutinize the World's Greatest Shot." *Yahoo! Sports*, January 29, 2021. https://www.yahoo.com/now/meet-the-coaches-that-scrutinize-the-worlds-greatestshot-064948893. html.

———. 2021. "Zion Williamson Blends Football with Basketball." *Yahoo! Sports*, April 5, 2021. https:// www.yahoo.com/now/zion-williamsons-football-frame-blended-with-basketball-finesse-could-benext-frontier-195906171.html.

Spears, Marc. 2007. "Smith's Mistakes the Start of Nuggets' Downfall." *Denver Post*, April 28, 2007.

Spears, Marc J. 2021. "Elgin Baylor, Underappreciated Superstar." *The Undefeated*, ESPN, March 22, 2021. https://theundefeated.com/features/elgin-baylor-underappreciated-nba-superstar/.

Sports Odds History. n.d. "NBA Regular Season Win Total Results by Team—2000s." *Sports Odds History.* https://www.sportsoddshistory.com/nba-regular-season-win-total-results-by-team-2000s/.

Springfield College. 2015. "Where Basketball Was Invented: The History of Basketball." *Springfield College*, December 16, 2015. https://springfield.edu/where-basketball-was-invented-the-birthplace-ofbasketball.

Statista. n.d. *U.S.-Seniors as a Percentage of the Population 1950–2050.* https://www.statista.com/statistics/457822/share-of-old-age-population-in-the-total-us-population/. Accessed 20 January2020.

Steele, Ben. "Budenholzer's First Practice with Bucks Emphasizes Transition Defense and Spacing on Offense." *Milwaukee Journal Sentinel*, September 25, 2018. https://www.jsonline.com/story/sports/nba/bucks/2018/09/25/bucks-coach-mike-budenholzer-emphasizes-fundamentals-firstpractice/1414121002/.

Stein, Marc. 2006. "Sources: Nelson to Return to Warriors as Coach." *ESPN*, August 19, 2006. https://www. espn.com/nba/news/story?id=2565022.

———. 2014. "NBA Has Discussed Bigger Court, 4–Point Shot." *ESPN*, February 25, 2014. https://www. espn.com/nba/story/_/id/10517078/nba-discussed-bigger-court-4–point-shot.

———. 2015. "Summer Scoop: Bucks Can Spend Cash - Marc Stein." *ESPN*, Disney, June 12, 2015. https:// www.espn.com/blog/marc-stein/post/_/id/3881/summer-scoop-bucks-can-spend-cash.

Steinberg, Dan. 2009. "LeBron, DeShawn and the Travel." *Washington Post*, January 4, 2009. http://voices. washingtonpost.com/dcsportsbog/2009/01/lebron_deshawn_and_the_travel.html.

Stites, Adam. 2021. "Warriors' Steve Kerr Says 'Game Has a More Authentic Feel' in 2021 Thanks to Rule Changes." *Yardbarker*, October 29, 2021. https://www.yardbarker.com/nba/articles/warriors_steve_kerr_says_game_has_a_more_authentic_feel_in_2021_thanks_to_rule_changes/s1_13132_36273008.

Strasburger, Hans. 2019. "Seven Myths on Crowding and Peripheral Vision." *Perception* 11 (3). https:// journals.sagepub.com/doi/10.1177/2041669520913052.

Strauss, Ethan Sherwood. 2020. *The Victory Machine: The Making and Unmaking of the Warriors Dynasty.* Kindle ed., PublicAffairs.

Surdam, David George. 2012. *The Rise of the National Basketball Association.* Kindle ed., University of Illinois Press.

Sykes, Mike D. 2020. "NBA Fans Don't Think Giannis Deserves DPOY." *For The Win*, USA Today, September 1, 2020. https://ftw.usatoday.com/2020/09/giannis-antetokounmpo-guard-jimmy-butlerfans-react.

Tamayo, Paul. "Ray Allen Reveals the NSFW Nickname Some Opposing Coaches Had for Him." *Clutch Points*, September 6, 2018. https://clutchpoints.com/nba-news-ray-allen-reveals-the-nsfwnickname-some-opposing-coaches-had-for-him/.

Tatler, Benjamin W., et al. 2017. "Latest: A Model of Saccadic Decisions in Space and Time." *Psychological Review* 124 (3): 267–300. https://doi.org10.1037/rev0000054.

Tax, Jeremiah. 1959. "Bunyan Strides Again." *Sports Illustrated*, April 6, 1959. https://vault.si.com/vault/1959/04/06/bunyan-strides-again.

Taylor, Ben. 2017. "A Visual History of NBA Spacing." *Back Picks*, WordPress, November 2, 2017. https://backpicks.com/2017/11/02/the-history-of-nba-spacing/.

———. 2020. "Is Marcus Smart the Best Defensive Guard in the NBA?" *Thinking Basketball*, July 15, 2020, YouTube video. https://www.youtube.com/watch?v=3IWiADg7IiU&.

———. 2021. "How the Referees Slowed Down James Harden, Damian Lillard & Other Stars." *Thinking Basketball*, November 22, 2021, YouTube video. https://www.youtube.com/watch?v=-tojc0cl680.

———. 2021."The Warriors Defense Is on Another Level!" *Thinking Basketball*, December 13, 2021, YouTube video. https://www.youtube.com/watch?v=jbNS09Rt4u8.

Taylor, Phil. 1995. "The Oldest Pick in The Book." *Sports Illustrated*, November 13, 1995. https://vault.si.com/vault/1995/11/13/the-oldest-pick-in-the-book-the-defense-usually-knows-its-coming-butthe-well-executed-pick-and-roll-is-still-pro-basketballs-most-dependable-play.

———. 1997. "Hey, It's My Move!" *Sports Illustrated*, November 10, 1997. https://vault.si.com/vault/1997/11/10/hey-its-my-move.

———. 1999. "A Turn for The Better." *Sports Illustrated*, March 15, 1999. https://vault.si.com/vault/1999/03/15/a-turn-for-the-better-all-it-took-were-missteps-harsh-critics-and-a-switch-to-anew-position-to-help-the-76ers-allen-iverson-develop-into-the-nbas-most-explosive-scorer.

The Encyclopadia Britannica: A Dictionary of Arts, Sciences, Literature & General Information. 1926. United Kingdom: Enclyclopadia Britannica.

Theeuwes, Jan. 2019. "Goal-Driven, Stimulus-Driven, and History-Driven Selection." *Current Opinion in Psychology* 29: 97–101.

Thompson, Adam. 2005. "Spurs Take Command." *Denver Post*, April 30, 2005.

Thompson II, Marcus. 2020. "Steph Curry's Offseason Regimen Has Him Ready for Anything This Season." The Athletic, November 27, 2020. https://theathletic.com/2224339/2020/11/27/thompson-stephcurrys-offseason-regimen-has-him-ready-for-anything-this-season/.

Thornton, Ian M., and Suncica Zdravkovic. 2020. "Searching for Illusory Motion." *Attention, Perception & Psychophysics* 82: 44–62.

Thorpe, David. 2021. "2022's Key NBA Skill: The Pass." *TrueHoop*, Substack, December 28, 2021. https://www.truehoop.com/p/2022s-key-nba-skill-the-pass.

Torralba, Antonio, et al. 2006. "Contextual Guidance of Eye Movements and Attention in Real-World Scenes: The Role of Global Features in Object Search." *Psychological Review*13 (4): 766–86, PubMed. https://pubmed.ncbi.nlm.nih.gov/17014302/.

Tread Athletics. 2020. "Pelvic Dissociations | Learning Hip/Shoulder Separation." December 8,2020, YouTube video. https://www.youtube.com/watch?v=-DK-U7sdcAU.

Treisman, Anne M., and Garry Gelade. 1980. "A Feature-Integration Theory of Attention." *Cognitive Psychology*, 12 (1): 97–136. https://doi.org10.1016/0010–0285(80)90005–5.

Tripathy, Srimant P., and Patrick Cavanagh. 2002. "The Extent of Crowding in Peripheral Vision Does Not Scale with Target Size." *Vision Research* 42 (20): 2357–69. Science Direct. https://www.sciencedirect.com/science/article/pii/S0042698902001979?via%3Dihub.

Turner, Broderick. "Brown Starts in Backcourt." *Los Angeles Times*, October 18, 2009. https://www.latimes.com/archives/la-xpm-2009-oct-18-sp-lakers-fyi18-story.html.

Turner, Jamie. 2009. "Talk the Walk: Bemused James Defends (Kind of) His 'Crab Dribble' Controversy." *Cleveland Plain-Dealer*, January 7, 2009. https://www.cleveland.com/cavs/2009/01/talk_the_walk_bemused_james_de.html.

USA Today. 2008. "The Passage Behind 'Traveling.'" *USA Today*, November 14, 2008, C.8.

Vardon, Joe. 2020. "'I Can Take Two Steps and Dunk': The Art of Being Giannis Antetokounmpo." The Athletic, August 1, 2020. https://theathletic.com/1966956/2020/08/01/i-can-take-two-steps-and-dunk-theart-of-being-giannis-antetokounmpo/.

Vater, Christian, et al. 2016. "Detecting Single-Target Changes in Multiple Object Tracking: The Case of Peripheral Vision." *Attention, Perception, & Psychophysics* 74: 1004–19.

———. 2017. "Detecting Target Changes in Multiple Object Tracking with Peripheral Vision: More Pronounced Eccentricity Effects for Changes in Form Than in Motion." *Journal of Experimental Psychology. Human Perception, and Performance* 43 (5): 903–13. https://pubmed.ncbi.nlm.nih.gov/28230396/.

Vater, Christian, et al. 2017. "Examining the Functionality of Peripheral Vision: From Fundamental Understandings to Applied Sport Science." *Current Issues in Sport Science* 2.

Velazquez, Matt. 2018. "Mike Budenholzer Has the Bucks—All of Them—Shooting Three-Pointers." *Milwaukee Journal Sentinel*, September 26, 2018. https://www.jsonline.com/story/sports/nba/bucks/2018/09/26/budenholzer-has-bucks-all-them-shooting-three-pointers/1426257002/.

Verghese, Preeti. 2001. "Visual Search and Attention: A Signal Detection Theory Approach." *Neuron* 31: 523–35. https://doi.org10.1016/S0896–6273(01)00392–0.

Verrier, Justin. 2016. "Steve Clifford Emphasizes Belief in Hornets' Plan in Postgame Sermon." *ESPN*, April 21, 2016. https://www.espn.com/blog/nba/post/_/id/18276/steve-clifford-emphasizes-his-belief-inhornets-gameplan-preperation-in-postgame-sermon.

———. 2018. "You Can't Stop NBA Offenses—and Now, You Can't Even Hope to Contain Them." *The Ringer*, October 30, 2018. https://www.theringer.com/nba/2018/10/30/18038802/nbadefense-offensive-boom.

Voigt, Will, performer. 2021. "Will Voigt on Peel Switching, Servant Leadership, and Building Systems." *Slappin' Glass Podcast*, created by Patrick Carney and Dan Krikorian, season 1, episode 24, January 22, 2021. https://podcasts.apple.com/us/podcast/will-voigt-on-peel-switchingservant-leadership-building/id1528050811?i=1000506230841. *Apple Podcasts*.

von Muhlenen, Adrian, and Alejandro Lleras. 2007. "No-Onset Looming Motion Guides Spatial Attention." *Journal of Experimental Psychology: Human Perception and Performance* 33 (6): 1297–310. https://doi.org10.1037/0096–1523.33.6.1297.

Vorkunov, Mike. 2021. "The 4–Point Revolution: How the Knicks Learned to Stop Worrying and Love the (3-Point) Bomb." The Athletic, May 21, 2021. https://theathletic.com/2603262/2021/05/21/the-4–point-revolution-how-the-knicks-learned-to-stop-worrying-and-love-the-3-point-bomb/.

Washington, Jesse. 2018. "Step into the Future: NBA Talent Redefines the Meaning of Traveling." *The Undefeated*, 15 February 2018, https://theundefeated.com/features/step-into-the-future-nba-talentredefines-the-meaning-of-traveling/.

Weiss, Jared. "Steph Curry and drop coverage? Here's why the Celtics are doing it in the NBA Finals." The Athletic, 13 June 2022, https://theathletic.com/3361968/2022/06/13/stephen-curry-celtics-defense-drop-nba-finals/.

Weitzman, Yaron. 2017. "Inside the NBA's Most Essential Defensive Tactic." *Bleacher Report*, Turner Sports, November 2, 2017. https://bleacherreport.com/articles/2739086–inside-the-nbas-most-essentialdefensive-tactic.

Whicker, Mark. 2004. "Dream Over: NBA Pros No Match Anymore for Rest of World, Will Play for Bronze." *Pittsburgh Post-Gazette*, August 28, 2004, D-1, ProQuest.

Whitehead, Todd. 2019. "How the Milwaukee Bucks Brought Their Offense into the 21st Century." *FiveThirtyEight*, ESPN, February 5, 2019. https://fivethirtyeight.com/features/how-the-milwaukeebucks-brought-their-offense-into-the-21st-century/.

Whitney, David, and Dennis M. Levi. 2011. "Visual Crowding: A Fundamental Limit on Conscious Perception and Object Recognition." *Trends in Cognitive Science* 15 (4): 160–8, HHS Public Access. https://www.ncbi.nlm.nih.gov/pmc/articles/PMC3070834/.

"Why The Warriors Screens Are No Different Than the Rest of the NBA." 2016. *Court Call*, created by Nick Hauseman, season 2016, BBALLBREAKDOWN, February 29, 2016, YouTube video. https://www.youtube.com/watch?v=sU1XSRC7el0.

Wilson, Chad. 2020. "How to Turn Out of Your Backpedal." *All Eyes DB Camp*, January 26, 2020, YouTube video. https://www.youtube.com/watch?v=jzGid_zzXQE.

———. 2020. "To T-step or Not to T-step." *All Eyes DB Camp*, March 4, 2020. https://alleyesdbcamp.com/to-t-step-or-not-to-t-step/.

Wilson, David. 2021. "Heat Flames Out in Four." *Miami Herald*, May 30, 2021, 23A.

Winderman, Ira. 1996. "In game's final seconds, Mourning a spectator." *South Florida Sun-Sentinel*, December 12, 1996, 44.

———. 1996. "NBA Officials Taking Steps, So Players Take Fewer." *South Florida Sun-Sentinel*, December 8, 1996, 5.C.

———. 2001. "NBA Changes Its Rules to Allow Zone Defense." *South Florida Sun-Sentinel*, April 13, 2001. https://www.sun-sentinel.com/news/fl-xpm-2001–04–13–0104121399–story.html.

———. 2005. "NBA Crackdown: Let's Don't Do the Flop." *South Florida Sun Sentinel*, October 12, 2005. https://www.sun-sentinel.com/news/fl-xpm-2005–10–12–0510110568–story.html.

———. 2021. "Bucks Go Big on Butler." *South Florida Sun Sentinel*, May 24, 2021, C3.

———. 2021. "Giannis Antetokounmpo on Jimmy Butler a New Heat-Bucks Twist." *South Florida Sun Sentinel*, May 23, 2021. https://www.sun-sentinel.com/sports/miami-heat/fl-sp-miami-heat-notebook-sunday-20210523–elr4lfv34jfnlor7xpdjgl2lhy-story.html.

Windhorst, Brian. 2004. "Cavaliers Fall to Jefferson (42 Points) and Nets." *Akron Beacon-Journal*, December 22, 2004, ProQuest.

———. 2009. "Cavs Walk Away with Loss." *Cleveland Plain-Dealer*, January 4, 2009, https://www.cleveland.com/cavs/2009/01/cavs_walk_away_with_loss.html.

———. 2009. "The Latest 'James Rules' May Make Life Easier for LeBron: NBA Insider." *Cleveland Plain-Dealer*, October 17, 2009. https://www.cleveland.com/cavs/2009/10/the_latest_james_rules_may_mak.html.

———. 2009. "LeBron James Pleased to Hear NBA Is Reconsidering Rules on Traveling." *Cleveland Plain-Dealer*, March 13, 2009. https://www.cleveland.com/cavs/2009/03/lebron_james_pleased_to_hear_n.html.

———. 2009. "Windhorst Beat Blog: Traveling backward in D.C." *Cleveland Plain-Dealer*, January 4, 2009. https://www.cleveland.com/cavs/2009/01/windhorst_beat_blog_cavs_at_wi.html.

———. 2021. "The Cleveland Cavaliers Were Mocked for Bucking the NBA's Small-Ball Trend—Now They're Contending for Home Court." *ESPN*, December 28, 2021. https://www.espn.com/nba/insider/insider/story/_/id/32947881/the-cleveland-cavaliers-were-mocked-bucking-nba-small-balltrend-now-contending-home-court.

Winfield, Kristian. 2017. "The Rockets Shoot Very Deep 3-Pointers on Purpose. Here's Why." *SB Nation*, Vox Media, January 20, 2017. https://www.sbnation.com/2017/1/20/14284896/houston-rockets-threepoint-stats-mike-dantoni.

———. 2018. "Giannis Antetokounmpo's Euro-Steps Are Unstoppable." *SB Nation*, Vox Media, April 26, 2018. https://www.sbnation.com/nba/2018/4/26/17288526/giannis-antetokounmpo-eurostep-unfair-cheat-code-bucks-vs-celtics-game-6–nba-playoffs-2018.

Wise, Mike. 2001. "Pro Basketball; N.B.A. Takes Quick Action to Get the Game Moving Again." *New York Times*, April 13, 2001. https://www.nytimes.com/2001/04/13/sports/pro-basketball-nbatakes-quick-action-to-get-the-game-moving-again.html.

———. 2002. "Pro Basketball: Inside the N.B.A.; Ties with Hawks May Attract West." March 17, 2002. https://www.nytimes.com/2002/03/17/sports/pro-basketball-inside-the-nba-tieswith-hawks-may-attract-west.html.

Woike, Dan. 2020. "Anthony Davis Is Disruptive Force on Defense in Game 4 Win." *Los Angeles Times*, October 6, 2020. https://www.latimes.com/sports/lakers/story/2020–10–06/anthony-davis-isdisruptive-force-on-defense-against-jimmy-butler.

———. 2021. "Elgin Baylor Dies: Dr. J, Other NBA Greats Describe Legacy." *Los Angeles Times*, March 23, 2021. https://www.latimes.com/sports/story/2021–03–23/elgin-baylor-dr-j-legends-revolutionizednba.

Wolfe, Jeremy M. 1994. "Guided Search 2.0: A Revised Model of Visual Search." *Psychonomic Bulletin & Review* 1 (2): 202–38.

———. 2017. "'I Am Not Dead Yet!' The Item Responds to Hulleman & Olivers." *Behavioral & Brain Sciences* 40: e161.

Wolfe, Jeremy M., and Todd S. Horowitz. 2017. "Five Factors that Guide Attention in Visual Search." *Nature & Human Behavior*, 1 (0058).

Wolfley, Bob. 2014. "Former Bucks Forward Marques Johnson: 'Who Wouldn't Want Their Number Retired?'" *Milwaukee Journal Sentinel*, July 15, 2014. http://archive.jsonline.com/blogs/sports/267236841.html.

Woodyard, Eric. 2019. "Quin Snyder, Igor Kokoskov Relationship Goes 'Beyond Basketball' Even as Opposing Jazz, Suns Coaches." *Deseret News*, February 6, 2019. https://www.deseret.com/2019/2/6/20665194/quin-snyder-igor-kokoskov-relationship-goes-beyond-basketball-even-as-opposing-jazz-sunscoaches.

Worell, Bill, et al., performers. 2013. "Golden State Warriors at Houston Rockets." *Houston Rockets Basketball*, season 2012–13, Game 50, Comcast SportsNet Houston, February 5, 2013.

Wright, Michael C. 2019. "Manu Ginóbili's San Antonio Spurs Career Defined by These 20 Moments." *ESPN*, March 28, 2019. https://www.espn.com/nba/story/_/id/23841819/manu-Ginóbili-sanantonio-spurs-career-defined-20–moments-nba.

Wyche, Sam. 2001. "NBA Debates Defense Rule." *Washington Post*, April 2, 2001. https://www.washingtonpost.com/archive/sports/2001/04/02/nba-debates-defense-rule/8f04015b-9659–4ced-9bb6–612f35a99e69/.

Wyche, Steve. 1999. "New NBA Rules Aim to Put Points on Board." *Washington Post*, September 25, 1999. https://www.washingtonpost.com/archive/sports/1999/09/25/new-nba-rules-aim-to-put-points-onboard/5c6698c6–c34e-4be8–8c02–f5a3953ff08c/?utm_term=.3c487f948240.

Yagoda, Ben. 2001. "The Rise of the Robo-Ref." *New York Times*, February 25, 2001, SM138, ProQuest.

Yang, Lindong, et al. 2017. "Shape Representation Modulating the Effect of Motion on Visual Search Performance." *Scientific Reports* 7: 14921. https://doi.org10.1038/s41598–017–14999–1.

Yeshurun, Yaffa, and Einat Rashal. 2010. "Precueing Attention to the Target Location Diminishes Crowding and Reduces the Critical Distance." *Journal of Vision* 10 (10): 1–12, https://jov.arvojournals.org/article.aspx?articleid=2121093.

Young, Alex. 2017. "How To: Improve Defensive Speed for Basketball!! (Become a Better Defender)." *THINCPRO Basketball*, November 28, 2017, YouTube video. https://www.youtube.com/watch?v=LwMb9ObC3D8.

Young, Damon. 2016. "Allen Iverson's Greatest Contribution to Basketball Is an Unstoppable and Completely Illegal Dribble Move." *The Root*, April 5, 2016. https://www.theroot.com/alleniversons-greatest-contribution-to-basketball-is-a-1822521382.

Young, Jabari. 2016. "Spurs Off-Topic Conversation: Manu Ginóbili." *San Antonio Express-News*, December 5, 2016. https://www.mysanantonio.com/sports/spurs/article/Spurs-Off-Topic-conversation-Manu-Ginóbili-10694547.php.

Young, Royce. 2021. "The NBA's Savvy Moves and the 'Innovators' Who Push the Limits of the Rulebook." *ESPN*, February 24, 2021. https://www.espn.com/nba/story/_/id/30947170/the-nba-savvy-movesinnovators-push-limits-rulebook.

Young, Shane. 2021. "Giannis Antetokounmpo's Defensive Brilliance Is Swinging the Momentum of the NBA Finals." *Forbes*, July 15, 2021. https://www.forbes.com/sites/shaneyoung/2021/07/15/giannisantetokounmpos-defensive-brilliance-is-swinging-the-momentum-of-the-nba-finals/.

Youngmisuk, Ohm. 2021. "Brooklyn Nets' James Harden Says He's 'Slowly' Regaining Form, but Still Limited." *ESPN*, October 28, 2021. https://www.espn.com/nba/story/_/id/32492304/brooklyn-nets-jamesharden-says-slowly-regaining-form-limited.

Zatzman, Louis. "More NBA Teams Are Using a Pick-and-Roll Hack: Sticking Two Guys in the Corners." *FiveThirtyEight*, ESPN, December 21, 2021. https://fivethirtyeight.com/features/morenba-teams-are-using-a-pick-and-role-hack-sticking-two-guys-in-the-corners/.

Zaucha, Evan. 2021. "The Art and Science of 'Feel' in Basketball." *EZ Hoops*, January 4, 2021. https://ezhoops.wordpress.com/2021/01/04/feel-and-feel-accessories/.

Zhang, Hang, et al. 2010. "Do Objects in Working Memory Compete with Objects in Perception?" *Visual Cognition* 18 (45): 617–40. ResearchGate. https://www.researchgate.net/publication/230754025_Do_objects_in_working_memory_compete_with_objects_in_perception.

Ziller, Tom. 2019. "Steph Curry's Double Stepback Political Statement, Explained." *SB Nation*, Vox Media, January 9, 2019. https://www.sbnation.com/nba/2019/1/8/18173485/stephen-curry-doublestepback-travel-james-harden-gmib.

Zillgitt, Jeff. 2012. "LeBron James, Miami Heat Find No Position Like No Positions." *USA Today*, October 18, 2012. https://www.usatoday.com/story/sports/nba/heat/2012/10/18/miami-lebron-james-positionversatility-flexibility/1642623/.

———. 2013. "NBA Teams Fully Embracing the Three." *USA Today*, January 21, 2013. https://www.usatoday.com/story/sports/nba/2013/01/21/nba-three-point-shot-evolving-team-strategy-stephencurry-dell-curry/1853357/.

———. 2019. "How Bigger Court Could Improve the Game." *USA Today*, March 9, 2019. https://www.usatoday.com/story/sports/nba/columnist/jeff-zillgitt/2019/03/09/expand-nba-court-improveflow/3070024002/.

———. 2021. "Elgin Baylor's Style Led to Julius Irving Who Led to Michael Jordan." *USA Today*, March 23, 2021. https://www.usatoday.com/story/sports/nba/columnist/jeff-zillgitt/2021/03/23/elgin-baylordies-led-dr-j-who-led-michael-jordan/6958820002/.

Zylberberg, Ariel, et al. 2014. "Variance Misperception Explains Illusions of Confidence in Simple Perceptual Decisions." *Consciousness and Cognition* 27C (1): 246–253.